UiPath Associate Certification Guide

The go-to guide to passing the Associate certification exam with the help of mock tests and quizzes

Niyaz Ahmed

Lahiru Fernando

Rajaneesh Balakrishnan

BIRMINGHAM—MUMBAI

UiPath Associate Certification Guide

Group Product Manager: Rohit Rajkumar
Publishing Product Manager: Ashitosh Gupta
Senior Editor: Hayden Edwards
Content Development Editor: Feza Shaikh
Technical Editor: Saurabh Kadave
Copy Editor: Safis Editing
Project Coordinator: Manthan Patel
Proofreader: Safis Editing
Indexer: Tejal Daruwale Soni
Production Designer: Joshua Misquitta
Marketing Coordinator: Deepak Kumar

First published: June 2022
Production reference: 2280622

Published by Packt Publishing Ltd.
Livery Place
35 Livery Street
Birmingham
B3 2PB, UK.

ISBN 978-1-80107-273-1

www.packt.com

To my father – your guiding hand on my shoulder will remain with me forever.

– Niyaz Ahmed

I'd like to thank my father, Sesha, my wife, Mihiri, and my daughter, Emmie, for holding my hand throughout all the hardships of my life. Also, special thanks go to my two amazing mentors, Erik Gillet and Lucas Pimenta, for always motivating and guiding me. Lastly, I would like to thank the entire UiPath Community, the UiPath team, my team at Boundaryless Group, and all my friends for all the opportunities and for helping me change my life in many ways.

– Lahiru Fernando

To anyone who wants to pass the UiPath Associate certification, start learning UiPath, change to a career in UiPath, or simply know about the technology – I'm sure this book will undoubtedly help you achieve your UiPath goals. Thanks to the amazing team efforts by the co-authors, reviewers, and the Packt Publishing team in creating the contents in the most simplified way to help anyone learn UiPath and earn the UiPath Associate Certification.

To my wife, Anusree, son, Saijesh, and daughter, Dakshya, for kindly letting me experience the writing process of this book.

– Rajaneesh Balakrishnan

Contributors

About the authors

Niyaz Ahmed is a technical program manager at UiPath, where he is working toward enabling the future and current workforce for the automation-ready world. He manages the UiPath Academic Alliance and Learning Partner program by working with leading institutions, including universities, colleges, and high schools. He is also an instructor at Udacity for the RPA Developer Nanodegree program. In addition, he continues to evangelize RPA by mentoring learners to develop professional-level skills focused on developing and deploying software robots.

A special thanks to Alok Shrivastava, Rajesh Nambiar, and all my colleagues at UiPath who have helped me in the different phases of the book.

Lahiru Fernando is a UiPath MVP, executive team lead for RPA, UiPath community leader, mentor, lecturer, and public speaker, and has over 11+ years of experience in the IT industry. He started his career in 2011 after completing a degree in specialized software engineering at Staffordshire University. He has been engaged in multiple business intelligence projects in the banking, finance, market research, and agriculture sectors. Moving into RPA in 2019, he has led multiple successful RPA projects in the finance, retail, banking, child welfare, oil and gas, telecommunication, and apparel sectors as a lead RPA solution architect. He also leads the RPA enablement and training fronts for Boundaryless Automation.

Rajaneesh Balakrishnan is the founder of 2AutomateAnything and has been a UiPath Advanced Certified RPA developer and UiPath MVP since 2020. He started his career as a quality analyst, progressed to become a software testing practice lead, and then became an RPA lead with immense automation tool implementation and multiple domain experience, including BFSI. Having over 15 years of experience in IT, he has successfully implemented RPA in UiPath for many reputable clients and has saved a significant amount of time and cost to organizations. He is also a passionate teacher, conducting various corporate and personalized training events and guiding the careers of many toward RPA in UiPath. He used to share educational content on YouTube, Udemy, and LinkedIn to support the UiPath community.

About the reviewers

After earning his master's degree in computer science, **Mukesh Kala** started his career as a software developer. He has over 8 years of professional experience and presently works as a senior RPA analyst, automating work in the banking and financial services industry.

A strong believer in the power of learning and knowledge sharing, Mukesh regularly attends UiPath community events, training and helping out beginners in technology. Mukesh was recognized as a UiPath MVP in 2021 and is behind the YouTube channel *Tutorials by Mukesh Kala*. In his leisure time, he loves to read books and speedcubing.

Andy Menon is a UiPath MVP for 2021. In his day job, he is an integrations engineer, with experience in integrating systems for the enterprise.

Andy is also the founder of RPA Vanguard and the namesake channel on YouTube, teaching RPA with real-world examples. His Udemy course on enterprise RPA is ranked amongst the top 20% of almost 100,000 courses on CourseMarks!

In his free time, Andy dabbles in hobby electronics, 3D printing, and the **Internet of Things (IoT)**, experimenting with Arduino, Raspberry Pi, and the ESP8266 family of microcontrollers.

Andy is also a Kindle-published author of the book *Give Yourself IoT Super Powers*.

He has published several of his hobby projects and designs online at Instructables and Thingiverse.

Table of Contents

2

UiPath Ecosystem

3

Introducing UiPath Orchestrator

4

Create, Deploy, and Execute RPA Process on the UiPath Ecosystem

Part 2: UiPath Studio

5

Learning about Variables and Arguments

6

Understanding Different Control Flows

7
Manipulating Data Using UiPath

8
Exploring UiPath Selectors

9
Learning the Uses of Data Tables and Exploring Excel Automation

10
Exploring User Interfaces and User/Robot Interactions

11
Automating PDF Data Extraction

12
Exploring UiPath Email Automation

Part 3: Use Case and Exam Preparation

13
Debugging

14

Invoice Processing – Dispatcher

15

Invoice Processing – Performer

16

How to Prepare and What to Expect

17
Mock Exam 1

18
Mock Exam 2

Appendix

Index

Other Books You May Enjoy

Preface

UiPath is the most popular vendor in the **Robotic Process Automation (RPA)** industry. If you're an RPA enthusiast or citizen developer who wants to succeed in the industry, achieving this certification can help you get accredited and ready for real-world challenges using UiPath.

UiPath Associate Certification Guide offers complete, up-to-date coverage of the UiPath RPA Associate certification exam to help you pass on the first attempt and get certified. The book is written in a clear, succinct way with self-assessment questions, quizzes with answers at the end of each lesson, exam tips, and mock exams with detailed answers and explanations. You'll start by getting to grips with the basic concepts of UiPath RPA, and then progress to an in-depth discussion of all the concepts required for Associate certification. Finally, you'll develop UiPath skills by gaining the required knowledge and implement these skills using sample business cases.

By the end of this UiPath book, you'll have covered everything you need to pass the exam, gained the knowledge you need to work on real-world case studies, and learned how to apply various concepts to build enterprise-level use cases.

Who this book is for

This RPA book is for those in technical and semi-technical roles such as citizen RPA developers, junior RPA developers, RPA developers, solution architects, business analysts, system administrators, college or university students and graduates, and UiPath and partner employees in pre-sales, services, support, and so on. If you are looking to get certified and meet the industry standard with the largest RPA vendor, then this book is for you.

What this book covers

Chapter 1, The Automation Journey and Identifying Suitable Business Processes, explores the importance of digital transformation and what factors drive it. The chapter also illustrates some RPA use cases in business, followed by the essential steps needed to identify a suitable automation process. Knowledge of these points is necessary before starting the RPA journey, as the topics addressed in this chapter give you an idea about the current state of process automation in the world, why it is important, and the critical resources involved.

Chapter 2, UiPath Ecosystem, provides an overview of each and every component of the UiPath Enterprise RPA platform for building simple to complex automation using UiPath Studio. Information about installing UiPath and setting up the UiPath Studio profile is also included in this chapter.

Chapter 3, Introducing UiPath Orchestrator, focuses on introducing the UiPath cloud platform and UiPath Orchestrator. UiPath Orchestrator plays a significant role in automation as it acts as the central controlling unit for all deployed robots and processes. Hence, it is crucial to understand the use and concepts of Orchestrator to manage your virtual workforce.

Chapter 4, Create, Deploy, and Execute RPA Process on the UiPath Ecosystem, provides step-by-step instructions to create a robot and establish a connection between the robot and UiPath Orchestrator. A sample automation project is created in UiPath Studio and then published to Orchestrator and executed by the Robots using the UiPath Assistant and attended automation.

Chapter 5, Learning about Variables and Arguments, looks at variables and arguments – two crucial components of any programming language. This chapter introduces you to how UiPath Studio works with variables and arguments, along with the most common data types used.

Chapter 6, Understanding Different Control Flows, covers control flows, which give more power to the robot to make crucial decisions while evaluating any business conditions. Various control flow activities, such as sequences, flowcharts, and loops, are explored using real-time examples for better understanding.

Chapter 7, Manipulating Data Using UiPath, focuses on data – the most critical resource in every organization. We need to modify, structure, format, and sort data to convert it into meaningful information. This chapter introduces different methods of manipulating data based on various data types.

Chapter 8, Exploring UiPath Selectors, looks at one of the major important topics when it comes to automation – selectors. Various selector types, such as full selector, partial selector, static selector, and dynamic selector are discussed with examples. Certain selector tools, such as UI Explorer and Selector Editor, are also used effectively for optimal usage of selector features.

Chapter 9, Learning the Uses of Data Tables and Exploring Excel Automation, homes in on Microsoft Excel – used almost every day to perform different functions. The data we process in Excel is more structured in a tabular form. In this chapter, we focus on learning how to automate Excel using UiPath, and how we can use data table variables to support our Excel automation.

Chapter 10, Exploring User Interfaces and User/Robot Interactions, looks at the automation of the user interface. Automation of UI elements such as windows, text fields, buttons, dropdowns, checkboxes, textboxes, and so on are discussed in this chapter. Various input actions and output actions are explored for effective automation. Some advanced UI automation such as image automation and text automation is also discussed.

Chapter 11, Automating PDF Data Extraction, covers PDF files – widely used across organizations to share information. This chapter focuses on learning how to automate PDF files using UiPath, and what activities are available to build a successful PDF automation.

Chapter 12, Exploring UiPath Email Automation, focuses on email – one of the most often used forms of digital communication by individuals and organizations. This chapter explores how to automatically send emails, receive emails, respond to emails, attach and download document attachments, and use defined message templates for emails. Various email activities and email features are explored with real-time examples for better clarity.

Chapter 13, Debugging, shows you how to debug a process that involves identifying and removing bugs from a given project to make it function correctly.

Chapter 14, Invoice Processing – Dispatcher, shows you how to design the dispatcher model of invoice processing to extract relevant details from the invoice and upload it to Orchestrator queues.

Chapter 15, Invoice Processing – Performer, shows you how to design the performer model of invoice processing by retrieving transaction items from Orchestrator queues and entering the invoice data onto the CRM.

Chapter 16, How to Prepare and What to Expect, helps you understand more about the exam and the certification credential.

Chapter 17, Mock Exam 1, is a practice test designed to help you prepare for the UiPath RPA Associate v1.0 exam. The practice test tests your knowledge and helps you get a feel for what the actual exam is like.

Chapter 18, Mock Exam 2, is a practice test designed to help you prepare for the UiPath RPA Associate v1.0 exam. The practice test tests your knowledge and helps you get a feel for what the actual exam is like.

To get the most out of this book

In this book, we use UiPath Studio, UiPath Orchestrator, and the UiPath Assistant, so ensure that you have the correct version installed.

You also need access to a few applications, as documented in the *Technical requirements* section of each chapter.

Software/hardware covered in the book	Operating system requirements
UiPath Studio 202X.X	Windows 8.1+
UiPath Orchestrator 202X.X	
UiPath Assistant 202X.X	

This book is compatible with the latest version of UiPath Studio, Orchestrator, and Assistant at the time of publishing (UiPath 202X.X).

The entire UiPath Associate Certification is based on the Classic Design experience of UiPath Studio. The Modern Design experience is not a part of the certification; hence, the book is also based on the Classic Design experience.

If you are using the digital version of this book, we advise you to type the code yourself or access the code from the book's GitHub repository (a link is available in the next section). Doing so will help you avoid any potential errors related to the copying and pasting of code.

Download the example code files

You can download the example code files for this book from GitHub at https:// github.com/PacktPublishing/UiPath-Associate-Certification-Guide. If there's an update to the code, it will be updated in the GitHub repository.

We also have other code bundles from our rich catalog of books and videos available at https://github.com/PacktPublishing/. Check them out!

Download the color images

We also provide a PDF file that has color images of the screenshots and diagrams used in this book. You can download it here: `https://static.packt-cdn.com/downloads/9781801072731_ColorImages.pdf`.

Conventions used

There are a number of text conventions used throughout this book.

`Code in text`: Indicates code words in text, database table names, folder names, filenames, file extensions, pathnames, dummy URLs, user input, and Twitter handles. Here is an example: "Create the `EmailAddress`, `Password`, `FirstName`, `LastName`, and `TermsAndConditions` variables of the `String` type, and have the default values of `EmailAddress`, `FirstName`, and `LastName`."

A block of code is set as follows:

```
"Hello " + In_UserName + ", It's nice to see you. This is my
first attempt to join two workflows."
```

Bold: Indicates a new term, an important word, or words that you see onscreen. For instance, words in menus or dialog boxes appear in **bold**. Here is an example: "Click on the **DataTable...** button on the activity to open the **Build Data Table** screen. This screen can be used to add columns, rows, and change column properties."

> **Tips or important notes**
> Appear like this.

Get in touch

Feedback from our readers is always welcome.

General feedback: If you have questions about any aspect of this book, email us at `customercare@packtpub.com` and mention the book title in the subject of your message.

Errata: Although we have taken every care to ensure the accuracy of our content, mistakes do happen. If you have found a mistake in this book, we would be grateful if you would report this to us. Please visit `www.packtpub.com/support/errata` and fill in the form.

Piracy: If you come across any illegal copies of our works in any form on the internet, we would be grateful if you would provide us with the location address or website name. Please contact us at copyright@packt.com with a link to the material.

If you are interested in becoming an author: If there is a topic that you have expertise in and you are interested in either writing or contributing to a book, please visit authors.packtpub.com.

Share your thoughts

Once you've read, we'd love to hear your thoughts! Scan the QR code below to go straight to the Amazon review page for this book and share your feedback.

https://packt.link/r/1801072736

Your review is important to us and the tech community and will help us make sure we're delivering excellent quality content.

Part 1: Importance of RPA

In this part, we will discuss the importance of **Robotic Process Automation** (**RPA**) and how we can use it to support the automation journey. The main objective of this section is to better understand the concepts behind automation and what factors to consider to identify the best processes for it. This is the most important aspect of any automation project. Furthermore, we will also be focusing on understanding the entire ecosystem of UiPath to get started with deep-dive sessions.

In this part, we will cover the following chapters:

- *Chapter 1, The Automation Journey and Identifying Suitable Business Processes*
- *Chapter 2, UiPath Ecosystem*
- *Chapter 3, Introducing UiPath Orchestrator*
- *Chapter 4, Create, Deploy, and Execute RPA Process on the UiPath Ecosystem*

1
The Automation Journey and Identifying Suitable Business Processes

Digital transformation is one of the big buzzwords of the day, as **robotic process automation (RPA)** is currently transforming the way we work.

UiPath, the leading vendor in RPA, provides a **state-of-the-art (SOTA)** platform for process automation. The UiPath automation platform includes more than 20 different products addressing different automation requirements. Compared to other RPA tools, the SOTA capabilities that UiPath offers are one reason the company has become the market leader. In addition, UiPath offers a high-stakes certification program and a learning platform to help users harness the technology's power.

The *UiPath Certified Professional* program offers two certification exams that include an Advanced-level certification and an Associate-level certification. The Associate certification is suitable for junior RPA developers, solution architects, **business analysts (BAs)**, and any business user who wants to pursue their career in RPA. The Advanced certification assesses a deeper level of RPA expertise and is designed for advanced developers. This book primarily focuses on providing a guide for the UiPath Associate certification by offering information on all required aspects of the exam.

In this chapter, we will explore the importance of digital transformation and which factors drive it. The chapter also illustrates some RPA use cases in business, followed by the essential steps needed to identify a suitable automation process. Knowing and understanding this information is essential before starting the RPA journey. The topics addressed in this chapter will give you an idea about the current state of process automation in the world, why it is important, and the critical resources involved.

In this chapter, we will cover the following topics:

- Understanding why automation is driving the digital transformation
- Implementing RPA in business
- What can RPA automate?
- Identifying processes for RPA
- Understanding the stages of an RPA journey
- Knowing the RPA resources and responsibilities in an RPA project

Technical requirements

We will be covering theoretical content in this chapter, so there are no technical requirements.

Understanding why automation is driving digital transformation

The way people work has changed over many years. People used to do a lot of complex activities manually before the era of computers; however, with the introduction of computers, people slowly moved into a digital way of working. Today, every employee in this world interacts with some software applications to get their daily work done. All these actions still have us (that is, humans) as the central point of contact. Therefore, although we developed many software applications to take care of our day-to-day activities, we were still busy doing the same mundane and repetitive actions. Over time, work started piling up again and people got into a standard set of repetitive tasks to work like robots every day.

What is the solution to get out of these repetitive actions? RPA is the answer.

RPA is a technology that has evolved over many years. During the initial stages, there were automation workflows that were specific and dependent on an application, such as macros in Microsoft Excel. These automation scripts worked only within the application's scope and automated some time-consuming manual activities. This technology slowly evolved, and next, we were able to use tools that replicate actual user activity, which increased the capabilities of automation and increased the efficiency of the tasks performed. The software industry is a fast-growing industry, and you will come across many new technologies every day. The evolution of the latest technologies—such as **artificial intelligence** (**AI**), **machine learning** (**ML**), Microsoft, Google, and other cognitive services—helped to widen robots' capabilities. Today, RPA combines multiple technologies such as workflow automation, ML, AI, **intelligent character recognition** (**ICR**), and so on.

RPA is a technology that automates tasks previously performed by humans in a digital interface. This software uses a computer robot to run applications the same way a person would do by interacting with the software **user interface** (**UI**). In addition to mimicking human interaction, RPA includes capabilities to consume background services such as **application programming interfaces** (**APIs**), databases, and many more to efficiently and accurately perform actions. RPA aims to replace repetitive tasks performed by humans with a digital workforce, to focus on more value-added activities in an organization. The software robot acts as your virtual assistant that will simply use your existing applications with no change in its existing infrastructure to perform its actions, documenting every step consistently for reporting and maintenance purposes. Such robots are capable of interacting with any software application, mimicking human actions.

Further, robots can work 24/7 without any errors and with minimal or no human intervention. RPA primarily targets highly manual, repetitive, rule-based processes with low exception rates and standard electronic readable input. These robots are considered virtual workforces where the business and the **information technology (IT)** teams manage their operations.

Not only is RPA a type of automation today, but it is also one of the most popular technologies available in the industry. RPA gained popularity because of its unique capabilities that made it the technology driving digital transformation. Some of those unique features of RPA are described in more detail here:

- **RPA is a non-invasive technology**: Using RPA in your organization does not require any significant changes in the existing IT infrastructure or deep integrations with existing software applications. RPA is a technology capable of providing a reliable, fast, and cost-effective solution for automating processes.

- **RPA is easy to scale**: RPA implementations are usually not limited to a specific process. Further, automated business processes are also subject to change over time. Organizations that implement RPA usually look for ways to quickly scale up and scale down, depending on their future requirements. Hence, RPA solutions are built in a way where they can be easily scaled without much hassle.

- **RPA is future-proof**: The automation solutions built today use the technology that is available today. However, these robots are easily extensible to use the technology that would be available tomorrow.

- **Customer expectations**: Every day, the demand for services increases. However, to meet the increasing demand, organizations have to spend a lot on costly resources. Using RPA helps organizations reduce the cost they pay on new resources as RPA brings with it a virtual workforce's power to meet the growing demand quickly. Apart from that, the utilization of a virtual workforce increases the efficiency and the reliability of the process, as robots can deliver a high accuracy rate.

- **Compliance and regulations**: Every organization has to adhere to government rules and regulations. Meeting compliance and regulations requires a lot of manual effort as there any many tasks to be done. However, using a virtual workforce helps comply with rules and regulations as robots generate execution logs for compliance reporting.

Digital transformation is an essential topic today because RPA is changing the way we work in our personal lives and at work. These virtual workforces can quickly meet customer expectations, compliance, and regulatory requirements with future-proof technology. It is essential to know that robots' capabilities have expanded over time, enabling them to mimic almost all the actions performed on a digital platform. Such robots today are being used in multiple industries at a large scale.

Implementing RPA in business

RPA in business enables the creation of partnerships between robots and human workers, allowing humans to focus on what they can do best. Once RPA is implemented in an organization, the first question that surfaces is this: *What will robots do and what will human workers do when their tasks are automated?* Robots are best at handling tedious, repetitive, and high-volume tasks that are automated with a high efficiency and accuracy level. While robots take care of manual tasks, human workers can stop worrying about painful mundane activities and can instead focus on face-to-face discussions with people to develop strategic solutions to manage the business. In addition, human workers can focus on upskilling themselves to better fit management-level opportunities within the organization.

Someone may ask whether the introduction of RPA will cause them to lose their job. RPA is **not** a replacement for human workers. RPA only handles repetitive and mundane activities that people used to do before. As a result, the introduction of RPA eliminates some of the tasks that people did before, allowing people to have more free time to focus on strategic activities rather than repetitive operations. Although robots have AI to take care of specific actions, when it comes to strategic decisions, robots cannot replace the experience and complex reasoning abilities people have accumulated over many years.

Today, organizations in different industries have already implemented RPA to automate their processes. The following screenshot illustrates some of the functions already automated in other sectors:

Industry	Automated Processes
Services	<ul><li>Customer invoicing</li><li>Claim processing</li><li>Call center processes</li></ul>
Financial	<ul><li>Fraud detection and prevention</li><li>Data integration (internal and external sources)</li><li>Account settlement</li><li>Automatic account opening</li><li>Automatic account closure</li><li>Loan processing</li><li>Credit card requisition</li><li>Enabling/disabling credit cards</li><li>Customer onboarding</li></ul>
Healthcare	<ul><li>Digitizing and updating patient records</li><li>Inventory management</li><li>Invoice settlement</li><li>Automated report generation</li></ul>
Education	<ul><li>Course registration</li><li>Attendance management</li><li>Course schedule management</li><li>Processing grades and report cards</li></ul>
Technology	<ul><li>Complaint management</li><li>Client management by updating data</li><li>Enable/disable client services</li></ul>
Manufacturing	<ul><li>Inventory management</li><li>Procurement management</li><li>Payment processing</li><li>Customer communication</li><li>Invoice processing</li><li>Purchase order management</li></ul>
Retail	<ul><li>Employee onboarding</li><li>Employee offboarding</li><li>Employee payroll processing</li><li>Invoice processing</li><li>Return processing</li><li>Sales analytics</li></ul>
Government	<ul><li>Benefit claims</li><li>Fraud prevention</li><li>Payer data updating</li></ul>

Figure 1.1 – RPA examples in business

More processes are also suitable for automation in every industry, outside of what is included in the table shown in *Figure 1.1*.

The preceding list illustrates some of the most popular use cases for automation. Some of these processes are explained in detail next.

Payroll processing

Payroll is a typical process in any organization. Payroll refers to actions taken to keep track of employees' attendance and salary (or incentive payments), done every month. Payroll calculations are quite time-consuming as payroll is calculated based on different factors— for example, to derive the total monthly salary, the respective person should figure out the number of hours/days worked, number of paydays, taxes, bonuses, allowances, and more. Performing this check for each employee is complicated and highly manual.

Further, there are sometimes scenarios where employees do not correctly update their attendance. In such cases, the **human resources (HR)** representative has to contact them personally, either via email or a phone call, and request they update their attendance before performing this operation. RPA can automatically access HR applications or even manually maintained timesheets to capture the required information and complete payroll calculations. The process could also be further automated by automating actual bank transfers to transfer money to employee salary accounts.

Client information management

One of the main objectives of a company is to maintain a good client relationship. Maintaining a good relationship requires every record related to clients to be accessible in a central system, such as a **customer relationship management (CRM)** application. However, large-scale companies are spread across different geographies; hence, this makes it challenging to maintain a proper CRM system, and it requires a lot of data entry and frequent updates. Maintaining and updating such information in CRM applications is now performed by introducing RPA. Robots connected to various data sources capture the required information and easily update the CRM without any human intervention.

Invoice processing

Almost all organizations have to deal with documents, one of the most common types being invoices. Organizations receive invoices in different ways, such as soft copies or hard copies. Further, some of these invoices are handwritten, and some are computer-generated to add to the complexity. Data-entry operators have to extract the critical information from these invoices and update downstream applications to maintain financial records on time. Usually, organizations receive many invoices per day that require on-time data entry, verification from management, and system updates, all of which take many human hours. Introducing RPA to such processes provides many benefits in terms of data accuracy, efficiency, and reliability. Robots have the intelligence to extract the required critical information from invoices, perform verification based on a predefined set of rules, and update downstream applications with minimal human involvement.

Financial statement reconciliation

Financial statement reconciliation covers a significant portion of a finance team's operations, including matching orders, payments, losses, margins, and so on with internal accounts and financial statements that it receives at the end of the month. This is a very time-consuming task that involves many finance employees, as the accounts they work with go through a considerable number of transactions every day. To make sure financial statements are ready by the end of the month, the finance team works hard every day, completing and matching the financial statements of prior days to reduce the workload at the end of the month. Introducing RPA into such processes has shown a significant improvement. Robots can perform the same operation much faster and accurately for all reconciliations that the finance team manages.

Call center automation

Call centers perform a significant role in providing better and faster customer support to their valuable customers. Once a call center agent receives a customer call, they must perform initial checks to validate and recognize the customer before providing a service. Let's take the call center of a bank as an example. In that case, a customer may reach out for queries such as requesting account information, complaints about credit/debit card faults, enabling and disabling services, or something else. The call center agent must access multiple systems, retrieve the required information to perform initial validation, and provide the customer with an essential service. Performing the aforementioned actions takes time, and it takes attention away from the discussion the agent is having with the customer. The introduction of RPA to such processes allows a robot to understand the conversation between the two parties. Based on the understanding, the robot performs the required data retrieval from the systems. The robot finally shows the information onscreen automatically, allowing the agent to focus on the conversation to provide a better service.

Loan processing

Though banks and financial institutes use many software applications to perform their activities, some processes such as loan processing activities still require a lot of manual processing. Further, some financial organizations still use paper-based loan application forms. Once the customer fills out an application form and submits an application with any other required documents, the bank representative verifies the submitted data. The data verification usually includes validating the customer's personal information, cross-checking for other facilities obtained from other banks, repayment capabilities, and so on. Such checks are done by connecting to multiple external applications, which usually takes a long time. After the background checks, approval is carried out by the manager of the bank, based on specific criteria. The introduction of RPA for loan processing has brought a lot of benefits as most of these functions—such as reading the application form, performing background checks, calculating the grantable loan amount, and so on—are easily automated.

As well as the processes mentioned, there are many more exciting processes out in the world that robots take care of, allowing them to focus on more value-added activities.

> **Important Note**
>
> RPA in businesses allows employees to focus on more strategic initiatives while robots take care of transactional activities. This section of the chapter covered some of the commonly automated processes across multiple organizations around the world. Most business processes that require automation are complex and require many steps to be carried out. It is essential to understand all the activities that an RPA robot can perform to meet such complex business requirements. The simple actions performed by RPA robots sometimes require a combination of multiple technologies.

What can RPA automate?

As we discussed in the previous sections, RPA robots can mimic human interactions in a digital platform. Listed here are some of the very few actions that RPA robots can manage:

- Automated reading, sending emails and attachments
- Logging in to web and enterprise applications
- Moving files and folders

- Copying and pasting data

- Filling out forms in web/desktop applications

- Reading and writing data into databases

- Reporting across multiple systems

- Scraping data from the web

- **Internet of Things** (**IoT**) data collection and analysis

- Performing simple-to-complex calculations

- Extracting data from scanned and computer-generated documents that are structured or semi-structured

- Collecting social media statistics and performing different analytics on them

- Automated customer service

- Standard letter writing

Given the technological advancements and the expansion of RPA robots' capabilities, robots could perform many more functionalities other than those seen in the preceding list. Today, new technological improvements have taken RPA to another level, known as **hyperautomation**. The concept of hyperautomation covers many more functions such as AI skills, ML, long-running workflows, process mining, native integrations, and advanced analytics.

The use of RPA with AI capabilities such as **natural language processing** (**NLP**), ICR, **optical character recognition** (**OCR**), and AI computer vision enables robots to perform more advanced and complex tasks. The use of AI also allows robots to learn by themselves through ML. The ability to train robots over time helps improve their accuracy and reliability. Further, with the concept of long-running workflows, robots can work on more diverse business scenarios, with humans interacting with the robots at specific decision points seamlessly without worrying about what is happening before and after the decision point.

We, as humans, interact with software applications by simple mouse or keyboard actions. However, we perform these steps in different environments such as our desktop or laptop computers and remote or **virtual machines** (**VMs**). Today's technology has allowed RPA robots to mimic the same actions with higher precision, irrespective of the environment in which they are working. All activities performed by robots require monitoring to ensure the best utilization of the digital workforce. Also, monitoring allows administrators to track and monitor execution times and failures and track the idle times of robots. Today's data analytics power provides precise tracking and analysis of such data to calculate the **return on investment** (**ROI**), utilization, robot idle times, and so on. Hyperautomation is a concept that not only covers the development and monitoring of robots but also enables organizations to precisely monitor and analyze the business process itself. Business process mining is a concept that hyperautomation offers to explore the process and identify the nature of the process, exceptions, different methods of performing the procedure, steps carried out, bottlenecks, and automation possibilities.

RPA today is not just one technology—it is a combination of multiple technologies such as AI, ML, NLP, ICR, and much more. The combination allows RPA robots to perform various simple-to-complex activities without human intervention. RPA has to be applied wisely to business processes, and there are many factors to consider to identify a business process for automation.

Identifying processes for RPA

There are a few main characteristics we look at when deciding the automation potential of a process. At a high level, we could categorize these characteristics into two main segments, as follows:

- Process fitness
- Automation complexity

A few factors are involved in the process of calculating the fitness of a process for automation. The following table illustrates the factors considered in identifying the fitness of a process:

Process fitness	
The process should be rule-based	The decisions taken on the data processed are required to be backed by a predefined set of rules.
Low exception rates	The process should not have many scenarios where we cannot complete the process due to unknown conditions.
Repetitive actions	Considering the repetitive nature of the processes, they require further categorization: • *Manual and non-repetitive*: Processes that require manual executions, but the steps executed in each run are different and nonrepetitive. The functions of such nature are not suitable for automation because automation requires a standard set of steps. • *Manual and repetitive*: The processes that require manual execution and the steps executed in each run are the same and repetitive. The functions of such nature are highly suitable for automation. However, the repeated actions require proper standards to ensure high efficiency. • *Semi-automated and repetitive*: The steps performed in the process are repetitive, but some of the steps are already automated using macros or other automation methods. With proper analysis of the process, possible automation opportunities can be identified. • *Automated*: If the process is already automated, introducing RPA is not required.
Standard input	Inputs provided to the process should either be electronic and easily readable, or readable using the technology that RPA is associated with (such as OCR).
Stable process	The process should not undergo frequent changes in the steps performed.

Figure 1.2 – Process fitness factors in identifying a process for automation

A business process should meet all the factors listed in *Figure 1.2* to qualify for automation. In addition to the process fitness factors, the automation complexity is also one crucial aspect of identifying a suitable automation process. The following screenshot illustrates the required characteristics to consider to determine the process automation complexity:

Automation Complexity	
Types of applications	Some of the applications we use today, such as the Office suite, are easy to automate. However, we do come across very complex applications such as mainframe applications that increase the automation effort. A complete process may require the interaction of multiple applications of such nature. This point plays a significant role when identifying the automation suitability of a process.
Number of screens that require interaction in the application	Similar to a human worker, RPA robots interact with the elements shown on a specific screen of an application. The actions performed might require navigation to multiple screens of an application. The robot is programmed to perform different actions based on the elements shown on the application screen. The higher the number of screens that require interaction, the more effort needed to program the robot.
Types of input	As stated already, the more standard the input is, the less effort is needed to manipulate and prepare the data. However, there are cases where the information is not standardized, and it requires conversion to a standard format, which requires additional effort. The complexity depends on how standard the input is. For example, if the RPA robot requires data extraction from a paragraph of text, it is one of the most complex inputs. On the other hand, if the RPA robot requires data extraction from a structured Excel file, it is one of the least complex inputs.
Number of input	The higher the number of inputs, the higher the complexity is.
Business decisions	The higher the number of decisions taken within the process flow, the higher the complexity is.

Figure 1.3 – Process complexity factors in identifying a process for automation

Deciding on the automation suitability of a process requires consideration of all the factors discussed. The process is mapped into a process assessment matrix based on the results of the factors discussed to compare and identify the best process. The following diagram illustrates a process assessment matrix that each process is mapped onto after assessment. Each process is assessed based on the complexity and benefits it generates after automation and is mapped into the matrix's respective box. The matrix shown here plays a significant role in prioritizing and categorizing the assessed processes:

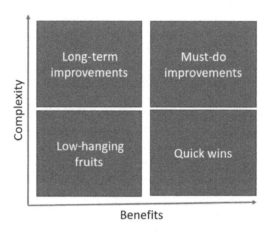

Figure 1.4 – Process assessment matrix

Having identified which bucket the process falls into, the organization can prioritize the automation initiatives based on the previous matrix. Organizations can prioritize quick-win processes in the initial stages, as those are less complicated and provide the highest benefits within a shorter period. Low-hanging fruits are the best to start off with and demonstrate how automation improved the way people work. The processes that fall into the long-term improvements bucket are usually ignored in automation since they do not offer a significant advantage compared to the effort required. The processes that fall into the low-hanging fruits and must-do improvements categories get prioritized for RPA based on the organization's strategic plans. Additionally, the processes that fall into the must-do improvements category usually require standardization to improve the process. The improved processes are assessed again and prioritized based on the bucket they fall into after the assessment.

It is not a good practice to automate every process in the organization or the department. It is important to identify the benefits gained, efforts and resources needed, and the suitability of the process itself for automation before implementing RPA. The inability to perform process assessment and standardization where necessary may lead to more inefficiencies and high costs after applying RPA without a proper strategy. Hence, the following assessment strategy is crucial in any RPA project.

Understanding the stages of an RPA journey

Analyzing the processes and correctly categorizing them can result in obtaining quick wins in RPA projects; however, not all functions are quick wins. To achieve long-term effects from these projects, the organization must have the proper mindset, proper resources, and reasonable goals to get the best outcome. Hence, every RPA project requires the involvement of multiple essential resources during different stages of the journey.

Every RPA project needs to go through six stages during its automation journey. These stages are depicted in the following diagram:

Figure 1.5 – RPA journey

The following sections describe each stage in more detail.

Discovery

Discovery is the initial phase of any RPA project. This phase's primary goal is to spread the word about automation within the organization and find the most suitable process candidates for automation. There are two approaches to perform discovery, as follows:

- The organization already knows the process that requires automation.

- Discover all possible candidate processes for automation.

If the organization does know the process that requires automation, the scope of the discovery phase will be limited to the already identified processes. Critical resources in the RPA team, such as BAs and RPA solution architects, can sit together with the business team to understand the process in detail. The RPA experts and the business teams conduct multiple requirement-gathering sessions to capture all the information needed to understand the process. The teams' tasks include process assessment and detailed mapping of the *as-is* process. The BAs draw the as-is process in detail, explaining all the subprocesses involved. The process map helps to discover standardization requirements and the steps that require automation. The RPA team documents all the information and presents two standard documents, as outlined here:

- **Process definition document (PDD)**: This contains details about the as-is process and how it is standardized and automated.

- **Solution design document** (**SDD**): This contains all the technical details of the automated solution.

However, if the organization does not have a specific process that requires automation, it requires a thorough analysis of all the available functions to identify possible candidates. In such scenarios, the RPA experts such as BAs and solution architects sit together with all the critical business people to understand the existing processes and identify suitable automation opportunities. The team follows the same steps as those explained previously to carry out the assessment. All the analyzed processes are documented and put into the assessment matrix discussed in the previous section. Once the assessment matrix is updated, the most important and the most suitable business processes are selected based on different factors such as cost, ROI, and so on. The rest of the functions are kept in the automation pipeline to keep track of the identified processes that require automation over the next couple of months. All these processes go through some level of standardization and governance procedures to improve the process before automating.

Build

Development of the automation opportunities identified in the discovery phase takes place in the build phase. There are two different approaches to carry out the development of the automation project, as outlined here:

- **Center of Excellence** (**CoE**)-**driven**: The core development team consists of RPA experts such as RPA solution architects, RPA developers, and experienced BAs who carry out discovering and developing automation solutions. The RPA team works with the business users throughout the automation journey to ensure successful delivery.

- **Democratized approach:** With this approach, business users carry out the development by themselves. Not all business users may have technical experience, hence they are enabled to perform actions using tools that do not require specialized or programming knowledge.

Once development is complete, all the automation solutions will undergo rigorous testing to ensure efficiency, accuracy, reliability, and that coding meets development standards and best practices.

Manage

The automation solutions that are built are required to be deployed and updated from time to time. It is vital to keep track of each deployment and update carried out for the project for many reasons, such as the following:

- Keeping track of the changes carried out
- Comparing different versions when needed for bug fixing
- Rolling back to previous versions in an emergency
- Monitoring the usage of automation solutions created
- Accessing management of the solutions

Run

The run stage is crucial in every automation project. Robots execute the solutions deployed in this stage. The execution and allocation of robots are configured based on organizational requirements. Depending on the organization's needs, the robots execute the processes developed in the user's machine or virtual environments without human intervention.

Engage

Every business process includes steps that require decision-making by the users who perform it. Some of these decisions are rule-based, but some require expertise and **user experience (UX)**. In such scenarios, the robot and the user must work together to perform certain steps while the robot takes care of the most complex activities. This concept is called "human in the loop", whereby robots assign tasks for the user, and once the user completes these, the robot takes over control of the rest of the activities.

Measure

Introducing RPA makes an impact within the organization. The effect created requires measurement to understand how to scale RPA initiatives. These measures provide insights into the automation outcomes and the impact made to align the RPA strategy to achieve organizational goals.

Similar to any software development project, RPA projects also have a life cycle. Every RPA project must go through a mandatory set of steps during its life cycle to ensure efficient and worthy delivery. Each stage of the life cycle requires different resources. The following section explains the resources needed during an RPA project and the responsibilities of each resource.

Knowing the RPA resources and responsibilities in an RPA project

As we discuss the different phases of the RPA journey, we also encounter many experts in various projects. These experts perform several tasks depending on their expertise to ensure high-quality and on-time delivery of RPA projects, and we'll now look at them in more detail.

RPA solution architect

The solution architect is in charge of designing the RPA solution's architecture for the proposed business process. The solution architect works alongside the BA to capture the requirement and translate the identified business scenario into a technical solution. The solution architect transfers the technical architecture knowledge to the BA, the business users, and the RPA developers to finalize the solution before development. The solution architect also acts as the development team lead (but does not perform code development) to ensure code quality and standards. The architect is involved from the first stage of the process until the solution is accepted and deployed.

RPA developer

The RPA developer is responsible for developing the solution architecture provided by the solution architect. An RPA developer interacts with development tools and has an excellent knowledge of different development techniques to deliver the final output within the expected standards. The RPA developer is mostly involved in the build stage of the project life cycle, performing development, testing, and bug fixes.

BA

The BA is primarily responsible for gathering all the required information to understand the process and map its as-is version. The BA also works hand-in-hand with the RPA solution architect to develop a *to-be* business process that involves process standardization and automation. The BA should also have a general idea of RPA capabilities and how they work to provide better solutions. Further, the BA is also responsible for transforming the captured requirements and the solution into a PDD to hand over to the business and development teams. The BA is mostly involved during the discovery stage of a project. However, BAs also get involved during a project's development stage from time to time to ensure the proper delivery of requirements.

Implementation manager

The implementation manager manages the overall project and the involved teams. The implementation manager ensures the timely achievement of project milestones by managing the project overall. Usually, the implementation manager is the single point of contact for the business stakeholders.

Infrastructure engineer/manager

Infrastructure is a crucial aspect of any RPA project. The infrastructure engineer/manager is responsible for robots' security and efficient execution of the processes developed by providing the required hardware and software configurations.

RPA support

This role provides support for business users during their day-to-day concerns or issues while working with robots.

The roles mentioned previously are involved in the project as a part of the CoE team. More stakeholders from the business users will also join the team to ensure successful project knowledge transfer and delivery.

Summary

This chapter introduced RPA and discussed why it is the driving force of digital transformation. We further discussed the benefits RPA brings to an organization, as well as which processes are automated across different industries using RPA, and their results. Some of those processes were discussed in more detail, explaining how RPA is applied. Further, we also looked at the factors that need to be considered to identify a business process as suitable for RPA.

Additionally, we also covered how these factors contribute to comparing processes in a process assessment matrix and segments in the matrix to consider for automation. The RPA journey is common to every process that goes through automation. This chapter also addressed the critical stages of an RPA journey and who the involved vital resources are. Finally, the chapter covered each essential resource's roles and responsibilities in the CoE team.

Now that we understand what RPA is, it's the right time to introduce you to the UiPath ecosystem and the tools UiPath has to build automation solutions. *Chapter 2, UiPath Ecosystem*, will introduce you to the UiPath ecosystem, development tools, and setting up the development environment.

2
UiPath Ecosystem

The UiPath platform is an end-to-end automation program that lets organizations achieve remarkable results by helping them improve resilience, adapt to changing market trends, and continuously improve their own process. This is an enhanced version of automation that includes advanced technologies such as Machine Learning, Process Mining, Task Mining, Computer Vision, and many others. The UiPath platform offers all the required tools and services and supports the digital transformation of companies into fully automated enterprises.

Let's have a look at an overview of the UiPath platform and see how we get started with UiPath Studio to build simple to complex automation.

This chapter consists of the following sections:

- An overview of the UiPath platform
- Setting up UiPath Studio
- The UiPath Studio interface

Technical requirements

You should have the following hardware and software to install UiPath Studio:

Particulars	Minimum	Recommended
CPU Cores	2 x 1.8 GHz 32-bit (x86)	4 x 2.4 GHz 64-bit (x64)
RAM	4 GB	8 GB
Operating Systems	Windows 8.1	Windows 10
.NET Framework	Version 4.6.1	Version 4.6.1 or greater

Figure 2.1 – Technical requirements

For downloading and installing UiPath Studio, please navigate to the UiPath Automation Cloud portal by visiting `https://www.uipath.com/start-trial` and follow the onscreen instructions to register to the UiPath portal.

> **Important Note**
> This chapter was created using UiPath Studio 2020.10. Some elements may be different in the latest Community Edition version.

An overview of the UiPath Enterprise RPA platform

The Enterprise RPA platform of UiPath offers you several tools and technologies, seamlessly integrating multiple applications and departments into a fully automated enterprise. The platform helps engage everyone in the organization as part of the Automation journey to automate more labor-intensive tasks.

To achieve successful end-to-end Automation, organizations need to rapidly identify and automate all possible business processes, empower everyone in the organization to contribute to the Automation journey, enable people and robots to automate together, and manage the complete automation cycle. The RPA life cycle consists of the following phases, which will be discussed in upcoming sections:

- Discover

  The processes that need to be automated are identified, analyzed, and documented by process experts using discovery tools.

- Build

  More processes are automated with less effort by developers using UiPath Studio.

- Manage

  Deploy the developed solutions to UiPath Orchestrator to perform automation execution.

- Run

  You can securely and flexibly execute the automation solution using UiPath Robots that access your applications and data to perform automation execution.

- Engage

  Humans and Robots join together in action to complete the automation goals.

- Measure & Govern

  Ensure the automation processes are aligned with the business expectations.

All of this can be achieved by implementing the UiPath Enterprise RPA platform, as shown in *Figure 2.2*, where you can see the key components in action.

The core components of the UiPath platform are **UiPath Studio**, **Orchestrator**, and **Robots**, and they have the option to utilize advanced tools such as Automation Hub, Task Mining, AI Fabric, and Insights, depending on the automation requirements of the enterprise. This process of achieving end-to-end automation in an RPA life cycle using a combination of tools and technologies can also be referred to as **hyperautomation**.

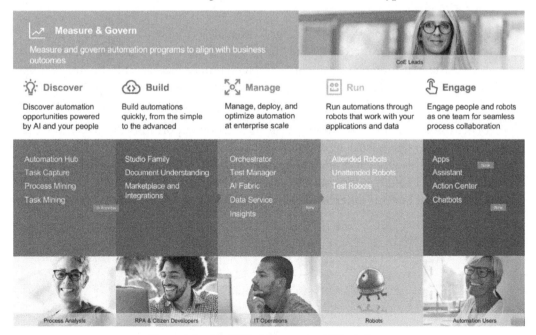

Figure 2.2 – The UiPath Enterprise RPA platform

You should have a fair understanding of hyperautomation and the stages of an RPA journey from the previous chapter. Now, let's explore a little further to see what tools and technologies are used in each stage to implement hyperautomation.

Discover

The Discover phase covers the process of understanding, identifying, and defining the requirements for the Automation process by engaging multiple stakeholders within the organization, such as business users, **Centre of Excellence** (**CoE**) leaders, and RPA developers. The different tools used in this phase are **Automation Hub**, **Task Capture**, **Process Mining**, and **Task Mining**; let's discuss each of these in more detail:

- **Automation Hub**: The main idea of this tool is to encourage any employees in the organization to contribute Automation ideas using a simple submission process so that the idea can be converted into a working solution by engaging relevant stakeholders. This tool has several features, such as exporting the process as XAML or PDD files, taking screenshots of the process, and checking the ROI forecast.

- **Task Capture**: UiPath Task Capture is used to understand more about the daily automation processes directly by gathering detailed information from employees. Once the potential automation candidate is identified, your **Subject Matter Experts** (**SMEs**) can provide their expertise about the particular task and help to achieve your RPA goals.

- **Process Mining**: Process Mining is a process analysis tool that offers solutions to the operational and procedural challenges experienced by organizations. It improves business and customer engagement by implementing a fact-based technique in order to clearly differentiate between useful processes and time-consuming processes, which shows the internal functionality of processes in a pictorial representation.

- **Task Mining**: UiPath Task Mining is an automation opportunity discovery tool that collects information, such as desktop data comprising of screenshot and log data (for example, mouse clicks and keystrokes), and then runs a **Machine Learning** (**ML**) model to analyze the data and suggest a list of processes with high automation potential that benefits different stakeholders in many possible ways.

Build

With the UiPath platform, everyone should be able to build automations, no matter their prior coding skills. The UiPath automation building tool comes in three types:

- **StudioX** (for citizen developers): UiPath StudioX is a complete solution for automating business applications. It aims to enable every business user to automate repetitive tasks by offering seamless integration with Microsoft Office applications and has an intuitive user interface that makes it easy to create automations. As a business user, you can create step-by-step graphical representations of your projects by dragging the corresponding activities to the designer panel. This can be further reviewed with the RPA stakeholders for analysis and development.

- **Studio** (for RPA developers): UiPath Studio is a professional development tool that addresses the creation of complex business processes. It enables team collaboration while enforcing standards, reducing errors, and cutting down on development times. UiPath Studio is ideal for developers with a programming background who are looking to create complex automation projects.

- **Studio Pro** (for specialized developers): In addition to all the capabilities of Studio, UiPath Studio Pro offers access to advanced features such as Test Automation, Application Testing, RPA Testing, API Testing, and Mobile Automation. In short, it is a superset of UiPath Studio with direct integration with UiPath Test Manager and specific capabilities for software test automation.

There is a single installer for all three products. Once you download and run the installation steps, you can select the profile that best suits you. Switching between profiles is allowed at any time from the **Settings** panel.

Manage

Once you have built a robot, it has to be efficiently managed so that it does not create any issues later in deployment or in production. The Manage phase is a centralized location to control all other automation resources. The Manage phase uses different tools for you to start from scratch and work up to production deployment in a minimal number of days. This can also be deployed in scenarios involving short and repetitive processes and fewer robots. Let's look at the tools one by one:

- **Orchestrator**: UiPath Orchestrator helps control robots remotely to perform single or multiple executions of business processes. It supports the management of various resources, such as Assets, Queues, and Triggers, and helps manage the robots and their environments. This can also be seamlessly integrated with third-party applications and solutions to perform continuous executions on multiple environments.

- **AI Fabric**: UiPath AI Fabric is used to integrate ML with RPA. The ML models developed for business processes can be imported to UiPath using AI Fabric for the robots to execute business processes. The ML models are built externally to UiPath using third-party applications, such as Python and AutoML, and then integrated with RPA using AI Fabric.

- **Test Suite**: UiPath Test Suite is a tightly integrated bundle of tools that consolidates the testing process through integrations with your test management and **Application Lifecycle Management** (**ALM**) tools. UiPath Test Suite consists of combinations of tools, such as Studio Pro, Orchestrator, Test Manager Hub, and Test Manager.

- **Data Service**: UiPath Data Service is a persistent data storage service bringing more advanced data modeling and powerful data storage features to your RPA projects. This central place is built to securely store and manage your business data within UiPath, and it is integrated with UiPath Studio and UiPath Robots, allowing you to build automations that can leverage capabilities such as rich relational data types, integrated security, and instantaneous provisioning and deployments, while taking scale into account.

- **Insights**: Insights provides a reporting platform in UiPath Orchestrator using the existing metrics and operational data in executing businesses processes. Using custom-designed dashboards to visualize company data across desired metrics, it enables you to discover new analytical insights and track performance indicators, and it can alert you to errors and irregularities.

Run

There are two types of robot development – separating the capabilities of the attended and unattended robot and adding integrations to make robots part of your work without too much struggle. Let's briefly look at both:

- **Attended robots**: These robots work together with human users to execute business processes. These are typical RPA candidates that do most of the repetitive and boring work, which the robot will take care of executing. Human intervention is still essential in these kinds of executions, mainly to enter credentials or authorize transactions during the business process execution.

- **Unattended robots**: These robots perform complex, repetitive tasks that are carried out in batches. They are also used in cases where human intervention is not required and few sensitive processes (such as signature verification and invoice approvals) are involved during execution.

Engage

In the Engage phase, people and robots work together to achieve common automation goals. There are certain actions the robots are not allowed to perform, such as approving an invoice or verifying signatures, which robots are entirely dependent on humans to complete. Similarly, people depend on robots to perform all repeated, manual, and boring tasks. In the Engage phase, we have different tools to achieve automation goals as follows:

- **Apps**: UiPath Apps is a cloud-based, low-code application development platform that enables you to build and share enterprise-grade custom applications that deliver engaging user experiences. Using UiPath Apps, you can quickly build custom business applications that connect to data in any underlying cloud or on-premises system using the power of automation.

- **Action Center**: UiPath Action Center offers a way for business users to handle actionable items and provide business inputs to robots. It enables support for long-running unattended workflows that require human intervention, as workflow execution is split into multiple manageable workflows and can be executed later based on the inputs from human users. For example, if signature verification is required to perform an approval process, the robot notifies the human approver and performs the approval process based on the input from the human.

- **Assistant**: UiPath Assistant is the center of all your attended automation needs. It is an application that allows you to view, manage, and set reminders for processes. As a client of the service, it can request to start or stop jobs and change settings based on user input.

In this section, we discussed the hyperautomation platform/life cycle of RPA. We also discussed different tools used in various stages of the RPA Enterprise platform. Although we have encountered several tools, UiPath Studio in the Build phase is our primary focus for the Associate Certification, and you will be learning about how to install and use UiPath Studio in the upcoming sections.

Setting up UiPath Studio

The best way to explore the UiPath Studio components is to start using them for your daily automation requirements. In this book, you will have lots of opportunities to learn and practice, so let's start by installing UiPath Studio.

Exploring the different editions

First, let's take a brief look at the different editions of UiPath:

- **Community Edition**: The Community Edition is always free and comes with two Studios, three Robots, and a cloud-hosted Orchestrator for designing automation. Users have access to UiPath Forum support and UiPath Academy courses.

- **Enterprise Server Edition**: This UiPath Studio version is mainly targeted at on-premises enterprise deployments for large businesses. It can have unlimited Studios, an on-premises Orchestrator, and unlimited Robots for designing automation. It offers premium support from the UiPath technical support team in case of any issues and provides access to specialized training from UiPath official training partners.

- **Enterprise Cloud Edition**: The UiPath Enterprise Cloud Edition accommodates the automation needs of both Community- and Enterprise-level users by maintaining the infrastructure in the cloud. It offers instant access to all tools and services required over the cloud to build automation processes and supports the unlimited scaling of automation resources for complete enterprise-level capacity. This edition is highly secure and compliant and provides access to centralized user access management. Additionally, this edition offers premium support from the UiPath technical support team in case of any issues and provides access to specialized training from UiPath official training partners.

Although there are three different UiPath Studio editions available, the one best suited to this book is the UiPath Community Edition.

Installing UiPath Studio

In this section, we are going to see how we can install UiPath Studio from scratch. You may come across two types of installers: `UiPath.Studio.msi` and `UiPathStudioSetup.exe`. UiPath.Studio.msi installs the Enterprise version, or Enterprise Trial version, of the UiPath platform. This supports all users logged in on the machine, offers command-line support and customizable installation, and requires Admin privileges to install Studio. UiPathStudioSetup.exe installs the Community Edition of UiPath Studio and is available for only the user who performs the installation and does not have command-line support or customizable installation and does not require admin privileges to install Studio. Follow these step-by-step instructions to download and install UiPath Studio Community Edition:

1. Navigate to the UiPath Start Trial web page by following this link: `https://www.uipath.com/start-trial`.

2. Sign up for UiPath Automation Cloud by entering information, as you can see in the following screenshot:

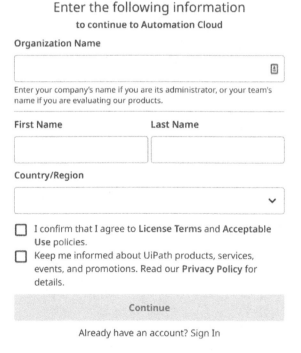

Figure 2.3 – Sign up to the UiPath Cloud platform

3. Once you sign up and verify your email address, click **resource center** on the right side of the **Automation Cloud** screen, as shown in *Figure 2.4*:

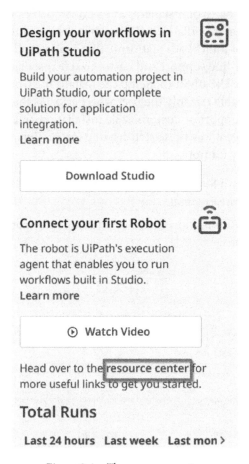

Figure 2.4 – The resource center

4. Click **Download (Preview)** on the Community Edition section of the **Automation Cloud** screen, as shown in *Figure 2.5*:

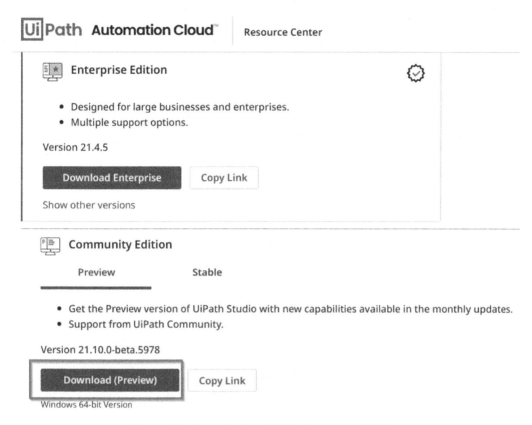

Figure 2.5 – Downloading UiPath Community Edition

5. Once the `UiPathStudio.msi` executable file is downloaded to your system, install the file by double-clicking on the file and following the onscreen instructions. Select the default or recommended options during the installation. You will see the following screen (*Figure 2.6*) once the setup is completed. Click on **Finish** to exit the setup screen.

Completed the UiPath Setup

Click the Finish button to exit the Setup

 Launch UiPath Studio

Finish

Figure 2.6 – UiPath Studio Setup wizard

6. To ensure UiPath is installed successfully, launch UiPath by entering `UiPath` in the Windows search bar. Click on **UiPath Studio** from the menu displayed.

7. Once UiPath Studio is launched successfully, you will be able to see the home screen of the software displayed, as shown in *Figure 2.7*:

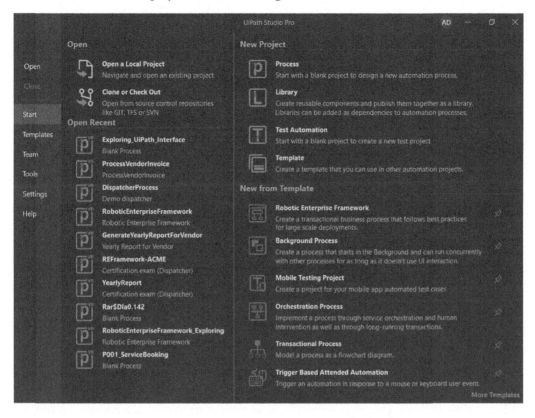

Figure 2.7 – Home screen of UiPath Studio

8. Navigate to **Settings | License and Profile** to configure the profile in UiPath Studio, as follows (*Figure 2.8*). Choose **UiPath Studio** from the options displayed.

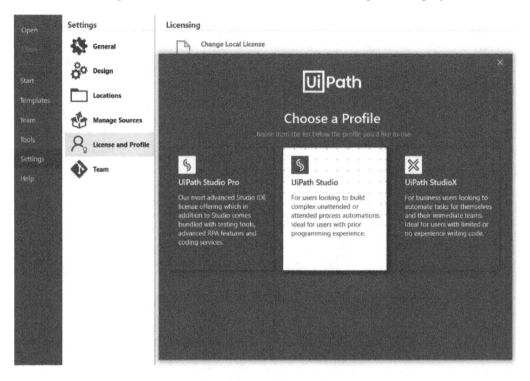

Figure 2.8 – Profile options

In this section, we have discussed different options to sign up to the UiPath Cloud platform and how to install UiPath Studio. Now, let's explore more features and see how we can automate using the different sections and features that are available within UiPath Studio.

Exploring the UiPath Studio interface

UiPath Studio has several menu options available for multiple purposes. Every item on the screen has a hover text to explain the functionality.

Let's explore various parts of UiPath Studio and get more familiar with the Studio interface by creating a basic process. To create a process, click on **Process** in the **New Project** section, as shown in *Figure 2.9*:

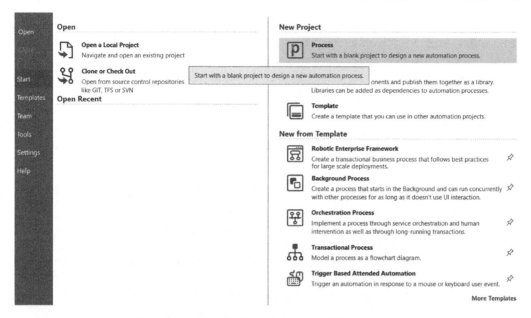

Figure 2.9 – New Project section on the Home screen

When you click **Process,** a pop-up window called **New Blank Process** appears with three fields:

- **Name**: To capture the name of the project

- **Location**: To capture the folder path of the project to be saved

- **Description**: To capture more details about the project

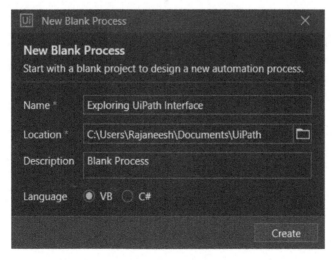

Figure 2.10 – New Blank Process

In this example, I have provided Exploring UiPath Interface as the process name and Blank Process as the process description. Once we have clicked on **Create**, we will be taken to a new project screen where we will see how we can best use the different panels and features for designing our automation workflows.

The Designer panel

The **Designer** panel is used to design automation projects by dragging and dropping activities into it.

Figure 2.11– The Designer panel

The **Designer** panel is the main space for designing or creating an automation project that has quick access to the **Activities**, **Properties**, **Variables**, and **Arguments** panels. Activities can be collapsed or expanded for better viewability and the panel is highly intuitive as it supports all Microsoft Windows operations, such as cut, copy, and paste.

The Project panel

The **Project** panel is displayed as a tree structure, where the root node is the name of the project and the branches contain the dependencies, inputs, settings, and project files. You can see the process you just created displayed in *Figure 2.12*:

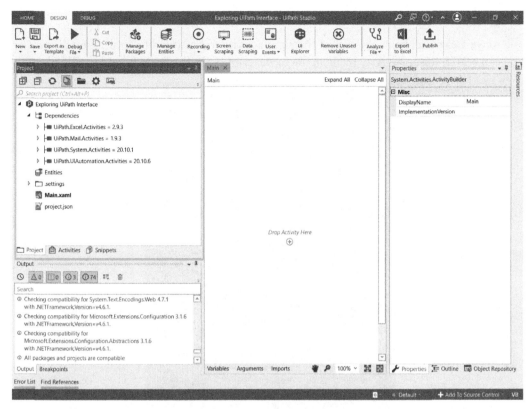

Figure 2.12 – The Project panel

In the **Project** panel, you can perform almost all the operations you perform on a Windows folder. You can copy and paste files, drag files from another folder, rename files, and change project settings. This section is used to manage the project files, dependencies, and project settings.

The Activities panel

The **Activities** panel helps you select the right activity to be added to your automation. You can search for an activity by its name or description in the **Search** field provided.

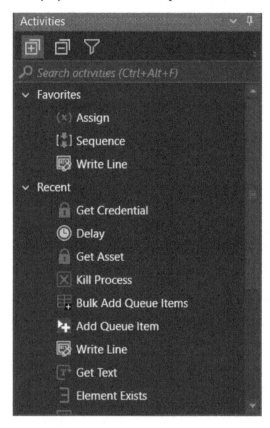

Figure 2.13 – The Activities panel

Once an activity is found in the panel, you can either click and drag it or press the *Enter* button on your keyboard to add it to the **Designer** panel. You can also right-click on the activity and add the activity to your **Favorites** panel.

The Properties panel

This section is used to manage the properties of various activities and to manage variables. The **Properties** panel looks similar to *Figure 2.14*, but changes based on the selected activities:

Figure 2.14 – The Properties panel

Once you have clicked on an activity from the **Designer** panel, the **Properties** panel is displayed on the right by default. This allows you to analyze or change the properties specific to the selected activity. Hovering over the **Properties** field provides more information regarding the field. There are certain properties, such as the **Text** field of a **Type Into** activity, or the **Output** field of an **OpenBrowser** activity, that allows variables to be created from the **Properties** panel.

The Variables panel

The **Variables** panel enables you to create variables and make changes to them.

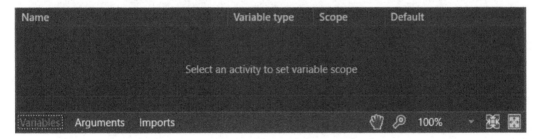

Figure 2.15 – The Variables panel

There are certain details you need to be aware of while creating a variable:

- **Name**: You should give an accurate and meaningful name to the variable, and it needs to be created in camel case (for example, userName), which helps the user to read the name easily. Renaming a variable in this panel automatically updates all occurrences in the current file.

- **Variable type**: You need to select the correct variable type from the list of options available in UiPath. Click on **Browse for Types…** in the **Variable Type** column to explore all the available variable type options. Examples of variable types are **String**, **Int32**, **Boolean**, **DataTable**, and **DateTime**.

- **Scope**: You need to decide the level of access the variable can have, either locally to a specific sequence or globally to the entire project.

Important Note

You can refer to the *Practicing variable creation* section in *Chapter 5, Learning about Variables and Arguments*, to find more information on best practices for using variables.

The Argument panel

The **Argument** panel is mainly used when accessing a workflow to pass input through an argument or get the output from an argument.

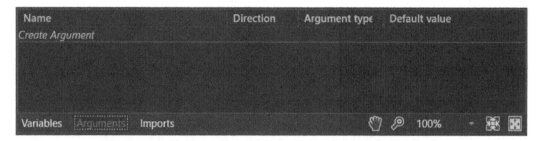

Figure 2.16 – The Argument panel

There are three mandatory fields to be filled:

- **Name**: You can use either lower or upper camel case, followed by the direction of the data flow of the variable. For example, the input username can be given as `in_username` or `in_UserName` and the output can be given as `out_username` or `out_UserName`.

- **Direction**: It can be either **In**, **Out**, or **In/Out**, depending on the direction of the data flow.

- **Argument type**: This needs to be selected based on the nature of the variables or the argument.

The Output panel

The main use of the **Output** panel is to verify the results of the workflow using log messages or writing line activities:

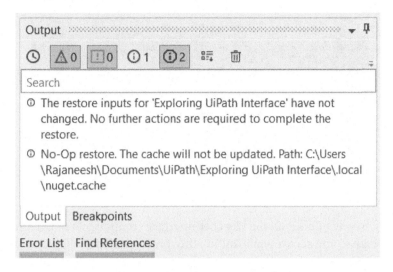

Figure 2.17 – The Output panel

There are different options available in the **Output** panel to display or hide messages based on the type of log messages, such as errors or warnings. There is also a search field to search for specific logs; the matched results are highlighted during this search. Clicking on the **Error List** panel displays any errors during the workflow execution, and clicking on the **Warnings** panel displays any warnings that are generated during the execution of automation workflows.

The Outline panel

The **Outline** panel is used to view the hierarchy of the selected workflow and all nodes available inside the workflow, as shown in *Figure 2.18*:

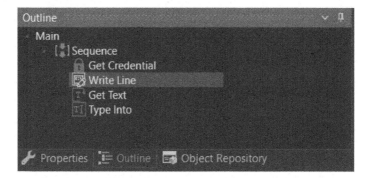

Figure 2.18 – The Outline panel

In this section, we introduced all the key user interface components of UiPath Studio that you will frequently come across while automating processes. This will help you to better understand UiPath Studio and create automation projects in the upcoming chapters.

Summary

This chapter introduced the UiPath Enterprise platform and its components. As part of this introduction, the chapter described each and every component of the UiPath Enterprise platform. Furthermore, we discussed how to install UiPath and set up a UiPath Studio profile. UiPath Studio is the core of the UiPath platform, as automations are created in Studio and then published to Orchestrator and executed by robots.

The next chapter describes UiPath Orchestrator and how automations can be created, published, and executed in Orchestrator.

3
Introducing UiPath Orchestrator

UiPath Orchestrator is a web application and an essential UiPath component through which the automation workflows developed in **UiPath Studio** are published, assigned to robots, and executed. It enables the management of robots, activity packages, data to be processed, execution schedules, and many other assets. Orchestrator can manage all types of processes, from simple to complex.

This chapter focuses on introducing the **UiPath Cloud** platform and Orchestrator. Similar to UiPath Studio, UiPath Orchestrator plays a significant role in automation. Orchestrator acts as the central control unit for all deployed robots and processes; therefore, it is crucial to understand Orchestrator's use and the key concepts used in Orchestrator to manage a virtual workforce.

This chapter consists of the following sections:

- Introducing the UiPath Automation Cloud platform
- Introducing UiPath Orchestrator
- Understanding the fundamental concepts of UiPath Orchestrator
- Creating your first Orchestrator instance in Automation Cloud
- Connecting a local robot to Orchestrator

Technical requirements

Before starting with this chapter, please have UiPath Studio and **UiPath Robot** installed. This chapter requires a general idea of how to use Studio and **UiPath Assistant**.

Additionally, use the following link to sign up or sign in to the Cloud platform: `https://cloud.uipath.com/portal_/cloudrpa`.

The features of the Cloud platform are discussed in detail throughout this chapter.

Creating your first cloud Orchestrator instance

UiPath offers the cloud platform in three versions: Community, Enterprise Trial, and Enterprise. In either version, signing up for the cloud platform creates the UiPath Orchestrator service automatically. The completed service is visible on the **Home** page. However, if the Orchestrator service is not available on the Home page, you can easily create it by navigating to the **Admin** page and then the **Services** page.

Follow these steps to create your first Orchestrator service if it is not available:

1. Log in to the Cloud platform via the following link: `https://cloud.uipath.com/portal_/cloudrpa`.

2. If the Orchestrator service is not available on the **Home** screen, navigate to the **Admin** page.

3. Navigate to the **Tenants** page and click on the **Add Tenant** button.

4. Fill in the **Tenant Name** field and make sure the Orchestrator service is checked in the service options.

5. Click on the **Save** button.

6. If the Orchestrator service is available, click on **Orchestrator service** to navigate to Orchestrator.

Following these steps helps to create the first Orchestrator service easily. Setting up the service is the first step. The UiPath Robot service requires a few configurations to connect with the created Orchestrator service.

Introducing the UiPath Cloud platform

The Cloud-based Enterprise platform is provided as a platform as a service to all users. The Cloud platform enables users to create and manage all automation resources. It allows users to automate instantly without any changes to their existing infrastructure, and to quickly scale up. Furthermore, the Cloud platform enables easy management of licensing plans by requesting a trial or purchasing additional licenses for other services that UiPath offers.

The following are some of the primary functions of the Cloud platform:

- Managing who can access the Cloud platform and their roles based on the task they are required to perform

- Managing licenses by allocating them to Orchestrator instances

- Managing multiple UiPath Orchestrator tenants and services associated with each tenant

- Managing the robots and the processes that require execution based on triggering schedulers

- Managing other cloud-based solutions offered by UiPath

- Managing logs for auditing purposes

UiPath manages all the system updates in the Cloud platform, removing the burden of system updates from the user. Further, the Cloud platform offers state-of-the-art defense mechanisms, proven by many government organizations to ensure data security. The Cloud platform is available for Enterprise users as well as Community users.

Signing in to the Cloud platform provides you with the ability to access the sections listed next.

Home screen and Resource Center

The Home screen presents a dashboard that gives you a high-level view of the Robot and Studio licenses, license usage, recently assigned tasks in Action Center, recently executed processes, and access to Orchestrator services. The latest version of the Cloud platform may look slightly different than *Figure 3.1*. In addition, the Community Cloud may also look different compared to the Enterprise version, as some of the features are restricted in terms of the environments based on the license type.

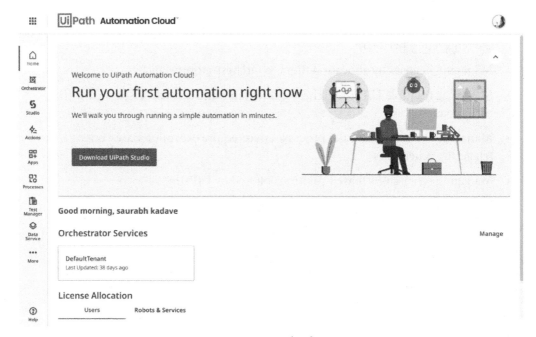

Figure 3.1 – Automation Cloud Home screen

As shown in *Figure 3.1*, the Home screen also gives you access to additional resources such as a download link to download UiPath Studio

Actions

Actions give you the ability to manage and attend to all the tasks robots create for humans to verify. *Figure 3.2* illustrates what Action Center tasks look like in the UiPath Cloud platform:

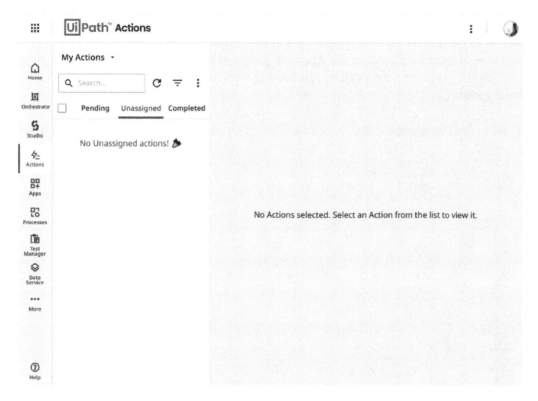

Figure 3.2 – Automation Cloud Actions screen

The **Actions** page shows all the completed tasks by users, including tasks that are
`Pending`, `Unassigned`, and `Completed`. Users can also assign tasks to themselves or
transfer them to a different user for further action.

Apps

The **Apps** screen provides users with the ability to build their applications. **UiPath Apps**
is a low-code platform that allows any user to quickly create a web interface by dragging
and dropping the elements needed. Applications designed through Apps interact with
the robots to execute automated processes using the data provided by the user through
the application.

Apps helps to present a simple single interface for users to interact with complex automation solutions that require interaction with multiple applications behind the scenes. *Figure 3.3* illustrates the **Apps** screen. Apps is not part of the Associate certification; however, we wanted to provide a glimpse of the other interesting features that are available.

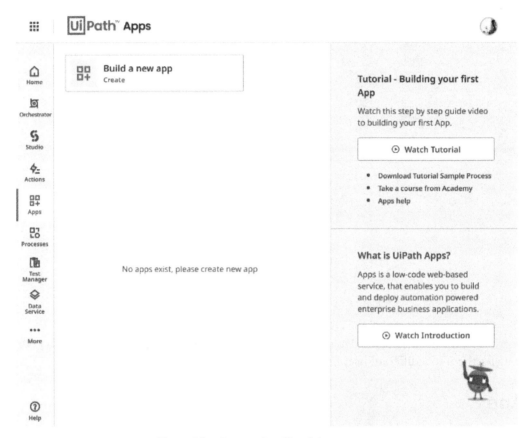

Figure 3.3 – Automation Cloud Apps screen

As illustrated in *Figure 3.3*, UiPath Apps can create multiple applications seamlessly for different needs. Users can publish and share the application with other users who require access and the ability to utilize the power of automation in their day-to-day activities.

Processes

The **Processes** page provides easy access to all automated processes that robots execute in Orchestrator, without *actually* logging in to Orchestrator. However, configuring these automated processes is required to be done through UiPath Orchestrator. *Figure 3.4* illustrates a sample **Processes** page available in the UiPath Cloud platform. Although processes are part of the certification program, what is shown in the **Processes** section is not a part of the Associate certification.

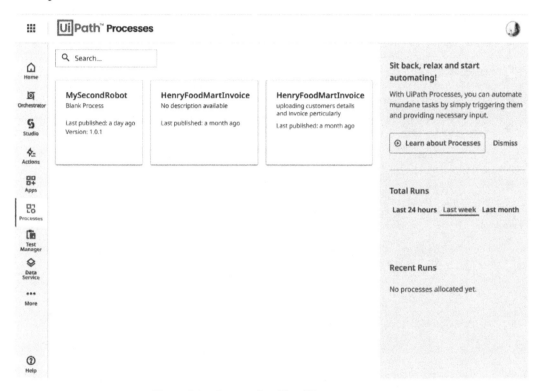

Figure 3.4 – Automation Cloud Processes screen

As shown in *Figure 3.4*, the **Processes** page shows all available processes and a few additional details such as the version, last run date, and package feed, which the user can click and execute.

Data Service

Data Service offers a platform for users to store the data passed through automated processes. This service provides cloud-based secure storage to store data in a relational model where robots can easily access the information to process. The goal of the Data Service is to provide a single point of storage for the data processed by the robots. The Data Service is an interesting feature to explore; however, it is not a part of the Associate certification.

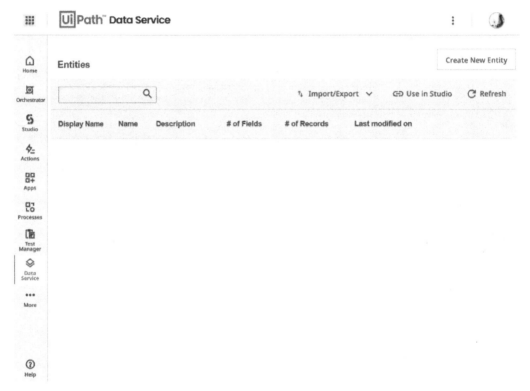

Figure 3.5 – Automation Cloud Data Service screen

Figure 3.5 showcases some sample storage entities created in the platform to store data. The **Entities** page summarizes each entity, by displaying the description, number of columns, number of records in each entity, and the last modified date.

AI Fabric

AI Fabric allows users to deploy and train AI models available out of the box or have custom-built AI models run within automation solutions. The AI models created in AI Fabric seamlessly integrate with the UiPath automation solutions built through UiPath Studio to provide intelligence to the tasks performed by robots. *Figure 3.6* gives you a general idea of what the **AI Fabric** main screen looks like. Building and connecting with AI models is interesting; however, there are more advanced features. As a result, AI Fabric is not included in the Associate certification.

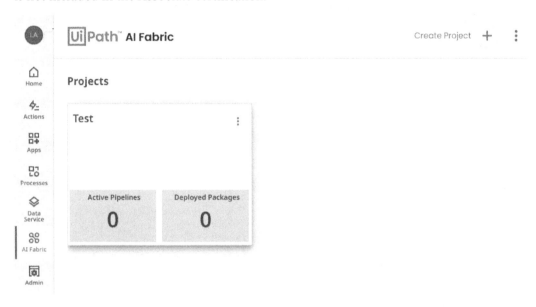

Figure 3.6 – Automation Cloud AI Fabric screen

All AI Fabric projects created will be listed on the main landing page of the AI Fabric platform.

Admin

The **Admin** page includes several sections that allow you to configure the services, licenses, user access, and organizational settings. The functions you see on the **Admin** page differ based on the version (Community or Enterprise) and the current release.

Tenants

The **Tenants** page includes the instances of different applications that you use in your cloud platform. One of these applications is UiPath Orchestrator. Currently, the **Tenants** page only supports instances of the Orchestrator application.

Figure 3.7 provides a glimpse of how the **Tenants** page appears in Automation Cloud. The **Tenants** page may include more than one Orchestrator tenant, thereby enabling multitenancy. By having multiple tenants, users are able to separate automation solutions into different environments. One of the best examples of multitenancy is the use of separate tenants for development, QA, and production.

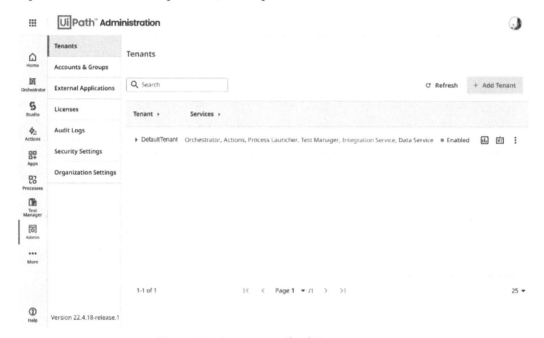

Figure 3.7 – Automation Cloud Tenants screen

As shown in *Figure 3.7*, the **Tenants** page lists all Orchestrator instances you have under your organization's instance. The page also allows users to edit the allocation of licenses to the tenants and manage the other services used, along with Orchestrator instances such as Action Center, Data Service, and AI Fabric.

Users and Groups

User and group management is one of the key features provided in Automation Cloud. The **Accounts and Groups** page gives you access to manage users and groups by creating users, customizing permissions at the organizational and service levels, inviting new users, and deleting existing users. *Figure 3.8* illustrates what the **Users** tab looks like in Automation Cloud:

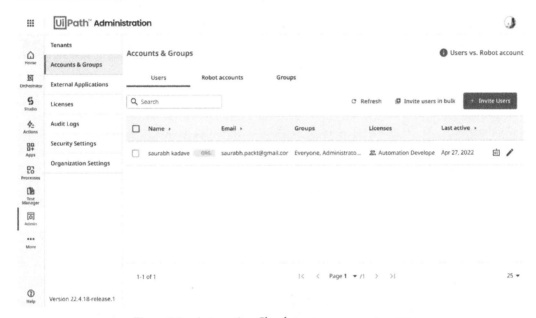

Figure 3.8 – Automation Cloud user management screen

In addition to the mentioned features, the **Accounts and Groups** page allows the bulk inviting of users through the **Invite Users** option.

Licenses

License management occurs under three different categories: Community Plan, Enterprise Trial, and Enterprise License Plan. The **Licenses** page displays the license plan assigned to you, along with the number of robots and other services you have access to in the Cloud platform.

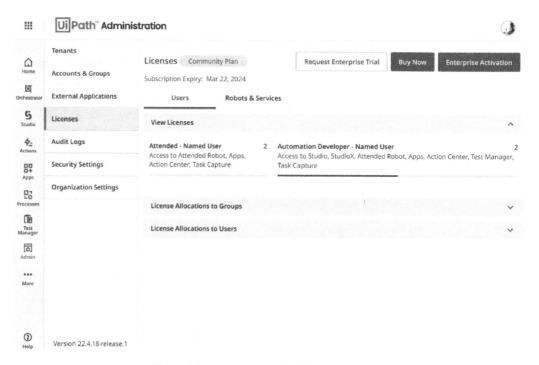

Figure 3.9 – Automation Cloud Licenses screen

As shown in *Figure 3.9*, the licensing information is displayed under three different tabs:

- The **Robots** tab illustrates how many attended, unattended, testing, and non-production robot licenses are available for the Cloud platform.

- The **Studios** tab displays the available named user Studio, Studio X, and Studio Pro licenses for the user.

- The **Other Services** tab showcases the license availability for services such as AI Fabric, Computer Vision, GPUs, and Document Understanding.

Audit Logs

The **Audit Logs** page displays all the logs related to user actions, such as new user creations and membership plans. *Figure 3.10* illustrates the **Audit Logs** page:

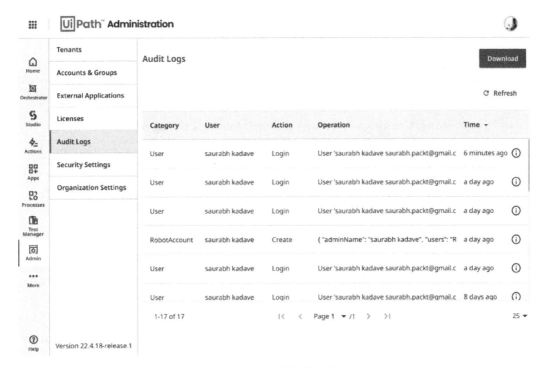

Figure 3.10 – Automation Cloud Audit Logs screen

The **Audit Logs** page also allows the user to download all the audit logs for auditing purposes. Additionally, the page will enable you to be compliant with the organization's rules and regulations by tracking user actions.

Organization Settings

The **Organization Settings** page provides the capability to change Orchestrator URLs, the Automation Cloud platform name, and language settings.

- Automation Cloud houses instances of UiPath Orchestrator and many other services. Knowing the Automation Cloud platform helps the user to easily configure and provision Orchestrator instances within minutes.

- Orchestrator uses the licenses available in the Automation Cloud platform to connect with robots and run automation processes. Each Orchestrator created in Automation Cloud is assigned several licenses to perform the required actions.

The next section of the chapter illustrates how to create Orchestrator instances on the Automation Cloud platform.

Introducing UiPath Orchestrator

UiPath Orchestrator is the heart of the entire automation suite, which manages all the published automation solutions developed in Studio, the execution of tasks by robots, and the execution schedules. Orchestrator is available as a cloud platform or as an on-premise solution. It offers many capabilities for its users. Some of those capabilities are as follows:

- **Provisioning**: Creating new robots and maintaining existing robots and users.

- **Deployment**: Deploying workflows created in UiPath Studio for execution on demand or using schedules to ensure efficient planning and execution.

- **Configuration**: Creating and maintaining user groups, robots, and user access for processes and other resources.

- **Monitoring**: Tracking the status of executed processes, robot status, and user permissions.

- **Logging**: Stores data related to executions, robots, audit logs, and other actions in a SQL database or Elasticsearch.

- **Queues**: Acts as an intermediary data storage and processing system for transactional data through queues by prioritizing the transactions processed. Each transaction is treated and monitored separately during the execution, ensuring the overall process is not affected by any transaction errors.

- **Integrated Connectivity**: Enables secure connections for communication between third-party services through API or other integration methods.

- **Version Control**: Orchestrator maintains the versions of the packages and libraries published. Orchestrator also allows the use of different package versions across multiple robots for execution.

UiPath Automation Cloud enables the users to manage the virtual workforce. To gain the best out of the capabilities that Orchestrator offers, understanding the key fundamentals is essential.

Understanding the fundamental concepts of UiPath Orchestrator

There are a few fundamental concepts that everyone needs to know before using UiPath Orchestrator. Some of these fundamental concepts are listed as follows.

Robots

Robots, also known as **execution agents**, execute the workflows created in UiPath Studio. Orchestrator manages these execution agents through the **Robots** page. The agent is installed separately or with Studio, depending on the license model. There are different types of robots available in Orchestrator. At the top of the Robot type hierarchy, Orchestrator categorizes robots into two categories, as shown in *Figure 3.11*:

Robot Type	Description
Standard	Configured when the machine that the robot works on does not change
Floating	Configured when the machine that the robot works on changes frequently or when the same user works on multiple devices

Figure 3.11 – Robot types in UiPath Orchestrator

Orchestrator allows the creation of either type according to how the robot allocation should occur. Each type mentioned is categorized into four additional robot types according to how the robot is triggered and the environment installed, as shown in *Figure 3.12*:

Robot Type	Description
Attended Robot	Is it triggered manually by the user or through user events. The robot agent runs in the same machine where the human user works, assisting the user's daily activities.
Unattended Robot	Runs in virtual machines and executes processes without any human intervention. The Orchestrator manages the unattended robots by controlling the executions, monitoring, and managing the data through queues.
Development Robot	Features are the same as the unattended robot but only used to connect the UiPath Studio to Orchestrator and for development purposes.
Non-Production Robot	Used only for development and testing purposes.

Figure 3.12 – Robot types in UiPath Automation Cloud

There can be more types other than these; however, for the purpose of the Associate certification, we will focus only on the robot types referenced in the preceding table.

Folders

The use of **folders** enables the user to better organize the processes, robots, assets, and queues for better management and access control. UiPath Orchestrator supports **Modern** and **Classic** folder types, each with a range of features.

Modern folders offer the following features:

- They allow the dynamic allocation of robots and user roles.
- They support a hierarchical structure where you can have up to six subfolders under each first-level folder.
- They enable large-scale automation initiatives by easily integrating with Windows Active Directory.
- Each folder has its package feed to store packages related to the context of the folder.

Classic folders do not have the same features that Modern folders offer. The following outlines the limitations of Classic folders compared with Modern folders:

- They contain robots and environments in the traditional way.
- They cannot create or maintain subfolders.
- Robots created in Classic folders can only work within the scope of the folder.

One important point to mention here is that Classic folders are a part of the Associate v1.0 certification. However, users may not be able to use them in the Community version as this feature is discontinued. The latest version of Orchestrator only uses Modern folders.

Folders are created and managed at the tenant level of Orchestrator. *Figure 3.13* illustrates the **Folder management** page of Orchestrator:

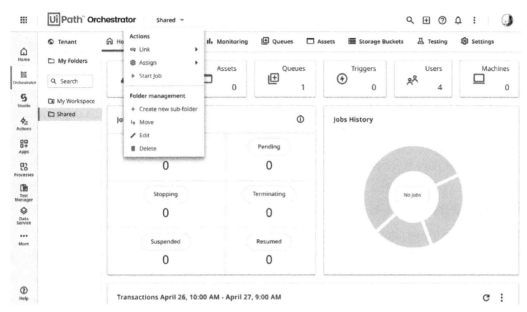

Figure 3.13 – Folder creation in UiPath Orchestrator

Folders provide better control over what users see and control. The folder management screen grants access to the folder's resources for different users with different permission levels. Orchestrator shows Classic folders in red, and Modern folders in blue. In addition, Modern folders allow the creation of subfolders for the further division of resources, whereas Classic folders do not allow subfolders.

On the other hand, there is another type of folder, named "MyWorkspace." Developers mainly use this option to separate their development work from other users. MyWorkspace is unique and other users cannot access another user's workspace. MyWorkspaces offer the same functionality as other folders, although they are restricted to the assigned users.

Environment

The **Environment** feature in UiPath Orchestrator allows the grouping of robots. Grouping was the traditional method of categorizing robots before the introduction of folders. Grouping is usually done based on the business groups that execute their automation solutions. For example, a Human Resource department may have multiple user groups running their automation solutions that are disconnected from the rest of the department. Each environment may consist of multiple robots, and a robot can be a part of more than one environment. The management of environments is handled through the **Environment** page in Orchestrator. Environments are only available in Classic folders.

Organizational units

UiPath Orchestrator allows the creation of multiple business units within the same Orchestrator instance. Each instance will consist of its dedicated environments, queues, assets, and robots. The separation of business units ensures the proper organization of processes, robots, and the security of the data and processes available in Orchestrator.

Packages

The published workflow solutions are known as **packages**. Packages can be published both locally and in UiPath Orchestrator. Uploading packages to Orchestrator can be done directly through UiPath Studio or manually through the Orchestrator UI. Orchestrator manages the versions of the packages deployed and used within Orchestrator. The **Packages** screen of Orchestrator allows the management of all packages and their versions.

The **Packages** screen displays the release notes and the versions of each package version. The user is given the ability to downgrade or upgrade packages depending on how they want to use them. Also, the same package management display allows the users to maintain the history of release versions by deleting or keeping track of release information for better visibility of changes. The usage of a package determines the status of the package as **Active** or **Inactive**. If the package is used in one or more processes, the status of the used package version is set as Active. *Figure 3.14* shows the **Packages** page with all the available packages:

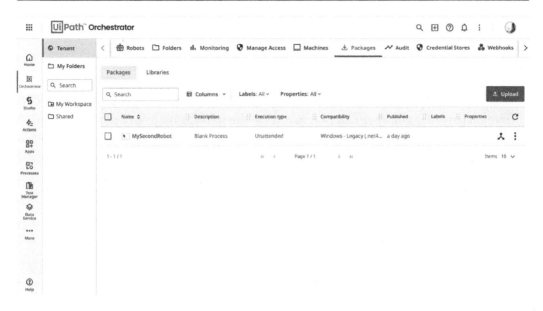

Figure 3.14 – UiPath Orchestrator Packages screen

Clicking on the **Options** button (the three dots) of each package takes you to a menu where you can select to view the package versions. The **View Versions** display shows the available versions of the package and which version the processes use. *Figure 3.15* shows the versions of a selected package:

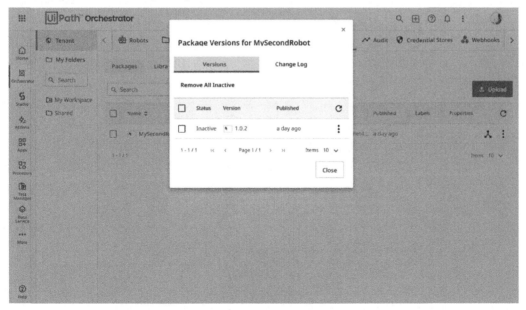

Figure 3.15 – Viewing package versions and usage

Processes

Processes are created using the packages published in Orchestrator. Multiple processes may use the same package within different environments. For example, let's assume that you developed and deployed a package that logs in to your core system to update customers' account details. The account details can be updated by different people in different departments in a bank. As a result, the same package may be used for different account updates through different teams by connecting with other processes. The robots look for the processes within their environment for execution. The `Main.xaml` file of each automation solution developed in UiPath Studio is the main file from which the execution starts. The Arguments available in the Main workflow file allow the user to pass pre-defined values during process execution and creation.

Figure 3.16 shows the **Processes** page of Orchestrator. The **Processes** page is available under the **Automations** tab, which is available for each folder. The package contains all the information about the process, the package used for the process, the package version, and the execution priority.

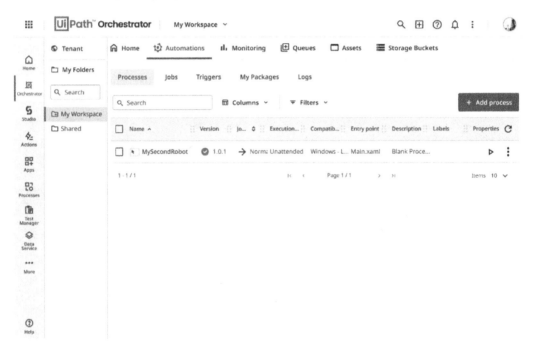

Figure 3.16 – Processes page in UiPath Orchestrator

Process creation takes place after uploading the package to Orchestrator. Clicking on the blue color **Add Process** button on the **Processes** page takes you to the process creation page. The process creation is configured in three stages, as shown in the following screenshot. Process creation requires the following inputs from the user (the input is provided in three stages):

- **Display Name**: A more user-friendly name for the process. Orchestrator and UiPath Assistant use this name to refer to the process.

- **Package Name**: Selected from the list of packages available in Orchestrator. It is mainly used to select the process that you want to create once it is published.

- **Package Version**: This shows the package version used for the process.

- **Job priority**: The priority you select is applied during the process execution. High-priority jobs will take precedence over medium- or low-priority jobs when executed/scheduled to run at a given time.

- **Description**: A short description of the process.

Providing the information referenced here and clicking on the **Create** button creates the process in Orchestrator. UiPath Assistant and the jobs will have access and will display the newly added processes. *Figure 3.17* shows the process creation screen of Orchestrator:

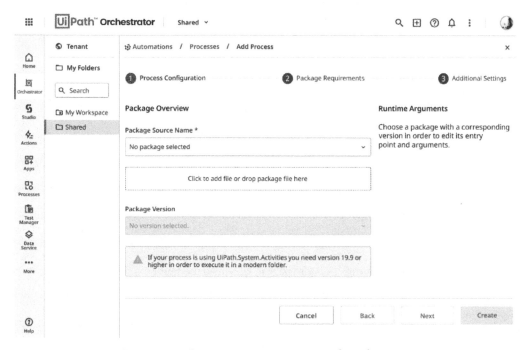

Figure 3.17 – Process creation page in UiPath Orchestrator

We need to navigate through the three stages shown in the screenshot and configure the fields described previously to create the process. The stages are introduced to simplify the configuration screen and have the options in an organized manner.

Job

A **job** is a task performed by a robot. Each job is managed separately in Orchestrator through the **Jobs** page. Orchestrator allows the creation of jobs on demand or based on schedules. **On-demand jobs** can start by creating the job from the **Jobs** page or by triggering the job from the UiPath Assistant screen. **Scheduled jobs** are triggered based on pre-defined schedules created in Orchestrator.

In addition, a job can automatically be triggered through a Queue. If the queue is configured to trigger a particular process upon inserting new items, the queue will automatically create the job without a schedule. *Figure 3.18* shows the executed jobs on the **Jobs** page. The **Jobs** page provides details of all the executed processes, execution time, user, machine (the name of the computer that the robot is connected to), the type of robot, and the status of the execution.

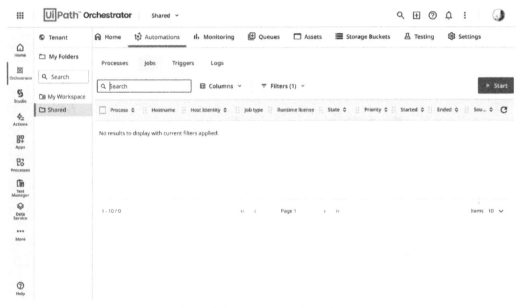

Figure 3.18 – Jobs page in UiPath Orchestrator

Similar to the **Processes** page, Orchestrator allows the creation of jobs from the **Jobs** page. This allows you to select the process to execute, the environment, and the robot assigned to perform the task. As shown in *Figure 3.19*, the execution target and the robot assignment is handled automatically if not specified by the user:

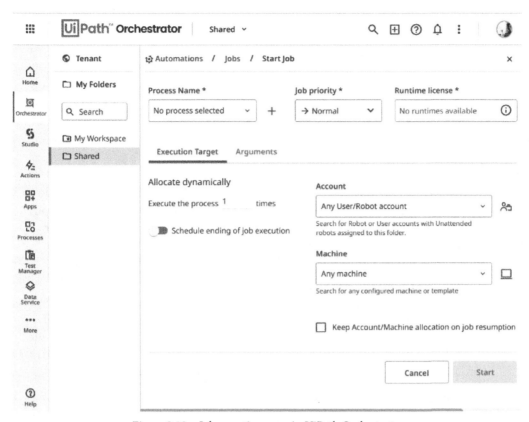

Figure 3.19 – Jobs creation page in UiPath Orchestrator

Job creation requires the user to configure the **Job creation** display fields before clicking the **START** button:

- **Process Name**: Select the process intended to run from the drop-down list. The drop-down menu shows the display names given for each process at the time of process creation.

- **Job priority**: The job priority has three values: **Low, Normal**, and **High**. The default priority is **Normal**.

- **Runtime License**: Orchestrator supports two main Runtime License options: Unattended and Non production. Unattended is used when you have production unattended runtime licenses assigned to the tenant. Non production is used for non production licenses, but it is also similar to unattended.

- **Execute the process X times**: Enables the process to run X number of times.

- **Account**: If not mentioned, the user/robot is dynamically allocated from the assigned group of users for the process.

- **Machine**: If not mentioned, the runtime machine is dynamically allocated for the process.

- **START** button: Clicking the **Start** button starts the job immediately and it will be visible on the **Jobs** page.

Triggers

Triggers enable the robot to run specific processes at a given timeslot. A Schedule allows users to trigger processes iteratively without human intervention. The **Triggers** page in Orchestrator gives you access to creating schedules based on regular working days or custom calendars that include non-working days.

The following screenshot of the **Triggers** page shows the two different types of triggers available:

- **Queue Trigger**: This trigger is associated with queues. It gets fired automatically whenever a specified number of new items are inserted into the queue. The queue trigger helps in situations where you cannot define a particular time frame to trigger a process, but you need to run it as soon as the data is available.

- **Time-Based Trigger**: This trigger is programmed to trigger a specific process at a particular time on an hourly, daily, weekly, or monthly basis. The users can configure custom time frequencies as required using cron expressions under advanced options. The **Trigger Details** column specifies the time and the running frequency of time-based triggers.

In addition, the **Triggers** page includes the trigger name, the process associated with the trigger, the execution environment, and the priority of the tasks.

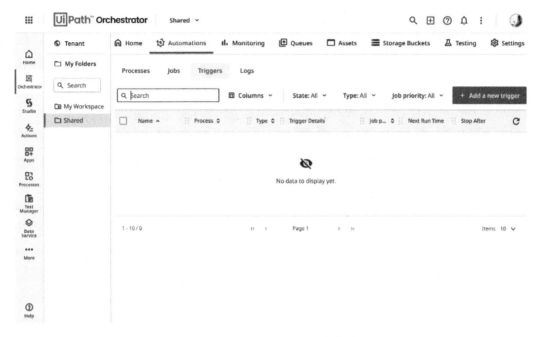

Figure 3.20 – Triggers page in UiPath Orchestrator

Clicking on the **Add New Trigger (+)** button on the **Triggers** page opens a new page to create a new trigger. The options shown on the screen depend on the type of trigger you select. *Figure 3.21* shows the inputs required to create a time-based trigger:

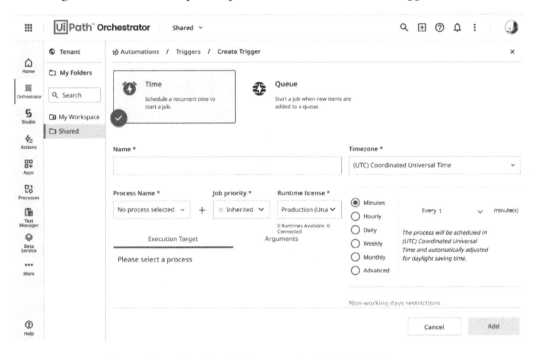

Figure 3.21 – Time-based trigger creation in UiPath Orchestrator

Time-based trigger creation requires the options shown in *Figure 3.21*. The following describes each option on the screen:

- **Name**: The name of the trigger.

- **Timezone**: The timezone to consider for the time-based trigger.

- **Process Name**: Includes a dropdown that consists of all the processes available in Orchestrator. The user must select which process to execute based on the trigger.

- **Job priority**: Similar to the job creation screen, this property describes which priority to consider when creating a job through a trigger.

- **Frequency**: Select the frequency at which the process is triggered. For example, if the process needs to be executed every 3 hours, the frequency must be set to **Hourly** and the time interval of **Every 3 hours** must be selected.

- **Non-working days restrictions**: If a custom calendar is built that includes non-working days, the user can select the calendar. The trigger does not get executed on defined non-working days.

- On the other hand, queue trigger creation has a different set of properties. *Figure 3.22* illustrates the inputs required to create a queue trigger:

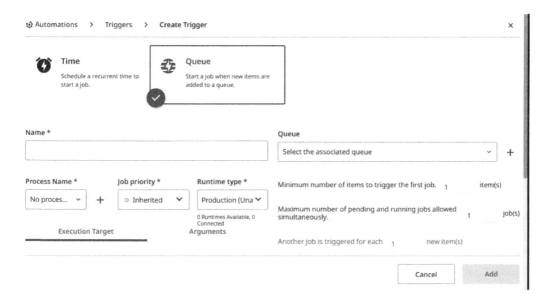

Figure 3.22 – Queue trigger creation in UiPath Orchestrator

An explanation of each input field required for a queue trigger is as follows:

- **Name**: The name of the trigger.

- **Process Name**: The name of the process the trigger should execute. The dropdown shows all the available processes in Orchestrator.

- **Queue**: The queue the trigger monitors for new items.

- **Job priority**: Similar to the job creation screen, this property describes which priority to consider when creating a job through a trigger.

- **Arguments**: If the selected process requires pre-defined input values for defined arguments, the necessary values are assigned through this option. However, the **Parameters** option is optional as the user may not need to provide the input, but it is taken automatically from another process.

- **Minimum number of items to trigger the first job**: Defines the minimum number of items required in the queue to trigger the process.

- **Maximum number of pending and running jobs allowed simultaneously**: Multiple jobs can use the items in the queue simultaneously. This property controls the maximum number of running or pending jobs the trigger creates to run simultaneously.

- **Timezone**: The timezone with which the queue is associated.

- **Non-working days restrictions restrictions**: If a custom calendar is built that includes non-working days, the user can select the calendar. The trigger does not get executed on defined non-working days.

Assets

Assets allow you to store a single data element for later use within the automation process. The typical types of assets available in Orchestrator allow the storage of text values, Boolean values, integer values, and credentials for applications.

Assets also provide the capability to store and pass different values for different robots. If an asset is configured to store a single value, all robots use the same value. However, if an asset is configured with the **Value Per Robot** option, different robots will obtain the value assigned to each. Assets can be created and configured through the **Assets** page in Orchestrator.

Assets come in handy when robots need credentials to access applications or in scenarios where it does not make sense to store values in a workflow. Orchestrator allows the creation of assets for each folder. An asset created in one folder will only be visible within the scope of the folder.

Figure 3.23 illustrates the **ASSETS** option on the Orchestrator home page for the selected folder:

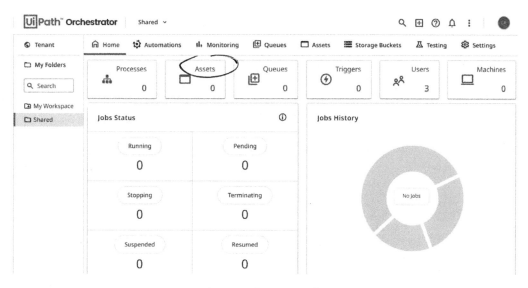

Figure 3.23 – Orchestrator home page folder Assets option

Clicking **Assets** navigates the user to the **Assets** page that lists all the available assets under that folder. *Figure 3.24* showcases the **Assets** page of a selected folder. The display also offers the capability to create, edit, and delete new assets.

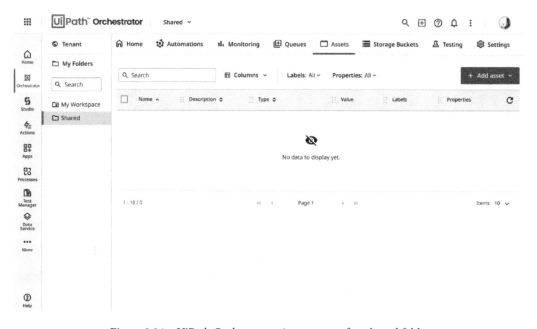

Figure 3.24 – UiPath Orchestrator Assets page of a selected folder

For asset creation, the user can click on the + button to navigate to the asset creation page. *Figure 3.25* shows the asset creation page and the fields required to create an asset:

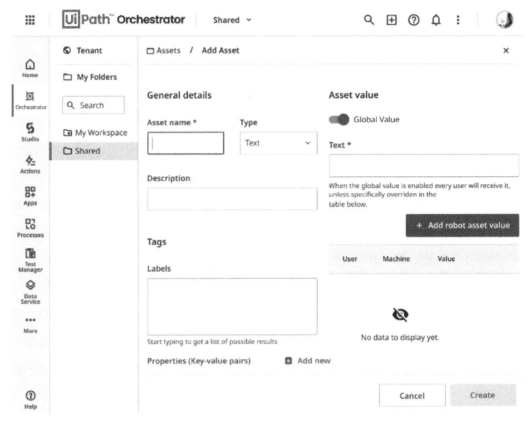

Figure 3.25 – UiPath Orchestrator asset creation page

The following provides an explanation of the required fields:

- **Asset name**: The asset should have a unique name as the workflows created in Studio refer to the asset using this name.

- **Type**: The data type of the asset. Depending on the data stored in the asset, the data type is selected. Currently, the asset supports only primitive data types such as Text, Integer, Boolean, and Credential. The Credential is a particular type that allows users to securely store credentials in different systems. The other data types, such as Text, Integer, and Boolean, are selected based on the asset's value and usage.

- **Description**: A short note that describes the use of the asset and what values it holds.

- **Global Value**: If enabled, every user will receive the value unless it is explicitly overridden by the user in the Specific Value section.

- **Add robot Asset Value**: The asset can provide different values for each user/robot if configured. The default is a single value.

UiPath Studio provides a set of activities that enables interaction with assets in Orchestrator. The following describes each activity and how they interact with assets:

- **Get Asset**: Retrieves the value of the specified asset

- **Set Asset**: Updates the specified asset with a new value

- **Get Credential**: Retrieves credentials from the specified Credential type asset

- **Set Credential**: Updates the specified Credential type asset with new credentials

Queues

Queues offer the capability to store and process items in the queue in sequential order. The records added to the queue are known as **transaction items**. The execution order of transactions is decided based on the priority and SLA levels of each transaction item. One or multiple robots access the queue to process each transaction separately. The queue can also trigger jobs upon inserting new queue items through the **Queue Trigger** option. There are many advantages of using queues in complex automation solutions. The following are some of these advantages:

- A central repository for all transaction items.

- Reporting capability for each transaction item as well as for the queue itself.

- In-built transaction item prioritization based on transaction priority and **Service-Level Agreement (SLA)** levels. SLAs are the agreed service delivery timelines that everyone in the organization needs to follow to ensure customer satisfaction and quality delivery.

- Efficient processing of items using one or many robots.

- Advanced auto retrying capabilities of failed transaction items.

These capabilities come in handy when processing large amounts of data that require independent processing and monitoring. For example, processing customer complaints, customer loan application processing, and client enrollments represent excellent use cases for queue processes. These examples are ideal candidates for processing queues because each complaint or each loan application is independent of one another. Each item has its unique characteristics that require separate processing.

Similar to assets, folders in Orchestrator house queues. A queue available in one folder is not visible to another folder. *Figure 3.26* shows the option available on the Orchestrator home page to access the **Queues** page:

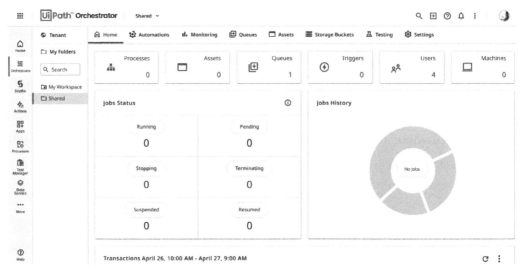

Figure 3.26 – Queues option on the Orchestrator home screen

The **Queues** page displays all the available queues in the selected folder with additional information related to the queue. *Figure 3.27* shows the information related to each queue on the **Queues** page:

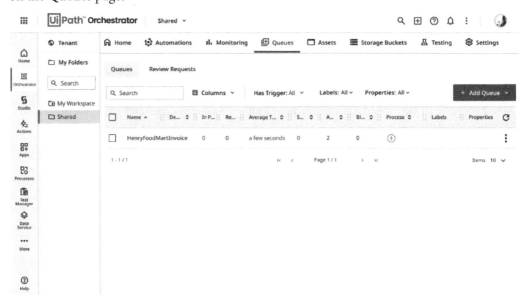

Figure 3.27 – Information shown on the Orchestrator Queues page

The following describes the information in more detail:

- **Name**: The name of the queue

- **Description**: A short description of the queue

- **In Progress**: The number of transaction items with the **In Progress** status

- **Remaining**: The number of transaction items remaining to be processed

- **Average Time**: The average time taken to complete a transaction

- **Successful**: The number of transaction items completed successfully

- **App Exception**: The number of failed transactions due to application exceptions

- **Biz Exception**: The number of failed transactions due to business exceptions

- **Process**: Displays the associated queue triggers

Clicking the + **Add Queue** button in the top-right corner navigates to the queue creation screen. *Figure 3.28* shows the required configurations to create a queue:

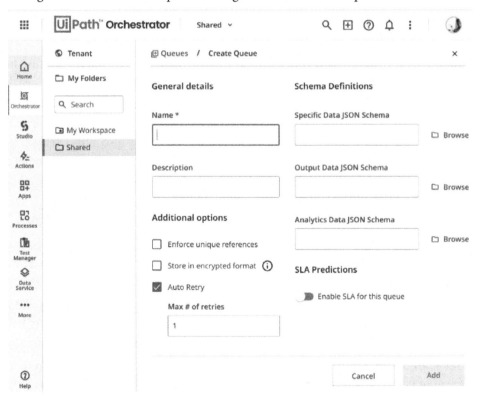

Figure 3.28 – Queue creation page in UiPath Orchestrator

The following describes each required field for easy understanding:

- **Name**: Workflows created in UiPath Studio refer to the queue using the name provided.

- **Description**: A short description of the queue and its usage.

- **Enforce unique references**: Each transaction created in a queue has a reference. This property is selected as **Yes** if you want the transaction references to be unique. The user cannot change this property after creating the queue.

- **Auto Retry**: This property is selected as **Yes** if the automatic retry of failed transactions is required.

- **Max # of retries**: Specifies the maximum number of times that a failed transaction needs to be retried. As a best practice, three maximum retries are recommended before terminating.

UiPath Studio offers a unique set of activities that can easily interact with the created queues. These activities allow robots to insert items, bulk insert items, retrieve queue items, and process them. The following are the activities used in UiPath workflows to interact with queues:

- **Add Queue Item**: Used to add a transaction item to a queue. Each transaction item may contain multiple data elements. Queue item uses a key-value to refer to each data element in the transaction. Each transaction item added with this activity gets added to the queue with the **New** status.

- **Add Transaction Item**: Like **Add Queue Item**, this activity also adds a transaction item to the queue, but with an **In Progress** status. This activity allows immediate processing of the item after adding it to the queue.

- **Get Transaction Item**: Retrieves the next available transaction item in the queue with the status of **New**. The status of each retrieved item is changed to **In Progress** automatically.

- **Postpone Transaction Item**: Used to add a date parameter that defines the date and time the item should get processed.

- **Set Transaction Progress**: Some transactions have longer processing times and may have several stages to pass depending on business requirements. This activity helps to introduce and track custom statuses for such transactions.

- **Set Transaction Status**: Used to change the status of the transaction item in the event of failure or success. The status gets changed to **Failed** if a failure is due to a business or an application rule exception. Similarly, the status gets changed to **Successful** when the transaction gets processed successfully.

- **Get Queue Items**: Retrieves all the queue items that have the defined status in the activity.

- **Wait Queue Item**: Waits for a transaction to be available in the queue for processing and sets its status to **In Progress**.

- **Bulk Add Queue Items**: Allows the user to add a set of items to the queue at one time. All added items will have a **New** status.

- **Delete Queue Item**: Used to delete specified items with the **New** status.

UiPath Orchestrator plays a significant role in the entire automation solution you build, so understanding the fundamentals is one of the main essential points when learning about the UiPath platform. The knowledge and familiarity gained from the topics discussed in this chapter will help in understanding and practicing the features discussed in the following chapters. The next section focuses on creating the first Orchestrator instance and connecting the local robot as the first step of the journey.

Summary

This chapter introduced the UiPath Cloud platform and UiPath Orchestrator. UiPath Orchestrator is the heart of UiPath's platform as it is the control center for all robots. As part of the introduction, the chapter described each available component of the Cloud platform and Orchestrator in detail. We also described some of the activities that can be used to interact with Orchestrator assets and queues. Finally, we looked at how to configure the Cloud platform to create the first UiPath Orchestrator instance.

The fundamental concepts of UiPath Orchestrator that have been discussed will be useful in the following chapters. The next chapter describes UiPath Robot, the different types of robots, and how they are configured and connected to Orchestrator. To better understand the configuration of robots, it is essential to have a good understanding of the concepts described there.

4

Create, Deploy, and Execute RPA Process on the UiPath Ecosystem

Once your robots have been created and assigned to processes, you are faced with the task of how to manage all their actions. This is where Orchestrator comes into the picture – it helps you to manage multiple robots in one place.

As part of this chapter, you will create a **robot** and establish a connection between your local machine robot and **UiPath Orchestrator**. Then, you will create your first **robotic process automation (RPA)** process in UiPath Studio, publish it to Orchestrator, and deploy the process. And finally, you will learn how the processes can be executed using **UiPath Assistant** and **attended automation**.

This chapter consists of the following sections:

- Connecting a robot to Orchestrator
- Creating your first RPA process
- Managing packages in Orchestrator
- Running the deployed process from UiPath Assistant

Technical requirements

This chapter requires you to have UiPath Studio and UiPath Robot installed, along with a basic understanding of Studio user interfaces. You can refer to *Chapter 2, UiPath Ecosystem*, to understand the basics of Studio. You also need the following prerequisites:

- Access to the UiPath Automation Cloud portal
- UiPath Studio already installed on your machine
- Access to Command Prompt

Connecting a robot to Orchestrator

In the previous chapter, you learned about Orchestrator and robots, but in this section, you will learn about how to create a robot and connect it to Orchestrator.

Once you have installed UiPath Studio, you may notice in the Orchestrator cloud that a default tenant, a machine, and a robot are created, and the connection between UiPath Studio and Orchestrator is already established. However, through the following sections, you will understand how to create a robot and establish the connection to Orchestrator manually.

Creating a machine template in Orchestrator

The machine that you will be using for automation needs to be registered with Orchestrator, and the robot that is installed in your machine needs to relate to Orchestrator for the RPA process to work seamlessly. Perform the following steps to create a **machine template** in Orchestrator:

1. Log in to UiPath Automation Cloud.

2. Launch the corresponding **Orchestrator Services** option, as highlighted in the following screenshot, using the URL `https://cloud.uipath.com/`:

Figure 4.1 – Orchestrator Services

3. Click on the **Tenant** menu on the left side of the Orchestrator window:

Figure 4.2 – The Tenant menu

4. Click on the **Machines** tab:

Figure 4.3 – The Machines menu

5. Click on the **+ Add machine** icon, which will display options such as **Standard machine** and **Machine template**.

We are creating a machine template as it allows multiple users to connect their robots to Orchestrator.

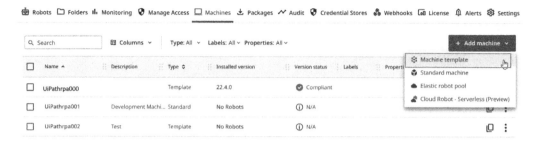

Figure 4.4 – Add machine options

6. Click on **Machine template**, which takes you to the **Add Machine template** window.

7. On the **Add Machine template** screen, enter the details of your machine. You will need to provide the machine name, a short description, and the intended **Runtime license (execution slots) | Production (Unattended)** number to register your machine. Then, click **Provision**:

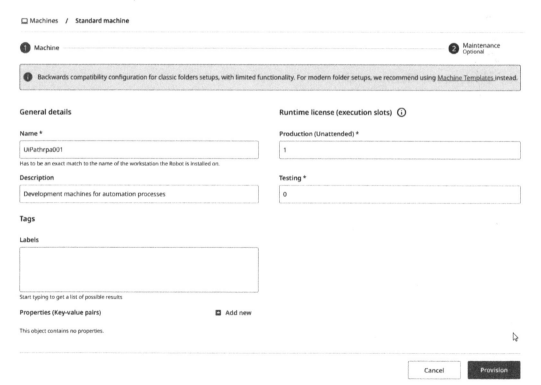

Figure 4.5 – Add Standard machine

8. Once **Provision** has been clicked, the machine is created in the Orchestrator, as follows:

Figure 4.6 – The available machines

9. You may copy the machine key for future use to connect UiPath Robot to Orchestrator by clicking the **Copy Machine Key to Clipboard** icon:

Figure 4.7 – Copying the machine key

10. You may also copy the Orchestrator URL for future use to connect UiPath Robot to Orchestrator. To do that, copy the URL until the **orchestrator** keyword, as highlighted in this screenshot:

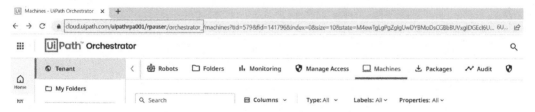

Figure 4.8 – Copying the Orchestrator URL

Now, you have successfully created a standard machine in Orchestrator, and you need to connect a robot to the created machine for the execution of the RPA processes. The following sections explain how to create a standard robot and connect it to Orchestrator.

Creating a Robot account

In this section, you will be creating a Robot account by performing the following steps:

1. Navigate to the **Robot accounts** section by clicking on the **Admin | Accounts & Groups** menu, as shown in the following screenshot:

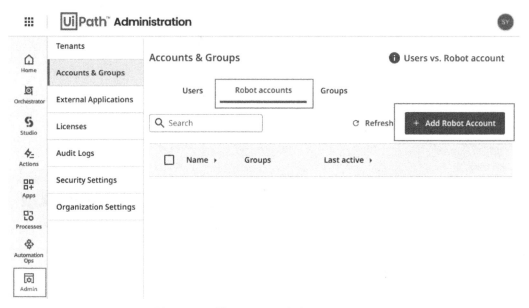

Figure 4.9 – The Accounts & Groups section

2. Click on the **+ Add Robot Account** button:

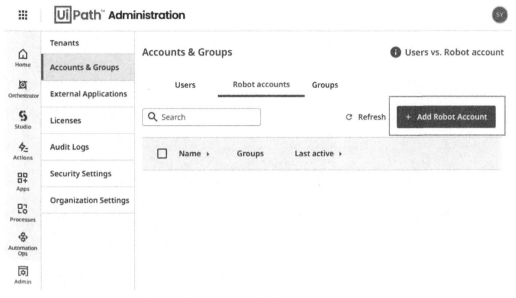

Figure 4.10 – The Robot menu

3. Enter a Robot name and select appropriate group names to create a robot service account. Click on the **Add** button to create a Robot.

4. If UiPath Assistant is not displayed on the taskbar, open **UiPath Assistant** from the Windows start menu, as shown in the following screenshot:

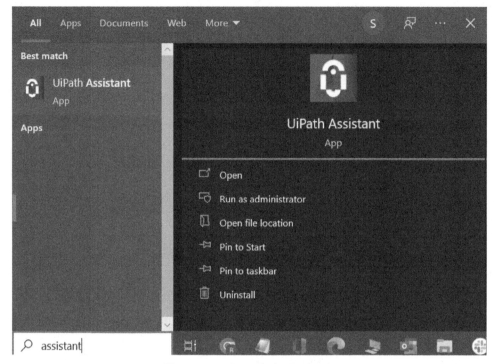

Figure 4.11 – Launch the Assistant

5. Now, you will be able to see UiPath Assistant on your taskbar.

6. Right-click on **UiPath Assistant** on the taskbar, and you will get a context menu. Select **Orchestrator Settings** from the list, which will display the **Orchestrator Settings** window:

Figure 4.12 – The context menu

7. Verify the connection status in the **Orchestrator Settings** window. If the status is **Connected, Licensed**, click on the **Sign out** button, as highlighted in the following screenshot:

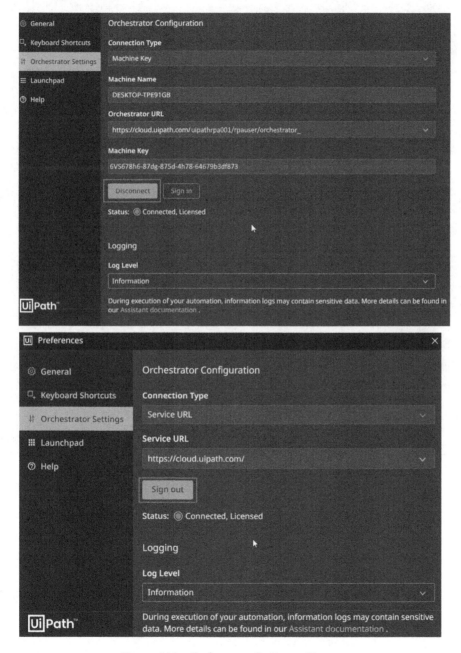

Figure 4.13 – Orchestrator Settings – Sign out

8. Ensure the connection status in the **Orchestrator Settings** window is **Offline**, as displayed in the following screenshot:

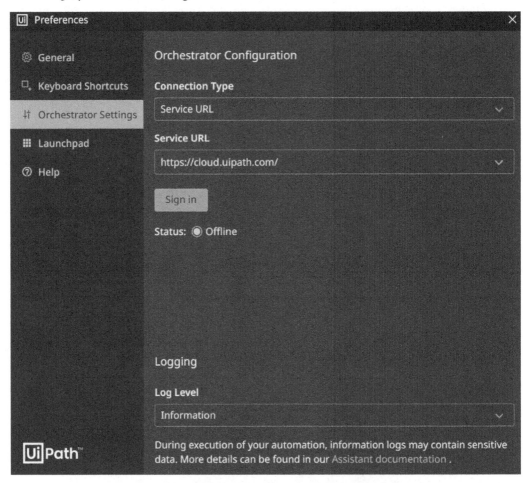

Figure 4.14 – Orchestrator Settings – Offline connection

9. Under **Connection Type**, select **Machine Key** on the **Orchestrator Configuration** screen. **Machine Name** is already populated automatically. However, you need the values of **Orchestrator URL** and **Machine Key** to connect to the Orchestrator, which are available from *steps 9* and *10* of the previous section, *Creating a machine template in Orchestrator*.

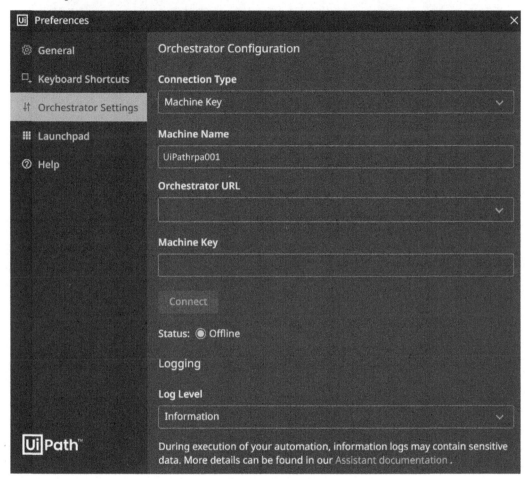

Figure 4.15 – Connection Type – Machine Key

10. Enter the **Orchestrator URL** and **Machine Key** details and click on **Connect** for the robot to connect to the Orchestrator. Once connected, the status changes to **Connected, Licensed**, as shown in the following screenshot:

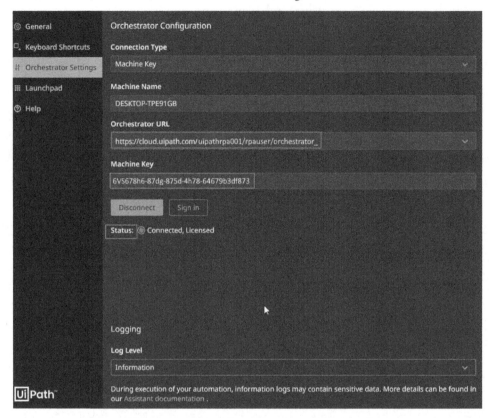

Figure 4.16 – Connection successful – Machine Key

The step-by-step instructions you have followed in this section give you a good understanding of the end-to-end process of creating a robot, machines, and an environment in Orchestrator, and then establishing a connection to it. Let's dive a bit deeper by creating your first RPA process, using a practical use case example.

Creating your first RPA process

To help you understand UiPath Studio and the RPA process better, let's implement what you have learned into a simple project to display `Hello World` in a message box.

Follow these steps to create your first automation process:

1. Launch UiPath Studio and navigate to the home view by clicking on the **HOME** tab:

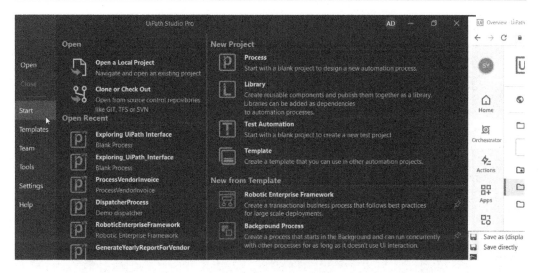

Figure 4.17 – The home page view

2. Click **Process** in the **New Project** section to create a new project. The **New Blank Process** window is then displayed:

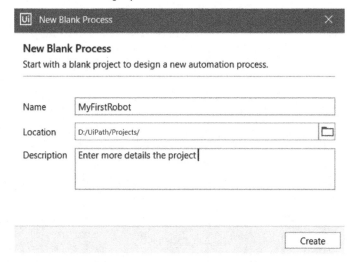

Figure 4.18 – A new process creation

3. Enter a suitable name for the project and select a drive location to save it. Note that the project name cannot exceed 128 characters, and the description cannot exceed 500 characters.

4. Click **Create** after entering all the details. The new project is opened in Studio.

5.   Click on **Open Main Workflow** on the **DESIGN** view of the newly created project:

Figure 4.19 – The design view

6.   Type Sequence in the search box of the **Activities** panel to drag and drop the sequence from the activity. Double-click on the **Sequence** title and rename it MyFirstRobot:

Figure 4.20 – Creating a sequence

7. Right-click on the sequence to add an annotation, or press *Shift + F2* to add more descriptive information about the project:

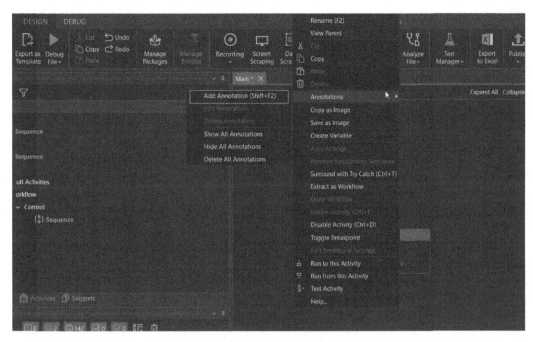

Figure 4.21 – Adding an annotation

8. Now, type `Message Box` in the search box of the **Activities** panel to drag and drop the **Message Box** activity into the **MyFirstRobot** sequence activity:

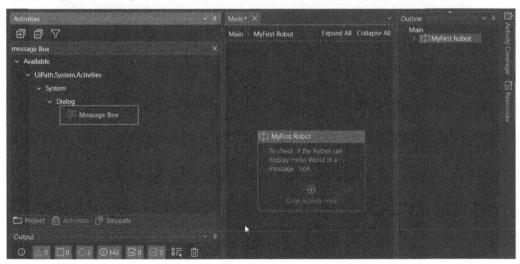

Figure 4.22 – Adding Message Box

9. By default, the message box does not have any default value. However, the message box displays an alert, expecting a text value for the message box:

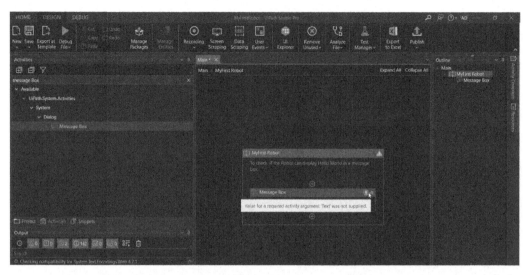

Figure 4.23 – Understanding the alert message

10. Enter the text `"Hello World!"` inside the **Message Box** activity within double quotes:

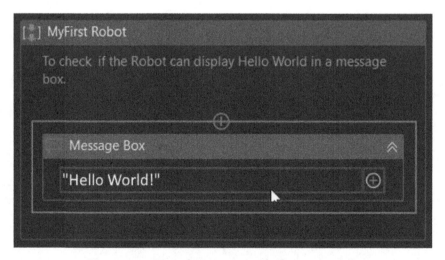

Figure 4.24 – Enter the message inside the message box

11. Now, run the workflow by clicking on the **Run** button or by pressing *Ctrl + F5*:

Figure 4.25 – Running the workflow

12. Verify the **Message Box** output generated by the robot. Click **OK** to end the robot execution:

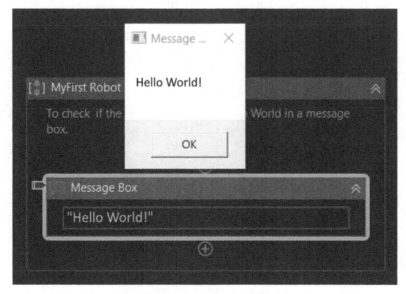

Figure 4.26 – Running the workflow

> **Important Note**
> As the screenshots displayed in this chapter were taken using UiPath Studio 2020.10, some elements may be different in the latest Community Edition version.

You have successfully created your first robot, which displays a **"Hello World!"** message. In the next section, you will be creating your second robot, which performs slightly more work with multiple applications.

Creating your second RPA process

Now, let's jump into creating a simple project to extract information from a web page to **Notepad**, the writing application.

Prerequisite

Try performing the following steps to identify any issue(s) launching Chrome related to Chrome extensions, as we will be using the Chrome browser for this exercise:

1. From the **Tools** page, click **Chrome** from **UiPath Extensions**:

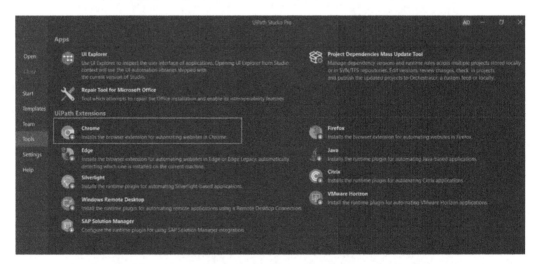

Figure 4.27 – Chrome extensions

2. Navigate in Chrome to `chrome://extensions/` and confirm that the extension is available:

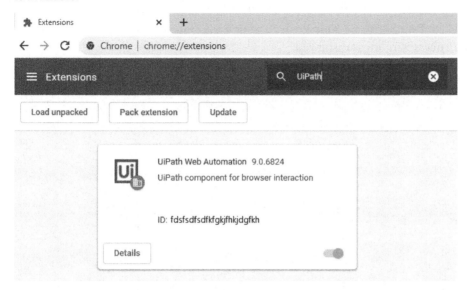

Figure 4.28– Enabling Chrome extensions

3. Ensure that the **UiPath** extension is enabled by default. If not, enable it manually by clicking the highlighted switch icon:

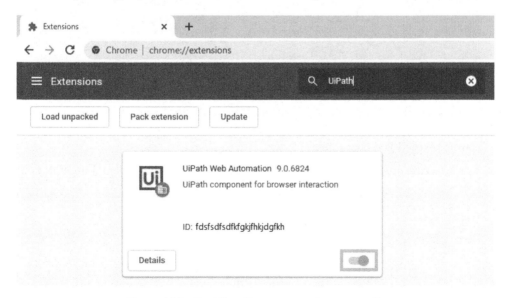

Figure 4.29 – Enabling Chrome extensions manually

Once the extensions are set up correctly, perform the following process design steps.

Follow these steps to create your second automation process:

1. Launch UiPath Studio and navigate to the home view by clicking on the **HOME** tab.

2. Click **Process** in the **New Project** section to create a new project. The **New Blank Process** window is displayed:

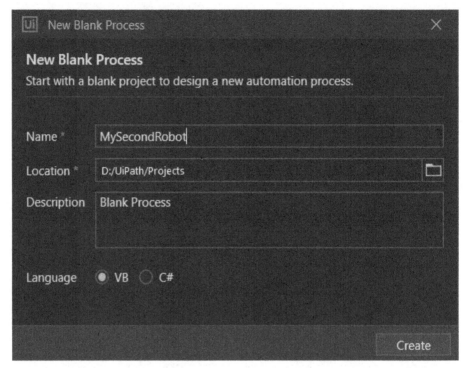

Figure 4.30 – A new process creation

3. Enter a suitable name for the project and select a drive location to save the project. Note that the project name cannot exceed 128 characters, and the description cannot exceed 500 characters.

4. Click **Create** after entering all the details. The new project is opened in Studio.

5. Click on **Drop Activity Here** and type Open Browser:

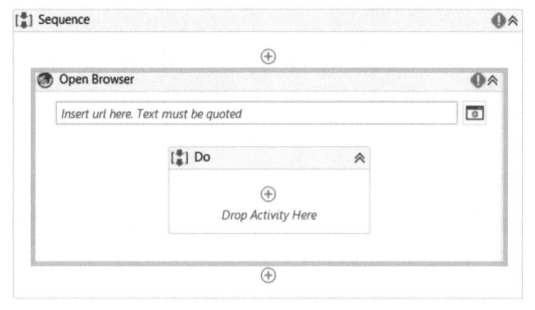

Figure 4.31 – Open Browser

6. Name the sequence Extract Text from Packt and insert the https://
www.packtpub.com/au/about URL:

Figure 4.32 – The Open Browser URL

7. Click **Open Browser**. From the **Properties** option, expand the dropdown by clicking **BrowserType**:

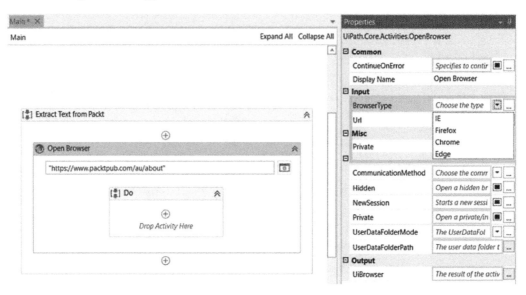

Figure 4.33 – The Open Browser type

8. Select Chrome as your preferred browser:

Figure 4.34 – The Open Browser type

9. Rename the **Do** sequence `Extract Text` and click **Drop Activity Here** to select the **Get Visible Text** activity:

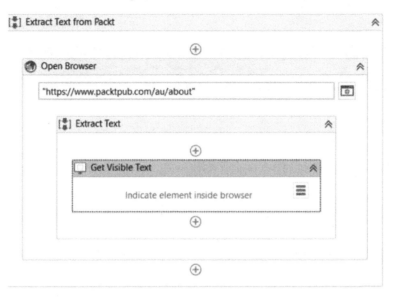

Figure 4.35 – Get Visible Text

10. Click the **Run** button to check whether the browser has launched successfully:

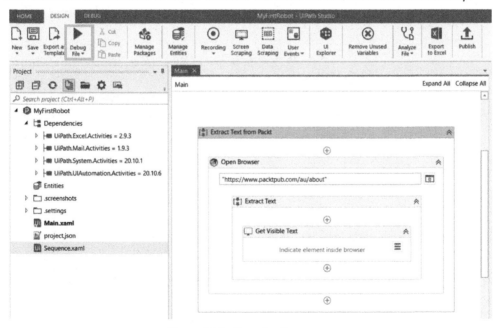

Figure 4.36 – Running the process

11. Verify whether the robot can launch the browser successfully with the expected web page:

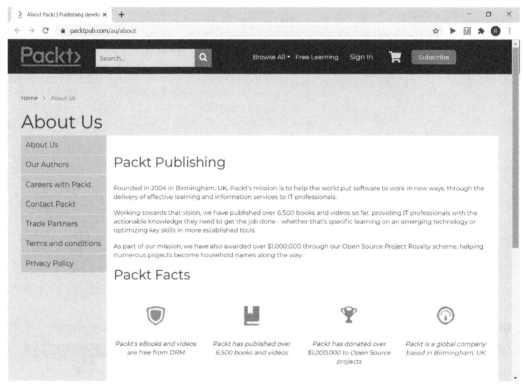

Figure 4.37 – The output result

12. Click **Indicate element** inside the **Get Visible Text** activity to extract the desired content from the browser:

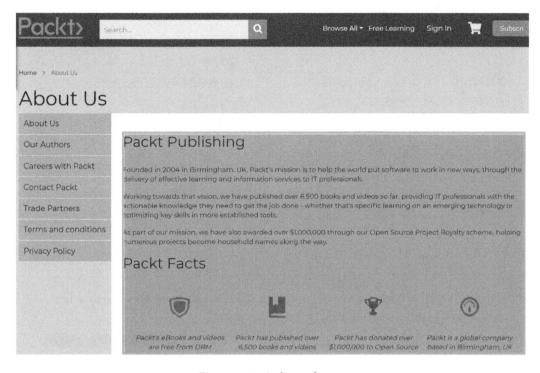

Figure 4.38 – Indicate element

13. Create a variable to save the extracted text by pressing *Ctrl + K* from the **Text** field in the **Properties** panel. This gives you the option to enter the variable name, as highlighted:

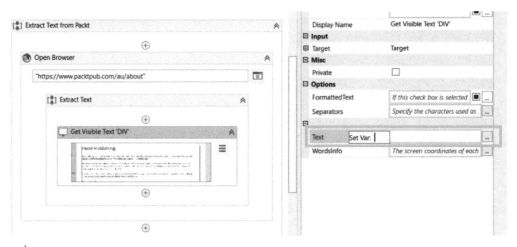

Figure 4.39 – Creating a variable

14. Set the variable name to txtAboutPackt and press *Enter*. This will save the extracted text to the txtAboutPackt variable:

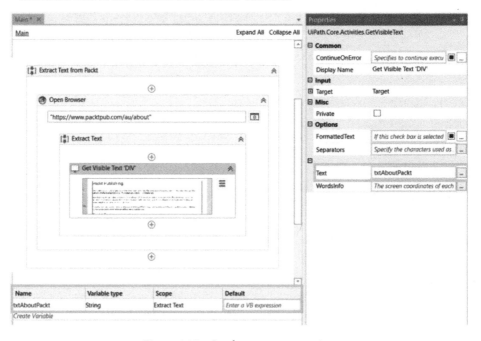

Figure 4.40 – Set the output properties

15. Click on the + symbol and add the **Open Application** activity.

16. From the **Open Application** activity, attach the Notepad app by clicking on **Indicate window inside browser** to output the extracted text from the previous steps:

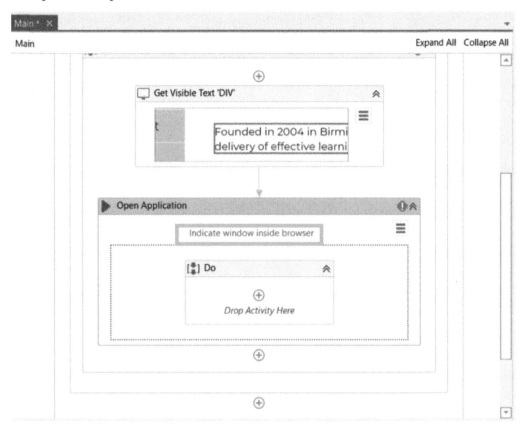

Figure 4.41 – Open Application

17. Ensure that the Notepad application is linked to the **Open Application** activity:

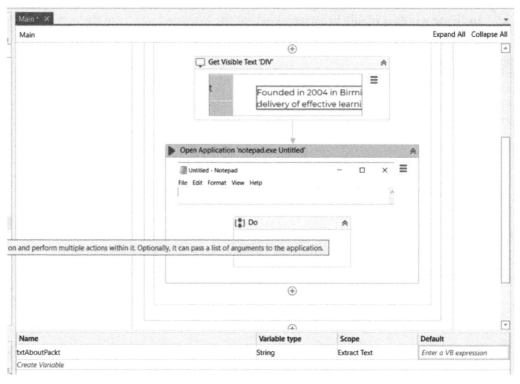

Figure 4.42 – Indicating Notepad as output

18. Change the sequence inside **Open Application** to **Enter Text**, and click on the +
symbol to include the set text:

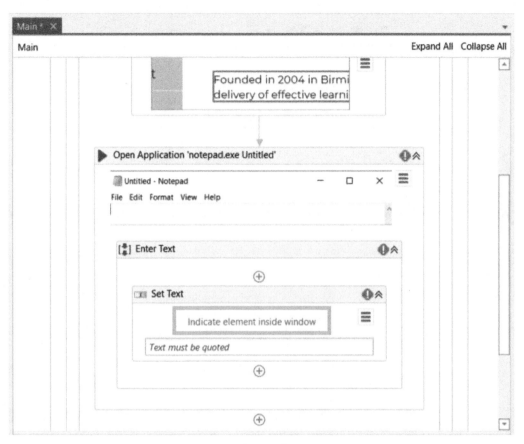

Figure 4.43 – Setting the output text

19. Click on the **Indicate** element to point to the blank notepad:

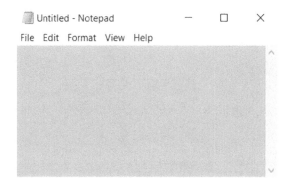

Figure 4.44 – Indicate Notepad to write the output text

20. Change the **Set Text** activity to **Enter the extracted text,** and modify the text field to accept the available `txtAboutPackt` string variable:

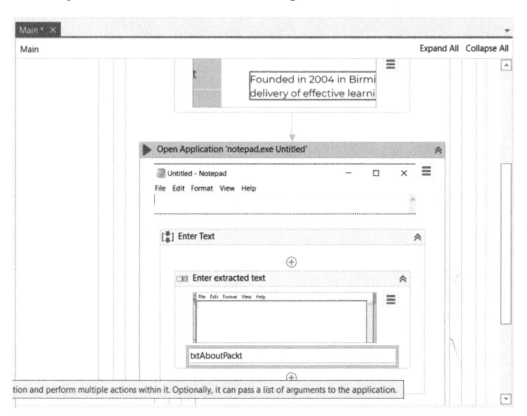

Figure 4.45 – The mapping of the text variable output

21. Finally, include the **Close Tab** activity for the robot to close the already opened browser during automation execution:

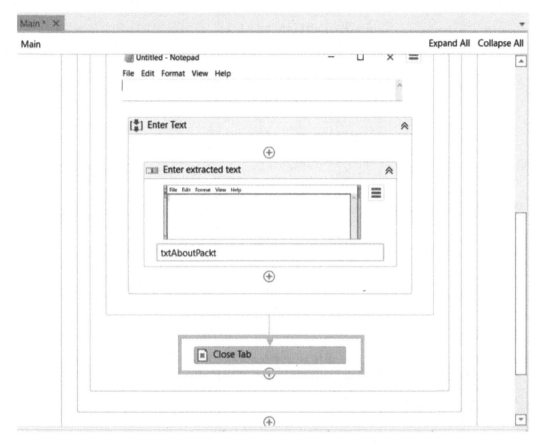

Figure 4.46 – Close Tab

22. Save the workflow by clicking the **Save** button (or by pressing *Ctrl + S* on your keyboard).

23. To execute the workflow, close any open browser or notepad applications and click the **Run** button from the **DESIGN** panel:

Figure 4.47 – Debug tab

24. Observe the output generated by the robot:

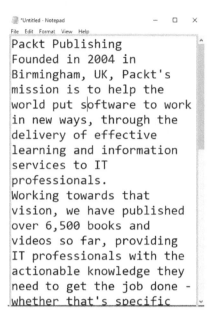

Figure 4.48 – The result verification output

25. Publish the project by clicking the **Publish** button on Studio:

Figure 4.49 – The publishing process

26. Click **Next** in the **Package properties** section:

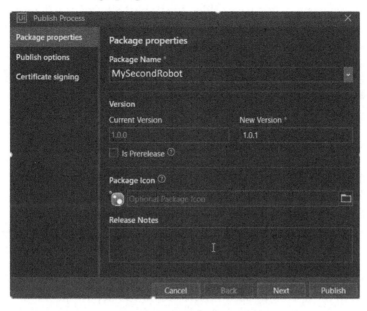

Figure 4.50 – Package properties

27. In **Publish options**, ensure that **Orchestrator Tenant Process Feed** is selected to publish to the **Tenant** level in Orchestrator, which is selected by default. You can also publish to your personal workspace folder directly if you select the **Orchestrator Personal Workspace Feed** option, as shown in *Figure 4.51*:

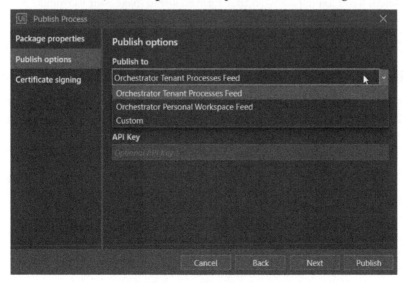

Figure 4.51 – Publish Process

28. Click **Next** and then the **Publish** button from the **Publish Process** popup. As we are using the default workspace folder, the published project will be available in the default folder of Orchestrator. You will see the following confirmation message upon publishing the project from Studio:

Figure 4.52 – The published project

In this section, you have successfully created your second RPA process and published it to Orchestrator. In the upcoming section, let's see how to deploy the published processes from Orchestrator to be executed by UiPath Assistant.

> **Important Note**
>
> Try the given project with the **Get Full Text** activity instead of **Get Visible Text** and observe the differences. You can similarly play around with the different web scraping activities that are available to make your learnings even more interesting!

Managing packages in Orchestrator

The package published from UiPath Studio must be available in UiPath Orchestrator. The package will be deployed further and assigned to the correct robot for execution. Let's see the step-by-step instructions on how to perform these operations.

Using the latest version of the published package

Every time you publish a package to Orchestrator, the version number is updated. Therefore, it is essential to use the latest package to get all the latest updates and/or code. Follow these step-by-step instructions to use the latest version:

1. Navigate to the **Packages** tab in Orchestrator:

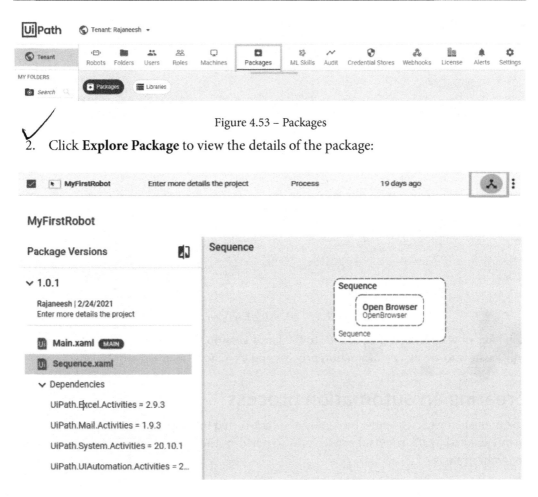

Figure 4.53 – Packages

2.   Click **Explore Package** to view the details of the package:

Figure 4.54 – Explore Package

3.   Click the **More Actions** icon:

Figure 4.55 – More Actions

4. Click **View Versions** if you want to view the available versions:

Figure 4.56 – View Versions

5. Select the package you want and click the upgrade package button:

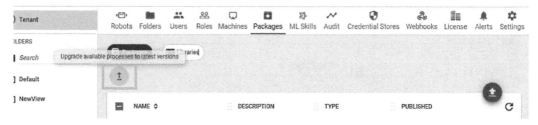

Figure 4.57 – Use the latest version

You have now upgraded the package to the latest version. In the upcoming section, you will see how to create an automation process and execute it from UiPath Assistant.

Creating an automation process

The published packages must be deployed or converted into an automation process to be executed by the robots. Let's see how to perform the automation creation process in Orchestrator:

1. Click on the **Default** folder on the left side of the display in which we are working, click the **Automations** tab, and then click the + add process button:

Figure 4.58 – Add processes

2. Enter the correct **Package Source Name**, **Package Version**, and **Environment** details, and then click the **CONTINUE** button:

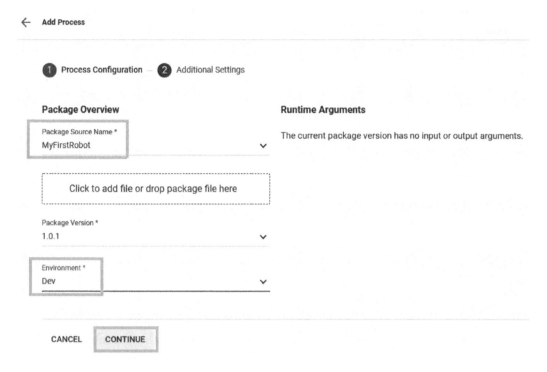

Figure 4.59 – Enter the process details

3.   Enter the **Display name** and **Description** details, and then click **CREATE**:

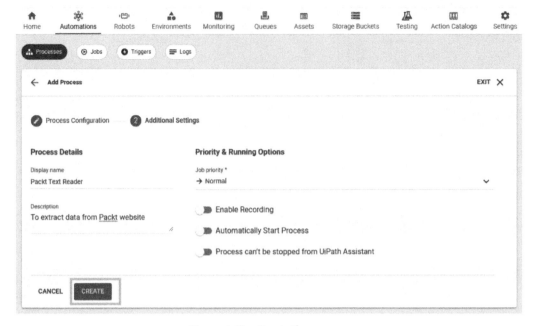

Figure 4.60 – Create the process

4.   Ensure that the process is created and displayed by viewing the **Automations** tab:

Figure 4.61 – The available process

In this section, we have seen ways of deploying a published package from Orchestrator. In the upcoming section, we will see how to execute the deployed process from UiPath Assistant.

Running the process from UiPath Assistant

In order to achieve attended automation (as discussed in *Chapter 3, Introducing UiPath Orchestrator*) that is to execute the automation process without any help from a human user, we need to perform the following steps:

1. Launch UiPath Assistant from the taskbar:

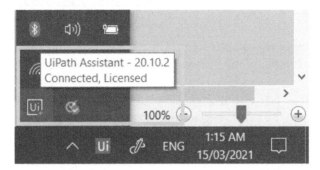

Figure 4.62 – The UiPath Assistant taskbar icon

2. Verify that the package published from Orchestrator is in the **Awaiting install** status in UiPath Assistant, as shown in *Figure 4.77*:

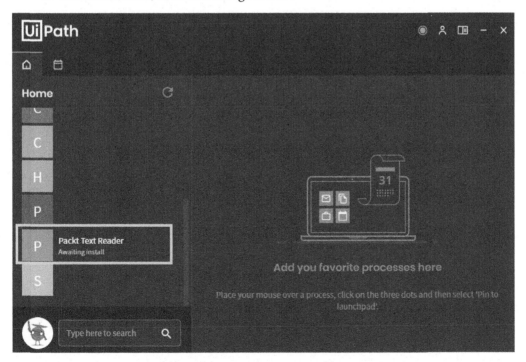

Figure 4.63 – UiPath Assistant – Awaiting install

3. Click the start button for the package to be installed and to start the execution of the process from UiPath Assistant:

Figure 4.64 – The UiPath Assistant installation and execution processes

4. Verify the status of the automation in UiPath Assistant, and ensure that the automation execution of the process has already been completed:

Figure 4.65 – The UiPath Assistant executed process

5. Verify the output text extracted from the **Packt Publishing** website by checking the Notepad app, as follows:

Figure 4.66 – The result verification output

In this section, we have seen the step-by-step instructions to execute the deployed process from UiPath Assistant, and we have verified the results.

Summary

This chapter has provided the opportunity to gain more experience in using all core components of the UiPath Enterprise platform. You have successfully created a machine, a robot, and environments in Orchestrator, and established a connection between UiPath Studio and Orchestrator.

In addition, you have created your first RPA process and published it in Orchestrator. The latest version of the published package was then deployed, and the automation process was executed using UiPath Assistant from your computer taskbar. Overall, you have experienced end-to-end automation by implementing a simple project.

The next chapter describes what UiPath Orchestrator is all about and how automation can be published and executed in it. It will also provide you with more information on variables and arguments to help you gain additional experience in building more robust automation processes.

Part 2: UiPath Studio

In this part, we will focus on understanding the basics of building automation workflows. The basics you learn here will be used in all the automation projects you work with. By the end of this section, you will be able to define the variables, arguments, control flows, and different data manipulation methods available in UiPath. Furthermore, by the completion of this part, you will understand how and when to use different data types and controls to build the logic required.

In this part, we will cover the following chapters:

5
Learning about Variables and Arguments

Variables and **arguments** are two critical components of any programming language. As with any other programming language, UiPath Studio also uses variables and arguments to store, read, and process data. Variables and arguments enable users to build an automation flow by connecting different actions based on each step's input and output.

By the end of this chapter, you will understand the most common data types used in UiPath and how to configure arguments and variables according to the requirements.

The chapter consists of the following sections:

- Exploring variables
- Practicing variable creation
- Exploring arguments
- Practicing argument creation
- Understanding data types

Technical requirements

Before starting this chapter, please ensure UiPath Studio and UiPath Robot are installed. This chapter requires a general idea of how to use Studio and the UiPath Assistant tool. You can refer back to *Chapter 2, UiPath Ecosystem*, to better understand the basics of UiPath Studio.

Exploring variables

A variable can be defined as a container that holds values of the same data type. There are different methods for changing the value of a variable, such as the following:

- **External input**: A user or another system provides a value to store in the variable.

- **Data manipulation**: A variable used in a data manipulation process may hold the derived values. A data manipulation process is a series of steps that are carried out to extract, filter, modify, and clean data. Data manipulation is further described in *Chapter 7, Manipulating Data Using UiPath*.

- **Passing from one activity to another**: Executing multiple workflow activities may use the same variable as the input or output of an activity.

Let's now explore the main properties of a variable.

Properties of a variable

There are four main properties used in UiPath to configure variables. You can find these four properties through the **Variables** panel of UiPath Studio, as shown in the following screenshot:

Name	Variable type	Scope	Default
SumValue	Int32	Sequence	Enter a VB expression
Create Variable			

Variables Arguments Imports   100%

Figure 5.1 – Variables panel in UiPath Studio

Let's explore each property in detail for a better understanding, as follows:

- **Name**: This property contains the name of the variable. The name specified here is used throughout the automation workflow to refer to the variable. It is always best practice to provide a short but descriptive name for a variable based on its use.

- **Variable type**: This defines the type of data stored in the variable. The type of the variable is defined when creating a variable and can be changed if needed. Some specific types are more generic and can accommodate different types of data. These data types are unique to UiPath. In general, the commonly used data types are **Text**, **Number**, **Array**, **Date/Time**, **Boolean**, and **Data Tables**.

- **Scope**: Describes the region of the workflow where a variable can be used. Containers such as **Sequence**, **Flowchart** and **Scope** `Activities` (described in detail in *Chapter 6, Understanding Different Control Flows*) define the region in which a variable can work. It is always good to assign a variable to the required scope to ensure efficient execution and avoid confusion because many variables are used in a real automation workflow.

- **Default**: Every variable is assigned with a default value by default. The default value property enables the user to set a custom default value to the variable.

As we now know the properties of a variable, let's take a look at the different approaches we can take to create variables. Variable creation involves configuring the properties described earlier.

Creating variables in UiPath

Variable creation and modification are quite frequent when building automation workflows. Hence, UiPath has introduced three methods of creating variables in a workflow, as described here:

- **Through the Variables panel**: Clicking on the **Create Variable** option in the **Variables** panel allows for the easy creation of variables by configuring the properties discussed previously. The following screenshot shows how this is done:

Name	Variable type	Scope	Default
SumValue	Int32	Sequence	*Enter a VB expression*
Create Variable			
Variables Arguments Imports		🖐 🔎 100% ∨ ▦ ▧	

Figure 5.2 – Variables panel in UiPath Studio

Clicking on the **Create Variable** option creates a new row in the panel to provide a name, variable type, scope, and the default value for the new variable.

- **Through the Designer panel**: Use the activity you want to associate the variable with, and press the *Ctrl + K* shortcut keys to enable variable creation mode in the **Designer** panel. You can provide the variable name and other additional configurations through the **Variables** panel as needed. The variable created through the **Designer** panel picks the scope and the data type of the variable automatically, based on the configurations of the activity and the scope of the activity. The container the activity is in determines the scope of the variable.

- **Through the Properties panel**: The **Properties** panel of the activity includes all configuration options for the activity. As with the **Designer** panel, pressing the *Ctrl + K* shortcut keys in the property that the variable needs to interact with will enable the variable creation mode. The rest of the variable's properties are automatically configured based on the activity's configurations and the activity's scope.

Variables are common containers that we use across all programming languages to hold different types of data. UiPath uses all the data types available with the Microsoft .NET Framework, with a few additional data types unique to UiPath. As we now know the basic properties of a variable, the next section of the book provides you with guidelines to practice the creation of variables and scope management. Practicing variable creation now will come in handy in future chapters as we talk about more complex scenarios.

Practicing variable creation

Since we have covered the basics of variables, let's now practice a little bit. The following steps will guide you on how to create a simple variable in a UiPath workflow:

1. Run UiPath Studio from the Windows **Start** menu.

2. Click on the **Process** option on the Studio **Start** screen under the **New Project** section to create a new blank project, as illustrated in the following screenshot:

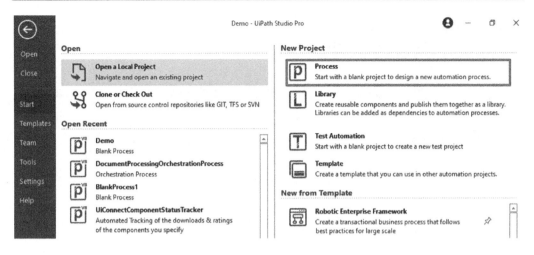

Figure 5.3 – Studio Start page

3. In the pop-up menu that appears, provide the solution name and the file path where you want to save your solution, and then click on the **Create** button to create your blank solution, as illustrated in the following screenshot:

Ui New Blank Process	×

New Blank Process

Start with a blank project to design a new automation process.

Name	MyFirstVariableCreation
Location	C:\Users\lahir\OneDrive\Documents\UiPath
Description	Blank Process
Language	⦿ VB ◯ C#

Create

Figure 5.4 – UiPath Studio project creation page

4. Once a project is created, your screen would look similar to the one shown in the following screenshot. Now, click on the `Main.xaml` file to open it in the **Designer** panel.

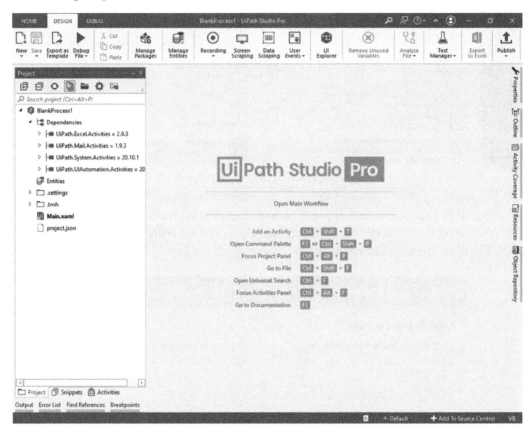

Figure 5.5 – UiPath Studio project home page

5. Click on the **Activities** panel, search for the **Sequence** activity, and drag and drop it into the workflow body.

6. Open the **Variables** panel and create a variable named `UserName` of the `String` type, as illustrated in the following screenshot:

Name	Variable type	Scope	Default
UserName	String	Sequence	*Enter a VB expression*
Create Variable			

Variables   Arguments   Imports

Figure 5.6 – Variable creation

7. Search for the **Input Dialog** activity from the **Activities** panel and drag it to the designer. The **Input Dialog** activity prompts a window for the user to enter a value during runtime.

8. Configure the **Input Dialog** activity, as shown in the following screenshot:

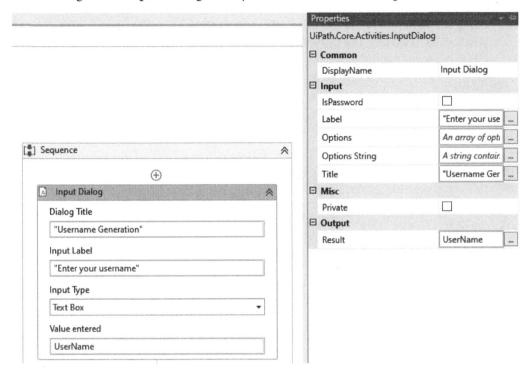

Figure 5.7 – Configuring the Input Dialog activity

9. Search for the **Message Box** activity from the **Activities** panel and place it below the **Input Dialog** activity.

10. Configure the **Message Box** activity by typing the following command:

```
"Hello " + UserName + ", Nice to see you!"
```

11. Now, click on the **Debug File** button on the **DESIGN** ribbon (or press *F6*) to run the process.

12. Once the **Input Dialog** activity shows up on your screen, provide a name and click **OK**.

13. You will see a **Message Box** activity that contains the text **"Hello John, Nice to see you!"** (if you provide John as the name). Based on the name you provide, the **Message Box** activity may change.

At the end of this practical task, you now know how to use a variable to assign a user-entered value and show it in a message box.

Now, let's take a look at a scenario where changing the scope of the variable affects the workflow, as follows:

1. Using the same workflow you just built, now select another **Sequence** container and position it in between the **Input Dialog** and **Message Box** activities, as shown in the following screenshot:

Figure 5.8 – Adding an inner sequence to the workflow

2. Double-click on the header of the newly added **Sequence** container and rename it **Inner Sequence**, as illustrated in the following screenshot:

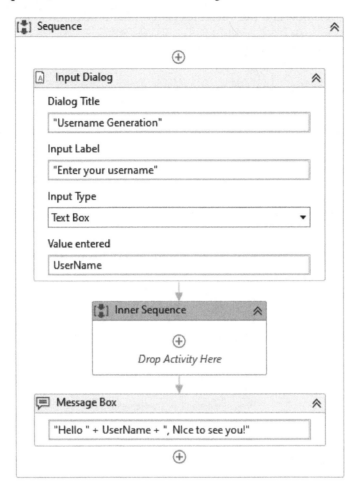

Figure 5.9 – Renaming the inner sequence

3. Search for the **Assign** activity from the **Activity** panel and place it inside the **Inner Sequence** container.

4. Provide the following value for the **Value** segment of the **Assign** activity:

```
"Welcome to my first RPA program"
```

5. Click on the **To** segment of the **Assign** activity, and press *Ctrl + K* to enable variable creation mode.

6. Provide the variable name as `WelcomeMessage` and press *Enter* to create this variable.

7. Now, your workflow and the **Variables** panel should look similar to this:

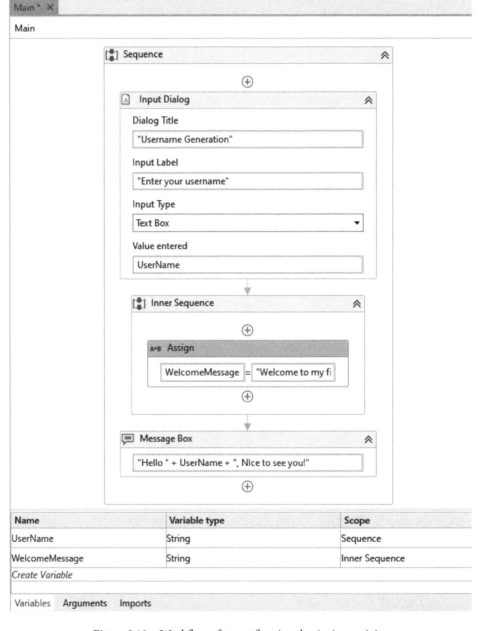

Figure 5.10 – Workflow after configuring the Assign activity

Taking a closer look at the **Variables** panel, we notice that the **Scope** value of the new WelcomeMessage variable is automatically set to **Inner Sequence**. This means that the WelcomeMessage variable is only accessible within the **Inner Sequence** scope. However, while you have the **Assign** activity selected, you can still see the UserName variable in the **Variables** panel. This means that you have access to the UserName variable within the **Inner Sequence** scope because the UserName variable's scope is the outer sequence that houses the inner sequence.

8. Now, click the **Message Box** activity while closely monitoring the **Variables** panel. As soon as you click on the **Message Box** activity, the WelcomeMessage variable disappears from the **Variables** panel, as shown in the following screenshot:

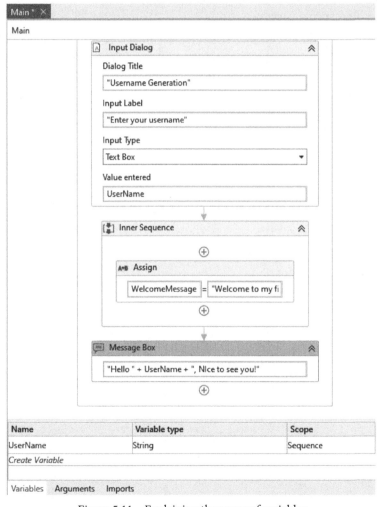

Figure 5.11 – Explaining the scope of variables

The variable disappeared because the **Inner Sequence** variable cannot be used outside of its defined scope.

9. If you try to configure the **Message Box** activity by including the `WelcomeMessage` variable, the activity will show you an error message, as follows:

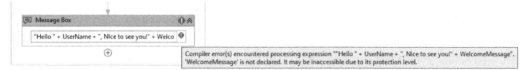

Figure 5.12 – Explaining the error due to incorrect scope

The error message indicates that the `WelcomeMessage` variable is not declared as it cannot find such a variable.

10. Now, select the **Inner Sequence** container again and change the **Scope** value of the `WelcomeMessage` variable to the outer sequence. Once you do the configuration, your **Variables** panel should look similar to this:

Figure 5.13 – Fixing the variable scope issue

You can now see that the **Message Box** activity's error has disappeared because the variable is accessible now.

11. Click on the **Debug File** button (or press *F6*) to run the process to experience the output.

The practice steps you followed in this section give you a good understanding of the different ways of creating a variable and how a variable's scope affects the workflow. The knowledge gained on variables will come in handy when we explore arguments. Arguments are quite similar to variables, but they have different properties. However, they use the same concept as variables, with slight differences.

Exploring arguments

In UiPath, the goal of a variable is to store data within the specified scope and pass it on to other variables or activities as required. A real-world automation project includes more than one workflow, hence the use of variables is not enough to connect the workflows. Arguments in UiPath come into play to fill this gap by acting as a container that allows the transfer of data between multiple workflows. Arguments are very similar to workflows as they store data dynamically based on their defined data types. However, the difference is that arguments have a **Direction** property that describes how the data is transferred between workflows. Further, the use of arguments enables users to reuse automation workflows in multiple projects.

Let's take a look at the properties of arguments.

Properties of an argument

Let's take a look at the properties of an argument, as follows:

- **Name**: Similar to variables, this property indicates the name of the argument. To differentiate between variables and arguments, we use the direction of the argument as a prefix for the name as a best practice (for example, In_UserName; Out_ CustomerData; IO_AccountData).

- **Data Type**: Specifies the type of data the argument holds.

- **Direction**: Specifies the direction from/to which the data is passed. There are three directions in UiPath, as shown in the following screenshot:

Direction	Description
In	Argument can only be used within the given workflow as the data is passed into the workflow
Out	Argument can be used to pass data outside the given workflow
In/Out	Argument can be used for both receiving and sending data out

Figure 5.14 – Argument directions

- **Default**: The default value the argument holds. However, this property is disabled for arguments with the **Direction** type defined as Out or In/Out.

As we now know the properties of an argument, let's take a look at the different approaches we can take to create arguments.

Creating arguments in UiPath

Arguments are created when you want to pass data between multiple workflows. Argument creation is similar to variable creation, described in the *Practicing variable creation* section. The following methods are used to create arguments:

- **Through the Arguments panel**: Clicking on the **Create Argument** option on the **Arguments** panel allows for the easy creation of arguments by configuring the properties discussed previously. The following screenshot illustrates this option:

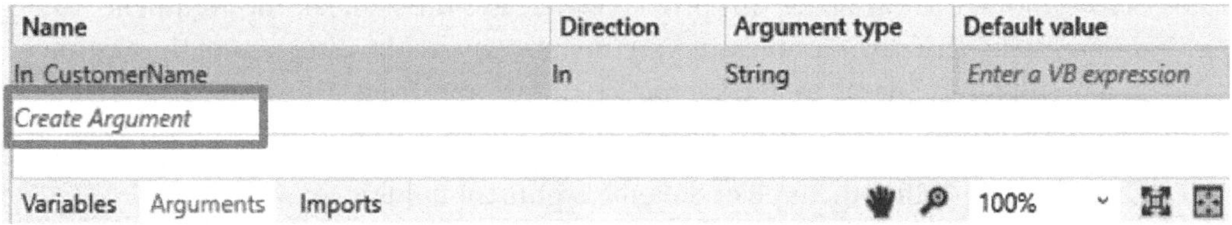

Name	Direction	Argument type	Default value
In CustomerName	In	String	Enter a VB expression
Create Argument			

Variables Arguments Imports   100%

Figure 5.15 – Arguments panel in UiPath Studio

Clicking on the **Create Argument** option creates a new row in the panel to provide a name, data type, scope, and a default value for the new variable.

- **Through the Designer panel**: Use the activity you want to associate the argument with, and press the *Ctrl + M* shortcut keys to enable argument creation mode in the **Designer** panel. You can provide an argument name and do additional configurations through the **Arguments** panel as needed. The argument created through the **Designer** panel picks the data type of the argument automatically based on the configurations of the activity.

- **Through the Properties panel**: The **Properties** panel of the activity includes all configuration options for the activity. As with the **Designer** panel, pressing the *Ctrl + M* shortcut keys in the property that the argument needs to interact with will enable argument creation mode. The **Direction** value of the argument is automatically set to In by default. However, if you want to change the **Direction** value, this must be done through the **Arguments** panel.

Similar to variables, arguments are containers that support the transfer of data between workflows, enabling component reusability. As you now know the properties of arguments and the methods to create them, the next section provides you with guidelines to practice the creation of arguments. This practice also helps you to understand how to use multiple workflows in a UiPath solution.

Practicing argument creation

Now, since we are familiar with variables and the properties of arguments, let's try building a simple workflow to test our knowledge, as follows:

1. Open UiPath Studio and create a new project.

2. Open the Main.xaml file from the **Project** panel.

3. Click on the **Activities** panel and drag and drop the **Input Dialog** activity.

4. Configure the **Input Dialog** activity to obtain the name of the user. The configuration of the activity should look similar to this:

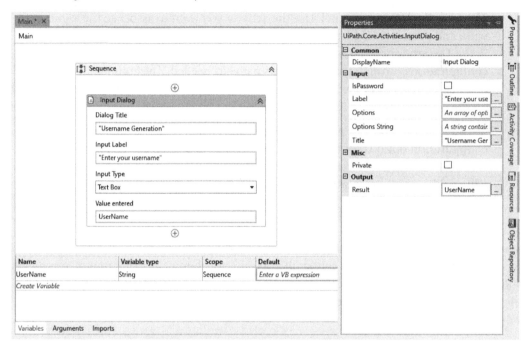

Figure 5.16 – Configuring the Input Dialog activity

5. On the **DESIGN** ribbon, click on **New** and select **Sequence** to create a new sequence workflow file, as illustrated in the following screenshot:

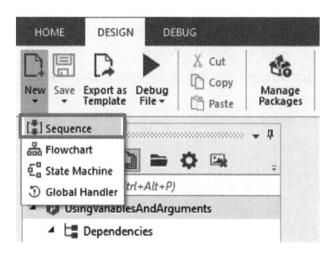

Figure 5.17 – Creating a new workflow file

6. Provide the workflow filename on the popup that appears and click on the **Create** button to create this workflow, as illustrated in the following screenshot:

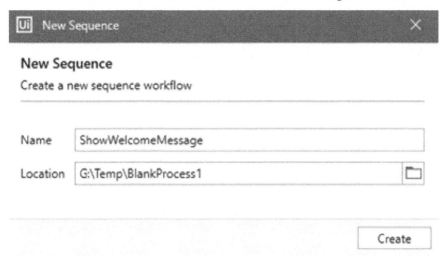

Figure 5.18 – Creating a new sequence workflow

7. The new workflow file will open on the **Designer** panel with an empty sequence.

8. Click on the **Arguments** panel of the new workflow file.

9. Click on **Create Argument** and provide the argument name as In_UserName, the **Direction** value as In, and the data type as String. The following screenshot illustrates the configuration:

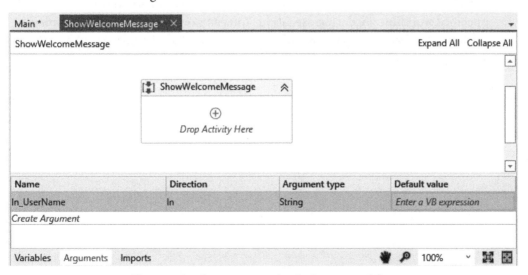

Figure 5.19 – Argument creation in the new workflow

10. Place a **Message Box** activity inside the **Sequence** container and configure it with the following code:

```
"Hello " + In_UserName + ", It's nice to see you. This is my
first attempt to join two workflows."
```

11. Save the new workflow. The configuration should look similar to this:

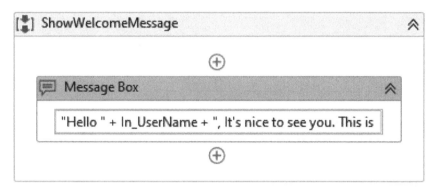

Figure 5.20 – New workflow: message box configuration

12. Click on the Main.xaml file.

13. Search for the **Invoke Workflow File** activity from the **Activities** panel and place it below the **Input Dialog** activity.

14. Click on the **Folder** icon on the **Invoke Workflow File** activity and select the new workflow file we created. This command instructs the robot to execute/invoke the specified workflow file during execution. You can now see the **Import Arguments** button of the **Invoke Workflow File** activity highlighted in orange on your screen, as illustrated in the following screenshot:

Figure 5.21 – Invoke Workflow File activity

15. Click on the **Import Arguments** button to configure the arguments. The popup that appears shows all the expected arguments of the indicated workflow. Now, you can see the input argument we created while configuring the workflow.

16. Provide the UserName variable in the **Value** field of the pop-up window. During the execution, the user-entered value is captured by the UserName variable through the **Input Dialog** activity. The configuration we perform here ensures that the UserName variable's value is passed to the In_UserName argument of the invoked workflow. The following screenshot illustrates the complete configuration of the **Invoke Workflow File** activity:

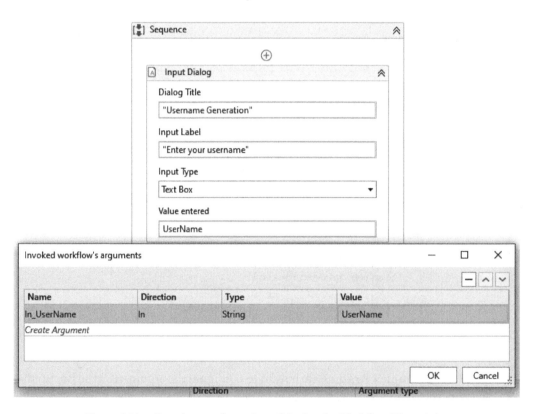

Figure 5.22 – Complete configuration of the Invoke Workflow File activity

17. Click on **OK** to close the pop-up window and then click on **Save** to save the workflow.

18. Click on the **Debug File** button on the **DESIGN** ribbon of UiPath Studio (or press *F6*) to test your workflow.

19. Once the execution starts, a popup will appear asking you to enter the name as we configured the workflow. Provide the name and experience the output. You should receive a **Message Box** activity that includes the name you provided, as illustrated in the following screenshot:

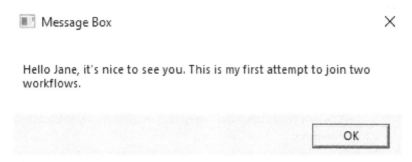

Figure 5.23 – Final output of the workflow after execution

With the completion of the steps, you now understand how to use arguments to pass data between workflow files. The use of arguments and variables is very important for the chapters to come. It is essential and mandatory that you practice using different variables and arguments. Variables and arguments may have many data types, and it is important to understand the different data types to use specific functions related to those data types. The following section of the chapter explains the different data types used in UiPath.

Understanding data types

UiPath uses multiple data types to perform and store different data elements. This section does not address all the available data types. However, it explains the commonly used data types across different automation solutions.

Let's take a look at some of the commonly used variables, as follows:

- **String variables**: Store any sequence of text. There are many methods specific for string processing, which are addressed later in *Chapter 7, Manipulating Data Using UiPath*.

- **Boolean variables**: Used to store only two values, True and False, to be used with control statements to help determine the flow of the program

- **Number variables**: Used to store numeric values to execute equations or perform comparisons, and so on. There are many sub-types of numeric variables, and the following screenshot describes some of those types:

Numeric Type	Description
Int16/32/64	Signed integers (for example, 10, 20, 100, -250).
Long	Holds signed integers ranging from -9,223,372,036,854,775,808 through 9,223,372,036,854,775,808
Double	Allows you to store the largest and smallest possible floating point integers.
Decimal	Decimal supports the storage of values up to 29 significant digits and can represent values above $7.9228 \times 10 ^\wedge 28$. The Decimal type is more suitable for financial calculations as it supports large numbers and does not provide errors while rounding values.

Figure 5.24 – Numeric data types

- **Date and time variables**: These variable types contain two categories of data, as shown in the following screenshot:

Data Type	Description
DateTime	Used to store specific date and time information regarding a given date. This allows you to perform date-related calculations, such as calculating date durations and substracting and adding dates.
TimeSpan	Used to measure the duration between two given Time values.

Figure 5.25 – Date-related data types

- **DataTable variables**: Used to store tabular data in rows and columns, hold large data pieces, and act as a database. `DataTable` variables are useful for performing operations such as filtering large amounts of data, searching, and copying.

- **GenericValue variables**: `GenericValue` variables come in handy when you are unsure what type of data is returned from a process. They have the capability of automatically converting their kind according to the first value assigned to the variable. UiPath recommends the use of `GenericValue` variables as a temporary solution in the workflow until the point you derive the actual data type. `GenericValue` variables can hold any data type, including `String`, `Number`, and arrays. For example, you are comparing two Excel sheets column by column and each column has a different data type. In such scenarios, we can use `GenericValue` variables to perform a comparison.

- **Collection type variables**: Includes all collection objects, such as arrays, lists, and dictionaries. The following screenshot describes commonly used collection objects:

Collection Type	Description
Arrays	Used to store multiple values of the same data type. The size of the object is defined at creation.
Lists	Used to store multiple values of the same data type (similar to Arrays). However, the size of the List may change during execution.
Dictionary	Used to store data values in the form of key-value pair where its unique key refers to each value. In simple words, every value in a Dictionary variable is referenced using a unique key that describes the value in the collection.

Figure 5.26 – Collection data types

By now, you should have an initial understanding of commonly used data types. We will discuss how to use these data types and their unique functions in *Chapter 7, Manipulating Data Using UiPath*.

Summary

This chapter introduced you to variables and arguments. Variables and arguments are containers of a specifically defined type that enable the user to hold data during execution. In UiPath, the properties of variables/arguments define the use of those within the automation workflow. The chapter described the properties and provided step-by-step practice guides to configure and use both variables and arguments. Further, the chapter also provided an initial introduction to commonly used data types, covered in detail in the data manipulation chapter.

The discussed concepts of variables and arguments and how they are used will come in handy in the following chapters. The next chapter describes the control flows used when designing an automation workflow. The control flow chapter enables you to understand how to build a workflow, including conditional statements and loops. The automation solutions built to support business processes include many decision points and may require you to perform the same steps iteratively, hence it is crucial to grasp the concepts of building your execution flow.

6
Understanding Different Control Flows

To create robust automation workflows using UiPath Studio, you must understand how to control the project efficiently using **control flows**. UiPath provides a lot of control flow activities so that you can effectively drive the automation workflows of the project. Control flows provide the robot with more power so that it can make decisions while evaluating any business conditions as it's being executed. In this chapter, we will learn about these essential skills by covering important control flow activities using real-time examples.

In this chapter, we will cover the following topics:

- Overview of control flows
- What are sequences?
- What are flowcharts?
- Exploring decisions and types of decisions
- Exploring loops and types of loops

By the end of this chapter, you will be able to understand all the key concepts behind control flows and be able to implement these ideas in your robots.

Technical requirements

To work on control flows, you need to have UiPath Studio and UiPath Robot installed.

For this chapter, you will need a general idea of how to use Studio and Robot. Please refer to *Chapter 2, UiPath Ecosystem*, and *Chapter 5, Learning about Variables and Arguments*, to learn about the basics of UiPath Studio.

Overview of control flows

Control flows are activities that are used to convert the decision requirements into business workflows in UiPath. In an RPA project, control flows are sequentially executed on RPA code. This code may contain UiPath activities, control statements, and workflows. There are two key workflows in an RPA project, as follows:

- **Sequence**: Sequence workflows are easy to read, and they are executed from top to bottom or executed in a sequence of activities. They are mainly used in simple or linear business processes, which involve performing a sequence of automation executions *once* for the given input data.

- **Flowchart**: Flowchart business processes are used to address complex business requirements that involve many decision points and complex logic.

RPA workflows use control flow activities to drive the execution of statements. The most frequently used control activities are as follows:

- **If**: This activity is used to verify a condition and the outcome is either `True` or `False`. It's useful for making decisions based on the input value of the variables. This rule uses the *If-Then-Else* rule to evaluate any given input. For example, if you want to check a voter's eligibility by reading the value from the `Age` field, you need to evaluate the business condition if the given age is greater than or equal to 18 to find their eligibility status, as shown in the following screenshot:

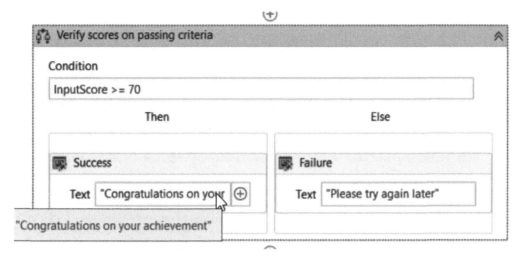

Figure 6.1 – Example of If-Then-Else

- **Loops**: These are used to verify a set of statements based on a conditional requirement or to execute statements multiple times until a certain condition is satisfied. The key loops are **DoWhile**, **While**, and **For Each**.

- **Switch**: This activity is used when there are more than two decision points and corresponding actions must be performed on each decision outcome.

In this section, we provided a high-level overview of control flows. We'll explore control flows in more detail in the upcoming sections.

What are sequences?

Sequences are easy to understand, and they are the simplest type of project. They are commonly used in processes that are linear and have step-by-step instructions to be performed one after the other in a single block of activity. The main use of sequences is **reusability**, in that they can be used in a single workflow or invoked from any other automation workflows by passing the arguments that we will discuss in *Chapter 5, Learning about Variables and Arguments*.

For example, you can create a sequence that takes information from a spreadsheet and enter it into a registration web page. Let's explore an example.

Example of a sequence

In this example, we will create a sequence that asks for `first name`, `last name`, and `age` and then displays the answer in a sentence:

1. Create a **New Blank Process** from the **New Project** section in UiPath Studio and name it `Sequence_Example`, as shown in the following screenshot:

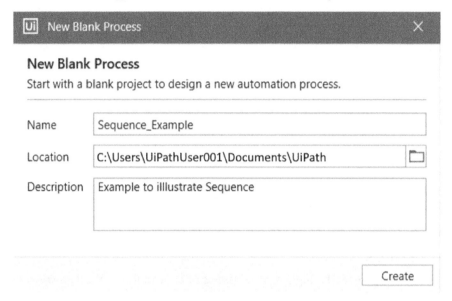

Figure 6.2 – Creating a New Blank Process

2. Enter your preferred project **Location** to save the project.

3. Enter details of the project in the **Description** field and click **Create** to create the **Designer** panel.

4. Drag and drop the **Sequence** activity from the **Activities** panel into the **Designer** panel.

5. Create three **String** variables called `FirstName`, `LastName`, and `Age` to store the information that's received from the user, as follows:

Name	Variable type	Scope	Default
FirstName	String	Sequence_Example	*Enter a VB expression*
LastName	String	Sequence_Example	*Enter a VB expression*
Age	String	Sequence_Example	*Enter a VB expression*

Figure 6.3 – Creating variables

6. Drag three **Input Dialog** activities to the project's sequence, one after the other.

7. Do the following to edit the properties of the Input Dialog so that it accepts and stores `FirstName` (these options are shown in the following screenshot):

    • Set the **Display Name** property of the first **Input Dialog** to `First Name`.

    • Set **Dialog Title** to `"Enter First Name"`.

    • Set **Input Label** to `"What's your First Name?"`.

    • Set **Input Type** to `Text Box`.

    • Set **Value entered** to be stored in `FirstName`:

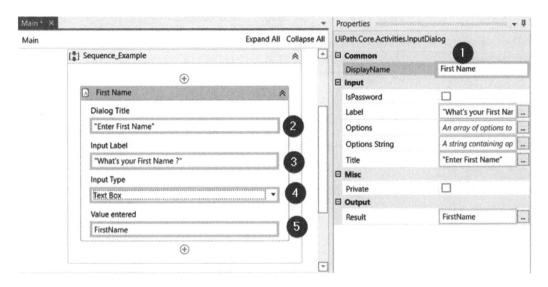

Figure 6.4 – Updating the Input Dialog properties – part 1

8. Do the following to accept and store **LastName** (these options are shown in the following screenshot):

    • Set the **Display Name** property of the second **Input Dialog** to `Last Name`.

    • Set **Dialog Title** to `"Enter Last Name"`.

    • Set **Input Label** to `"What's your Last Name?"`.

    • Set **Input Type** to `Text Box`.

- Set **Value entered** to be stored in `LastName`:

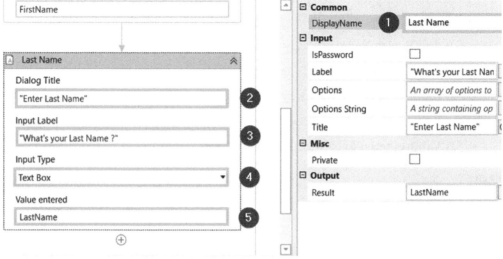

Figure 6.5 – Updating the Input Dialog properties – part 2

9. Do the following to accept and store `Age` (these options are shown in the following screenshot):

    - Set the **Display Name** property of the third **Input Dialog** to `Age`.

    - Set **Dialog Title** to `"Enter Age"`.

    - Set **Input Label** to `"What's your Age?"`.

    - Set **Input Type** to `Text Box`.

    - Set **Value entered** to be stored in `Age`:

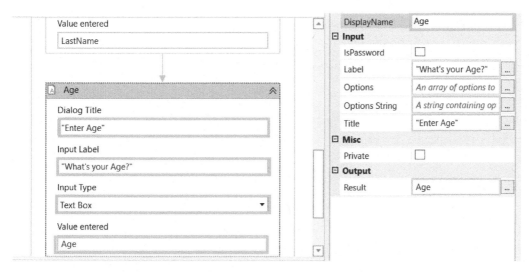

Figure 6.6 – Updating the Input Dialog properties – part 3

10. Drag a **Message Box** activity to the sequence and change **Text** from the **Properties** section so that it includes "The Age of " + FirstName + " " + LastName + " is " + Age +".", as shown in the following screenshot:

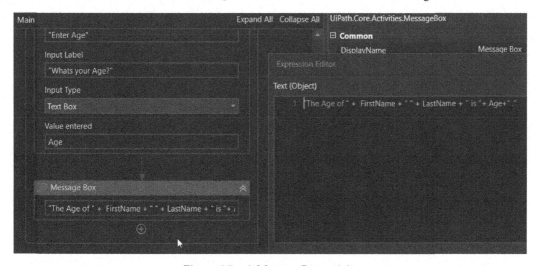

Figure 6.7 – A Message Box activity

The project outline sequence should look as follows:

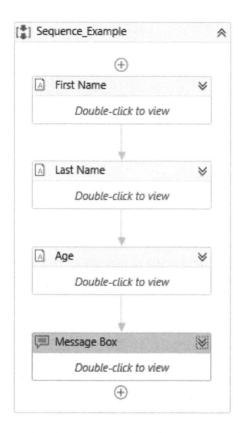

Figure 6.8 – Sequence outline

11. Click the **Run** button from the **Design** tab and follow the prompts to enter your input to ensure the final output looks as follows:

Figure 6.9 – Output Message Box

In this section, we learned how sequences can be used in automation. In the next section, we will explore other control flow options.

What are flowcharts?

Flowcharts are used in project settings where the business processes are complex and have multiple decision points. Flowcharts support multiple logical branching using various types of activities such as **If/Else**, **loops**, and **switches**.

For example, you can create a flowchart that takes input information, such as Year, from a user through an **Input Text Box** and verify whether it is a leap year. In this example, it can have two possible outcomes. One is *leap year*, while the other is *not a leap year* based on the input provided. Let's look at an example.

Example of a flowchart

In this section, we will create a flowchart example that identifies whether a given year is a leap year. Perform the following steps to build the automation using a flowchart:

1. Create a **New Blank Process** from the **New Project** section in UiPath Studio and name it Flowchart_Example, as shown in the following screenshot:

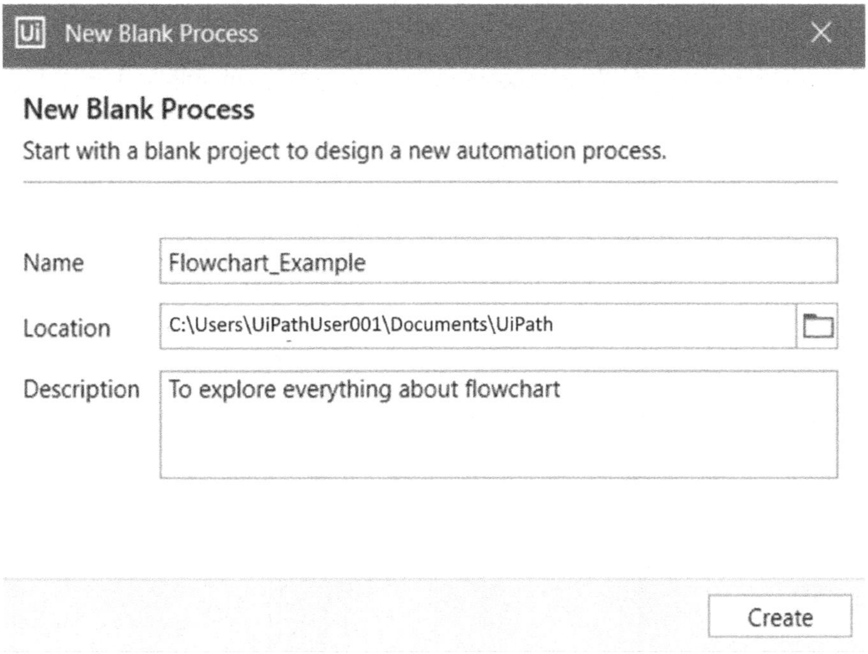

Figure 6.10 – Creating a New Blank Process

2. Enter your preferred project **Location** to save the project.

3. Enter details in the **Description** field and click **Create** to create the **Designer** panel.

4. Click **New > Flowchart** from the **Design** tab and set **Name** to LeapYear, as shown in the following screenshot:

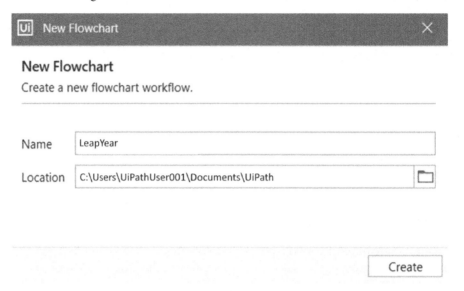

Figure 6.11 – New Flowchart

5. Click **Create** to update the **Designer** view, as shown in the following screenshot:

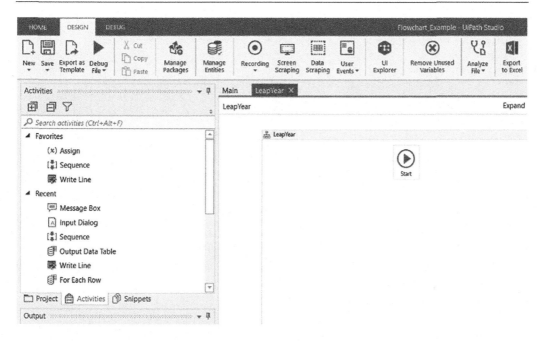

Figure 6.12 – The Flowchart Designer view

6.   Create a **Name variable** called inputYear and a **Variable type** called Int32 to store the information that's received from the user, as follows:

Name	Variable type	Scope	Default
inputYear	Int32	LeapYear	*Enter a VB expression*

Create Variable

Figure 6.13 – Creating a variable

7. Drag an **Input Dialog** activity onto the project flowchart, as follows:

Figure 6.14 – Input Dialog

8. Do the following to accept and store `Input Year`, as shown in the following screenshot:

- Set **Dialog Title** to `"Input Year"`.

- Set **Input Label** to `"What's the Input Year?"`.

- Set **Input Type** to `Text Box`.

- Set **Value entered** to be stored in `inputYear`:

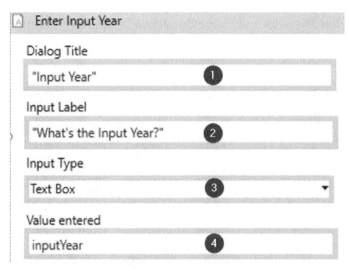

Figure 6.15 – Updating the Input Dialog properties

9. Connect the **Start** node to your **Input Dialog** by dragging the pointer, as shown in the following screenshot:

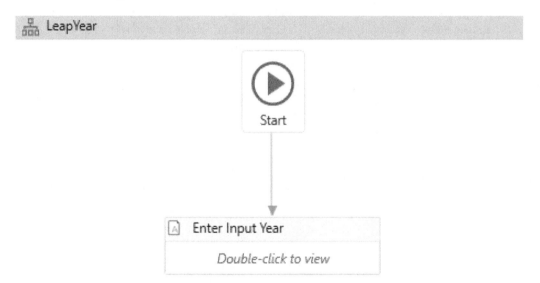

Figure 6.16 – Connecting the Input Dialog

10. Drag a **Flow Decision** activity and place it next to your **Input Dialog**.

11. Click on **Flow Decision** and, in the **Condition** field, enter `"inputYear mod 4 = 0"` as a VB expression to verify whether the given input is a leap year. Otherwise, it is not a leap year, as shown in the following screenshot:

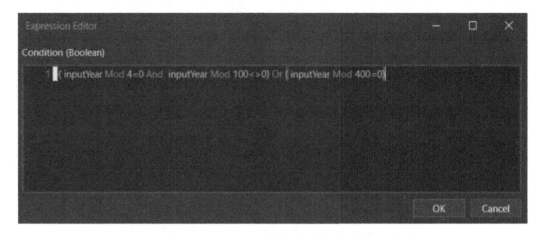

Figure 6.17– Updating the condition in the Condition (Boolean) panel

12. Drag a **Message box** activity to the **True** side of the flow decision and add a message stating `"The given year " + inputYear.ToString + " is a Leap Year"` to the **Text** field of **Properties**, as shown here:

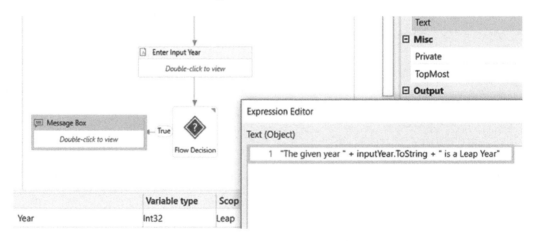

Figure 6.18 – True decision message box

13. Drag a **Message box** activity to the **False** side of the flow decision and add a message stating `"The given year " + inputYear.ToString + " is not a Leap Year"` to the **Text** field of **Properties**, as shown here:

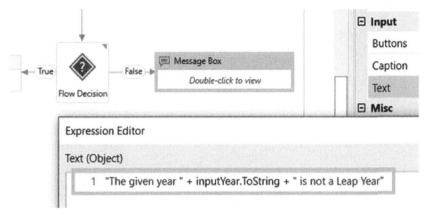

Figure 6.19 – False decision message box

The project's outline flowchart should look as follows:

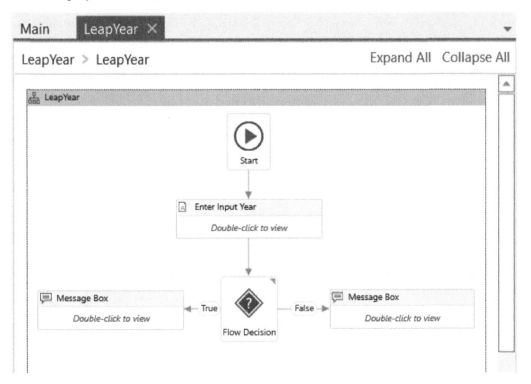

Figure 6.20 – Flowchart outline

14. Click the **Run** button from the **Design** tab and follow the prompts to enter your input. The final output should look as follows for a leap year:

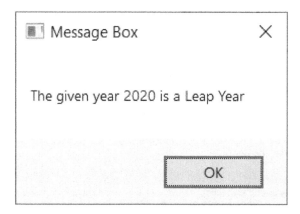

Figure 6.21 – Final true decision output message

15. Click the **Run** button from the **Design** tab and follow the prompts to enter your input so that the final output looks as follows when it is not a leap year:

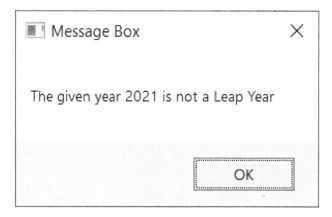

Figure 6.22 – Final false decision output message

So far, we have seen how sequences and flowcharts can be used in the **Designer** panel for automation using real-time examples. In the upcoming sections, we will learn how control flow activities can be used to enhance automation.

Exploring decisions and types of decisions

The decision activities allow you to control the execution of the data flow when a decision must be evaluated on a business scenario. Based on that, one of two actions must be performed. These two actions form the branches of the decision activity and are performed based on the outcome of the decision, which can be either `True` or `False`. In cases where multiple outcomes are expected, it is recommended that the **Switch** activity is used.

The **If** statement activity is used in a sequence, while a **flow decision** activity is used in a flowchart. For example, you can check for a specific value in some input text and act based on the outcome of the text. Let's look at this in more detail.

Example of an If activity

In this example, we will create a sequence that asks for an input number and then displays whether the given number is even or odd. Let's get started:

1. Create a **New Blank Process** from the **New Project** section in UiPath Studio and name it `Decision_Example`, as shown in the following screenshot:

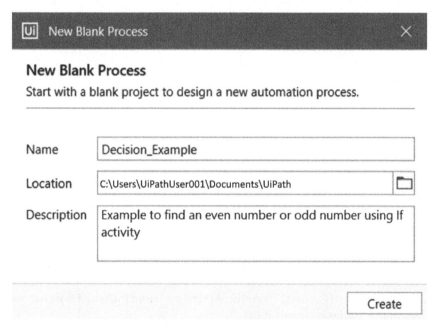

Figure 6.23 – Creating a New Blank Process

2. Enter your preferred project **Location** to save the project.

3. Enter some details in the **Description** field and click **Create** to create the **Designer** panel.

4. Create an integer called `InputNumber` to store the information that's received from the user, as shown in the following screenshot:

Name	Variable type	Scope	Default
InputNumber	Int32	Sequence	*Enter a VB expression*
Create Variable			

Figure 6.24 – Creating a variable

5. Drag an **Input Dialog** activity to the project's sequence.

6. Do the following to accept and store `InputNumber`, as shown in the following screenshot:

    ▪ Set **Dialog Title** to `"Input Number"`.

    ▪ Set **Input Label** to `"Enter Input Number"`.

    ▪ Set **Input Type** to `Text Box`.

    ▪ Set **Value entered** to be stored in `InputNumber`:

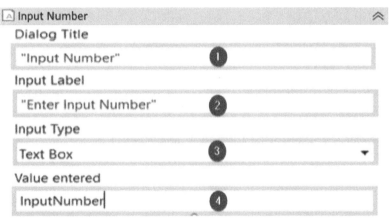

Figure 6.25 – Updating the Input Dialog properties

7. Drag and drop the **If** activity from the **Activities** panel into the **Designer** panel, as shown in the following screenshot:

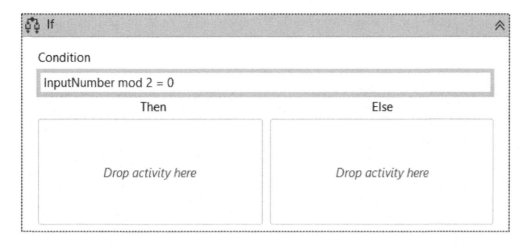

Figure 6.26 – Creating an If activity

8. In the **Condition** field, write `InputNumber mod 2 = 0`, as shown in the following screenshot:

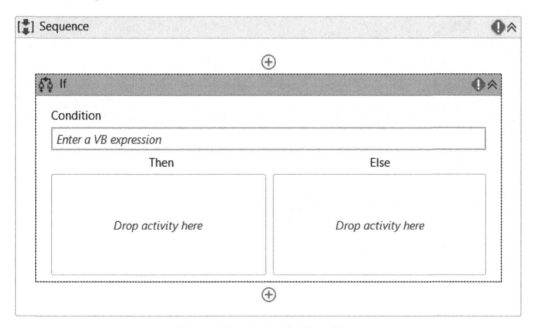

Figure 6.27 – Setting the If condition

9. In the **Then** branch, drag a **Message box** activity and write `"The given number is an even number"`.

10. In the **Else** branch, drag a **Message box** activity and write `"The given number is an Odd number"`.

The project's outline sequence should look as follows:

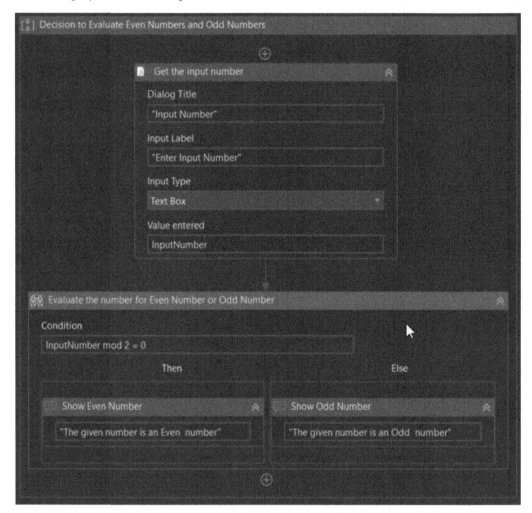

Figure 6.28 – Sequence outline

11. Click the **Run** button from the **Design** tab and follow the prompts to enter your inputs so that the final output looks as follows for an even number:

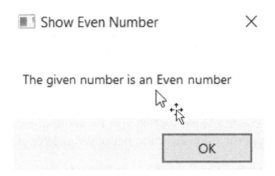

Figure 6.29 – Output message for an even number

12. Click the **Run** button from the **Design** tab and follow the prompts to enter your inputs so that the final output looks as follows for an odd number:

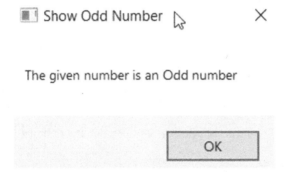

Figure 6.30 – Output message for an odd number

In this section, we have seen how If, Else, and Then can be used to evaluate a condition and perform actions based on the evaluation result. In the next section, we will learn how to automate repeated tasks using loops.

Exploring loops and types of loops

Loops are used to execute a given statement on repetitions based on a specific condition in an automation process. They are mainly used to automate repetitive automation tasks. The key loops in UiPath are **Do While**, **While**, and **For Each**. Let's explore these in turn.

Do While

The statements inside the **Do While** loop are executed first and then the execution is repeated until the specified condition is satisfied.

Example of a Do While loop

In this example, we will create a sequence that asks for an input number and then performs actions to output the value a set number of times. Let's get started:

1. Create a **New Blank Process** from the **New Project** section in UiPath Studio and name it DoWhile_Example, as shown in the following screenshot:

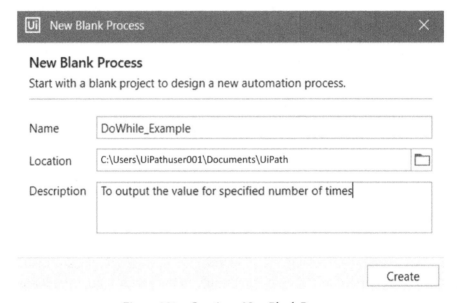

Figure 6.31 – Creating a New Blank Process

2. Enter your preferred project **Location** to save the project.

3. Enter some details in the **Description** field and click **Create** to create the **Designer** panel.

4. Create an integer called Counter to get information from the user, as shown in the following screenshot:

Name	Variable type	Scope	Default
Counter	Int32	Sequence	Enter a VB expression

Figure 6.32 – Creating a variable

5. Drag an **Input Dialog** activity to the project's sequence.

6. Do the following to accept and store InputNumber, as shown in the following screenshot:

    - Set **Dialog Title** to "Input Number".

    - Set **Input Label** to "Enter Input Number".

    - Set **Input Type** to Text Box.

    - Set **Value entered** to be stored in InputNumber:

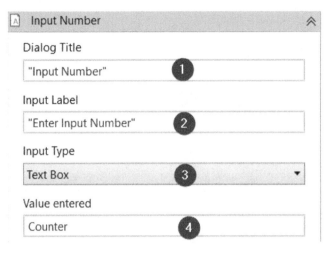

Figure 6.33 – Updating the Input Dialog properties

7. Drag and drop the **Do While** activity from the **Activities** panel into the **Designer** panel, as shown in the following screenshot:

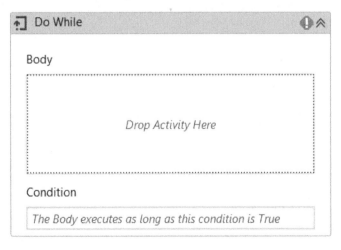

Figure 6.34 – Creating a Do While activity

8. In the **Condition** field, write `Counter < 10`.

9. In the **Body** branch, drag a **Write Line** activity and write `Counter.ToString`.

10. Change the name of the `Do While` sequence to *Do While_Count Numbers,* and change the name of the `Body` sequence to *Increment Counter by .1*

11. Drag an **Assign** activity inside the *Increment Counter by 1* sequence and write `Counter = Counter + 1`.

12. The project's outline sequence should look as follows:

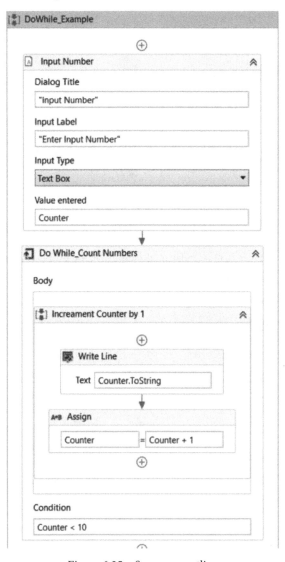

Figure 6.35 – Sequence outline

13. Click the **Run** button from the **Design** tab and follow the prompts to enter 1 as input so that the final output looks as follows for a number that's less than 10:

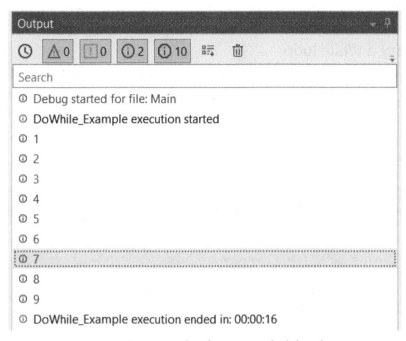

Figure 6.36 – Output window for an input that's less than 10

14. Click the **Run** button from the **Design** tab and follow the prompts to enter 99 as your input so that the final output looks as follows for a number that's greater than 10. The number **99** will be displayed in the output because a **Write Line** activity has been used to display the number that is read as input through the **Input Dialog** activity and saved in the **Counter** variable.

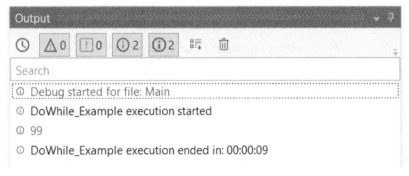

Figure 6.37 – Output window for an input that's greater than 10

While

The statements inside a While loop are executed if the specified condition is satisfied any number of times.

Example of a While loop

In the following example, we will create a sequence that asks for an input number and then performs actions to output the value, as long as the condition has been satisfied. Let's get started:

1. Create a **New Blank Process** from the **New Project** section in UiPath Studio and name it `While_Example`, as shown in the following screenshot:

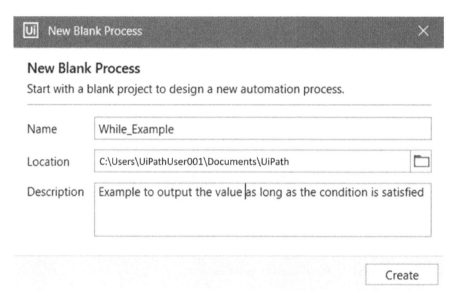

Figure 6.38 – Creating a New Blank Process

2. Enter your preferred project **Location** to save the project.

3. Enter some details in the **Description** field and click **Create** to create the **Designer** panel.

4. Create a `Counter` integer to get information from the user, as shown in the following screenshot:

Name	Variable type	Scope	Default
Counter	Int32	Sequence	*Enter a VB expression*

Figure 6.39 – Creating a variable

5. Drag an **Input Dialog** activity to the project's sequence.

6. Do the following to accept and store `InputNumber`, as shown in the following screenshot:

- Set **Dialog Title** to `"Input Number"`.

- Set **Input Label** to `"Enter Input Number"`.

- Set **Input Type** to `Text Box`.

- Set **Value entered** to be stored in `Counter`:

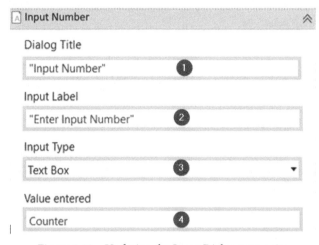

Figure 6.40 – Updating the Input Dialog properties

7. Drag and drop the **While** activity from the **Activities** panel into the **Designer** panel, as shown in the following screenshot:

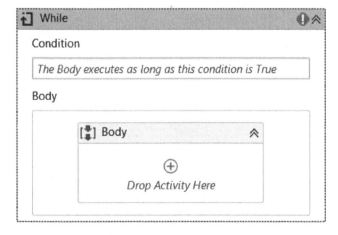

Figure 6.41 – Designer view of the While activity

8. In the **Condition** field, write `Counter < 10`.

9. In the **Body** branch, drag a **Write Line** activity and write `Counter.ToString`.

10. Drag an **Assign** activity and write `Counter = Counter + 1`.

The project's outline sequence should look as follows:

Figure 6.42 – Sequence outline

11. Click the **Run** button from the **Design** tab and follow the prompts to enter 1 as your input so that the final output looks as follows for a number that's less than 10:

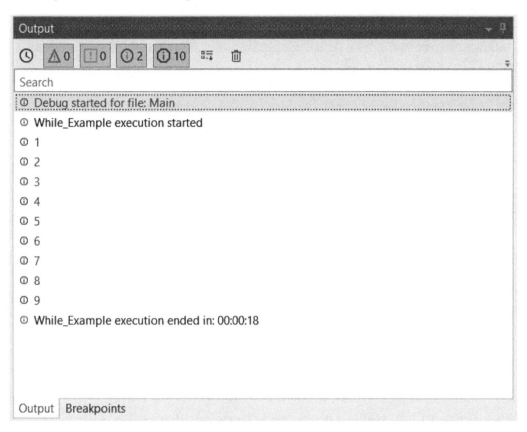

Figure 6.43 – Output window for an input that's less than 10

12. Click the **Run** button from the **Design** tab and follow the prompts to enter 99 as your input so that the final output looks as follows for a number that's greater than 10, that is, 99:

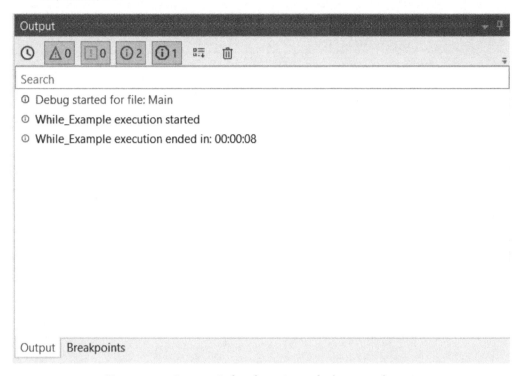

Figure 6.44 – Output window for an input that's greater than 10

In this section, we have explored the Do While activity, which is used in many programmatic situations to loop through inputs or values until a specific condition is satisfied. In the next section, we will learn about the For Each activity to see how we can process each and every available piece of input data.

For Each

The For Each activity helps you go through every item in your data collection defined in a list, array, or dictionary, as you learned in *Chapter 7, Manipulating Data using UiPath*. The statements inside the For Each activity are executed once for each item so that its operations are performed based on that item's information.

Example of a For Each activity

In this example, we will create a sequence that performs actions on a list of numbers. Let's get started:

1. Create a **New Blank Process** from the **New Project** section in UiPath Studio and name it `For_Each_Example`, as shown in the following screenshot:

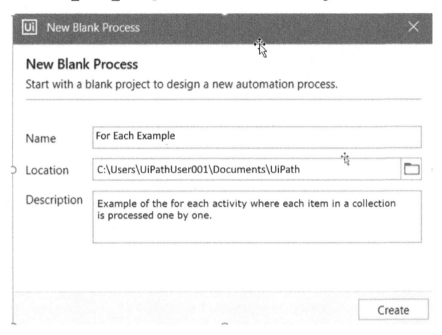

Figure 6.45 – Creating a New Blank Process

2. Enter your preferred project **Location** to save the project.

3. Enter some details in the **Description** field and click **Create** to create the **Designer** panel.

4. Create a variable and name it `Counters`. Then, set **Variable type** to **Array of** [T] and select `Int32` from the dropdown, as shown in the following screenshot:

Name	Variable type	Scope	Default
Counters	Int32[]	Sequence	Enter a VB expression

Figure 6.46 – Creating a variable

5. In the **Default** column of **Variables**, define the default list as
    {1,2,3,4,5,6,7,8,9,10}, as shown in the following screenshot:

Name	Variable type	Scope	Default
Counters	Int32[]	Sequence	{1,2,3,4,5,6,7,8,9,10}

Figure 6.47 – Setting the default values

6. Drag and drop the **For Each** activity from the **Activities** panel into the **Designer**
    panel, as shown in the following screenshot:

Figure 6.48 – Creating a For Each activity

7. Update the default value inside the **For Each** field to Counter and the **in** field to
    Counters, as shown in *Figure 6.49*. In the **Body** branch, drag a **Write Line** activity
    and write "The Current item in process is " + Counter.ToString.
    As the data type of each item of **Numbers** is Int32, we need to convert them into
    String format for the item to be displayed in the **WriteLine** activity.

The project's outline sequence should look as follows:

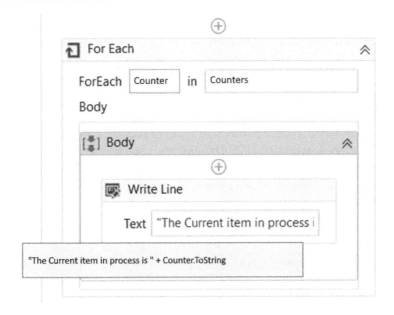

Figure 6.49 – Sequence outline

8. Click the **Run** button from the **Design** tab and follow the prompts to enter your input so that the final output looks as follows:

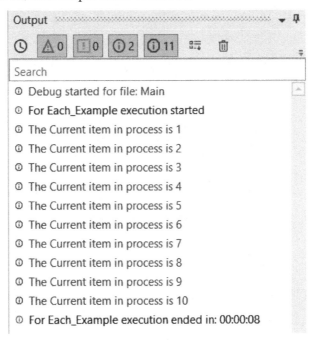

Figure 6.50 – Output window

In this section, we looked at the different types of loops that we can use to automate repeated tasks and enhance our automation effectively. These concepts can be applied to different situations, based on the automation requirements.

Summary

In this chapter, we learned about the different types of control flow concepts, control flow statements such as loops, switches, and If statements, and their implementations. We also learned how to apply these control flow concepts. The examples that were provided in this chapter will help you decide which activity to use when you encounter similar data handling situations while creating robots.

In the next chapter, you will learn how to manipulate different types of data using control flow activities.

7
Manipulating Data Using UiPath

Today, every software application, business process, or human deals with data. Data is the most critical resource in every organization and it's available to us in many different forms. We need to modify, structure, format, or sort data to convert it into meaningful information in a business process.

This chapter focuses on introducing different methods of manipulating data based on various data types. Data used in a business process undergoes many transformational steps before it's ready for consumption at various stages of the process, hence it is crucial to understand how to perform such manipulations.

This chapter consists of the following sections:

- Explaining the concept of data manipulation
- Understanding string manipulation
- Understanding date and time manipulation
- Understanding list manipulation
- Understanding numeric calculations
- Understanding dictionary manipulation
- Understanding pattern-based data extraction using **regular expressions** (**regexes**)

Technical requirements

As a prerequisite, please have UiPath Studio and UiPath Robot installed and connected with Orchestrator. Furthermore, it is essential to understand the different data types, control flows, and UiPath Studio features before starting this chapter.

Explaining the concept of data manipulation

Data manipulation is a process that alters data through various operations to convert it into a usable format. It is a vital function for business operations and management as it provides many benefits, such as the following:

- Converts data into a more consistent format to improve reliability, readability, and organization

- Enables customization and generation of more meaningful data according to business requirements

- Removes unwanted data to ensure only the required information is processed

Data manipulation operations consist of four primary functions, as outlined here:

- Extracting data by specifying extraction conditions such as filtering, summarizing, and so on

- Adding new data

- Removing unwanted data

- Changing existing data by updating new values or converting unstructured data into a more meaningful and process-friendly format

There are many different methods of manipulating data, depending on the type of data. Let's now take a look at various data manipulation techniques.

Understanding string manipulation

Strings are one of the most commonly used data types in any automation solution. A string data type refers to a series of text values that we frequently use to extract, display, process, and send data between multiple applications for further processing. String operations help perform business scenarios such as sending out emails for users, extracting a portion of text from a larger text, and so on.

UiPath uses string manipulation methods in **Visual Basic .NET (VB.NET)** or C#, depending on the language you choose to use in UiPath Studio. In this chapter, we will use the methods in VB.NET. The following sections describe some of the commonly used string manipulation methods in UiPath.

Concat function

The Concat function enables the user to concatenate two or more string representations into one string representation. The Concat function is capable of concatenating up to four string objects at a time. The following code snippet shows the expression we use to concatenate strings:

```
String.Concat(StrVariable1, StrVariable2)
```

Let's take a look at a simple example of how to use this function. Proceed as follows:

1. Open UiPath Studio and create a new project.
2. Once the project is ready, double-click on the Main.xaml file on the **Project** panel to open it in the **Designer** panel.
3. Click on the **Activities** panel, search for a **Sequence** activity, and drag it to the **Designer** panel.
4. Select the **Sequence** activity you added, and click on the **Variables** panel.
5. Create a new variable named DisplayText of type String.
6. Drag and drop an **Assign** activity and assign the following value to the DisplayText variable: "Hello... My name is".
7. Create another String variable named FirstName.
8. Use another **Assign** activity below the previous and assign a FirstName variable with the value "John".
9. Create a third String variable named LastName.
10. Use a third **Assign** activity below the previous one and assign a LastName variable with the value "Doe".
11. Now, search for a **Message Box** activity in the **Activities** panel and drag and drop it after the last **Assign** activity.
12. Configure your **Message Box** activity with the following code:

```
String.Concat(DisplayText, FirstName, LastName)
```

Once you reach this point, your workflow should look similar to this:

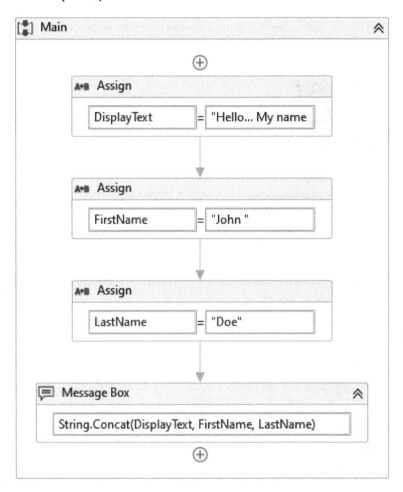

Figure 7.1 – String.Concat function example

Now we know how to combine two strings, let's look at how we can check whether a particular string exists in another string.

Contains function

The `Contains` function checks whether a specified substring exists in another string. The function returns a Boolean value depending on the result. The function returns `True` as the output when the substring exists in the main string and returns `False` if not. An important point to remember is that this function is case-sensitive; hence, it may return `False` as the output even when two strings match, but the casing of the letters is different. As we discussed in *Chapter 5*, *Learning about Variables and Arguments*, Boolean results enable the user to control the workflow execution. Since the `Contains` function returns a Boolean result, this function is mainly associated with a control flow activity. We can either use an **If** activity or **Flow Decision** activity depending on whether we are using a **Sequence** or a **Flowchart** container.

Let's look at the same workflow we designed and change it by adding this function to test its functionality, as follows:

1. In the same workflow, drag and drop an **If** activity from the **Activities** panel and place it in between the last **Assign** activity and the **Message Box** activity.

2. Configure the **If** activity using the following code for the **Expression** section:

```
String.Concat(DisplayText, FirstName, LastName).
Contains("John")
```

   The expression concatenates all the string variables and checks whether the "John" substring is available in it.

3. Select the **Message Box** activity located below the **If** activity, and move it into the **Then** segment of the **If** activity.

4. Drag and drop a **Write Line** activity from the **Activities** panel into the **Else** segment of the **If** activity.

5. Configure the **Write Line** activity with the following string:

```
"The name you are looking for is not available"
```

Once you configure the **Write Line** activity, your workflow should look similar to this:

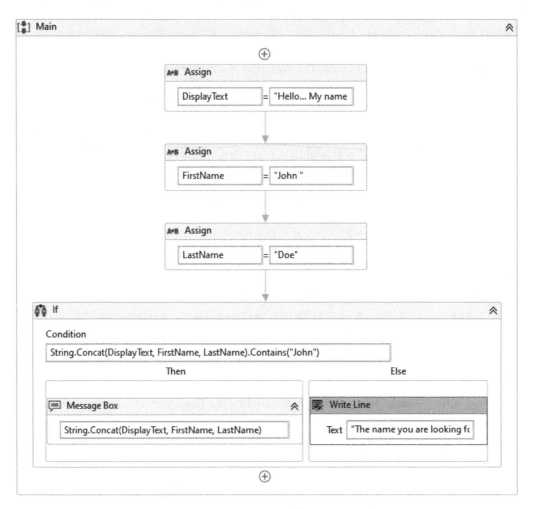

Figure 7.2 – String.Contains function example

The `String.Contains` function gives you `True` as the result if the searched string is available. If you want the function to return `False` when the string exists (simply by reverting the result), you can introduce the `Not` keyword into the expression. In the previously described example, the expression would look like this after introducing the `Not` keyword:

```
Not String.Concat(DisplayText, FirstName, LastName).
Contains("John")
```

We can also look at another function that is similar to `String.Concat`. The `String.Format` function, however, provides the ability to change values at designated locations in a defined string. The next section explains this concept in detail.

Format function

The `Format` function is similar to the `Concat` function. However, the `Format` function can convert objects into strings and insert them into another string at specified locations. The `Format` function also allows the combining of any number of strings into one string variable. The `Format` function uses specific **identifiers** (**IDs**) to locate where to insert new text in the primary string. Such IDs are referred to as {0}, {1}, and {2}, in which the numeric values describe the order of merging text.

Let's take a look at how we can apply the `Format` function through a simple example, as follows:

1. Let's continue to work on the same workflow we built previously. Drag and drop an **Assign** activity below the **If** activity.

2. Create a new string variable named `ConcatenatedText` and specify it in the **To** segment of the **Assign** activity.

3. Use the following code in the **Value** segment of the **Assign** activity to assign it a value. This function assigns the concatenated value to another string variable for us to further process the output:

   ```
   String.Concat(DisplayText, FirstName, LastName)
   ```

4. Drag and drop another **Assign** activity below the previous activity.

5. Configure the **To** segment of the **Assign** activity by creating a new string variable named `FormatString` and assign it the following string:

   ```
   "Good day... Let me introduce myself. {0} and I am {1}
   years old. I'm currently based in {2}"
   ```

6. Use another **Assign** activity and place it below the previous activity.

7. Create a new string variable named `DisplayResult` and configure the **To** segment of the **Assign** activity with the variable name.

8. Configure the **Value** segment of the same **Assign** activity using the following code. The following code uses the `String.Format` function to fill in the text portions for {0}, {1}, and {2} indicators:

   ```
   String.Format(FormatString, ConcatenatedText, "29", "Sri
   Lanka")
   ```

If you look at the function closely, the `FormatString` variable is the primary string that we need completed. The {0}, {1}, and {2} indicators are replaced by the values specified in the expression in the specified order.

9. Add a **Message Box** activity and configure it by specifying the `DisplayResult` variable to show the output as a message.

Once you complete the configuration, your workflow should look similar to this:

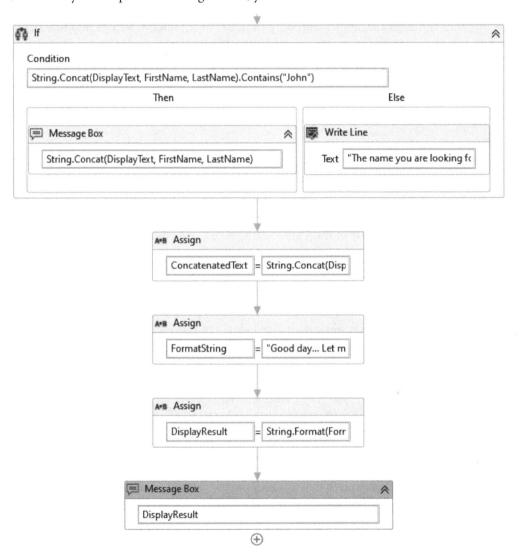

Figure 7.3 – String.Format function example

10. Execute the program, and you will see the following output from the last **Message Box** activity:

Figure 7.4 – String.Format function output

The `String.Format` option can be helpful in scenarios where you have to replace dynamic parts of a string with values retrieved during execution. One good example is updating the body of a standard email message with the name of the person addressed. So, let's look at the `Replace` function.

Replace function

The `Replace` function enables the user to replace all occurrences of a specified substring in the primary string. Similar to the `Contains` function, this function is also case-sensitive. It uses the following expression to replace text:

```
VarName.Replace(<String to Replace>, <New Value>)
```

The `Replace` expression requires two parameters: the string to be replaced and the new text.

Let's apply this function to the same workflow and try replacing some values, as follows:

1. Open the previously built workflow in UiPath Studio.
2. Drag and drop an **Assign** activity after the last **Message Box** activity into the workflow.
3. Configure the **To** segment of the **Assign** activity by creating a new string variable under the name `CleansedValue`.
4. Configure the **Value** segment of the **Assign** activity by providing the following code:

```
DisplayResult.Replace("Hello…", "")
```

This code would look for the word `"Hello..."` in the string value in the `DisplayResult` variable and replace it with a blank string.

5. Place a new **Message Box** activity below the last **Assign** activity and configure it to display the value in the `CleansedValue` variable. The final workflow should look similar to this:

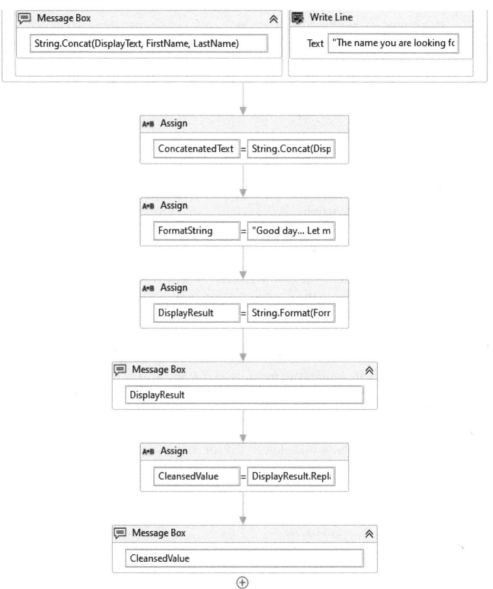

Figure 7.5 – String.Replace workflow example

6. Execute the workflow and see the result of the last message that pops up. It should look similar to the following output:

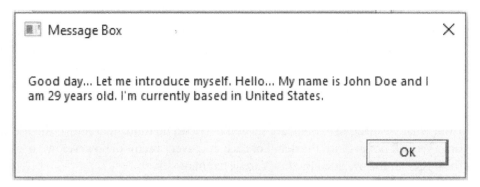

Figure 7.6 – String.Replace function output

So, the `Replace` function is beneficial when you want to remove special characters or any unwanted text from a string.

At this point, you are now familiar with several methods under string manipulation. Along with these methods, we sometimes need to search for a location of a string and get the position to perform certain actions. The following section describes the use of the `IndexOf` method to perform search operations.

IndexOf function

The `IndexOf` function returns the index of the first occurrence of a specified character in a string. An index in programming always starts at 0. Hence, in an actual string, the first letter is the zeroth letter, the second letter is the first letter, and so on. It is not just another method; it is one of many overload methods in VB.NET that perform several search mechanisms based on different input parameters we provide. In general, it uses the following expression to obtain the index of a specified character:

```
StrVariable.IndexOf("<search string>")
```

Let's get the index of the first occurrence of a letter in our previous output string, as follows:

1. Open the same workflow file we worked on previously.

2. Place a **Message Box** activity at the end of the workflow.

3. Configure the new **Message Box** activity with the following code:

```
CleansedValue.IndexOf("d").ToString
```

This configuration would provide the index of the first occurrence of the letter `"d"` in the `CleansedValue` string. The index is next converted into a string using the `.ToString` method to print it as text in the **Message Box** activity.

4. Run the program and see the output. The final **Message Box** activity should return `"3"` as the output. If you look closely in the `CleansedValue` variable string, the first occurrence of the letter `"d"` is in the word `"Good"`. It is the fourth letter in the string; hence, in a zero-based string, the index of the letter is `"3"`, which is similar to the output we got.

Apart from what we discussed, there are several overload methods that return the index of a string. We will not get into the detail of each and every method; however, we need to know the basics. Some overload methods are listed here:

*   `IndexOf(String, Int32, Int32, StringComparison)`: Provides the index of the first occurrence of a specified string in the current string. The parameters specify the starting search position in the current string, the number of characters in the current string to search, and the type of search to use for the specified string.

*   `IndexOf(String, Int32, StringComparison)`: Provides the index of the first occurrence of a specified string in the current string. The parameters specify the starting search position in the current string, along with the type of search to use for the string.

*   `IndexOf(Char, Int32, Int32)`: Provides the index for the first occurrence of a specified character. The parameters specify the starting search position and the number of characters to search in the current string.

*   `IndexOf(String, StringComparison)`: Provides the index of the first occurrence of a specified string in the current string. The parameters specify the type of search to use for the specified string.

*   `IndexOf(String, Int32, Int32)`: Provides the index of the first occurrence of a specified string. The parameters define the search position in the current string and the number of characters to search.

*   `IndexOf(Char)`: Provides the index of the first occurrence of a specified Unicode character in the current string.

As we tried one type out of the different overload methods, you can also try out some of the other types mentioned to get more practice on obtaining the index of a given string.

Let's now apply the knowledge gained on indexes and try out another method for string manipulation.

SubString function

There are scenarios where you need to extract only a particular portion of a string from a longer string to process it further. For example, from all the text in a **Portable Document Format** (**PDF**) file, you might want to extract only the invoice number to use it in another application. The `SubString` function comes in handy in such scenarios as it allows extraction of text by providing the starting index and the length of the substring. It uses the following expression to extract a portion of a text from a longer string:

```
StrVariable.SubString(<starting index>, <length of substring>)
```

Applying our knowledge of indexes, let's use the same working solution and try to extract the name of the person from the string variable, as follows:

1. Let's open the same working solution we worked on previously.

2. The `CleansedValue` string variable contains the name `"John Doe"`. Let's count the starting index of the word `"John"` in the string. The word `"John"` starts from the 47th position.

3. Now, we have to check how many characters we need to extract. The name `"John Doe"` includes eight characters, including the space in the middle. Hence, the length of the string we require for extraction is 8.

4. Using the starting index and the length we calculated, let's configure the last **Message Box** activity to show the name. The following code example illustrates the configuration to apply in the **Message Box** activity:

    ```
    CleansedValue.Substring(47, 8)
    ```

    We can try to get the same output using the `IndexOf` function without hardcoding the positions. As we explored several `IndexOf` functions, let's explore a bit how we can combine these two functions together to get the same output.

5. Start the program and see the output of the last **Message Box** activity. It should show the name `"John Doe"`.

As a quick recap, this section focused on extracting the desired part of a string from a larger string by providing start and end index points. This function comes in very handy on many occasions where you want to extract certain parts of a string based on a specific string pattern. Apart from this function, we also have the ability to split a string into multiple elements and access each part separately. Let's now see how we can split a text and retrieve individual elements after splitting.

Split function

The `Split` function enables the user to split a long string based on a specific character. This functionality can be used when you need to work with **comma-separated values** (**CSV**) files or delimited string variables to split to access each component. Splitting a single string based on a delimiter converts the entire string into a string array representing each element by a zero-based index. It uses the following function to split string values. The arrays are of fixed size; hence, you cannot add or remove items from an array after creation:

```
StrVariable.Split("<split character>"c)
```

The letter `c` after the split character converts the character specified within double quotes to a character type.

Let's use our previous examples and split the values in a `CleansedValue` variable, as follows:

1. Open the same working solution.
2. After the last **Message Box** activity, place a new **Assign** activity.
3. Configure the **To** segment of the **Assign** activity by creating a new string array-type variable. Press *Ctrl + K* and provide the variable name as `SplitArray`. Now, if you look at the **Variables** panel, the variable's data type is a string.
4. Click on **Variable Type** in the **Variables** panel of the variable and click on the **Array of [T]** option to find more data types.
5. From the **Select Types** pop-up screen, select the data type of the array as **String** and click **OK**.
6. Now, you can see the data type of the `SplitArray` variable as `String[]` in the **Variables** panel.
7. Configure the **Value** segment of the **Assign** activity with the following code to split the value in the `CleansedValue` variable by `"<space>"`:

```
CleansedValue.Split(" "c)
```

The aforementioned configuration will split the entire sentence in the `CleansedValue` variable by a space delimiter. Each word will represent a specific element in the array based on its position in the string. For example, splitting the `"Hello World"` string with a space places the two words in the zeroth and first indexes in the array.

8. Use another **Message Box** activity below the new **Assign** activity and configure it to retrieve the text in a specified index, as follows:

```
SplitArray(0).ToString
```

Once you reach this point, the workflow you built should look similar to this:

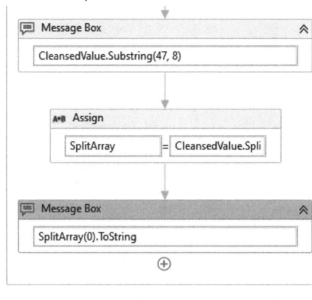

Name	Variable type	Scope
DisplayText	String	Main
FirstName	String	Main
LastName	String	Main
ConcatenatedText	String	Main
FormatString	String	Main
DisplayResult	String	Main
CleansedValue	String	Main
SplitArray	String[]	Main
Create Variable		

Figure 7.7 – String.Substring and String.Split functions' output

9. Run the program and observe the output of the last **Message Box** activity. Since we split by space, the first word of the `CleansedValue` string is placed in the zeroth position. The output you get is the first word, which is Good. Try changing the index and run it a couple of times to observe the output. The following screenshot illustrates the output of the workflow we built:

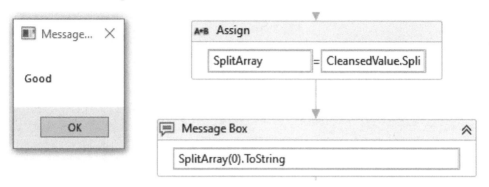

Figure 7.8 – String.Split function output

This section focused on learning how to split a string by providing the split character. This function comes in handy when you want to extract specific text elements from a given string. Further, we also learned that the elements in the split array can be accessed through a zero-based index. Having said that, let's now look at how we can merge data in collection variables—such as arrays—into one string.

Join function

The `Join` function combines all the elements in a string array into one string by introducing a character as a separator between each element. For example, if the array consists of two elements such as `"Hello"` and `"World"`, the separator introduced in the `Join` function is included in the output string to indicate which position it was split originally. Hence, in our example here, if we introduce `" | "` as the separator, the `Join` function returns `"Hello|World"` as the output. The expression used for the `Join` function is shown here:

```
String.Join("<separator>", <Collection Variable>)
```

Let's apply this function to our previous working solution to join the elements in the `SplitArray` variable, as follows:

1. Open the previous working solution.

2. Add a new **Message Box** activity at the end of the workflow.

3. Configure the new **Message Box** activity with the following code to join the elements in the `SplitArray` variable:

   ```
   String.Join(" ", SplitArray)
   ```

   We specified the space as a separator to return the string to its original form.

4. Run the program and observe the result of the last **Message Box** activity. It shows the string back in its original form.

String manipulation methods help us to understand which standard functions we can perform using text values. The concept of indexes we learned in this section of the chapter is common across all connection-type variables such as arrays, lists, data tables, and so on. All collection variables in VB.NET use the same concept using zero-based indexes when referring to individual elements. Each data type has its specific functions.

Similar to `String` functions, date-related functions are unique to the `DateTime` data type. Date-related calculations are quite common across any automation, hence it is essential to understand functions related to date values.

Understanding date and time manipulation

Date and time are two types of values that we come across almost all the time. Similarly, organizations deal with data that is of different dates, months, and years. .NET Framework offers many functionalities related to date values, enabling the user to calculate and manipulate dates easily. However, it is not required to know all the functionalities for the *Associate* exam. Hence, let's only look at some of the functionalities, which include the following:

- Date addition and subtraction

- Format conversion

- Extracting individual elements of a date

Let's explore some of the functionalities with the following scenario. We need to obtain a list of dates between 7 days before the current date and 7 days after the current date. Further, we also want to print the date, month, and the name of the date. The following steps provide a guide on generating the required output:

1. Open UiPath Studio and create a new **Empty** process.

2. Double-click on the `Main.xaml` file on the **Projects** panel to open the file in the **Designer** panel.

3. Create three variables named `CurrentDate`, `ProcessDate`, and `MaximumDate`, and configure all three by changing their data type to `System.DateTime`.

4. If `DateTime` is not listed in the dropdown under **Variable Type**, click on **Browse for More**, and search for the `System.DateTime` data type in the **Browser for .Net Types** popup.

5. Drag and drop an **Assign** activity from the **Activities** panel into the workflow.

6. Configure the **To** segment of the **Assign** activity by providing the first variable named `CurrentDate`.

7. Configure the **Value** segment of the **Assign** activity by providing `System.DateTime.Now` to assign the current date and time to the variable.

8. Drag and drop another **Assign** activity and use the `CurrentDate.AddDays(-7)` code to generate the date 7 days before the current date and assign it to the `ProcessDate` variable.

   The specified code deducts 7 days from the date held in the `CurrentDate` variable to generate a new date.

9. Similarly, use the following code in another **Assign** activity to assign the maximum date in the range to the `MaximumDate` variable:

   ```
   CurrentDate.AddDays(7)
   ```

   The specified code adds 7 days to the date specified in the `CurrentDate` variable to generate the maximum date we need to extract.

10. Search for a **While** activity from the **Activities** panel and place it below the three **Assign** activities. We use a `While` loop to loop through the days between the days specified in the `ProcessDate` and `MaximumDate` variables. The condition of the `While` activity uses the following code:

```
ProcessDate<= MaximumDate
```

11. Place a **Write Line** activity inside the `While` loop and configure it with the following code:

```
"Date: " + ProcessDate.ToString("dd-MMMM-yyyy") +
" | Month: " + Microsoft.VisualBasic.DateAndTime.
MonthName(ProcessDate.Month) + " | Day: " + ProcessDate.
ToString("dddd")
```

The `ProcessDate.ToString("dd-MMMM-yyyy")` code segment converts the date to the specified format to output the date in string format. For example, the date is printed as `01-January-2021`.

The `Microsoft.VisualBasic.DateAndTime.` `MonthName(ProcessDate.Month)` code segment generates the month name of the date value stored in the variable. For example, if the provided date is `01/12/2020`, this code's output would be `"December"`.

The `ProcessDate.ToString("dddd")` code segment converts the current day into the day's name, such as Sunday, Monday, and so on.

12. Place a new **Assign** activity below the **Write Line** activity and increment the `ProcessDate` variable's date by 1 day. The following code provides sample code for the activity:

```
ProcessDate.AddDays(1)
```

Once you reach this point, you have completed creating a date manipulation workflow. The developed workflow should look similar to this:

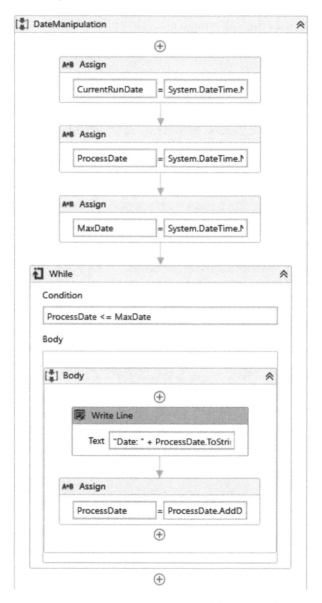

Figure 7.9 – Date manipulation workflow example

13. Run the automation and observe the output in the **Output** panel. Further, try simple configurations around the same workflow and understand which other functions are available to perform manipulations related to date values.

There are many functions related to a date. However, this section of the chapter covers only a few of the most commonly used functions. Based on the general idea obtained by going through the previously mentioned steps, you can easily use other functions to manipulate the data to retrieve the required output. On the other hand, the `Lists` data type offers the capability to hold a list of values of a specific data type, including strings, date-times, integers, and so on. The next section of the chapter focuses on some of the commonly used functions when working with list variables.

Understanding list manipulation

array → fixed size [handwritten]

Lists are data types of a specific type that can contain multiple data values. All list data values have a fixed memory location, which is known as an **index**. Arrays are of fixed size and defined at the creation of a variable. However, lists allow us to add, modify, and remove items during runtime. Similar to arrays, lists provide specific methods to manipulate their data, such as the following:

- Adding items
- Removing items
- Looping through elements in the list and performing specific actions on each
- Sorting items in the list
- Searching for an item
- Clearing items in a list

UiPath offers a collection of activities to perform the aforementioned actions efficiently. The activities that UiPath offers are listed here:

- **Add to Collection**: Adds new items to a specified collection variable. It is the equivalent of the `List.Add()` function.

- **Clear Collection**: Deletes all data from a specified collection variable. This function comes in handy when working with list variables that hold data temporarily. This activity helps such scenarios by deleting everything in the list before loading it with the next batch.

- **Remove from Collection**: Removes a specified item from a collection variable. In addition to the removal operation, the activity also returns a Boolean result indicating whether the removal operation has been successful or not.

- **Exists in Collection**: The activity returns a Boolean result indicating whether a specified item exists in the collection or not. This activity provides an efficient mechanism to check the existence of items without looping through the list.

Let's now practice some simple list manipulation methods. The steps outlined next provide a guideline to perform the required actions.

Declaring list variables

In this section of the chapter, we will take a look at how to declare list variables through the **Variables** panel.

Open UiPath Studio and create a new **Process** activity, as follows:

1. Open the Main.xaml file.

2. Drag and drop a **Sequence** activity from the **Activities** panel into the **Designer** panel.

3. Select the **Sequence** activity and click on the **Variables** panel.

4. Create a new list variable named StudentsList with the type List<String>. The list data type will not show in the dropdown initially. Hence, click on the **Browse for Types** option in the dropdown, and look for System.Collections.Generic.List in the **Browse and Select a .Net Type** pop-up window.

5. Select List<T> under System.Collections.Generic, select the data type from the dropdown as **String**, and click on the **OK** button to create a variable. The following screenshot shows the configuration in the **Browse and Select a .Net Type** pop-up window:

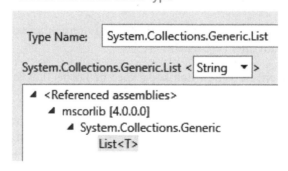

Figure 7.10 – List variable creation

6. Configure the **Default** section in the **Variables** panel with the following code to initialize the variable with a few values:

```
New List(Of String) from {"John", "Daniel", "Keith"}
```

7. Create another list variable of type `string` named `EmployeeList` following the same steps as before, and configure the **Default** section of the **Variables** panel with the following code:

```
New List(Of String) from {"Diana", "Lizi", "Peter",
"Daniel"}
```

You are now familiar with the creation of list variables. Let's now focus on using variables in workflows.

Adding items to a list

In this section, we will look at the usage of the **Add to Collection** activity to add items to one of the lists we created earlier. Proceed as follows:

1. Search for the **Add To Collection** activity in the **Variables** panel and drag it to the **Sequence** container we created earlier. Let's add a new item to the `StudentList` variable.

2. Select the **Add To Collection** activity and modify the `DisplayName` property in the **Properties** panel with `Add item to StudentList` to rename it.

3. Configure the `Collection` property of the activity by providing the `StudentList` variable. This property indicates to which collection variable you want to add data.

4. Configure the `Item` property of the activity by providing a new name within double quotes, as follows:

```
"Andrew"
```

5. You can now see in the following screenshot that UiPath Studio is showing an error message on the Collection property:

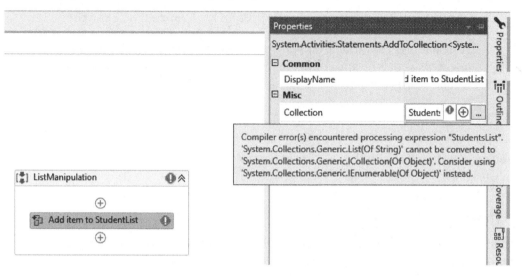

Figure 7.11 – Configuring Add To Collection activity data types

This error is thrown because the collection expects a string data type, but the activity is automatically configured to add object data types. You can see this configuration in the TypeArgument property of the activity.

6. Configure the TypeArgument property of the activity by selecting the data type as **String** from the dropdown.

7. Drag and drop another **Add To Collection** activity and configure it using the same steps to add a new name, "Jane", to the EmployeeList collection variable.

As we have built the workflow to add items to list variables, the next section of the chapter focuses on merging the two lists.

Merging list variables

Merging lists cannot be done directly—it requires converting the List type into an Enumerable type. To do this, proceed as follows:

1. Place an **Assign** activity below the two **Add To Collection** activities.

2. Configure the **To** segment of the **Assign** activity by creating a new list variable named CombinedPeopleList.

2. Configure the **Value** segment of the **Assign** activity using the following code. The `Enumerable.Concat` method concatenates the list variables that are converted As Enumerable. All lists that require merging need conversion from a `List` type to an `Enumerable` type. The `ToList()` function converts the combined `Enumerable` list into a `List` data type for further processing:

```
Enumerable.Concat(StudentsList.AsEnumerable,
EmployeeList.AsEnumerable).ToList
```

By now, we have one `List` variable that we can use for further processing. Further, if we look closely at the data values we have in both lists, we can see that the name `"Daniel"` is available in both lists. Once we merge the two lists into `CombinedPeopleList`, the new list now contains duplicate entries for `"Daniel"`. The next section of the chapter focuses on how to remove duplicate entries.

Removing data in lists

Data removal from a list is made easy by the **Remove From Collection** activity. We can use this activity to remove the duplicate entry we have for `"Daniel"` by following these next guidelines:

1. Search for the **Remove From Collection** activity from the **Activities** panel and place it below the **Assign** activity.

2. Configure the **Remove From Collection** activity by configuring the `Item` property as `"Daniel"` and configuring the `Collection` property by providing the `CombinedPeopleList` variable. This activity removes the first occurrence of the name `"Daniel"` from the list.

The data is now ready for modification. The next section of the chapter focuses on how to convert data in a list to uppercase.

Modifying data in lists

Lists contain multiple data values that we can access using an index. Similarly, this functionality also enables the user to loop through data elements while performing different actions for each data element.

Let's take a look at how to loop through items and update each item in a list. In our scenario, we will update items in the list by converting them to uppercase letters. Proceed as follows:

1. Search for a **For Each** activity from the **Activities** panel and place it below the **Add To Collection** activities.

2. Change the `TypeArgument` property in the **Properties** panel of the **For Each** activity to **String**. This property indicates the data type of each element within the list. Hence, our list is a **String** list, so we have to change the property to **String**.

3. Configure the `Values` property of the **For Each** activity by indicating the `CombinedPeopleList` list variable. It also updates the **In** segment of the **For Each** activity with the same configuration. The `item` variable specified in the `ForEach` segment of the loop is a particular variable that is only applicable within the `For Each` loop. The `item` variable holds the data element of the current iteration during execution.

4. Search for an **Assign** activity from the **Activities** panel and place it inside the **Body** container of the **For Each** activity.

5. Since we need to update the item in the list, let's place the `item` variable in the **To** segment of the **Assign** activity.

6. Configure the **Value** segment of the **Assign** activity using the following code, which converts the value in the `item` variable to uppercase:

    ```
    StrConv(item, VbStrConv.Uppercase)
    ```

7. Create another list variable of type `String` through the **Variables** panel and name it `ModifiedList`.

8. Change the **Scope** field of the `ModifiedList` variable to the outermost sequence.

9. Change the default value of the `ModifiedList` variable to `New List(Of String)` to initialize the `List` variable as a string list.

10. Place another **Add To Collection** activity below the **Assign** activity in the **For Each** loop.

11. Configure the `Collection` property of the activity by specifying the newly created `ModifiedList` variable.

12. Configure the `Item` property of the activity by providing the `item` variable. The **Assign** activity above the **Add to Collection** activity converts the value in the `item` variable to uppercase and overwrites its value. Hence, we are using the same variable to add the updated value to the new collection variable.

13. Let's now print the results. Search for a **Write Line** activity and place it below the **For Each** loop.

14. Configure the **Write Line** activity using the following code, which converts the final list into one string variable that we can print in the **Output** panel:

```
String.Join("|", ModifiedList)
```

Once you reach this point, the workflow you built should look similar to this:

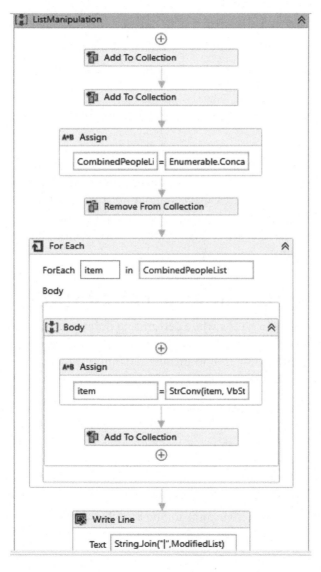

Figure 7.12 – List data manipulation workflow

Similarly, the final configuration of the variable you created in the **Variables** panel should look similar to this:

Name	Variable type	Scope	Default
StudentsList	List<String>	ListManipulation	New List(Of String) from {"John", "Daniel", "Keith"}
EmployeeList	List<String>	ListManipulation	New List(Of String) from {"Diana", "Lizi", "Peter", "Daniel"}
CombinedPeopleList	List<String>	ListManipulation	*Enter a VB expression*
ModifiedList	List<String>	ListManipulation	New List(Of String)
Create Variable			

Figure 7.13 – List data manipulation variables in Variables panel

15. Execute the program and observe the output in the **Output** panel. You should receive the following output:

JOHN | KEITH | ANDREW | DIANA | LIZI | PETER | DANIEL | JANE

The steps performed in this section give you a good understanding of how to manipulate data using List variables. Compared to arrays, the additional features List variables offer—such as adding or removing elements during runtime—make life easy when processing data elements. Lists are capable of holding any type of value, including numeric values. Numeric data has its unique functionalities such as summing up, division, multiplication, and so on. The next section of the chapter focuses on a few commonly used numeric calculations.

Understanding numeric calculations

Numeric data types come in handy while performing different simple-to-complex calculations. We can perform many calculations using numeric values, such as summing up, calculating averages, finding minimum and maximum values, and so on. Performing numeric calculations in UiPath is pretty easy. Let's try a straightforward example.

Create a List variable that holds the marks a student obtained during the last semester for all five subjects. Our task is to calculate the total and the average of the marks. Proceed as follows:

1. Open UiPath Studio and create a new **Blank Process** activity.

2. Double-click on the Main.xaml file to open the file in the **Designer** panel.

3. Search for a **Sequence** activity and add it to the **Designer** panel.

4. Create a new `List` variable of type `String` using the following code. The variable includes the results the student obtained for five subjects:

```
New List(Of String) From {"75", "34.4", "54", "34", "55"}
```

The scores on the list are of the `String` type. We cannot use the `String` data type to perform the calculations. As a result, we need to convert them to numeric data types while we perform the calculation.

5. Create a new variable named `TotalScore` of type `Int32`.

6. Create another variable named `AverageScore` of type `Double`.

7. Drag and drop a **For Each** activity to allow us to loop through the items in the list.

8. Configure the `TypeArgument` property of the loop with the `String` type.

9. Drag and drop an **Assign** activity into the body of the **For Each** loop. We will be using the **Assign** activity to calculate the total of scores by adding up each item's value in the loop.

10. Configure the **To** segment of the **Assign** activity by providing the variable name `TotalScore`.

11. Configure the **Value** segment of the **Assign** activity with the following code. There are values with decimals in the list. Decimal values cannot be converted directly to `Int32`. Therefore, for our scenario, we will first convert the string to `Double` and round it off to the nearest integer before converting it to `Int32`:

```
TotalScore + Convert.ToInt32(Math.Round(Double.
Parse(item)))
```

12. Drag and drop a **Write Line** activity below the **For Each** activity and configure it to write the `TotalScore` variable value as a string in the **Output** panel.

13. Place another **Assign** activity below the last activity and configure the **Value** segment with the following code, which uses the value in the `TotalScore` variable to generate the average score. We need the number of items in the list to calculate the average—the `StudentMarks.Count` code gives us the number of subjects the student completed:

```
TotalScore / StudentMarks.Count
```

14. Configure the **To** segment of the **Assign** activity by specifying the `AverageScore` variable. The `AverageScore` variable will hold the average marks derived from the previous calculation.

15. Place a **Write Line** activity below the For Each activity and configure it by converting the value in `AverageScore` to `String` to print the value in the **Output** panel. Once you reach this point, the workflow you have built should look similar to this:

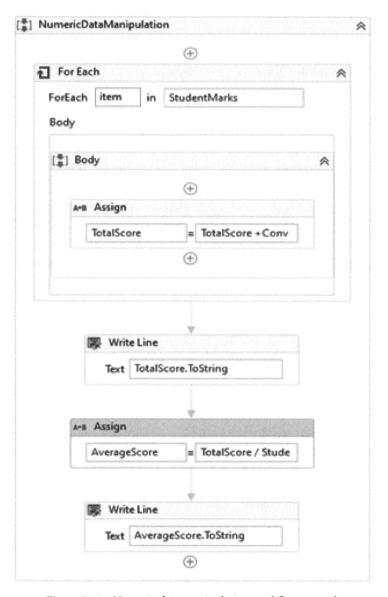

Figure 7.14 – Numeric data manipulation workflow example

16. Run the workflow and observe the results in the **Output** panel. You should see the total shows up as a whole number, whereas the average consists of decimal values.

There are many functions available in .NET Framework to perform numeric calculations. The example provided here is fundamental. It is intended to give you a high-level idea of performing some numeric manipulations such as rounding up values, calculating totals, and deriving averages. The knowledge you already gained through this chapter will give you the foundation to explore other functions in the `Math` library and the different other functions available for numeric calculations. Explore other methods and familiarize yourself with those functions as they will be useful when building automation solutions for your organization.

While numeric data types have their unique capabilities, `Dictionary`-type variables offer a unique way of managing data using the key-value pair concept. The next section of the chapter explains how to manipulate data using `Dictionary` variables.

Understanding dictionary manipulation

The `Dictionary` type has a key difference compared with `List` and `Array` types. While lists and arrays hold multiple data elements of the same data type, a dictionary can hold each data element along with a unique key. This combination is named **key-value** pairs. The user chooses the data type of the key and the value during variable creation.

The `Dictionary` type is mainly used for storing configuration details or other similar information. You may wonder why you should not use a `List` type to store and access configuration data. In real-world scenarios, each configuration data element has a descriptive name that describes what the configuration represents. For example, if the configuration file has data on **Uniform Resource Locators (URLs)**, timeouts, and file paths, the file may look like this:

Key	Value
BusinessURL	https://www.google.com
InputExcelFolderPath	C:\Invoice Files\
ProcessTimeout	10000

Figure 7.15 – Sample structure of a configuration file

`Dictionary` variables in similar scenarios make it easier for the user to understand which values are used within the workflow because of the descriptive key. This same concept is impossible with `List` or `Array` variables because values are accessed only by an index in lists and arrays.

UiPath Studio offers an environment to work with dictionaries with ease to perform actions such as initiation, addition, removal, extraction, and reassigning values. Let's work on a simple example to understand how to work with dictionaries.

Initialization of dictionaries

A dictionary is also a collection variable like lists and arrays. Therefore, the initialization procedure is similar to those data types. Initialization occurs when creating a variable through the **Variables** panel or within a workflow using an **Assign** activity.

Let's create a simple `Dictionary` variable that holds personal information such as a person's name, age, country, and birth date. Proceed as follows:

1. Open UiPath Studio and create a new **Empty** process.

2. Open the `Main.xaml` file in the **Designer** panel.

3. Drag and drop a new **Sequence** activity to start building the workflow.

4. Drag and drop an **Assign** activity from the **Activities** panel into the **Sequence** container.

5. Open the **Variables** panel and click on the **Create Variable** option to create a new `Dictionary` variable by providing the name `"PersonalData"`. The default data type of the variable is `String`.

6. Click on the **Variable Type** field of the variable to access the dropdown and select **Browse for Types**. This action will open up the **Browse and Select a .Net Type** window.

7. Search for the `Dictionary` type in the window and select the `Dictionary<Tkey, TValue>` item that resides under `mscorlibSystem.Collections.Generic`, as shown in the following screenshot:

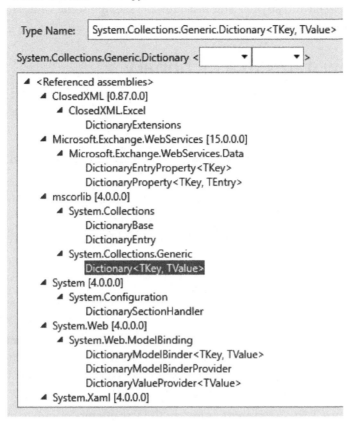

Figure 7.16 – Creating a Dictionary-type variable

8. Select the `String` data type for **Key** and `String` for **Value** from the two drop-down options that appear at the top, and click on the **OK** button. Once you create the variable, the **Variables** panel should show the data type of the variable as `Dictionary<String, String>`.

9. Configure the **To** segment of the **Assign** activity by providing the new variable name to initialize it by providing the following code in the **Value** segment:

```
New Dictionary(Of String, String)
```

The code provided initializes the dictionary with a new `Dictionary` object of the specified type to make it ready for later use. Now, let's assign some values to the new `Dictionary` variable.

Adding new items to a dictionary

Since we now have a usable variable, let's add new values to the dictionary. This section will add new items such as the name, age, country, and date of birth of a person to the dictionary. Proceed as follows:

1. Search for the **Invoke Method** activity from the **Activities** panel and place it below the **Assign** activity.

2. Configure the `TargetObject` property of the **Invoke Method** activity by providing the name of the `PersonalData` dictionary variable.

3. Configure the `MethodName` property of the **Invoke Method** activity by providing the method name as `Add`. The `Add` method is a method available in. NET Framework to add new items to a dictionary variable.

4. Expand the **Properties** panel to view the properties of the **Invoke Method** activity.

5. Click on the button next to the `Collection` property in the **Properties** panel to open the **Parameters** pop-up window to provide the new values for the key-value pair. The dictionary expects two input arguments for each item you add to the `Dictionary` variable.

6. Click on the **Create Argument** option in the **Parameters** popup to create the first input argument. The first argument refers to the key of the new value. We plan to add a record that describes information on a person such as `Name`, `Age`, `Country`, and `Birth Date`. These IDs are keys that we should place in the dictionary.

7. Configure the **Direction** value as `In` and the **Type** value as `String` since the dictionary expects a string as the key.

8. Provide the first key value as `Name`.

9. Create a new argument following the same method to provide a value for the new key you added. Specify the name of the person as `John Doe` in the second argument. The `Name` key would refer to the second argument that holds the value of the person.

The **Parameters** screen should look similar to this once you complete the aforementioned steps:

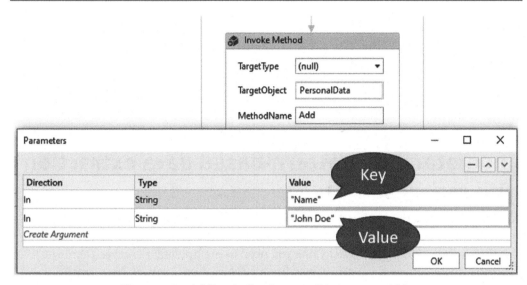

Figure 7.17 – Adding the first item to a Dictionary variable

10. Click the **OK** button to close the **Parameters** screen.

11. Add three more **Invoke Method** activities and configure them accordingly to add **Age**, **Country**, and **Date of Birth** values to the dictionary.

We now have data in the variable. Let's try to extract the data we inserted to use it in our workflow.

Extracting data from Dictionary variables

You are familiar with extracting data from lists and arrays. We used an index to access data elements in `Array` and `List` variables. Similarly, in `Dictionary` variables, we use the key to access data elements instead of the memory index. To do this, proceed as follows:

1. Open the solution we previously worked on to create and assign data to a `Dictionary` variable.

2. Place a **Write Line** activity below the last **Invoke Method** activity.

3. Configure the **Write Line** activity with the following code to print the name of the person:

```
PersonalData("Name").ToString
```

4. Run the program and observe the value printed on the **Output** panel.

5. Configure the **Write Line** activity to show the rest of the values, and test it to understand better how to extract values from `Dictionary` variables.

Now that you have reached this point, you should be familiar with manipulating data in `Dictionary` variables. The steps provided in this section enable you to easily initialize, assign, and retrieve values from `Dictionary` variables to use in real-world use cases. The use of `Dictionary` variables is similar to `List` and `Array` variables. The only difference is that `Dictionary` variables' values are accessed through a unique key instead of the memory location.

Understanding pattern-based data extraction with regexes

We discussed extracting, converting, and performing several other manipulations on different data types during this chapter. Up to now, we discussed pretty straightforward situations where you had the exact value you need to manipulate. However, there are scenarios where you need to extract specific values based on a pattern from larger datasets, such as text paragraphs. We need to use unique functionalities such as regexes to extract only the value we need in such scenarios.

The importance of regexes is that it enables the user to match, locate, and extract values based on a specific pattern. For example, if you have a text paragraph that contains account numbers and email addresses, you can use regexes to extract only email addresses from the input string.

However, building regexes can be challenging. UiPath provides a regex builder to simplify the complexities around these expressions. Regexes are commonly used to parse text and for input validation, data scraping, and string manipulation. Hence, regexes are a part of string manipulation. However, we thought of addressing regexes separately as they are quite different from the other manipulation methods that we have covered.

UiPath provides three methods that use regexes along with RegEx Builder. Each method is a separate activity in UiPath that is associated with RegEx Builder. The three methods are listed here:

- `Matches`: Used to search for a specific pattern in an input string and returns all matching values as `IEnumrable<Match>`. You can access values in this type by using a **For Each** activity by setting the **Type Argument** field to `System.Text.RegularExpressions.Match`.

- `IsMatch`: Used to check whether a specific pattern exists in the input string. This function returns a Boolean value based on the result.

- **Replace**: We already discussed the `String.Replace` function. However, the `String.Replace` function expects us to give the exact string to replace. The `Replace` function provided with RegEx Builder enables the user to replace values that fall under a specific pattern mentioned by the regex with a new value.

Each activity includes a button that enables you to navigate to the **RegEx Builder** screen, allowing you to build the activity's regex. The **RegEx Builder** screen looks like this:

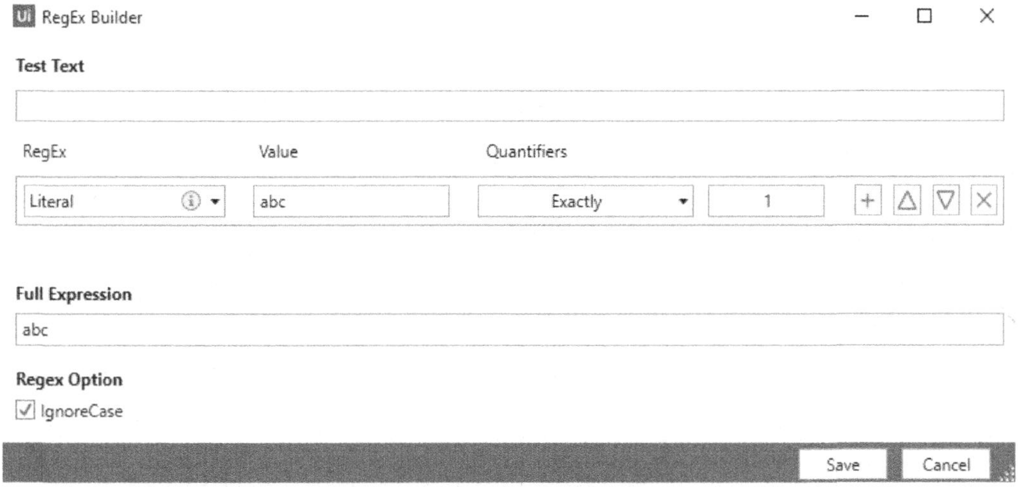

Figure 7.18 – RegEx Builder screen

The sections of the **RegEx Builder** screen are explained as follows:

- **Test Text**: A text editor where the user can test a specific text against an expression. The parts of matching text patterns in the test text will be highlighted, validating the expression.

- **RegEx**: Allows searching for a given text, number, character, or a combination of many.

- **Value**: Contains precisely the text, number, or character that needs to be retrieved.

- **Quantifiers**: A drop-down list that consists of types of results to be retrieved based on the user requirement. The drop-down list enables the user to extract the exact match or decide whether the expression can expect zero or more matching text values.

- **Full Expression**: Indicates the final expression built by adding one or more expression types.

Let's try some of these options with a simple example. We are given the following string:

```
"You have an amazing opportunity to connect with one of the
celebrities to ask questions. Please reach out to John.Doe@
mail.com or Jane.Doe@mail.com to reserve your seat today. For
more information, reach out to 5992754159."
```

We need to use and extract all the email addresses available in the string. To do this, proceed as follows:

1. Open UiPath Studio and create a new **Blank Process** activity.
2. Open the `Main.xaml` file in the **Designer** panel to start building your workflow.
3. Place a **Sequence** activity in the **Designer** panel.
4. Create a new string variable named `InputString` to hold the input string given to us.
5. Place an **Assign** activity within the **Sequence** container and assign the `InputString` variable The string given above in the block section.
6. Search for the **Matches** activity from the **Activities** panel and drag and drop it below the **Assign** activity.
7. Configure the `Input` property of the **Matches** activity by providing the `InputString` variable name. The `Input` property provides the string with the regex applied.
8. Click on the **Configure Regular Expression** button on the **Matches** activity to open the **RegEx Builder** window.
9. Copy the input string that we want to use and paste it in the **Test Text** section of RegEx Builder.
10. Select the regex type as **Email** from the **Expression Type** dropdown. Once you select the type, you can see the prebuilt regex for emails that show up in the **Full Expression** section. Further, it will highlight the two email addresses we have in the **Test Text** section.
11. Configure the `Result` property of the activity by creating a new variable named `EmailList` using the *Ctrl + K* variable creation shortcut.
12. Search for a **For Each** activity and place it below the **Matches** activity.
13. Configure the **Type Argument** field of the **For Each** activity by searching for `System.Text.RegularExpressions.Match` as the type of each item.
14. Place a **Write Line** activity inside the loop and configure it with the `item.ToString` code to print the matching email address of the current iteration.

15. Execute the workflow and monitor the **Output** panel for the extracted email addresses.

16. Similarly, try doing the same steps to extract the phone number from the text.

The data we receive during any process may not always be perfect. As a result, extracting the expected data and transforming it to the format we need is always mandatory. We always work with data; therefore, knowing how to manipulate data using different methods comes in handy when building automation solutions. There are straightforward transformation methods, such as the methods we have for string, integer, and date-time formats. However, regexes come in handy when we work with unstructured data where extraction is not straightforward.

Summary

Manipulating data while building automation workflows is very important. Data manipulation enables you to read, filter, sort, extract, and perform calculations to derive meaningful data out of raw input data. Different variable types have their unique ways of manipulating data. Therefore, it is essential to understand which functionalities UiPath offers to perform various manipulations based on each data type. This chapter provided you with a good understanding of how to manipulate data in the most commonly used variable types such as strings, arrays, lists, and dictionaries.

The concepts learned in this chapter are very helpful in building complex workflow solutions with many manipulations. The following chapters use the basic knowledge gained in this chapter to perform complex actions such as interacting with Excel files, emails, **user interfaces (UIs)**, and so on. As a result, it is essential to understand the concepts and methods described in this chapter. The next chapter covers one of the most critical topics in UI automation: selectors. The concepts you learned throughout this chapter will prove useful while performing UI automation.

8

Exploring UiPath Selectors

Selectors are one of the major and most important topics when it comes to automation. Selectors are automatically created using **standard XML code**, which *identifies* the **user interface elements**. The XML code consists of several **nodes**, which is a combination of **tags and attributes** in a structured and hierarchical order.

In this chapter, you will learn what selectors are, how they work, and how to use the correct selector types and settings when automating. You will learn about the user interface, how to perform element exploration, and how to fine-tune selectors to improve the accuracy of element identification.

In this chapter, we will cover the following topics:

- Tags and attributes of selectors
- Selector Editor
- UI Explorer
- Full versus partial selectors
- Dynamic selectors
- An example implementation of dynamic selectors using Packtpub.com

Technical requirements

This chapter requires that you have UiPath Studio and UiPath Robot installed, along with a basic understanding of Studio's user interfaces. Please refer to *Chapter 2, UiPath Ecosystem*, to learn about the basics of Studio.

Tags and attributes of selectors

In this section, we'll learn more about how to use the **tags and attributes** of selectors. As we mentioned previously, selectors consist of a group of nodes of a specific element in a detailed hierarchical order. This is very similar to the address order we use for identification; that is, country > city > ZIP code > street name > street number > apartment number. The structure of selectors can be represented as follows:

```
<Node_1 >

<Node_2>

…….

<Node_N>
```

Figure 8.1 – Structure of selectors

<Node 1> will primarily be the parent node or root node; the last node, <Node n>, will be the one you are likely to be be interested in because it usually represents the UI element and the previous nodes are the parents of that element. Each node has attributes to help you identify the element in the user interface such as windows, tables, links, text boxes, buttons and so on and it's essential to understand the attributes of each node to apply constant values to accurately identify the correct element. Let's look at an example of such selectors:

```
<wnd app='notepad.exe' cls='Notepad' title='Untitled -
Notepad' />
<wndcls='Edit' />
<ctrl name='Text Editor' role='editable text' />
```

Figure 8.2 – Example of selectors

In the <Node 1> code section, wnd (Window) is a **tag** and app='notepad. exe' cls='Notepad' title='Untitled – Notepad is an **attribute**. Similarly, in <Node 2>, Ctrl (Control) is a tag and name='Text Editor' role='editable text' is an **attribute**.

Now that you are aware of selectors and their usage, you need to how to edit them so that you can identify the target element based on your requirements. We will learn how to edit selectors in the next section.

Selector Editor

Selectors are usually stored inside the **Properties** panel of the activities used in the workflow and can be accessed via **Input > Target > Selector**, in the Properties window as shown in the following screenshot:

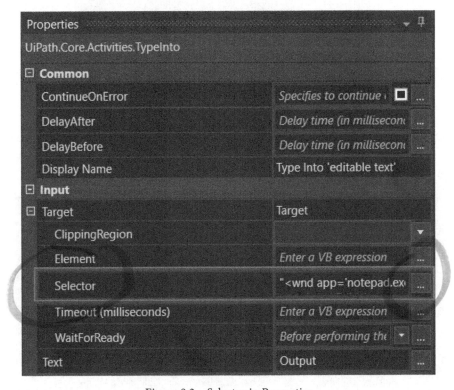

Figure 8.3 – Selector in Properties

The **Selector Editor** tool helps you view the selectors that have been used and edit their attributes to fine-tune the selector for better reliability. To access the tool, you can either click on the three dots in the **Properties** panel, as highlighted in the previous screenshot, or click on the **Edit Selector** option via the **Options** menu for any specific activity. In this case, the activity used in Type Into, as shown in the following screenshot:

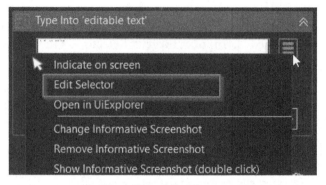

Figure 8.4 – Edit Selector

A new window will appear, where you have multiple options. Each has significance in terms of **overcoming** any selector challenges. Let's explore these options one by one; they are shown in the following screenshot:

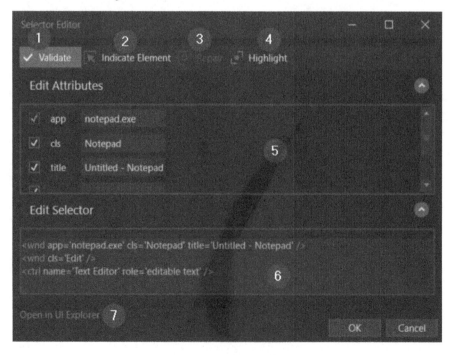

Figure 8.5 – Selector Editor

The various options are as follows:

1. **Validate**

    The **Validate** button displays the *status of the selector* based on the availability of the target UI element that's displayed on the screen. It has three different states:

    I.   **A green Validate button with a tick** (as shown in the following screenshot) indicates that the target element is *valid* and can be executed:

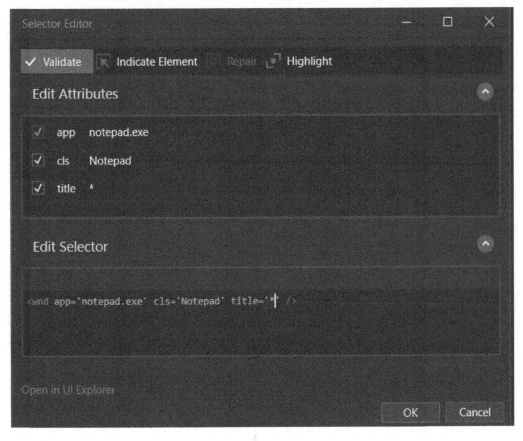

Figure 8.6 – Valid selector

II. **A red Validate button with a cross** indicates that the target element is *invalid* and cannot be executed:

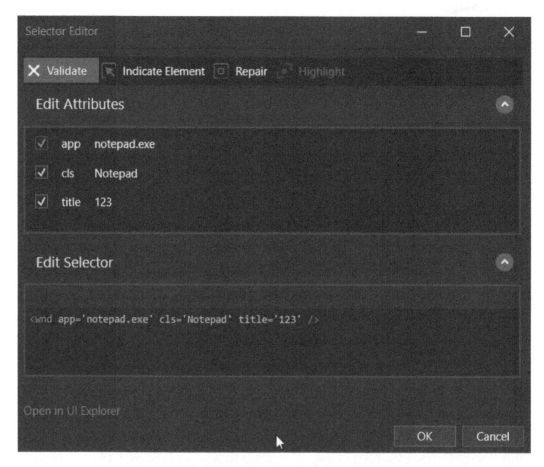

Figure 8.7 – Invalid selector

III. **A yellow Validate button with a question mark** indicates that the selector that corresponds to the target element has been modified and needs to be *revalidated* to correct its status:

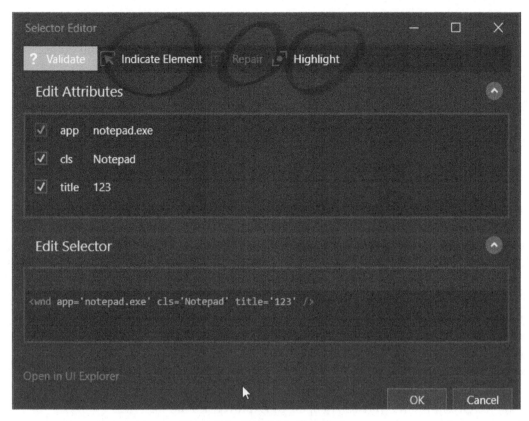

Figure 8.8 – Revalidate the selector

2. **Indicate Element**

   This is used to select the new UI targets or to *overwrite* the previously selected targets on the screen.

3. **Repair**

   This button is enabled when the selector is *invalid* and is used to *repair the existing selector* by indicating the same target UI element on the screen.

4. **Highlight**

   This button is used to *ensure* that the modified selector is still *valid* for the target element. Once clicked, the target element will be highlighted on the screen.

5. **Edit Attributes**

   This option lists all the target element attribute's tag names and attribute values.

6. **Edit Selector**

   This box contains the XML fragment that provides the tag names and attribute values of the target element. These can be edited to help *fine-tune* the selector.

7. **Open in UI Explorer**

   This is a separate tool that can be used to *refine* the selector options and is only displayed for valid selectors.

In this section, we looked at the various options within the Selector Editor and how to manipulate selectors and attributes using the basic options provided. For more advanced editing options, we can look at UI Explorer.

UI Explorer

UI Explorer is used to *analyze* and *edit* selectors, particularly when the **existing selectors** are not stable enough for automation. "Not stable enough" means that the properties of the selectors of the target application keep changing on every execution. UI Explorer has several options to overcome these challenges by fine-tuning the **properties** of the selector to make it more reliable. Let's explore these options one by one. Click on **Open in UI Explorer**, as shown in *Figure 8.5*, to open **UI Explorer**, as follows:

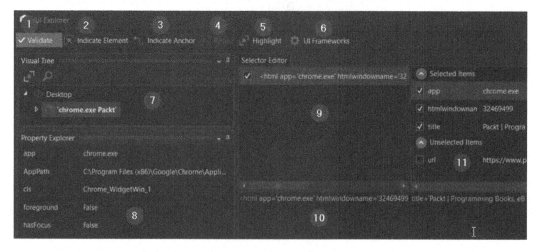

Figure 8.9 – UI Explorer

Let's look at the available options in more detail:

1. **Validate**

   Click on this button if you want to *verify* the validity of your Selector. The target element must be on the screen before you click this button.

2. **Indicate Element**

   Click on this option to *select* the target element and generate the selector with all the necessary properties.

3. **Indicate Anchor**

   This option is used to *identify* the target element by using the relative elements surrounding the target element.

4. **Repair**

   This button is enabled when the selector is invalid and is used to *repair* the existing selector by indicating the same target UI element on the screen.

5. **Highlight**

   This option is used to *highlight* the target on the screen for the current selector to ensure it is working.

6. **UI Frameworks**

   The **Framework settings** options are *changed* based on the application being used. There are three types of frameworks:

   - **Default**

     This specifies the **default settings**, which typically work with all types of user interfaces.

   - **Active Accessibility**

     This option is used for **legacy applications** such as mainframes or if the Default option did not work as expected.

   - **UI Automation**

     This is used **for any new applications** or if the other two types did not work as expected.

7. **Visual Tree**

   This section gives you the option to *explore the elements* of the target user interface in a **folders and subfolders** tree structure. To make the analysis more effective, a **Highlight** option is provided so that you can examine the UI elements from the tree.

8. **Property Explorer**

   This section gives the option to *explore* the available properties of the target application.

9. **Edit Selector**

   This section contains the **XML fragment** that has the **tag names** and **attribute values** of the target element. These can be *edited* to fine-tune the selector.

10. **Edit Attributes**

    This section is used to *edit* the attributes of the selected items in the **node**.

11. **Select Unselect Attributes**

    This section *displays* the list of selected and unselected attributes of the selector. This gives us the option to analyze the selector by selecting and unselecting attributes.

In this section, we explored the different options that are available within **UI Explorer** to enhance the selector so that it can handle dynamic target elements. In the next section, we'll compare the different selector types and how they can be applied in different scenarios.

Types of selectors

The selector types depend on the type of recorders or activities that are being used inside the UiPath workflows. There are two types:

- Partial selectors
- Full selectors

Let's look at them in more detail.

Partial selectors → *common in Classic Design Exp*

Partial selectors are generated when you use the **Desktop Recorder**. It does not contain information about the top-level window. Partial selectors are enclosed inside a container. While we're on the same application screen and interacting with multiple elements, it is a good option to use partial selectors. With partial selectors, the top element (which is grayed out) is inherited from the parent. Let's look at an example where an **Attach Window** activity is being used in a Notepad application and the selector of the **Click** activity looks as follows, where the first line can't be edited:

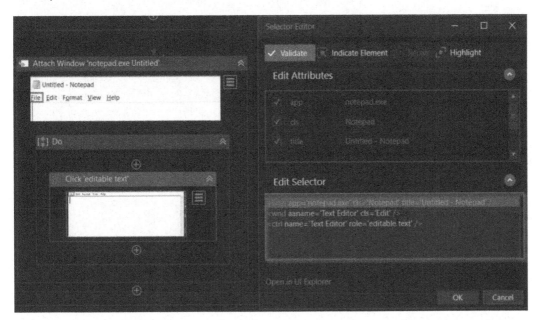

Figure 8.10 – Partial selector

If you want to edit the attributes of the top-level window, you may need to take a different recording approach known as full selectors, which we will look at in the next section.

Full selectors

Full selectors are generated when we are using the **Basic Recorder**. Full selectors contain all the necessary nodes, including the top-level window. This contains the application node and the final node, which are required to identify the UI element.

Full selectors should be used when you're switching between **multiple windows** or **activities**.

For example, when you're switching between multiple applications for data such as Notepad, Word, or Excel, you should use full selectors:

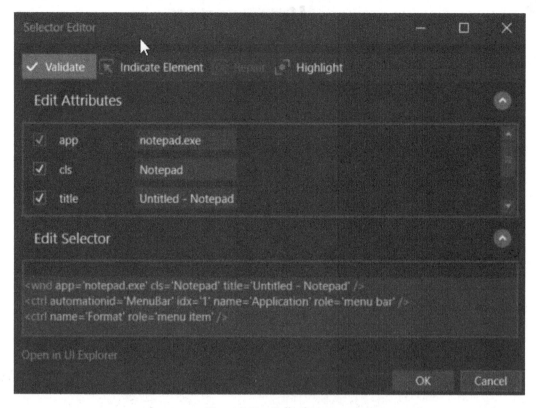

Figure 8.11 – Full selector

The following table shows the differences between partial selectors and full selectors:

Partial Selector	Full Selector
Generated by the Desktop Recorder.	Generated by the Basic Recorder.
Does not contain top-level elements.	Contains top-level elements.
Used when switching between multiple windows.	Used when staying inside the same window.
Enclosed inside containers.	Containers are not needed.
All attributes are editable.	Only elements related to partial selectors can be edited.

Figure 8.12 – Comparison of partial selectors and full selectors

In this section, we looked at the differences between partial selectors and full selectors. In the next section, we will learn about dynamic selectors and see how they can be implemented by looking at a real-life example.

Dynamic selectors

Before we begin discussing dynamic selectors, let's look at static selectors. **Static selectors are used to indicate an element in the user interface that does not change its properties** or that the element is stable enough. So, we do not need to change the properties in the **Selector Editor** window, such as the tags and attributes of the selector. **A dynamic selector is used to easily identify the target element, which changes its selector properties more frequently at runtime.** A dynamic selector is created using a **variable** or **argument** instead of the static attributes in the selector tags. Instead of hardcoding the values of the target element, the attribute values can be represented using a variable or an argument to handle the target dynamically. The syntax of the dynamic selector is shown here:

```
<tag attribute = '{{Value}}' />
```

Figure 8.13 – Syntax of the dynamic selector

Dynamic selectors can be *analyzed* and *modified* inside the **Edit Selector** window. This window displays all the basic options, such as **Edit Attributes** and **Edit Selector**, so that you can dynamically modify the selector. However, for more advanced options, such as **Visual Tree**, **Property Explorer**, and **Selected Items**, you can use **UI Explorer** to easily identify the dynamic properties.

The following table shows the differences between static selectors and dynamic selectors:

Static Selector	Dynamic Selector
Used to identify elements that are highly stable by having standard properties.	Used to identify elements that are unstable by changing their properties frequently.
You can hardcode the Property values inside the Edit selector window.	You can parameterize the Property values using variables or arguments inside the Edit selector window.
Uses tags and attributes to identify the target element.	Uses tags, attributes, variables, and arguments to identify the target element.
Indicates the target element for any required changes.	Indicates the target element and makes the necessary changes to the value of the variable or argument.

Figure 8.14 – Comparison of static selectors and dynamic selectors

Now, let's look at a real-life example that's available on the **PacktPub** website about dynamically reading the names of three books using a single selector. To understand this example better, we will analyze the web page, selectors, and their properties using UI Explorer.

Dynamic scenario

The following is a typical example of using dynamic values. The book name keeps changing over a certain period and the UiPath robot should dynamically read the name of the book. In this example, we'll have the **robot** read the names of the first three books. Let's get started:

1. Launch the **PacktPub** website by going to `https://www.packtpub.com/`, as shown in the following screenshot:

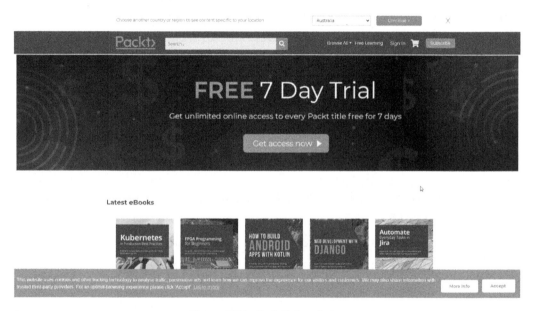

Figure 8.15 – PacktPub website

2. Click on **Browse All** (*1*) and then **All Books** (*2*), as shown in the following screenshot:

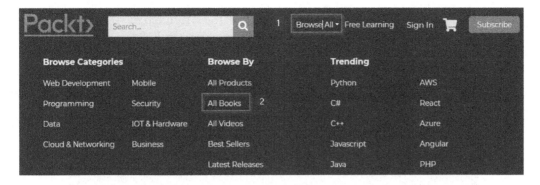

Figure 8.16 – All Books

3. Verify that the **Books** page is displayed, as shown in the following screenshot:

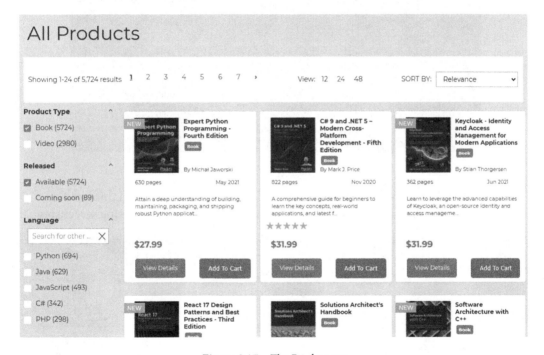

Figure 8.17 – The Books page

4. Launch **UiPath Studio** and create a **Process**. Name it `DynamicSelectors_`
    `Packt` and click **Create**, as shown in the following screenshot:

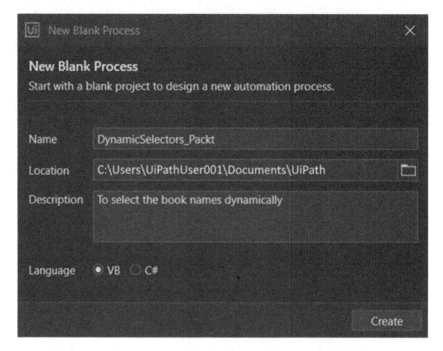

Figure 8.18 – New Blank Process

5. Using a **Click** activity, inspect the selectors of the first, second, and third books.
    Observe the similarities and the differences, as shown in the following screenshot:

Figure 8.19 – Click activity

6. Open **Edit Selector** by clicking on the respective button:

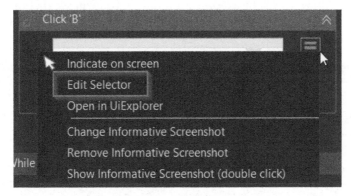

Figure 8.20 – Edit Selector

7. Observe the **Edit Attributes** and **Edit Selector** options. Here, you can modify the selectors so that they dynamically identify the targets:

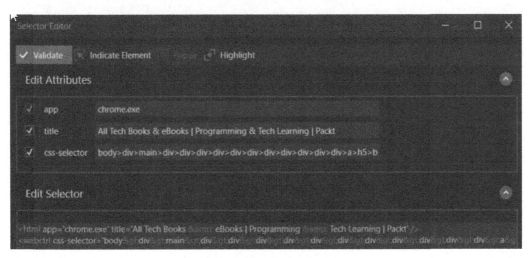

Figure 8.21 – Selector Editor

8. Open **UI Explorer** and observe the similarities and differences between the first, second, and third books. Based on your analysis, you will see that the **idx** value keeps changing when you select **css-sselector** (*2*) and unselect **aaname** (*1*), which is the name of the book:

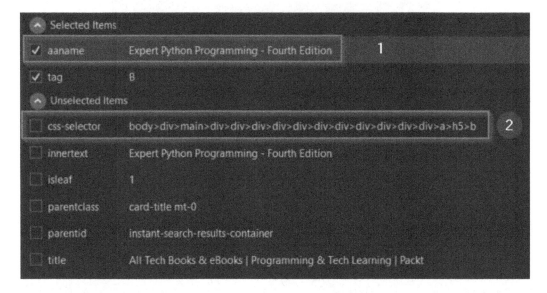

Figure 8.22 – Edit selector

9. Now, let's finalize the dynamic selector by clicking the **Save** button in UI Explorer. The following selector values will be displayed:

```
<webctrl tag='B' css-selector='body&gt;div&gt;main&gt;div&gt;
div&gt;div&gt;div&gt;div&gt;div&gt;div&gt;div&gt;div&gt;div&gt;
div&gt;a&gt;h5&gt;b' idx='1' />
```

Figure 8.23 – Selector values

If the highlighted idx='1' value needs to be changed for you to select the next book, then we need to **parameterize** this value.

10. Parameterize the `idx` value using the following selector options. Select the **idx** value and right-click and select **Create variable**, as shown in the following screenshot:

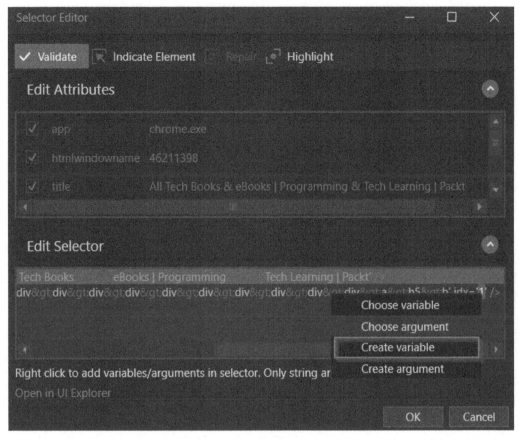

Figure 8.24 – Selector values

11. Set the **Set Name** value to idx (*1*) and the **Set Value** value to 1 (*2*). Then, click **OK** (**3**):

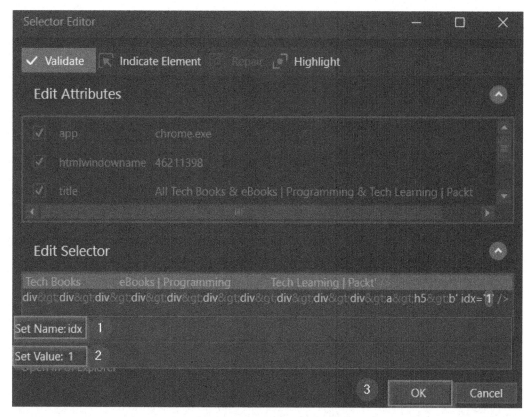

Figure 8.25 – Parameterized values

12. The selector will look similar to the following and will be ready to select the values dynamically. However, we must change the values accordingly:

```
<html app='chrome.exe' title='All Tech Books &amp; eBooks |
Programming &amp; Tech Learning | Packt' />
<webctrl css-selector='body&gt;div&gt;main&gt;div&gt;div&gt;
div&gt;div&gt;div&gt;div&gt;div&gt;div&gt;div&gt;div&gt;
a&gt;h5&gt;b' idx='{{idx}}' />
```

Figure 8.26 – Parameterized selectors

13. Inside the UiPath Studio sequence, specify the PacktPub website using the **Attach Browser** activity, as shown in the following screenshot:

Figure 8.27 – The Attach Browser activity

14. Create a **While Loop** activity to go through all three books with the `idx<=3` condition (*1*) and copy the selector that you created in *Step 8* to the **Get Text** activity (*2*). Then, write the result that you obtained using the **WriteLine** activity and increment (*3*) the value to read the name of the next book, as shown in the following screenshot:

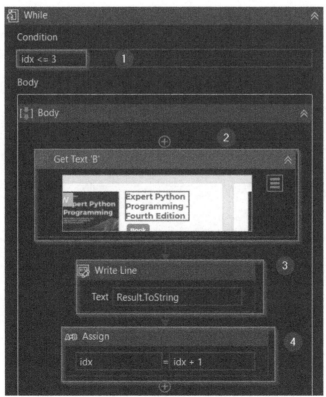

Figure 8.28 – Extracting book names

15. Execute the robot using the **Run** option under **Debug File** or press *Ctrl + F5*, as shown in the following screenshot:

Figure 8.29 – Run Project

16. Observe the output that's been generated in the **Output** section, as shown in the following screenshot:

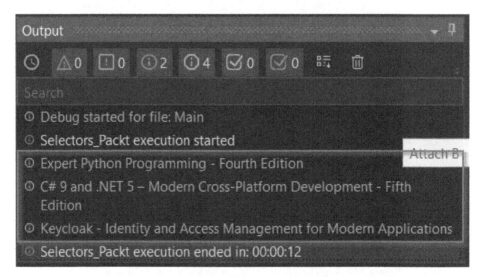

Figure 8.30 – Verifying the result

With that, we have successfully implemented dynamic selectors using a practical example from the **PacktPub** website to *dynamically* retrieve the names of books. You can apply the same concepts to different scenarios so that you can work with **dynamic target elements**.

Summary

In this chapter, we looked at selectors, including how to work with tags, attributes, and selector properties. Then, we explored the differences between static, dynamic, partial, and full selectors. After that, we learned about UI Explorer and how to work with the selector properties in challenging situations. Finally, we looked at a practical example of using dynamic selectors to implement the concepts we learned about in this chapter.

In the next chapter, you will be manipulating data using Excel and data tables. Here, you will use selectors to retrieve data from applications that communicate with Excel and data tables.

9

Learning the Uses of Data Tables and Exploring Excel Automation

We discussed different types of variables and arguments in the previous chapter. However, there is another very special type of variable, which we call **data tables**. We use data table variables to process more structured data that is organized in a tabular form. We use Microsoft Excel almost every day to perform different functions in an organization. For example, a finance department may use Excel regularly to generate reports, perform calculations, and reconcile financial data. As a result, many companies and/or departments have already started automating the actions performed manually in Excel.

This chapter focuses on learning how to automate Excel using UiPath and how data table variables can be used to support Excel automation.

The chapter consists of the following sections:

- Exploring data tables
- Creating and customizing data table variables
- Interacting with Excel files
- Practicing Excel automation

At the end of this chapter, you will understand the most common methods used to perform data manipulation in Excel using different Excel interaction methods.

Technical requirements

Before starting with this chapter, please have UiPath Studio and the Assistant installed. This chapter requires a general idea of how to use Studio to create variables and simple workflows. Furthermore, you must have the Microsoft Office package installed on your machine.

Exploring data tables

We have all used Microsoft Excel at some point in our life. In every Excel file, we see the following concepts:

- *Workbook*: This refers to the Excel file itself. From now on in our course, we will be using this word to refer to Excel files.
- *Worksheet*: Every workbook can have multiple worksheets that contain data.
- *Row*: Every worksheet consists of rows of data.
- *Column*: Every data row consists of multiple columns that contain different data values referring to the type of data each column holds.
- *Cell*: A cell in an Excel sheet contains a single value or a formula. Every row consists of multiple cells.

Similarly, a data table is a variable type that can store data in the same structural format as an Excelsheet.

You might wonder about the differences between a data table and a worksheet. A data table is a memory representation of a single database table that can hold multiple rows consisting of multiple columns of different data types. Alternatively, a worksheet has the same structure, but it can visually represent its data using tables and graphics.

Creating and customizing data tables

This section of the chapter will look at how we can create and customize data tables.

Creating data tables

If you have covered *Chapter 5, Learning about Variables and Arguments*, you are now familiar with creating variables and arguments in UiPath Studio. The same concept applies to data table variables. The only difference is that, for the **Data Type** property of the variable/argument, we have to select **System.Data.DataTable** from the drop-down menu.

Apart from the variable/argument creation, you will also encounter specific activities that help to create data tables:

- **Build Data Table**: This activity provides a wizard that you can use to graphically build your data table by adding columns, changing column properties (auto increment, null value handling, the maximum length of a value, and the default value), and adding rows with static values. This activity is handy when you explicitly expect data table output with a particular structure from an operation.

- **Read Range**: This is an activity that enables the user to read data from an Excel worksheet. The output of this activity is a data table that holds all columns and rows of a specified range in the sheet. The activity requires configuring the output property by creating a data table variable using variable/argument creation shortcut keys or creating it through the **Variables/Arguments** panel.

- **Read CSV**: Similar to **Read Range** but used to read data from CSV files. The configuration of the output properties is identical to the Read Range configuration.

- **Data Scraping**: This is an advanced functionality provided by UiPath to extract structured data from web pages or documents and save it in data table variables. This topic is covered in more detail in *Chapter 10, Exploring User Interfaces and User/Robot Interactions*.

- **Generate Data Table**: Used to generate data tables from unstructured data. The user can configure the activity to specify how to split the rows and columns based on separators.

We can perform multiple manipulations on data in created data tables, such as sorting, filtering, cleansing, and joining with other data tables. These manipulation functions are made easy by a wide range of activities that UiPath offers specifically for data tables. Some of those activities are as follows:

- **Clear Data Table**: Erases all the data in the data table variable. Clearing does not remove the structure of the data table. This activity can come in handy when working with temporary data generated inside a loop or an iterative part of the workflow to prepare the final data set. Clearing the data in the temporary data table ensures that the intermediary variable is cleared and ready for the next round of data.

- **Add Data Column**: Adds a new column to an existing data table variable. We could provide different inputs to this activity. The input can be an existing **Data Column** variable, or we could give the column name and the data type to create an empty column. The **Properties** panel for this activity contains several other configurable properties such as default value, auto-incrementing, unique value check, and an option to allow null values.

- **Remove Data Column**: Removes a data column from an existing data table variable. We could provide different inputs to this activity. The input can be an existing Data Column variable, or we could give the column name or column index of the column to be removed.

- **Add Data Row**: Adds a new data row to an existing data table variable. We could provide different inputs to this activity. The input can be an existing **Data Row** variable, or we can give the column values of the row as an **Array Row** that contains values for each column. The number of objects in the Array Row should match the number of columns in the data table.

- **Remove Data Row**: Removes an existing row from an existing data table variable. We could provide different inputs such as a **Data Row** variable or the index of the row to be removed.

- **Remove Duplicate Rows**: This activity provides an easy mechanism to look for all duplicate rows and remove them from the provided data table.

- **Filter Data Table**: Provides the user the ability to filter data in an existing data table according to their requirements. The filtering can be done in a couple of different ways. It allows the user to filter out unwanted columns by specifying the columns they need to remove or keep. Alternatively, you can write the conditions to filter data rows.

- **Sort Data Table**: Sorts the data table using a specified column in ascending or descending order.

- **For Each Row for Data Table**: Like the **For Each** activity, this activity is specially designed to loop through data tables. By default, the activity allows looping through rows. If you want to access a specific column in the row while looping, the CurrentRow("<Column Name>").ToString or CurrentRow(<Column Index>).ToString command can be used.

- **Join Data Table**: There are scenarios where we need to work with multiple data table variables to generate the required output. The **Join Data Table** activity enables the user to join two data tables using one or more commonly available columns in both data tables. The table join is carried out in different ways, as specified in the following table.

Let's explore joins by using a simple example to provide a better understanding. Imagine you have two data tables:

- **Data Table 1**: Contains information about all employees.

- **Data Table 2**: Includes information on all the available departments in the organization.

- **Join rule**: Two tables have a common column, Department ID, that specifies which employee is assigned to which department.

The following figure describes the different join rules available in the **Join Data Table** activity along with their use:

Join Type	Description
Inner Join	It is used when we are sure that we only need the records that match the join conditionspecified. The records that do not match are removed from the resulting data table. In simple words, it checks for matching records based on the defind commonly available columns and returns only rows that have match on both data tables. Example: Returns only the employees that is assigned to a department
Left Join	As we know, a Join includes two data tables. The first data table we specify for the Data Table 1 property is considered as your Left data table. The data table you specify for the Data Table 2 property is considered as your Right data table. You are giving priority to your Left data table the momemt you select the join condition as Left Join. Unlike in Inner Join, Left join returns all the rows on your Left data table. However, it also returns all the matching rows it finds from the second data table and empty rows that did not have a match. Example: Returns all the employees along with the information of their assigned department. Further, the result also contains employees with no assigned department.
Full Join	Keep all the records from both data tables irrespective of the join condition. It is more like a combination of both Left Join and Right Join. Full Join adds null values for both sides for the records that do not match.

Figure 9.1 – The join types in the Join data table activity

We can also look at these joins using the following diagrams to understand the concept graphically. According to the explanations, the inner join looks for similar data points. If we include the two data tables in a Venn diagram, it should give us the following result:

DataTable 1: Employee   DataTable 2: Department

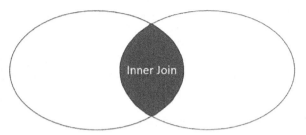

DT1 Department ID = DT2 Department ID

Figure 9.2 – A Venn diagram for the data table inner join

The left join is slightly different. According to the explanation, the left join provides everything on the first data table and the common section, as follows:

DataTable 1: Employee   DataTable 2: Department

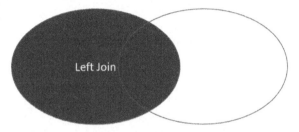

DT1 Department ID = DT2 Department ID

Figure 9.3 – A Venn diagram for the data table Left Join

The next join type, the full join, provides results from both data tables. In this case, the diagram looks as follows:

DataTable 1: Employee   DataTable 2: Department

DT1 Department ID = DT2 Department ID

Figure 9.4 – A Venn diagram for the data table full join

This is a very common concept when working with multiple datasets to find similar values. It is important to understand the difference between these join types, as they are used quite often in real-world projects.

Join rules enable users to join two data tables to generate the required data as described. However, data table variables support many more functions, as specified in the following points:

- **Lookup Data Table**: This function allows the user to look up a value in a specified data table and return the row index at which it was found. The activity also allows the user to configure it to return the value from a cell with given coordinates. The coordinates are usually the row index of the lookup result and the column name of the cell from which you want to extract the value.

- **Merge Data Table**: This is used to append another data table to the current data table. Merging requires handling the changes in the schema (structure) of the two data tables. The activity provides a property that handles missing schema in four different ways.

The following figure illustrates the options provided to handle the missing schema in the **Merge Data Table** activity:

Missing Schema Handle Option	Description
Add	Adds the missing schema to the destination data table
Ignore	Ignores the schema changes and merges columns already available on both data tables
Error	Throws an error if any schema changes detected
Add with Key	Adds new columns with a built-built key

Figure 9.5 – Schema change handling while merging

- **Output Data Table**: This converts the data in a data table variable into a single string using CSV format.

The data table variables are used quite often to handle manipulations on structured data. By now, you are familiar with the functions that data tables support and the activities available in UiPath to perform those functions. The knowledge gained on these functions and activities comes in handy when working with almost all RPA projects. The following section provides practical experience in using some of the activities discussed previously.

Creating and customizing data table variables

Since we have covered the basics of data tables, let's now practice. The following steps will guide you on how to use some of the activities we discussed earlier. Let's consider a scenario where you have one data table that consists of employee information and another with department information.

Let's build a workflow by completing the following steps:

1. Open UiPath Studio and create a new **Blank Process** project.

2. Open the **Main.xaml** file in the **Designer** panel.

3. Search for the **Build Data Table** activity from the **Activities** panel and drag it to the canvas.

4. Click on the **DataTable…** button on the activity to open the **Build Data Table** screen. This screen can be used to add columns, rows, and change column properties.

5. Remove all columns and rows by clicking on the **X** mark next to them.

6. Click on the + sign to add a new column named `EmployeeID` with the **Int32** data type and the **Auto-Increment** property set to `True`. Configure the **Allow Null** property to `False` and the **Unique** property to `True`, and then click on **OK** to create the new column. This configuration will enable the data table to automatically create a new unique ID for each new row added.

The following figure illustrates the configuration of the `EmployeeID` field in the **Build Data Table** activity:

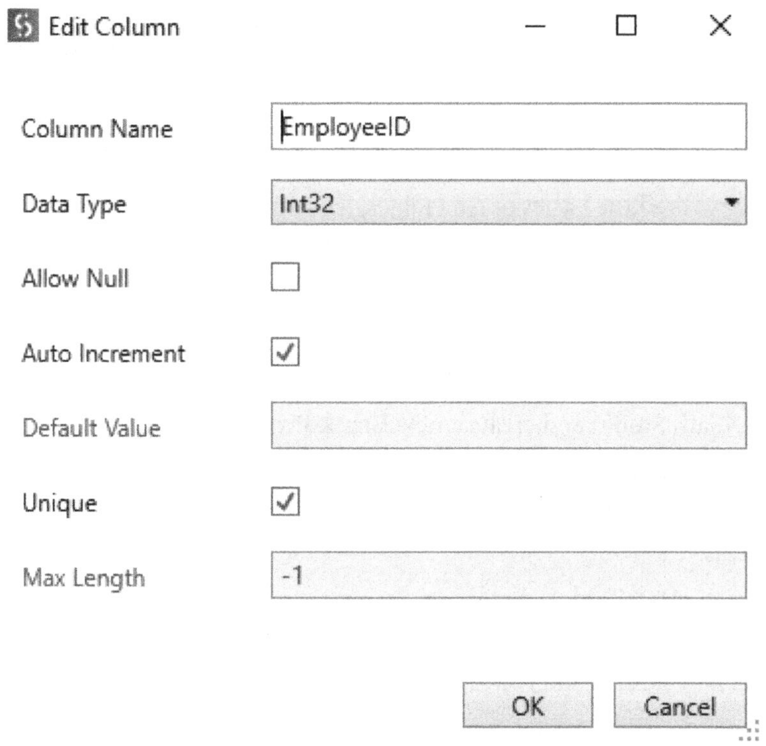

Figure 9.6 – Creating columns in the Build Data Table activity

7. Create another column with the name `FirstName` with the **String** data type. The remaining properties don't need to be changed.

8. As with the `FirstName` column, create another two columns named `LastName` and `City` of the **String** data type, and another column called `DeptID` of the **Int32** data type.

9. Populate the table with rows, as shown in *Figure 9.7*:

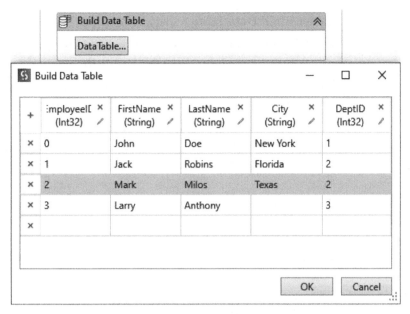

Figure 9.7 – Building the Employee data table

10. Click **OK** and close the configuration window.

11. Click on the **Properties** panel and configure the **Output Data Table** argument of the activity by creating a new data table variable and assigning it. You can create the variable through the **Properties** panel by using the *Ctrl + K* shortcut keys. Name the new data table EmployeeDT. Once you have configured the property, your configuration should look similar to the one provided in the following figure:

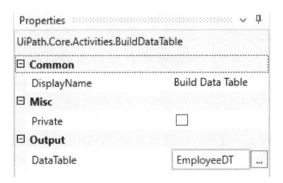

Figure 9.8 – Configuring the Output property of the Build Data Table activity

12. Drag and drop another **Build Data Table** activity below the previous activity.

13. Configure the activity as you did previously to build the following structure. Note that the Department ID column in this data table is **auto-incrementing**. Populate and configure the data table, as shown in the following figure:

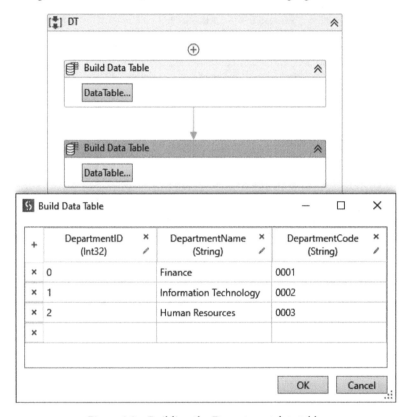

Figure 9.9 – Building the Department data table

14. Configure the **Output Data Table** property of the activity and assign it to a new data table variable named DepartmentDT. As of now, we have two data tables with data. Let's do some manipulations on the data.

15. Let's remove some unwanted columns from the **DepartmentDT** data table. We have two ID columns. We will remove **DepartmentCode** from the data table.

16. Let's use the **Remove Data Column** activity below the two activities:

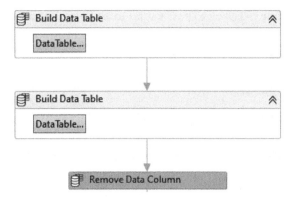

Figure 9.10 – Adding the Remove Data Column activity

17. Configure the **DataTable** property of the **Remove Data Column** activity by specifying the DepartmentDT variable. This property specifies which data table is affected by the activity.

18. Configure the **Column Name** property of the activity by specifying the "DepartmentCode" column, which we need to delete:

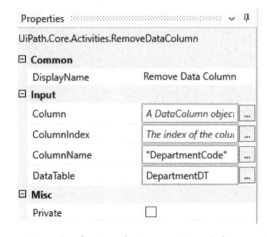

Figure 9.11 – Configuring the Remove Data Column activity

19. Now, let's add a new row to the Employee table. Use the **Add Data Row** activity and place it below the last activity.

20. Configure the **DataTable** property of the **Add Data Row** activity by specifying **EmployeeDT**, as that is the data table that we need to add the new row to.

21. Configure the Array Row property of the activity with the following code:

```
{Nothing, "Amy", "Woods", "New York", Nothing}
```

The array we define here has to pass values to all the columns. However, we do not need to assign a value to the **EmployeeID** field because it is an auto-incrementing field. In that case, we will be passing an empty field defined by the keyword `Nothing`. In the same command, we will also be giving a blank value for **DepartmentID** as well.

22. Add a **Filter Data Table** activity below the **Add Data Row** activity. Let's filter the **EmployeeDT** data table by removing employees that do not have a valid **City**:

23. Configure the **DataTable** and the **Filtered DataTable** properties with the same **EmployeeDT** variable. This configuration will overwrite the data in **EmployeeDT** with the filtered results.

24. Click the **Configure Filter** button on the **Filter Data Table** activity to open **Filter Wizard**.

25. Configure **Filter Wizard**, as shown in the following figure:

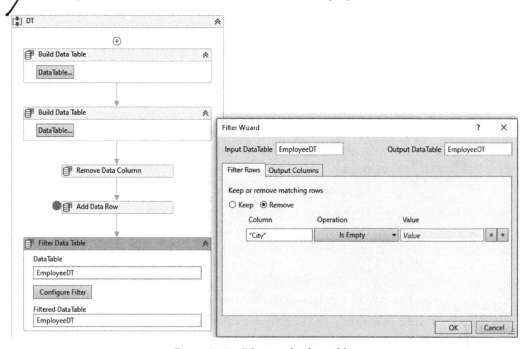

Figure 9.12 – Filtering the data table

26. Before we join the two data tables, print the values in the data tables and see how they look. Use an **Output Data Table** activity, and configure the **DataTable** property with **EmployeeDT** and the output **Text** property to a new string variable. Use a **Write Line** activity and configure it with the new string variable you created.

27. Run the workflow and check the output of **EmployeeDT**. You will see the final outcome of the manipulations we performed on the data table. Feel free to use the combination of **Output Data Table** and **Write Line** anywhere in the workflow to explore the output after each manipulation action.

28. Use a **Join Data Tables** activity to join the two data tables using the common **Department ID**. Configure the **Join Data Tables** activity, as shown in the following figure. Note that the **Join Type** option is set to an **Inner** join:

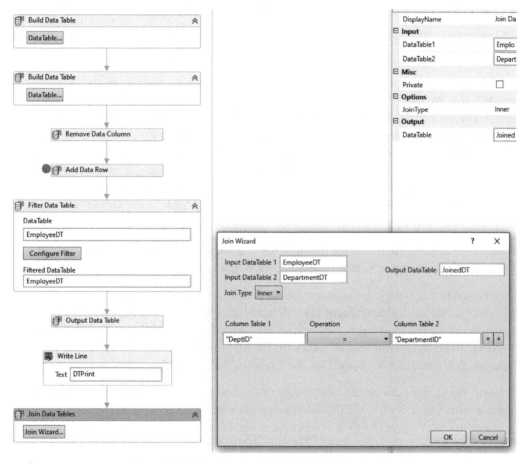

Figure 9.13 – Configuring the Join Data Tables activity

29. Use another combination of the **Output Data Table** and **Write Line** activities pointing to **JoinDT** (the data table that contains the result after joining) and examine the output.

30. The following is the output we get for the preceding workflow with the join type as an **Inner** join:

```
© EmployeeID,FirstName,LastName,City,DeptID,DepartmentID,DepartmentName
0,John,Doe,New York,1,1,Information Technology
1,Jack,Robins,Florida,2,2,Human Resources
2,Mark,Milos,Texas,2,2,Human Resources
```

Figure 9.14 – The data table output with an inner join

31. Configure the join type as **Left** and **Full** and explore how the output differs from the one previously.

In addition to the points covered, explore the different operation types available in the Join Wizard. We used the operation = for our matching because we wanted an exact match. However, there are many operations available that may fit into different types of joins based on the scenario. Alternatively, sometimes, you may receive data tables without a proper column name. In scenarios where you do not know the exact column names, you can always refer to the columns using the column index. Similar to the Collection type variables, **DataTable** also has zero-based indexes for rows and columns. In other words, if you want to access the first row in a data table using an index, it would always be zero. The same concept is applied to accessing columns.

Imagine we want to use the index to configure our Join Wizard instead of the column names. In such a case, we need to use the following approach.

The first data table (employee) has five fields, and **Department ID** is the last. Considering the zero-based index, **Department ID** will hold index 4. Regarding the `Department` data table, you need to use index 0 because the **Department ID** field is the first column. If you are to configure the Join Wizard with the identified indexes, you use index 4 for the **Column Table 1** field and index 0 for the **Column Table 2** field.

By now, you should have an understanding of the basic concepts of a data table and how to use it with our activities in UiPath. As you have already seen, there is a wide range of activities in UiPath to perform different manipulations with data tables. Try exploring the other activities on the same example and see what other things you can do. You can expect the same functionality when working with Excel files; therefore, data in Excel files is easy to export into data tables. The next section explains how to interact with Excel files. There are many automation solutions built around Excel data manipulation. It is essential to understand the different methods available to interact with Excel files.

Interacting with Excel files

Many business users use Excel to carry out their daily activities, such as performing financial calculations and maintaining expense records. Excel is one of the most widely used applications in all the departments of any organization. UiPath offers a fantastic set of activities that enables seamless integration and interaction with Excel files with or without Excel installed on your computer. The Excel dependency is added to the new solutions you create in Studio by default. However, if you specifically need to add it to your solution, you can look for **UiPath.Excel.Activities** from the Dependency Manager.

UiPath offers two different ways of interacting with Excel files:

- **File access level**: We call these **workbook activities**, which are part of Excel activities. Workbook activities do not require the Microsoft Office package to be installed on your computer. These activities work in the background and are faster compared to actual Excel integration. These activities only work for .XLSX files.

- **Excel app integration**: We call these **Excel activities**, which allow us to directly integrate with excel. Unlike the workbook activities, Excel activities require the Microsoft Office package to be installed on a computer. The use of these activities will open the Excel application, just as a human user would do before interacting with it. Excel activities enable the user to interact with CSV, XLS, SLSB, and XLSM files. Furthermore, all Excel activities can be configured to be visible or hidden when executing.

Regardless of the method used to interact with Excel files (the access level), both approaches share common actions. However, though the action is common, there are different activities to perform for each type. For example, you can find activities that can read an excel file under both Excel and Workbook activities. These are located in two separate sections in the **Activities** panel, as shown in *Figure 9.12*.

The following screenshot shows the **Read Range** activity, which is used to read data from Excel files. As shown in *Figure 9.15*, all CSV and Excel activities are located in the **App Integration** category, whereas workbook activities are located in the **System** -> **File** -> **Workbook** category. The main difference between the two types is that activities under the **App Integration** category require the **Excel Application Scope** activity to hold all the other activities, whereas the others do not. The following figure shows the two activities located separately under the **Workbook** and **Excel** categories:

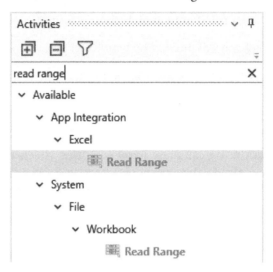

Figure 9.15 – The Excel and workbook activities location

Let's explore the common activities that are available for both methods:

- **Read Range**: Reads data from a specified range in an Excel file into a data table variable. Using the **Read Range** activity with **Excel Application Scope** enables the user to read the data based on the filters applied in the Excel file. Alternatively, the workbook activities read all the data available in the sheet irrespective of filters.

- **Write Range**: Provides the ability to write data in a data table variable to a spreadsheet. The writing starts from the cell indicated by the user.

- **Read Cell**: Reads the content of a specified cell into a string variable.

- **Write Cell**: Writes to the content of a variable into a specified cell in the specified worksheet.

- **Read Cell Formula**: Enables the user to read the available formula in a specified cell and store it in a string variable.

- **Read Column**: Enables the user to read the content of a specified column in the Excel file. The extracted content is stored in an `IEnumerable<object>` type variable.

- **Read Row**: Similar to **Read Column**, but this activity reads the content of a row, starting with the cell identifier provided by the user. The extracted data of the row is stored in an `IEnumerable<object>` type variable.

- **Append Range**: Enables the easy addition of content in a data table variable to the end of a specified spreadsheet without overwriting data. Furthermore, if the specified sheet is not available in the Excel file, the sheet is created automatically.

- **Get Table Range**: Works especially with the tables we have created in the Excel file. This activity enables the user to locate the specified table in a selected spreadsheet and extract the range of the table. This activity's output can be fed into other activities such as **Read Range** to extract the data from the range returned from the **Get Table Range** activity.

Apart from the common activities described, there are many other activities that UiPath offers to interact with Excel files through **Excel Application Scope**.

Excel Application Scope

Excel Application Scope is a container that holds all the Excel app integration category activities. The **Excel Application Scope** activity triggers the Excel file to open to perform the actions specified within the activity scope. You now have a general idea about the commonly available activities for both categories. However, Excel App Integration offers more functionalities apart from what we discussed earlier. There are many other functions that we can perform using the app integration approach. These actions can be categorized based on the different aspects of Excel functions.

CSV activities

Excel app integration offers the capability to interact with CSV files using data table variables easily. Although CSV activities are placed under the Excel app integration category, the main difference between CSV and Excel app integration activities is that they can still work without **Excel Application Scope**. UiPath offers three unique activities to interact with CSV files:

- **Read CSV**: Reads all the records from a CSV file and stores them in a data table variable.

- **Write CSV**: Writes the content of a data table variable into a CSV file. The activity is also capable of creating the CSV file if the file is not available.

- **Append to CSV**: Like **Append Range**, the **Append to CSV** activity adds the content of a data table variable at the end of an existing CSV file without overwriting the data. However, the activity also can create the file if it does not exist.

Range activities

The activities that fall under this subcategory can easily interact with specified ranges in Excel. These activities are similar to the activities we came across when learning data table activities. However, these activities directly perform the same function in the Excel file itself:

- **Select Range**: Enables the user to select a specific range in an Excel file. This action is similar to the function that the user performs to highlight a particular range in an Excel spreadsheet.

- **Delete Range**: Enables the user to delete a specific range in an Excel spreadsheet.

- **Get Selected Range**: Returns the given range as a string that can be used in other activities that work with ranges.

- **Insert Column**: Like **Add Data Column**, this activity directly adds a new table column at a particular position in the Excel file itself.

- **Delete Column**: Removes the specified Excel table column from the spreadsheet. The deletion takes place based on the column name.

- **Insert/Delete Columns**: This activity can either add blank columns or remove existing columns from a spreadsheet.

- **Insert/Delete Rows**: This activity can either add blank rows or remove existing rows, based on the action type the user selects.

- **Auto Fill Range**: Like auto-population in Excel, this activity will apply the given formula over a specified range in a spreadsheet.

- **Copy Paste Range**: Enables the user to copy and paste an entire range from one spreadsheet to another. The copied content can include values, formatting, and formulas.

- **Lookup Range**: Similar to the Lookup function in data tables and Excel, the **Lookup Range** activity can search for a value in all cells in a given range.

- **Remove Duplicate Range**: Deletes all duplicate rows in the specified range.

Excel table activities

The table activities interact with the tables you have created in Excel spreadsheets. The activities allow you to perform the basic functions related to sorting, filtering, and creating tables. The following activities are available to complete the previously mentioned functions on tables:

- **Create Table**: Creates the specified table in the specified range.

- **Filter Table**: Filters a table on an Excel spreadsheet based on the conditions provided. The **Filter Table** activity can be used with **Read Range** when you want to read filtered results. The filtering action is identical to the filter function in Excel. Once the filter is applied, the rows that do not qualify will be hidden in the spreadsheet.

- **Sort Table**: Sorts a specified table based on the values of a given column in ascending or descending order.

Excel file activities

The file activities are mainly associated with the file itself:

- **Save Workbook**: Saves a specified workbook. The **Excel Application Scope** activity automatically saves the file before exiting if the **Save Changes** option is enabled in the **Properties** panel. However, this activity can also be used to save the file.

- **Close Workbook**: Enables the user to close a specific Excel spreadsheet.

Cell color activities

Preparing Excel files often requires a little bit of coloring to highlight specific values. The activities under the cell color subcategory enable the user to perform coloring actions as follows:

- **Get Cell Color**: Returns the background color of a specific cell in an Excel file and stores it in a `Color` variable.

- **Set Range Color**: Enable the user to change the background of a specified cell range to the user-specified color. The input is a `Color` variable type.

Sheet activities

The sheet activities provide the ability to perform different actions related to Excel worksheets, such as copying and retrieving the sheet information. The following activities enable you to work with Excel sheets:

- **Copy Sheet**: This enables the user to create a copy of a sheet in the same Excel file or a different file.

- **Get Workbook Sheet**: Retrieves the name of the sheet by its index.

- **Get Workbook Sheets**: Retrieves all the available sheets in a workbook file as a `String` array.

Pivot table activities

Working with financial information often requires pivoting and converting the data into a more graphical and summarized format for better insights. Usually, once the pivot is created, it needs refreshing. UiPath provides two activities to create and refresh pivot tables:

- **Create Pivot Table**: Creates a pivot table using specified parameters. The data in Excel has to be first converted into a table in order to use this activity for the `Pivot` function.

- **Refresh Pivot Table**: Enables the user to refresh a pivot table to update its content based on the source.

Macro activities

Microsoft Excel is capable of automating simple application-specific actions using macros and VB scripts. UiPath can interact with the macros available and even create macros using VBA scripts:

- **Execute Macro**: Executes a macro available in a `.xlsm` file

- **Invoke VBA**: Invokes a macro available in another file using VBA scripts

Based on the content we covered, you are now familiar with the activities that UiPath can perform on Excel files. A few of these activities function similarly to data table activities. However, the rest mainly focus on functions that Microsoft Excel offers. The following section focuses on some hands-on practice on some of the Excel activities. The practice session does not cover all the activities we described. However, the practice session will help you to better understand how to use the activities discussed, when needed.

Practicing Excel automation

In this section, you will practice the concepts learned by interacting with some data in an Excel file. The Excel file consists of employee information such as `employee ID`, `first name`, `last name`, `hourly rate`, and `work hours`. Our task is to go through the data and add two new columns in the Excel file.

One column should include the full name (combining the first and the last name) and the other column should consist of the total payment (the hourly rate * work hours) for the employee. Once the report is generated, the robot should also filter the data to find employees who earn more than $2,000 and create a separate Excel file for this data.

Go through the following steps to complete this task:

1. Open UiPath Studio and create a new project.

2. Open Microsoft Excel and create the data as shown in *Figure 9.16*:

	A	B	C	D	E	F	G
1	ID	First Name	Last Name	Age	Hourly Rate ($)	Work Hours	
2	E0001	Dany	Joe	25	5	20	
3	E0002	John	Smith	36	25	100	
4	E0003	John	Doe	27	15	120	
5	E0004	Mary	Ann	30	15	50	
6	E0005	Emmy	Elissa	21	10	200	
7							

Figure 9.16 – Excel integration sample data

3. Save the Excel file in a folder that can be used as the input for our process.

4. Open the `Main.xaml` file in UiPath Studio.

5. Drag and drop an **Excel Application Scope** activity and configure the **Workbook Path** property by giving the file path to the Excel file you created.

    The **Excel Application Scope** activity has a **DO** sequence within it. This is where you place all the activities that you need to perform on the Excel file. Place a **Read Range** activity within the **DO** sequence by dragging it from the **Excel App Integration** section of the **Activities** panel. The following figure illustrates how to read data using **Excel Activity Scope** by placing the **Read Range** activity inside it:

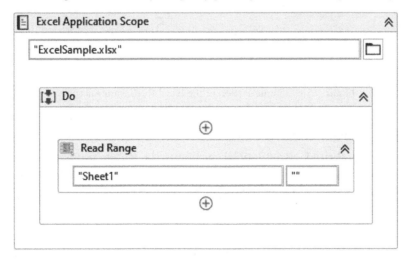

Figure 9.17 – Reading data from Excel

6. Configure the **SheetName** property of the **Read Range** activity by providing the sheet name you see on the Excel file. By default, both have the "Sheet1" value, which is a match.

7. Configure the **Range** property of the activity by specifying from where to start reading data. Our data starts from the **A1** cell, and you need to configure it by setting "A1".

8. Configure the **Output DataTable** property of the activity by creating and specifying a new data table variable to hold the data it reads from the file:

Figure 9.18 – Configuration of the Excel Read Range activity

9. Specify our two new columns in Excel. Drag a **Write Cell** activity from the **Excel App Integration** section and place it below the **Read Range** activity.

10. Configure the **Write Cell** activity by specifying the **Range** property as "G1" and the **Value** property by specifying the cell value (column name) as "Full Name".

11. Add another **Write Cell** activity and configure the **Range** property with "H1" and the **Value** property by specifying the new column name, "Total Payment", as shown in the following screenshot:

Figure 9.19 – Adding the Write Cell activities

12. Now, loop through the data in the data table and perform the manipulations. Add a **For Each Row** activity below the last **Write Cell** activity.

13. Configure the **For Each Row** activity by specifying the data table variable name you created earlier for **Read Range**.

14. Configure the **Output Index** property of the activity by creating and specifying a new **Int32** variable named `CurrentRowIndex`. This property generates a zero-based index of each row that is being processed. The value generated by this activity will help you later when updating the rows in the Excel file. The following figure shows the configuration of the **For Each Row** activity properties to obtain the row index:

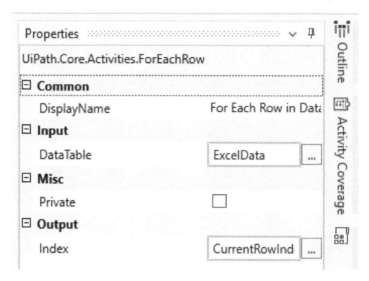

Figure 9.20 – Generating the current iteration value in the For Each loop

15. Search for the **Get Row item** activity and place it in the body of the **For Each Row** activity. This activity enables a user to get data from a specified column of the current row.

16. Configure the **Row** property of the activity by specifying the `CurrentRow` variable of the **For Each Row** activity.

17. Configure the **Column Name** property of the activity by specifying the `"First Name"` column of the Excel file. Column names have to be identical to what you see in the Excel file.

18. Configure the output **Value** property of the activity by creating and specifying a new string variable named `FirstName`, as shown in the following figure:

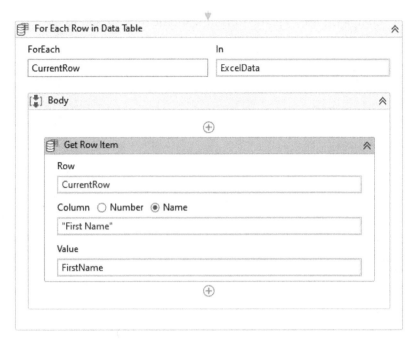

Figure 9.21 – Extracting data from CurrentRow

19. Place three more **Get Row Item** activities and configure them for each column that needs to be extracted. The columns are **Last Name**, **Hourly Rate**, and **Work Hours**. Create individual variables to hold the data of each column as you did for the first one. Ensure that the variables you create for **Hourly Rate** and **Work Hours** are of the System.Double type:

Name	Variable type	Scope
FirstName	String	Body
LastName	String	Body
HourlyRate	Double	Body
WorkHours	Double	Body
ExcelData	DataTable	Do
CurrentRowIndex	Int32	Do
ProcessedData	DataTable	ExcelAutomation
Create Variable		

Variables   Arguments   Imports

Figure 9.22 – Defining the variables for the process

Once you have completed the step, the workflow should look similar to the following screenshot:

Figure 9.23 – Extracting data to perform manipulations

Now, start updating the Excel file from the data we extracted.

20. Place a **Write Cell** activity below the last **Get Row Item** activity to update the **Full Name** column with data for the current row.

21. Since you are updating each row for the **Full Name** column, you cannot have a hardcoded value for the **Range** property because the row number is dynamic. As a result, you need to use the `CurrentRowIndex` variable of the **For Each Row** activity to find the row number in the Excel file.

22. Remember that the variable generates a zero-based index, whereas in Excel, the rows start with 1. Now, take a look at the Excel file again. The first row in Excel has the headers. The actual data starts from row number 2. Therefore, you need to match our zero-based index to the row numbers starting from 2 in Excel. Use the following expression in the **Range** property of the **Write Cell** activity.

    Note that you need to convert the row number generated dynamically to a String type because the field only accepts string values:

    ```
    "G" + (CurrentRowIndex + 2).ToString
    ```

23. Configure the **Value** property of the activity using the following expression to combine the first and last names:

    ```
    FirstName + " " + LastName
    ```

24. Place another **Write Cell** activity below the previous activity to update the rows for the next column, **"Total Payment"**.

25. Configure the **Range** property of the activity using the following formula. It is almost similar to the previous formula. The only difference is the column in Excel:

    ```
    "H" + (CurrentRowIndex + 2).ToString
    ```

26. Configure the **Value** property of the activity by specifying the following expression:

    ```
    (HourlyRate * WorkHours).ToString
    ```

27. Place a **Save Workbook** activity *below* the **For Each Row** activity to save the changes before closing the file.

28. Run the process and explore the output you receive in the Excel file. Once the process completes, you should see the following output in the Excel file:

	A	B	C	D	E	F	G	H	I
1	ID	First Name	Last Name	Age	Hourly Rate ($)	Work Hours	Full Name	Total Payment	
2	E0001	Dany	Joe	25	5	20	Dany Joe	100	
3	E0002	John	Smith	36	25	100	John Smith	2500	
4	E0003	John	Doe	27	15	120	John Doe	1800	
5	E0004	Mary	Ann	30	15	50	Mary Ann	750	
6	E0005	Emmy	Elissa	21	10	200	Emmy Elissa	2000	
7									

Figure 9.24 – Exploring the output of the workflow

In the second part, you need to read the data from Excel and filter the results to show only employees who have a total payment greater than or equal to 2,000.

29. Place another **Read Range** activity below **Excel Application Scope**. This time, use the **Read Range** activity under the **File/Workbook** category. This activity does not require the Excel file to be open.

30. Configure the activity by providing **Workbook Path**, the **Range** property as " ", and the **DataTable** output to a new data table variable named ProcessedData.

31. Use a **Filter Data Table** activity and configure it as shown in *Figure 9.25*:

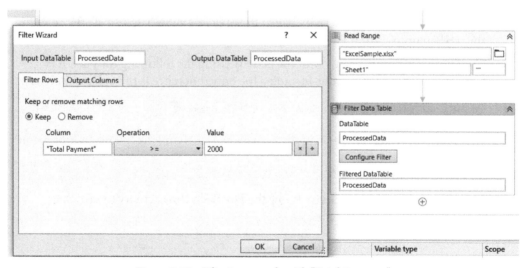

Figure 9.25 – Filtering records with "Total Payment"

32. Add a **Write Range** activity from the **File/Workbook** category and place it below the **Filter Data Table** activity.

33. Configure the activity as shown in *Figure 9.26*:

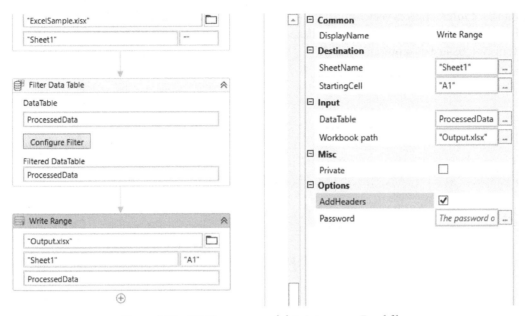

Figure 9.26 – Writing processed data into a new Excel file

34. Run the workflow and review the output in the newly created Excel file. You should only see two records.

You have now been shown the basic actions that can be performed on data tables and Excel files. There are many other functions that you can explore and try out. It is recommended to use the same solution you built to practice the different functions. Exploring and getting to know how these activities work will help when it comes to large projects with multiple files that contain complex data structures such as pivots.

Summary

This chapter introduced you to data tables and Excel files. The data table variable type is a widely used data type to hold structured and tabular data. Data tables interact easily with Excel files as they share the same data structure. Data tables and the concepts used with them go hand in hand when interacting with Excel files, as you experienced while doing the hands-on sessions. The concepts and activities learned in this chapter will come in handy when working with large Excel-related automation projects.

In addition, the concepts that have been discussed regarding the use of Excel files and data tables will be very helpful in later chapters, especially in the use case sections. The next chapter describes how UiPath robot can interact with user interfaces to perform different actions such as clicking, typing, and data scraping. Learning how to perform user interface interaction is very important for any RPA project. UI automation is a complex but important topic that enables the user to program the robot to interact with software applications just as a human would.

10

Exploring User Interfaces and User/ Robot Interactions

The automation of **user interfaces (UIs)** is one of the most important automation topics and is most frequently used in today's automation world. UI elements are the building blocks of the UI (for example, windows, text fields, buttons, drop-down menus, checkboxes, and text boxes). Your robot should be capable of communicating with the UI elements easily to perform actions such as clicking, typing inputs, and reading output values to achieve a perfect automation solution.

As part of this chapter, you will understand various techniques to interact with UI elements faster and more easily. You will learn about recorders and see how to efficiently use them for faster automation. You will also learn about some advanced UI automation, such as image and text automation. Finally, you will learn more about input and output actions, and explore various useful methods for effective automation.

This chapter consists of the following sections:

- Introducing UI interactions
- Recording the graphical user interface

- Advanced UI automation
- Input actions and methods
- Output actions and methods

Technical requirements

This chapter requires you to have UiPath Studio and Robot installed, along with a basic understanding of Studio UIs, variables, data types, control flows, and data manipulation. You can refer to *Chapters 5* to *9* to gain all the required knowledge.

Introducing UI interactions

The **graphical user interface** (**GUI**) is made up of various graphical objects, such as windows, text fields, buttons, dropdowns, checkboxes, text boxes, tables, and URLs. UiPath can seamlessly interact with most types of desktop and web applications as it has deep integration with major GUI frameworks, such as HTML, Java, .NET, and SAP. GUI automation interacts with these GUI objects by clicking, typing, selecting, checking values, copying data, and pasting data using various UiPath activities. The interaction of the UiPath robots exactly replicates the human interaction in a logical, faster, and error-free way as instructed by the RPA developer who designs or develops the process workflows or automation projects.

Foreground versus background automation

Foreground processes are run by attended robots and are usually performed under human supervision. The Robot uses foreground activities to interact with the GUI elements. **Background processes** are performed by unattended robots in a dedicated machine that uses background activities. You need to use the appropriate activities to achieve efficient UI automation and, for that, let's explore the key UiPath UI Automation elements in UiPath Studio as follows:

- **Activities**: This instructs the Robot to perform actions on the GUI bases on the type of activities selected, configured inputs, properties of activities, and output generated by the GUI. As a prerequisite, you need to ensure the `UiPath.UIAutomation.Activities` dependency package is available by default in the **Dependencies** node. In case the package is not available or has been removed by mistake, you need to install the same package from **Manage Packages**. We will explore more about the key activities in the upcoming sections, as shown in *Figure 10.1*:

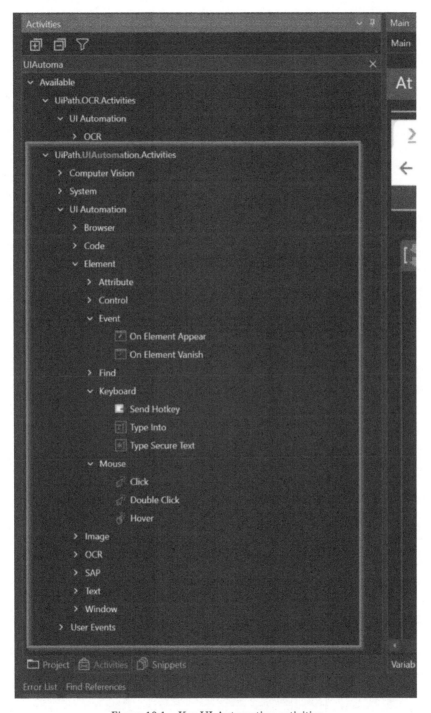

Figure 10.1 – Key UI Automation activities

- **Recording**: This enables the RPA developer to capture the step-by-step process and all the key interaction with the GUI elements, and convert them into a sequencing workflow in UiPath Studio for developing UI automation much faster, as shown in the following figure:

Figure 10.2 – Recording

- **Target**: This instructs the robot on which UI elements need to be actioned based on the **Target** properties configured, as shown in *Figure 10.3*. The most important element is **Selector**, which we have already discussed in *Chapter 8, Exploring UiPath Selectors*.

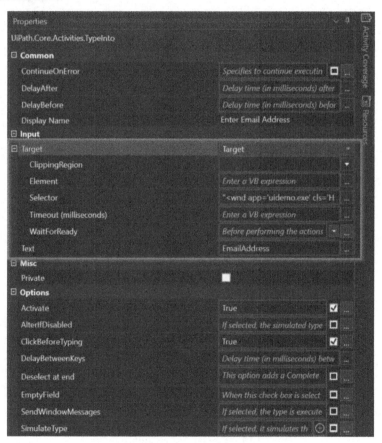

Figure 10.3 – Targeting methods

- **Input** and **Output**: These are important features in UiPath to decide the type of UI automation you are developing, such as foreground or background automation. You will be enabling **SendWindowsMessages** or **SimulateType**, as shown in *Figure 10.4*. These options are selected if your automation needs to run in the background without any human intervention:

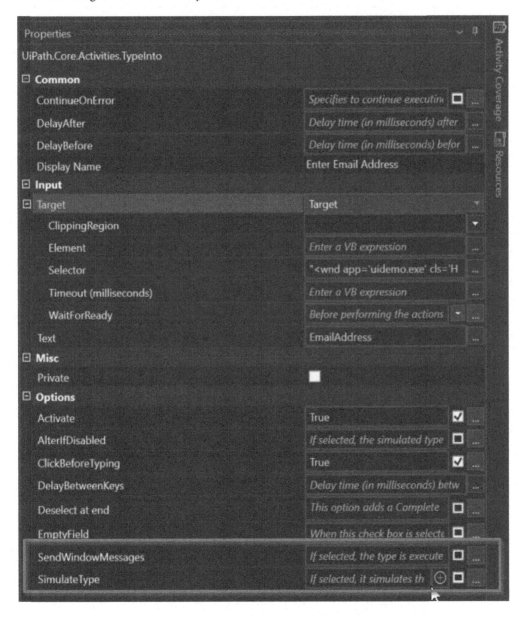

Figure 10.4 – Input and output methods

Activities

UI Automation activities are used to develop **tasks** or **workflows** for the robot to communicate with the GUI of several applications. Activities are essentially classified into four different types. These are shown in *Figure 10.5*:

Activities	Description
Containers	These are used to locate any GUI applications (desktop, web, or mainframes) or to identify active windows or pop up windows to communicate with the elements within the scope of the selected window. Open Browser, Open Application, Attach Browser, and Attach Window are examples of containers.
Input	These activities are used to provide inputs or perform actions on the UI elements. Examples are Click, Type Into, and Send Hotkeys.
Output	These activities instruct the robot to extract data from the GUI. Examples are GetText, GetURL, and GetOCRText.
Synchronization	These activities instruct the robot to perform defined operations based on the GUI behaviors to overcome any unexpected UI behavior. Examples are Element Exists, Image Exists, and Wait Element Vanish.

Figure 10.5 – Types of UI Automation activities

Properties

The properties of the activity decide how the robot will interact with the GUI based on the activity used. The different properties options can be found in the **Properties** panel section, usually displayed by default on the right-hand side of UiPath Studio. Let's explore some key properties used in GUI automation as follows:

- **DelayAfter** and **DelayBefore**: Instructs the robot to wait for a specified time in milliseconds before or after performing the activity. The default amount of delay time for **DelayAfter** is 300 milliseconds, and the wait time for **DelayBefore** is 200 milliseconds. You may increase or decrease the delay time depending on the responses of the UI element.

- **ContinueOnError**: Instructs the robot to wait for a specified time in milliseconds before or after performing the activity. By default, **ContinueOnError** is **False**, which means the remaining activities will not be executed in case of any errors or exceptions. You may select this as **True** if you want to continue with the execution despite an application exception.

- **ClippingRegion**: Used to target a specific region using coordinates such as **Left**, **Right**, **Top**, and **Bottom**. The values in the clipping regions are blank by default. You may input the values of the coordinates if available.

- **SendWindowMessages**: Sends specific messages to the target application and can run in the background, but it is not the fastest option and is not compatible with all desktop applications. By default, the **SendWindowMessages** checkbox is not selected.

- **SimulateType** and **SimulateClick**: Sends specific messages to the target application and can run in the background; this is the fastest option and compatible with all desktop applications. By default, the **SimulateType** or **SimulateClick** checkbox is not selected.

- **Target**: Helps the robot in different ways to identify target elements by providing inputs in the form of selectors, fuzzy selectors, images, or anchors. **Selector** is a commonly used method to identify elements; it's a key property for the robot to identify the target element using an XML fragment that has several attributes to locate the unique target element.

- **Output**: Used to store the output of the activity using variables or arguments to be used within the project. By default, the **Output** field will be empty. You may create a variable within the field to store the output generated in the selected activity.

Let's explore an example using `https://www.packtpub.com/` to apply a few of the UI Automation activities and properties learned so far to ensure that we can communicate with the web application. I can see a *Free 7 Day Trial* page at this URL while writing this lesson. If you do not find the same, you can use any other similar pages. In this example, you will be accessing a web application and interacting with the web elements to provide input, and access the data from the web page:

1. Launch `https://www.packtpub.com/`.

2. Click on the **Start 7-day FREE trial** button, as shown in *Figure 10.6*:

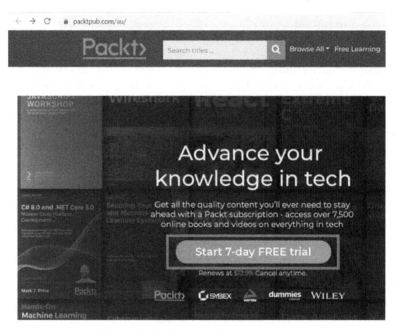

Figure 10.6 – Packtpub free trial access

3. The next page shows the **Account details** section, which we are going to automate, as shown in *Figure 10.7*:

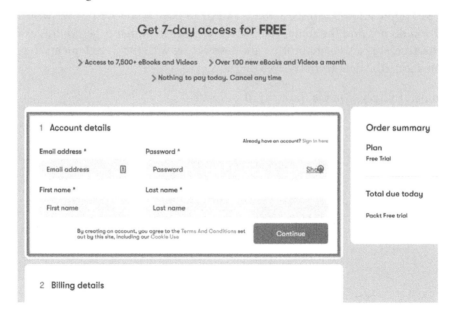

Figure 10.7 – Packtpub free trial registration

4. Apply the following steps to launch UiPath, and create a Sequence workflow for handling data in the **Account details** section, as shown in *Figure 10.8*:

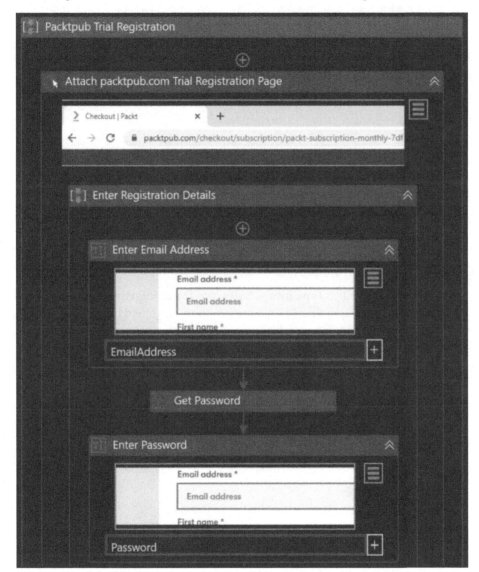

Figure 10.8 – Enter the email address and password

I.   Launch UiPath Studio.

II. Create a new **Sequence** and name it Packtpub Trial Registration.

III. Create the `EmailAddress`, `Password`, `FirstName`, `LastName`, and `TermsAndConditions` variables of the `String` type, and add default values for `EmailAddress`, `FirstName`, and `LastName`, as shown in the *Figure 10.9*:

Name	Variable type	Scope	Default
EmailAddress	String	Packtpub Trial Registration	"uipathadmin@gmail.com"
FirstName	String	Packtpub Trial Registration	"UiPath"
LastName	String	Packtpub Trial Registration	"Admin"
Password	String	Packtpub Trial Registration	*Enter a VB expression*
TermsAndConditions	String	Packtpub Trial Registration	*Enter a VB expression*

Figure 10.9 – Variable definitions

IV. Drag and drop the **Attach Browser** activity and connect to the `Packtpub Trial Registration` page by using the **Indicate** option.

V. Drag and drop the **Sequence** activity into the **Attach Browser** activity and name it `Enter Registration Details`.

VI. Drag and drop the **Type into** activity into **Enter Registration Details** and name it as `Enter Email Address`. In the text field of the properties, use the `EmailAddress` variable.

VII. Drag and drop the **Get Password** activity into **Enter Registration Details** and type your password in the **Password** field of **Properties**. Use the `Password` variable in the **Result** field of **Properties** to save the secured password, as shown in *Figure 10.10*:

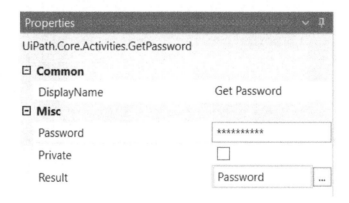

Figure 10.10 – Password properties

VIII. Drag and drop the **Type into** activity into **Enter Registration Details,** and name it Enter Password. In the text field of the properties, use the Password variable.

IX. Enter **First name** and **Last name** using the **Type into** activity and extract the TermsAndConditions text using the **Get Text** activity, as shown in *Figure 10.11*:

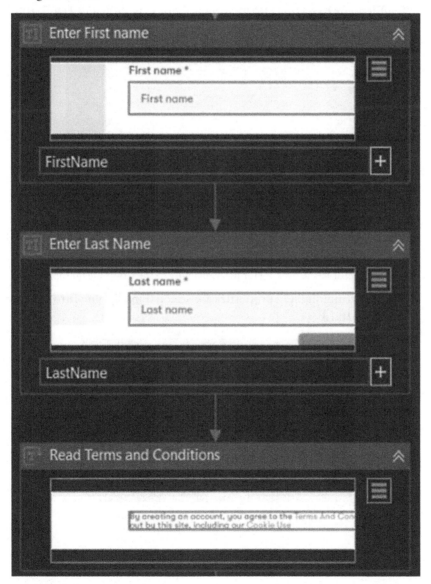

Figure 10.11 – Enter First Name, Enter Last Name, and Read Terms and Conditions text

X. Drag and drop the **Element Exists** activity into `Enter Registration Details`, and name it `Check the Continue Button Exists`. In the **Output** field of the properties, create a `ContinueAvailable` variable. Next, drag and drop the **Write Line** activity to output the value of the `ContinueAvailable` variable, as shown in *Figure 10.12*.

XI. Check for the availability of the **Continue** Button and write the output using the **Element Exists** and **Write Line** activities, as shown in *Figure 10.12*:

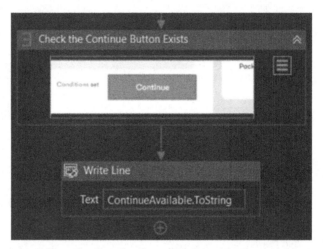

Figure 10.12 – Checking for the availability of the Continue button

XII. Ensure the highlighted properties are selected in all **Type Into** fields, as shown in *Figure 10.13*:

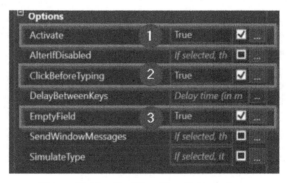

Figure 10.13 – Enabling Type Into options

5. Run the process to find the robot, navigate to the **Account details** page, and enter the account details as per your input data, as shown in *Figure 10.14*:

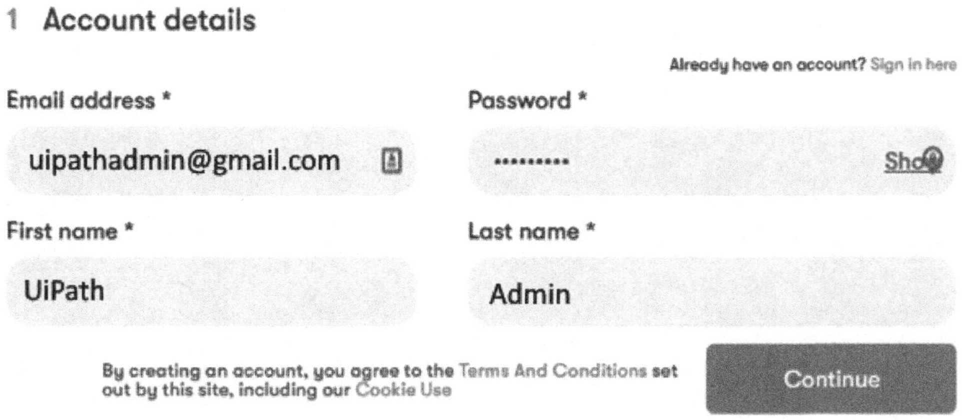

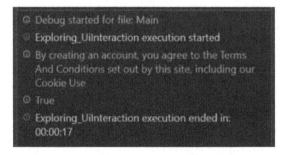

Figure 10.14 – Checking the output on the Packtpub page

6. Verify the output in the **Output** panel to ensure the **TermsAndConditions** text has been extracted from the web page and the **Continue** button is available as shown in *Figure 10.15*:

Figure 10.15 – Checking the output in UiPath Studio

In this section, we have seen how the robot interacts with a web page to read and write data. We have also seen how the robot interacts with the GUI using automation activities and properties to automate a web application. You have been introduced to the different types of activities and properties you need to be aware of while doing GUI automation. We have also used the activities and properties in an example to understand their functionality better. You will understand more about the different recording options available, and input and output methods in the upcoming sections, which will help you to perform the development faster and perform background automation.

Methods of recording the GUI

Recording is one of the important features in UiPath Studio, and allows users to capture the actions performed on the screen and convert them into sequences; this saves a lot of time and effort in automating business processes. To start recording, you need to access the **DESIGN** (1) panel and click on **Recording** (2), which will display all the available recording options (3), as shown in *Figure 10.16*:

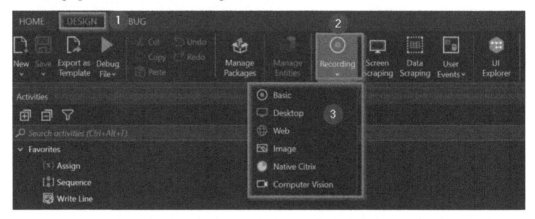

Figure 10.16 – Different recording options

There are six types of recordings: **Basic, Desktop, Web, Image, Native Citrix**, and **Computer Vision**. However, we will be exploring only the first three types (Basic, Desktop, and Web), as those are the most commonly used options and are more relevant for the RPA Associate certification.

Basic

Basic generates a **full selector** for each activity but does not create a container for the activities. This is better suited for creating *linear sequences within a container* and can be used for recording both web applications and desktop applications but is the *slowest* of all recorders.

Let's use the same example of the Packtpub web page to read and write data used in the previous section, but this time using the **Basic** recording:

1. Create a new sequence and name it Recordings.
2. Click on **Recording** (1) and then on **Basic** (2), as shown in *Figure 10.17*:

Figure 10.17 – Launching Basic recording

3. The **Basic Recording** panel is displayed with different options and you are able to perform the following actions, as shown in *Figure 10.18*.

4. Record a series of actions or events (such as launch an application, click on a menu, and type into a field), using the **Record** option (**1**). For this, you need to click on the **Record** button and perform all the required actions, and stop the recording by pressing the *Esc* key once your actions are completed. Perform step-by-step recording (such as launching the application using **Start App**, clicking on a menu using **Click**, and typing into the text field using **Type**) using the different recording tools (**2**) or you can perform combinations of both options 1 and 2. Press the *Esc* key to stop recording once you have completed all your actions.

Figure 10.18 – Starting a basic recording

5. Click on the **Record** button from the previous screen to record the elements from the **Account details** section of the **Subscription** page at https://www. packtpub.com/, in the order of elements numbered as shown in *Figure 10.19*:

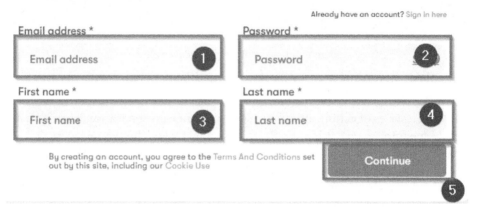

Figure 10.19 – Packtpub Account details section

6. Press the *Esc* button on the keyboard or right-click on the mouse to stop recording, and once the recording has been completed, you will find the following, where you can see the option to save your recording or to start a new recording using the various recording options:

Figure 10.20 – Basic Recording tool

7. Click on the **Save & Exit** button for the recorded activities to be saved to the workflow and to exit from **Basic Recording**:

Figure 10.21 – Basic Recording Save & Exit

8. Verify whether the username and password were generated from the recording, as shown in *Figure 10.22*:

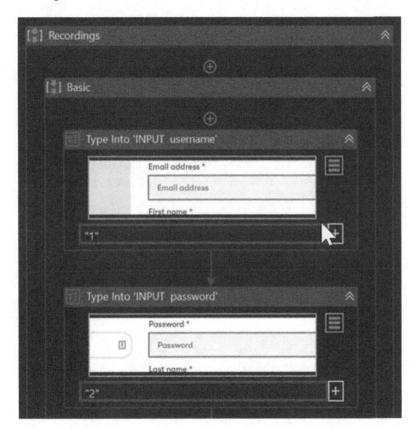

Figure 10.22 – Workflow verification of username and password

9. Verify whether **First name**, **Last name**, and the **Continue** button were recorded, as shown in *Figure 10.23*:

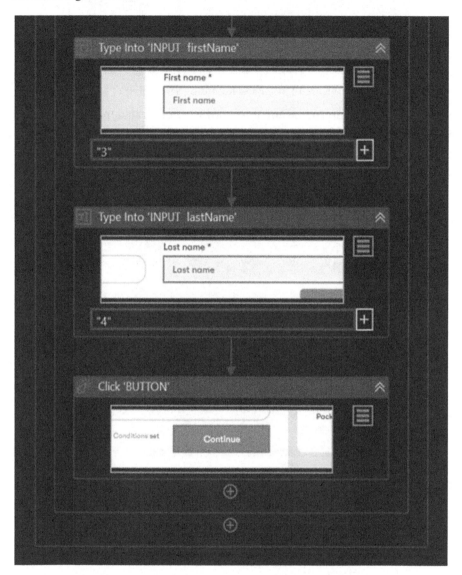

Figure 10.23 – Workflow verification, other recorded fields

10. Click on the **Options** menu (1) and then click on **Edit Selector** (2) from one of the activities, as shown in *Figure 10.24*:

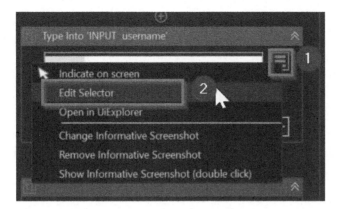

Figure 10.24 – Edit Selector menu option

11. Verify the **Edit Selector** section to ensure that the full HTML fragment of the selector is displayed and editable. Also, verify the browser details displayed; this is the reason we call the **Basic** recording a **full selector** as shown in *Figure 10.25*. Note that the HTML fragment section is non-editable in **partial selectors.**

Figure 10.25 – Edit Selector – Full selector

12. Note that even though it is recorded from a web application, there are no containers, such as **Open Browser** or **Attach Browser**, recorded within the **Basic** sequence, as shown in *Figure 10.22*.

Now, let's explore another example of basic recording, where the robot enters the text UiPath into Notepad. To perform that, follow these steps to generate the **Basic** sequence, as shown in *Figure 10.26*:

1. Launch Notepad.

2. Click on the **Basic Recording** option from UiPath Studio.

3. Click on the **Type** option from the Basic Recording tool (2) as shown in *Figure 10.18* during the recording and navigate the cursor to the Notepad.

4. Type UiPath in Notepad.

5. Press the *Esc* button to stop recording.

6. Click on the **Save & Exit** button.

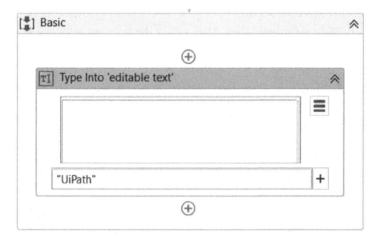

Figure 10.26 – Type into Notepad application (Basic recording)

7. Click on the **Options** menu (**1**) and then click on **Edit Selector** (**2**) from one of the activities, as shown in *Figure 10.27*:

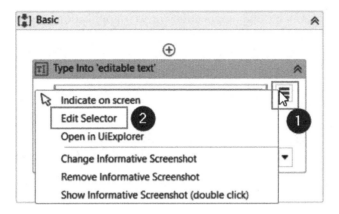

Figure 10.27 – Edit Selector

8. Verify the **Edit Selector** box of the Type Into activity to ensure the HTML code generated follows the structure of a **full selector**, which means each and every attribute within the HTML tags is editable as shown in *Figure 10.28*:

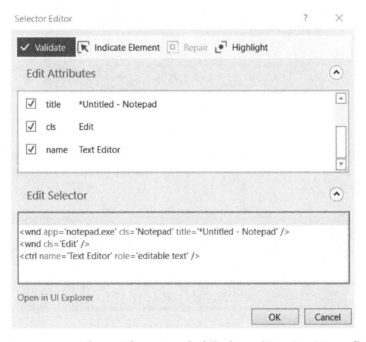

Figure 10.28 – Selector Editor view of a full selector (Type Into Notepad)

No matter whether it is a desktop applications or web-applications, the Basic recording generates full selectors, which means there are no separate containers generated, such as **Attach Browser** or **Attach Window**. Therefore, this recording is the *slowest* and most suitable for single activities within containers or for linear workflows.

Desktop

Desktop generates a **partial selector** for each activity and creates a container for the activities. This is better suited for automating desktop applications. This is *faster* than a Basic recording. Let's look at an example of automatically entering texts in to a notepad application:

1. Create a new sequence and name it Desktop Recording.

2. Click on the **Recording** button (**1**) and then **Desktop** (**2**), as shown in *Figure 10.29*:

Figure 10.29 – Launching Desktop recording

3. The **Desktop Recording** panel is displayed with the multiple recording options as shown in *Figure 10.30*. Refer *Step 3* of *Basic recording* to understand more about the recording features:

Figure 10.30 – Desktop Recording tool

4. Launch a new Notepad application and click on the **Record** button. Then, type UiPath (**1**), click on the **Format** tab (**2**), change the font size to 55 (**3**), and finally, click **OK** (**4**), as shown in *Figure 10.31*:

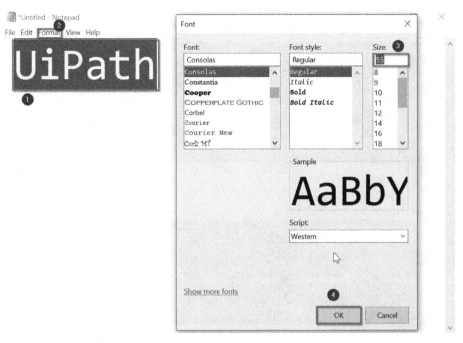

Figure 10.31 – Notepad during recording

5. Press the *Esc* button on the keyboard once the recording has been completed to find the options to either save the recordings or to start new recordings, as shown in *Figure 10.32*:

Figure 10.32 – Desktop Recording tool

6. Click on the **Save & Exit** button for the recorded activities to be saved to the workflow, as shown in *Figure 10.33*:

Figure 10.33 – Save activities

7. Verify whether the Notepad entry is recorded, as shown in *Figure 10.34*:

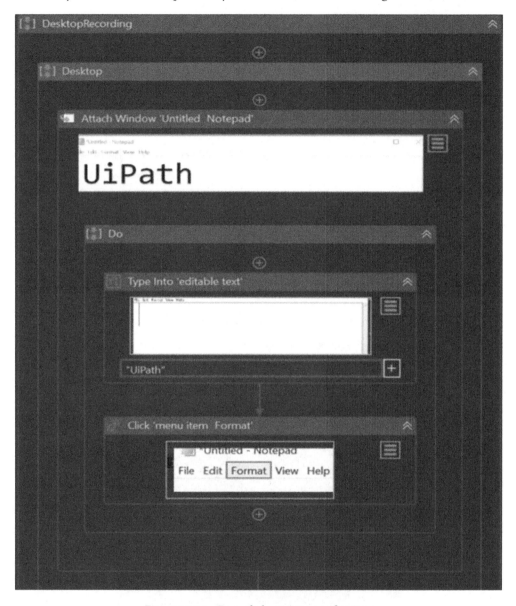

Figure 10.34 – Recorded activities verification

8. Verify whether the **Font…** changes are recorded, as shown in *Figure 10.35*:

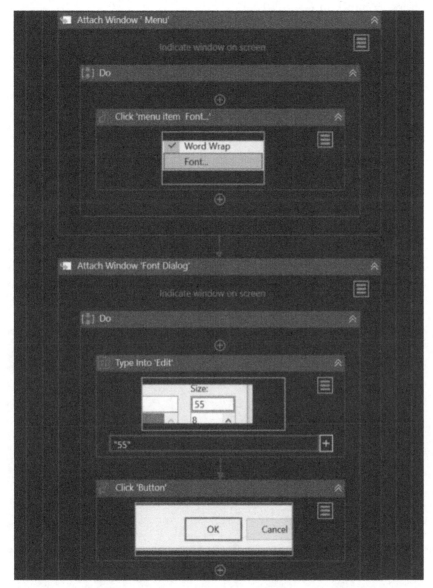

Figure 10.35 – Recorded activities verification continued

9. Click on the **Options** menu (**1**), and then click on **Edit Selector** (**2**) from one of the activities, as shown in *Figure 10.36*:

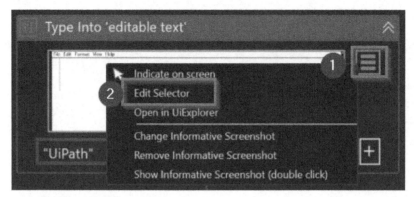

Figure 10.36 – Edit Selector

10. Verify the **Edit Selector** section to ensure that the HTML fragment of the selector is displayed, and part of the HTML is non-editable, which is grayed out in the first line of the **Edit Selector** section. This is the reason we call the Desktop recording a partial selector, as shown in *Figure 10.37*:

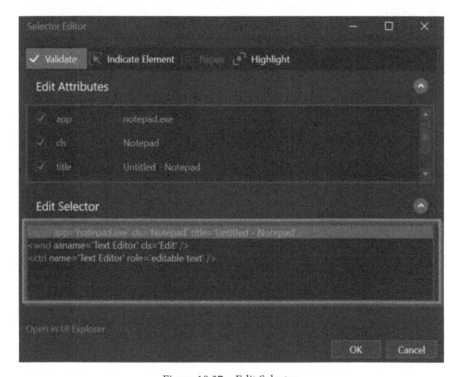

Figure 10.37 – Edit Selector

11. Verify the recorded activities have containers, such as **Attach Window** or **Use Application**, to ensure the desktop recording supports containers, as shown in *Figure 10.38*:

Figure 10.38 – Container verification

We have seen how to record desktop applications using Desktop recording and experienced how fast and easy it is to record every event.

Web

Web generates a partial selector for each activity and creates a container for the activities. This is better suited for automating web applications, and is faster than Basic recordings.

Let's see an example of automatically entering texts in to a notepad application with Web:

1. Create a new sequence and name it `Web_Recording`.

2. Click on the **Recording** button (**1**), and then click on **Web** (**2**), as shown in *Figure 10.39*:

Figure 10.39 – Launching Web recording

3. The **Web Recording** panel is displayed with multiple options, as shown in *Figure 10.40*. This is similar to the **Basic** recording from the earlier section except that **Web Recording** has the **Open Browser** option instead of the **Open Application** in the **Basic** recording.

Figure 10.40 – Web Recording tool

4. Click on **Record** as shown in the previous srceenshot to record the **Account details** sections from the **Subscription** page of https://www.packtpub.com/, and capture the elements in the order numbered in *Figure 10.41*:

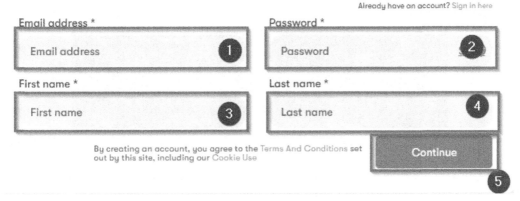

Figure 10.41 – Packtpub account details during recording

5. While typing the password during the recording, a pop-up box is displayed, as shown in *Figure 10.42*, in which you need to perform the following:

- Type your secure password in **Type the desired value (1)**.

- Check the **Type password (2)** option to enable secure text.

- Press the *Enter* key.

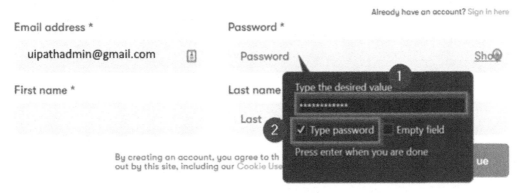

Figure 10.42 – Packtpub password during recording

6. Press the *Esc* button on your keyboard once the recording has been completed to find the options to either save the recordings or to start new recordings, as shown in *Figure 10.43*:

Figure 10.43 – Web Recording options

7. Click on the **Save & Exit** button for the recorded activities to be saved to the workflow and to exit from **Web Recording**, as shown in *Figure 10.44*:

Figure 10.44 – Web Recording Save & Exit

8. Verify whether the username and password are generated from the generated workflow, as shown in *Figure 10.45*:

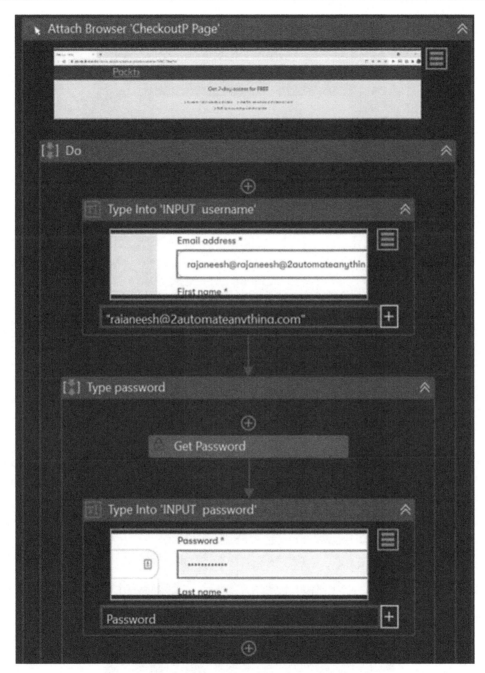

Figure 10.45 – Web Recording activities verification

9. Verify whether **First name** and **Last name** are recorded, as shown in *Figure 10.46*:

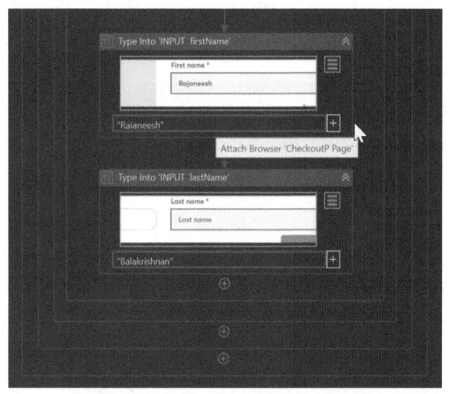

Figure 10.46 – Web Recording activities verification continued

10. Click on the options menu (1) and then click on **Edit Selector** (2) from the activities, as shown in *Figure 10.47*:

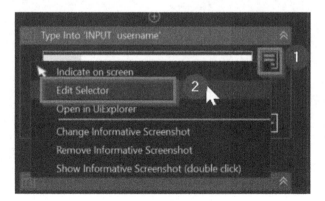

Figure 10.47 – Edit Selector

11. Verify the **Edit Selector** section to ensure that the full HTML fragment of the selector is displayed, and part of the fragment is non-editable. This is the reason we call the **Web** recording a partial selector, as shown in *Figure 10.48*:

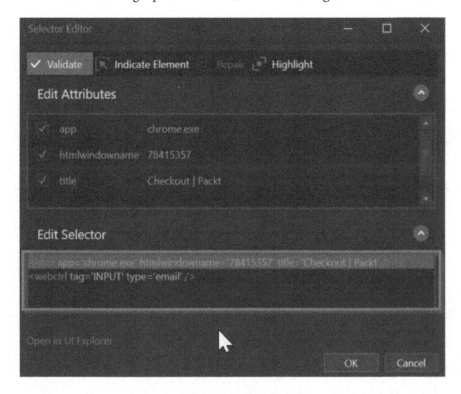

Figure 10.48 – Edit Selector

12. Note this recording is the fastest and most suitable for web application recording. You will find activities such as **Open Browser** or **Attach Browser** are recorded within the **Web Recording** sequence, as shown in *Figure 10.49*:

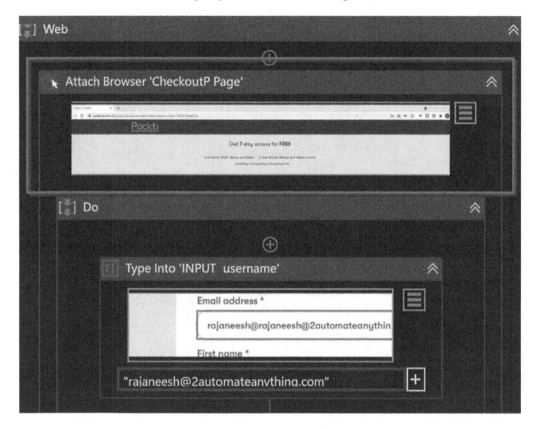

Figure 10.49 – Container verification

We have seen how to record web applications using Web recording and experienced how fast and easy it is to record each event within a browser. We have also seen that Web recordings use a partial selector and is the fastest of all the recording options.

So far, we have seen the different recording options we have in UiPath and have explored some key recording concepts with examples. Now, you have a better idea of how to choose the correct recorder based on the given application being automated. We have come across different activities and properties and have applied them in our examples. In the next section, let's explore some more advanced recording options.

When to use which types of recording?

Let's discuss the different types of available recordings, their usage, advantages, and disadvantages, as shown in *Figure 10.50*:

Recording Type	Usage, Advantages, and Disadvantages
Basic	• Best suited for linear workflows where not many windows or web pages are involved. • It is the slowest type of recording. • Can automate desktop and web applications. • **SimulateType** / **SimulateClick** is not enabled (**False**) by default.
Desktop	• Suitable for all types of desktop applications where multiple windows and web pages are involved. • Generates partial selectors for each activity. • It is faster than the **Basic** recording.
Web	• Best suited for recording web applications where multiple pages and actions are involved. • Generates partial selectors for each activity (for example, Attach Browser). • It is faster than the **Basic** recording. • **SimulateType** / **SimulateClick** is enabled (**True**) by default.
Image	• Only use it if you want to record virtualized environments (such as Virtual Networking Computers, virtual machines, and Citrix) or SAP. • It allows only image, text, and keyboard automation, and requires explicit positioning.
Native Citrix	• Only used in native Citrix automation projects. • As a prerequisite, you need to install the UiPath Citrix extension on the client machine and the UiPath Remote Runtime component (Citrix XenApp) on the application servers. • You can use activities such as **Click, Type Into, Get Text,** and **Extract Data**. • Selectors are natively generated for Citrix application elements.
Computer Vision	• It uses computer vision neural networks to identify UI elements such as buttons, texts, and checkboxes. • It does not use selectors. • Used to record virtualized environments (such as VNC, virtual machines, Citrix, and remote desktops). • Automating local applications where the other mentioned recording options are not reliable.

Figure 10.50 – Different types of recordings and their uses

This has provided us with better clarity about recordings and guided us to select the right recording tool for different situations.

Advanced UI Automation tools

Let's discuss a few advanced recording options available to automate complex GUIs, such as Citrix, SAP, and mainframes:

- **Image**: This recording is used to record images, text, and keyboard inputs, and is suitable for virtual environment automations such as VMs, Citrix, SAP, and mainframes. It captures the exact user interface position of the element and the value of the coordinates of elements to automate the GUI.

- **Native Citrix**: This recording is used to record images, text, and keyboard inputs, and is suitable for applications within the Citrix environment. It is like the desktop recorder, which can be used for recording different types of applications inside the Citrix environment.

- **Computer Vision**: This recording is mainly used to record images, text, and keyboard inputs, and is suitable for applications within the Citrix environment and Windows environment where any other previously discussed recording options failed to identify UI elements. It is a smart recorder that uses a built-in neural network to capture the UI element more accurately to overcome any selector inconsistency.

- **Object repository**: An advanced feature used to capture UI elements from applications and store them as **reusable objects** in the repository so that they can be used as and when required, or can be shared with other projects. These objects can be dragged and dropped from the object repository to the workflows for faster automation development, which is easily manageable, reusable, and reliable.

We have discussed a few advanced concepts and have seen how the GUIs such as Citrix, mainframes, and SAP can be automated using different tools and techniques. In the next section, we will explore a bit more about the input and output methods to develop a more efficient automation solution.

Input actions and methods

Automation requires certain properties to be configured to work seamlessly during the execution of the process. To perform either foreground or background automation, the input needs to be actioned in a GUI either directly by the user or by the robot. There are three types of input methods, which we will discuss now.

Default or hardware events

The default application mimics a mouse event or keyboard event using the hardware driver to communicate with the GUI. This is selected when **SendWindowMessages** and **SimulateType** are disabled by default, as shown in *Figure 10.51*. In the case of this event, the robot exactly mimics human actions, such as moving the cursor and clicking on a UI element. The UI elements need to be visible for this event to be successful.

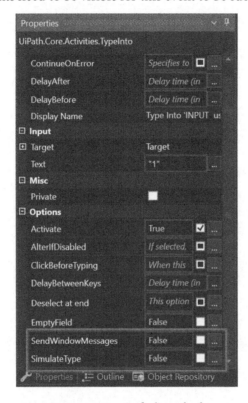

Figure 10.51 – Default method

The key characteristics of the default method are as follows:

- It is 100% compatible with all applications.
- It runs only in the foreground and no background execution is possible.
- The execution speed is generally slow and is only 50% of Simulate Type.
- This supports hotkeys by default.
- It does not auto-empty the input fields by default, which means it does not clear any existing values available in the input field that may include any spaces or previous executed input values.

SendWindowMessages

SendWindowMessages mimics a mouse event or keyboard event by sending a specific message directly to the GUI element. This can be activated when **SendWindowMessages** is selected in the **Options** section, as shown in *Figure 10.52*. The UI element does not need to be visible for this event to be successful as its work in the background.

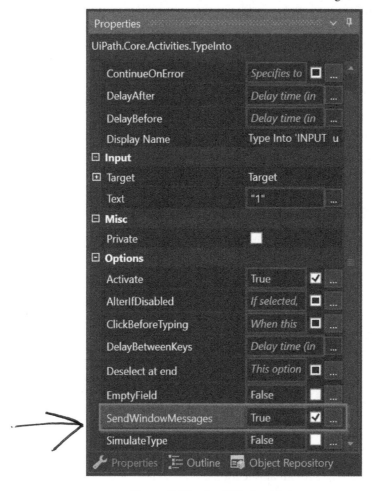

Figure 10.52 – SendWindowMessages

The key characteristics of the **SendWidowsMessages** method are as follows:

- It is 80% compatible with all applications.
- It runs only in background execution.
- The execution speed is slightly better than the default and is around 50% of Simulate Type.

- This supports hotkeys by default.
- It does not auto-empty the input fields by default.

SimulateType

The **SimulateType** method mimics a mouse event or keyboard event by communicating using the API, which provides a set of functions that allows applications to access specific features or data from the target application and is the fastest of all three input methods. This is selected when the **SimulateType** method is selected in the **Options** section, as shown in *Figure 10.53*. It is compatible with both desktop and web applications, and the UI element does not need to be visible for this event to be successful as its works in the background.

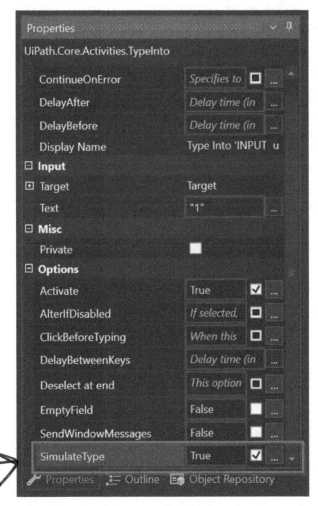

Figure 10.53 – SimulateType

The key characteristics of the SimulateType method are as follows:

- It is 99% compatible with web applications and 60% compatible with desktop applications.

- It runs in both foreground and background execution.

- The execution speed is the fastest of all three types of input actions.

- It does not support hotkeys by default.

- It auto-empties the input fields by default.

In this section, we have explored the different input methods and have seen how to use them in practical situations. In the next section, we will learn about output data extraction using **output methods**.

Output actions and methods

Automation requires certain screen scraping methods and scrape options to be configured to extract values from GUI elements, PDFs, or documents. There are three types of output methods, which we will discuss here.

FullText

FullText is the default output method and is the most frequently used. You need to follow the next steps to work with the **FullText** method:

1. Click on **Screen Scraping** from the **Design** panel, as shown in *Figure 10.54*, which gives you a cursor to select the **Target** element:

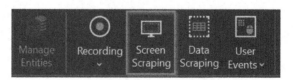

Figure 10.54 – Screen Scraping

2. Click on the element to be extracted, which will open **Screen Scraper Wizard**, and then complete the following:

    I.   Select **FullText** (**1**) for Scraping Method.

    II.   Check **Ignore Hidden** (**2**) under **Scrape Options** to ignore any hidden texts.

    III.   Click on the **Refresh** (**3**) button if there's any change in **Scrape Options**.

    IV.   Verify the output in **Scrape Result Preview** (**4**).

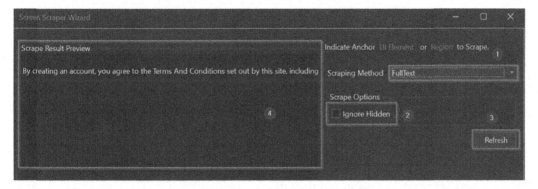

Figure 10.55 – Screen Scraping Wizard

The characteristics of the **FullText** scraping method are as follows:

- The fastest execution of all scraping methods.
- The accuracy of the method is 100%.
- It supports background execution.
- It does not extract text position.
- It can extract hidden text.
- It does not extract output from Citrix.

Native

The Native method is capable of extracting data from applications that are compatible with the **graphics device interface (GDI)** and **Microsoft API,** which are used for identifying graphical objects.

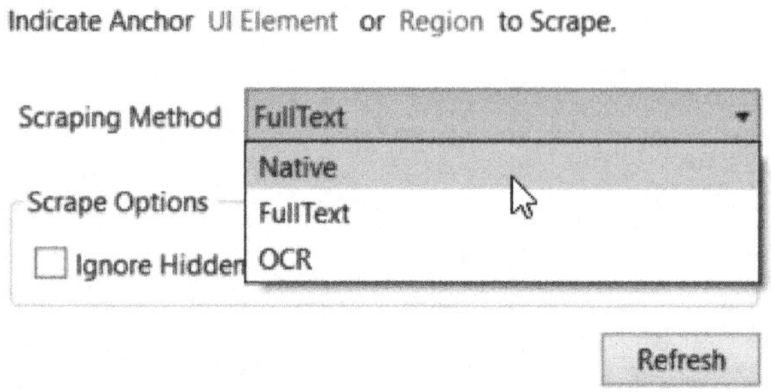

Indicate Anchor UI Element or Region to Scrape.

Scraping Method   FullText   ▾

Native

Scrape Options   FullText

☐ Ignore Hidden   OCR

Refresh

Figure 10.56 – Screen Scraping Wizard – Native

The characteristics of the Native scraping method are as follows:

- It has the fastest execution and the rate of speed is 80% of FullText.

- The accuracy of the method is 100%.

- It does not support background execution.

- It can extract text position.

- It cannot extract hidden text.

- It does not extract output from Citrix.

OCR

If the other two methods do not provide the desired results, then it is advisable to go for **OCR.** That extracts data from scanned documents or images and converts the inputs into machine-readable text. It is not 100% accurate and works with different types of applications. By default, OCR uses the **Google Tesseract** and **Microsoft Modi OCR** engines.

Figure 10.57 – Screen Scraping Wizard – OCR

The characteristics of the Native scraping method are as follows:

- It is the slowest of all three output methods and a rate of speed of 30% of FullText.
- The accuracy of the method is 98%.
- It does not support background execution.
- It can extract text position.
- It cannot extract hidden text.
- It can extract test outputs from Citrix.

In this section, we have explored the different output methods and have seen the applications of each method to use in extracting outputs from various applications.

Summary

We have explored everything about UI Automation interaction in this chapter: analyzed how to deal with different UI Automation activities, the different types of recording, and different types of input and output methods. We have explored more about activities and have performed a few projects to scrape data from web applications and desktop applications. We have also introduced some advanced UI Automation concepts, such as image and computer vision recording.

In the next chapter, you will be working with **PDF automation**, where you can implement the concept of UI interaction to retrieve data from PDFs using **Get Full Text** as well as **OCR**. You will be also implementing most of the activities, input, and output methods to deal with PDF data.

11
Automating PDF Data Extraction

In previous chapters, we discussed different interaction methods that you can use to interact with multiple applications. In addition, we discussed how PDF files play a significant role in our day-to-day operations. PDF files are one of the most used document types across organizations/individuals to share information. The information shared in PDF files could include invoices, purchase orders, letters, financial information, legal documents, and more. Therefore, it is essential that you gain an understanding of how you can use UiPath to extract data from PDF files to perform manual actions automatically.

This chapter focuses on learning how to automate PDF files using UiPath and what activities are available to perform a successful PDF automation.

This chapter consists of the following sections:

- Creating robots that read PDF text
- Extracting text from a PDF using the Extract PDF Text and Extract PDF with OCR activities
- Extracting PDF text using Screen Scraping
- Extracting single dynamic values from PDF files
- Extracting individual values using the Anchor Base activity

At the end of this chapter, you will have a clear understanding of the most common methods used to perform PDF automation.

Technical requirements

Before starting with this chapter, please ensure UiPath Studio and the robot have been installed.

This chapter requires a general idea of how to use Studio to create variables and simple workflows. In addition, a general idea of how to work with UI selectors (as explained in *Chapter 10, Exploring User Interfaces and User/Robot Interactions*) will help you to understand some of the concepts presented in this chapter. Further, you must have Adobe Reader installed on your machine.

Creating robots that read PDF files

Based on our previous experience in creating automation solutions, we know that the UiPath solution, by default, has the following dependencies:

- `UiPath.Excel.Activities`
- `UiPath.System.Activities`
- `UiPath.UIAutomation.Activities`
- `UiPath.Mail.Activities`

However, the default activities do not contain specialized activities for PDF automation. Therefore, we need to add a new dependency to the automation project that requires PDF interaction. Let's go through the following steps to create a project that contains PDF automation activities:

1. Open UiPath Studio and create a new project by providing the **Project Name** and **Path** details.

2. Once the project has been opened, click on the **Manage Packages** button from the top-level ribbon of the **Design** tab. This will open the **Manage Packages** window, as follows:

Figure 11.1 – The Manage Packages option

3. Select the **All Packages** option in the **Manage Packages** window and search for **UiPath.PDF.Activities** using the **Search** option.

4. Select **UiPath.PDF.Activities** from the package list panel. Then, click on the **Install** button to install the package for your solution:

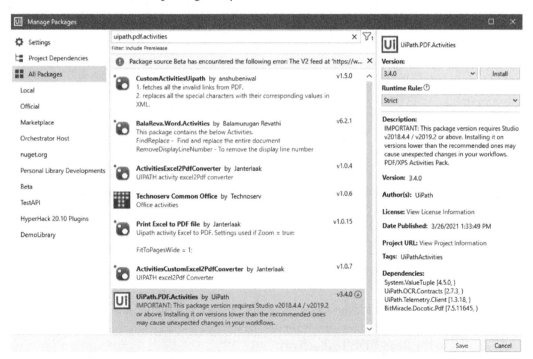

Figure 11.2 – Installing UiPath.PDF.Activities

5. Click on the **Save** button to complete the installation process and close the **Manage Packages** window.

6. Click on the **Activities** panel and navigate to **App Integration** and **PDF** to locate all of the activities related to PDF interaction.

Now we are ready to build our first PDF automation. However, first, we need to understand the usage of each activity:

- **Export PDF Page As Image**: This option enables a user to export a specified page of a PDF file as an image file. This feature can be used whenever a user needs to export specified pages from a large PDF file into multiple files for later usage.

- **Extract Images From PDF**: This option enables a user to extract all of the images of a PDF file and save them in a specified folder for later use.

- **Extract PDF Page Range**: This option enables a user to extract specified pages or a range of pages into another PDF file. Using this activity to only extract the required pages can reduce any unnecessary processing times in the downstream process actions. A user can provide the page range or individual page numbers separated by a comma, as shown in the following example: `"1, 2, 10, 15-20"`.

- **Get PDF Page Count**: This option returns the number of pages that are available in a specified PDF file.

- **Join PDF Files**: This option enables a user to merge two specified PDF files into one PDF file.

- **Manage PDF Password**: This option enables a user to password protect or unprotect a PDF file.

- **Read PDF Text**: This option reads all of the text from a specified PDF file and stores the extracted text inside a string variable. This activity can only read text from computer-generated PDF files. Note that the images or scanned documents of the PDF file are not extracted through this activity.

- **Read PDF with OCR**: This option enables users to use any OCR engine to extract and read a PDF file text. This activity enables the user to extract text from a PDF file that contains scanned documents.

- **Read XPS Text**: In addition to the PDF files, the PDF activities also enable a user to read text from XPS files and store the data inside a string variable. This activity is similar to the **Read PDF Text** activity.

- **Read XPS With OCR**: This option enables a user to read all the characters of an XPS file using an OCR engine. This activity is similar to the **Read PDF with OCR** activity.

Now that you have an initial idea of the activities available in the PDF package, we will see how we can use some of these activities. In the next section, we will focus on using some of the activities that have been discussed to generate some output.

Extracting text from a PDF using the Extract PDF Text and Extract PDF with OCR activities

Data extraction from PDF files can be done in columns of text or on individual elements. First, we will look at how we can extract all of the data from a page. Using the **Read PDF Text** and **Read PDF with OCR** activities enables a user to read large text files. A page of a PDF file might contain computer-generated text and also text in image format. Once the file is open in Adobe Reader, you can easily highlight the computer-generated text individually, whereas the text in image format gets highlighted as a section. Find a PDF file that contains such text and try to use it for our assignment. Let's try to build a simple workflow with the previously mentioned activities by going through the following steps:

1. Open the UiPath Studio solution that you created in the previous section.

2. Open the `Main.xaml` workflow file to start editing the workflow.

3. Drag and drop the **Read PDF Text** activity from the **Activities** panel by searching for it.

4. Select the activity to view the properties of the activity.

5. Provide the full file path for the **FileName** property of the activity.

6. Create a string variable in the **Output Text** property to hold the extracted text by pressing *Ctrl + K*.

7. By default, the **Range** property is set to `All`. The default value of `All` means that it extracts text from all pages of the document. However, if you only want to extract data from a specific page or a range of pages, you can define that using this property. If you are going to provide a particular page, you can enter the page number. If it is a range of pages, you can provide the starting page and the ending page separated by a `"-"`, for example, `12, 15, 20-24`. For our scenario, we will use the default value.

8. The **Preserve Formatting** property of the activity enables a user to preserve the format of the text in the PDF file while extracting. For example, if the document contains text in two columns, as shown in *Figure 11.3*, the option enables you to extract text as is. Set the property of the activity to `True`:

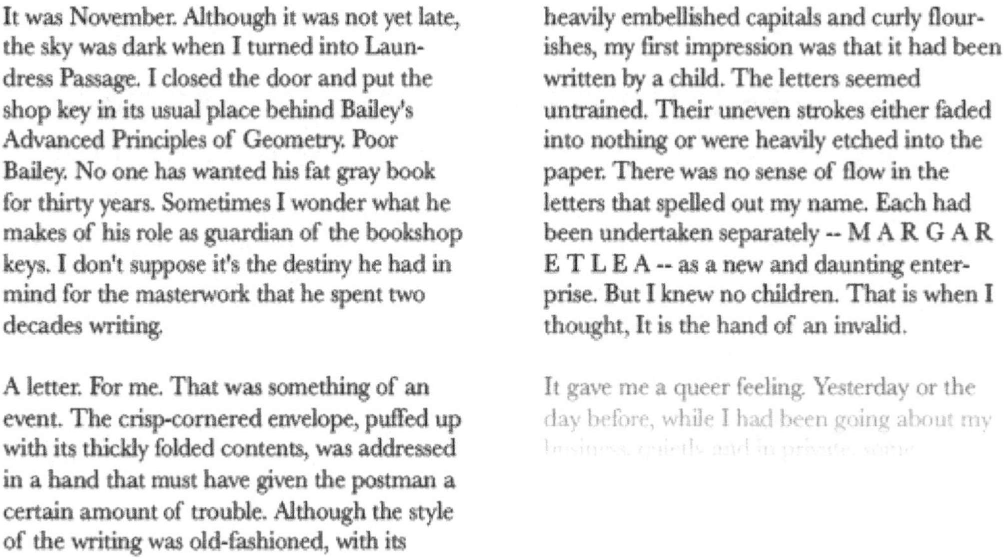

It was November. Although it was not yet late, the sky was dark when I turned into Laundress Passage. I closed the door and put the shop key in its usual place behind Bailey's Advanced Principles of Geometry. Poor Bailey. No one has wanted his fat gray book for thirty years. Sometimes I wonder what he makes of his role as guardian of the bookshop keys. I don't suppose it's the destiny he had in mind for the masterwork that he spent two decades writing.

A letter. For me. That was something of an event. The crisp-cornered envelope, puffed up with its thickly folded contents, was addressed in a hand that must have given the postman a certain amount of trouble. Although the style of the writing was old-fashioned, with its

heavily embellished capitals and curly flourishes, my first impression was that it had been written by a child. The letters seemed untrained. Their uneven strokes either faded into nothing or were heavily etched into the paper. There was no sense of flow in the letters that spelled out my name. Each had been undertaken separately -- M A R G A R E T L E A -- as a new and daunting enterprise. But I knew no children. That is when I thought, It is the hand of an invalid.

It gave me a queer feeling. Yesterday or the day before, while I had been going about my business, quietly and in private, some

Figure 11.3 – A sample PDF file with two columns of text to preserve the format

9. Drag and drop a **Write Text File** activity.

10. Configure the **Write Text File** activity by providing the previously created string variable into the **Text** property.

11. Configure the **Write Text File** activity by providing the output file path for the new text file in the **Write to Filename** property.

12. Once the configuration is complete, your workflow should look similar to the following screenshot:

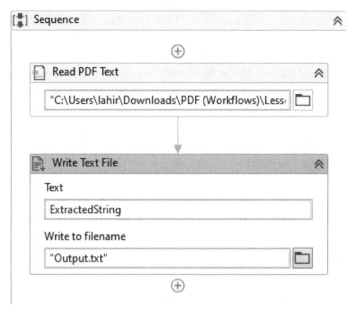

Figure 11.4 – Reading PDF files using Read PDF Text

13. Run the workflow and examine the output of the extracted data in the text file. The sample PDF file we used for this exercise and the result of the workflow are shown in the following screenshot:

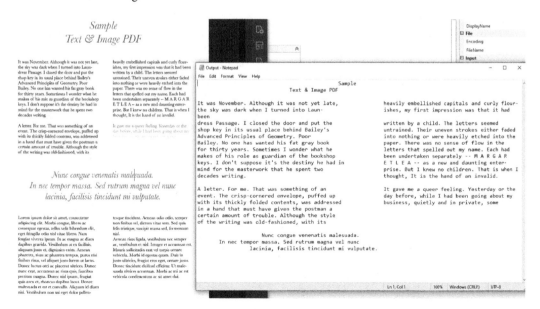

Figure 11.5 – The output of Read PDF Text

Look closely at the output and the text in the PDF file. You will notice that the **Read PDF Text** activity did not extract the text in the two columns below the center-aligned statement. The reason is that the text below the center-aligned text is an image. As a result, we need to use the **Read PDF with OCR** activity to extract the text in an image. To change the workflow to capture the missing text, follow these steps:

1. Delete the **Read PDF Text** activity.

2. Search for the **Read PDF with OCR** activity and place it at the top where the **Read PDF Text** activity was before.

3. When examining the properties of the activity, you should see properties that are similar to what you saw in the **Read PDF Text** activity. Change the **FileName** property with the file path as you did for the **Read PDF Text** activity.

4. By default, the **Range** property is set. For now, we will not change it and simply use the same value.

5. Change the output **Text** property by providing the string variable that you created earlier. The configuration should look similar to *Figure 11.6*:

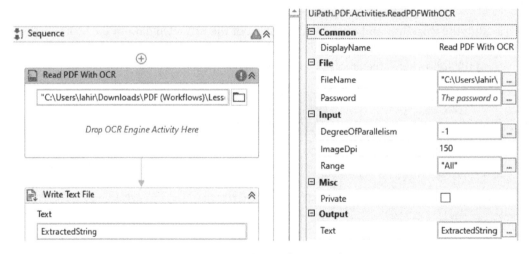

Figure 11.6 – Configuring the Read PDF With OCR activity

6. You can also see that there are a few additional properties specific to OCR. You
    need to drag and drop an OCR engine to the **Read PDF with OCR** activity for
    this activity to work. Search for OCR in the **Activities** panel to find all of the OCR
    engines that are available. Your search in the **Activities** panel should look similar to
    Figure 11.7:

Figure 11.7 – Searching for available OCR engines in the Activities panel

7. We have multiple OCR engines at our disposal. Use the **Microsoft OCR** activity.
    Drag and drop the **Microsoft OCR** activity into the **Read PDF With OCR** activity
    to complete the configuration.

8. Delete the output text file and run the workflow to generate the new output based
    on the OCR configuration.

9. Open the output text file and compare the generated result. You will notice that the data extract does not have the format preserved. All of the text appears in raw form, as shown in the following screenshot. However, it was able to extract all of the text from the image portion of the page:

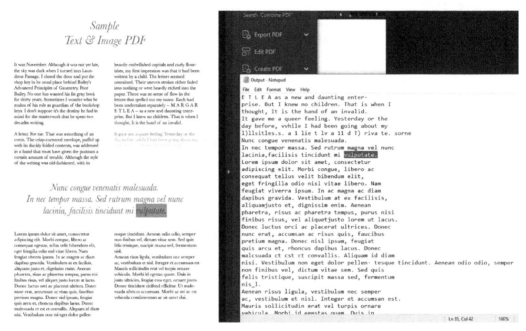

Figure 11.8 – Sample data extract using the Read PDF With OCR activity

The lesson to learn from this example is that using OCR does not provide us with the format. In addition, the accuracy of the text extracted using OCR engines can depend on the quality of the image in the PDF file. You could try to change the `ImageDPI` property to different values to determine which configuration provides you with the highest level of accuracy.

As you now know, two basic activities enable us to extract text from PDF files. You can practice the XPF-specific activities on your own in an XPF file. Additionally, explore the remaining activities to see how you can obtain the page count and extract a range of pages to familiarize yourself with the activities. Now that you have a basic understanding of PDF interaction, we will move on to the next section, which explains how we can use the Screen Scraping wizard to extract text from PDF files.

Extracting PDF text using Screen Scraping

Screen Scraping in UiPath offers the capability to extract text from a specific application or UI element. The same Screen Scraping wizard that we used in *Chapter 10*, *Exploring User Interfaces and User/Robot Interactions*, can extract data from PDF files. Now that you have a general understanding of Screen Scraping, let's try to build a new workflow to extract text from the same PDF file using Screen Scraping:

1. Open the PDF document that we need to screen scrape.
2. Open the same UiPath solution you were working on in the previous section of the chapter.
3. Create a new **Sequence** workflow file.
4. Click on the **Design** tab in the top-level ribbon.
5. Locate the **Screen Scraping** option and click it to open **Screen Scraping Wizard**. Clicking on it will automatically activate the UI element detection, and you will be able to highlight elements as you move the mouse pointer.

6. Highlight the area of the entire page and *left-click* using your mouse. The wizard detects the area, extracts the given region's data, and shows you in the Screen Scraping Wizard screen:

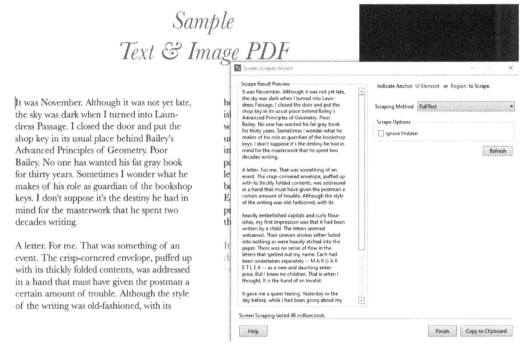

Figure 11.9 – A sample data extract using Screen Scraping Wizard

As shown in *Figure 11.9*, you can see that the **FullText** method was used to scrape the data. The use of the **FullText** method also preserves the format to some extent. Try changing the scraping method and refreshing the result to see the different outputs you receive.

7. Once you are ready to proceed, set the scraping method back to **FullText** and click on the **Finish** button to complete the wizard. UiPath Studio will automatically create a couple of activities in the workflow file based on your configuration. Once the wizard completes, you should see the workflow, as shown in *Figure 11.10*. Additionally, you should see a new variable automatically created in the **Variables** panel to hold the screen scraping output:

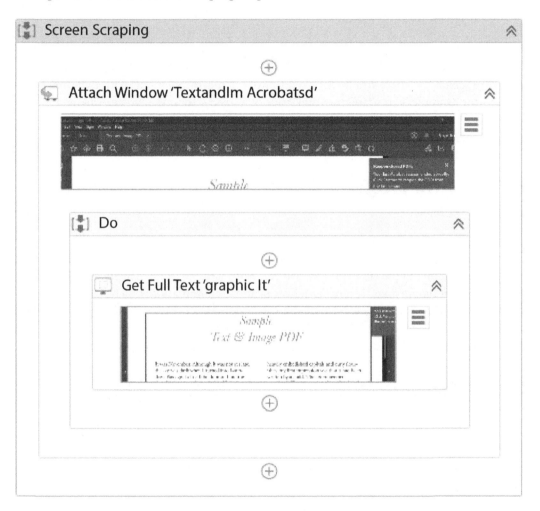

Figure 11.10 – A snippet of the automatically created workflow through Screen Scraping

8. Add a **Write Text File** activity and configure it, as you did earlier, to get the output of the screen scraping activity to a text file.

9. Rerun the workflow to examine the output. You should be able to see the paragraphs separated by white space. However, the last part of the document is not extracted, as it is an image.

10. Try changing the screen scraping method to Native or OCR and see how the output looks in each configuration.

By now, we have tried different methods of extracting text from PDF files. However, all of the approaches we used extracted text from the entire page or a specified UI element. There are scenarios where you might need to extract specific elements with dynamic values—for example, extracting the total price of a fixed structure invoice. The next section of the chapter focuses on how to extract dynamic values from the specific UI elements of a document.

Extracting single dynamic values from PDF files

Extracting single dynamic values requires the use of UI automation activities. However, this approach only supports fixed structure documents as the elements are identified based on selectors. Applying the concepts you learned from *Chapter 10*, *Exploring User Interfaces and User/Robot Interactions*, regarding selectors and UI automation, let's build a simple workflow to extract a specific value from an invoice document. We will be using a sample invoice PDF file that looks similar to *Figure 11.11*. Let's imagine a scenario where we get multiple similar PDF files of the same structure. We will continue to build our workflow:

ThisWebHost LTD
337 Bath Road
Slough
Berkshire
SL1 5P
United Kingdom

Invoice #38645

Invoice Date: 21st Sep 2016

Due Date: 28th Sep 2016

Invoiced To
Some Company LTD - Robotic Automations
3216 Maple Court, California, MO 63101 USA

Description	Total
Starter Shared Hosting - (28/09/2016 - 27/10/2016)	$30.00 USD
Hosting Location: United Kingdom (UK)	
Late Fee (Added 02/10/2016)	$10.00 USD
Sub Total	$40.00 USD
Credit	$0.00 USD
Grand Total	$40.00 USD

Transactions

Transaction Date	Gateway	Transaction ID	Amount
4th Oct 2016	Wire Transfer	44M54677JH991194L	$40.00 USD
		Balance	$0.00 USD

PDF Generated on 4th Oct 2016

Figure 11.11 – A sample invoice document for single value extraction

As we can see in *Figure 11.11*, the document is a well-structured native PDF file. Now it's time to focus on how we can extract the invoice number from this document:

1. Open the same UiPath solution that we created in the previous section.

2. Create a new **Sequence workflow** file.

3. Open the document in **Adobe Reader**, as we need to use UI automation to capture the invoice number from the document.

4. Use an **Assign** activity and configure the **Value** section of the activity with the
    `Directory.GetFiles("FolderPath")` command to retrieve all the PDF
    files in the specified folder. Use the command and replace the folder path with
    your folder path.

5. Create a **String Array** variable with the name of `FileList`, and add it to the **To**
    section of the **Assign** activity. This configuration will populate the string array with
    all the file paths of the files available in the specified directory.

6. Now, use a **For Each** activity to loop through each file. Drag and drop a **For Each**
    activity and configure the **Type Argument** setting of the activity to `String`.

7. Add the **String array** variable in the **Value** property of the **For Each** activity. Up to
    this point, the configuration should look similar to *Figure 11.12*:

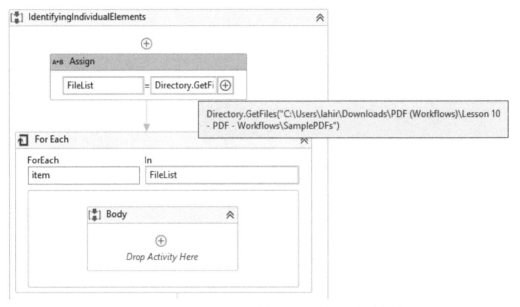

Figure 11.12 – Building a workflow to read individual fields

8. As we learned in the UI automation chapter, we need to use the **Get Text** activity to
    retrieve the data of a UI element. Search for the **Get Text** activity from the **Activity
    panel** and add it to the new workflow file.

9. Make sure that **Adobe Reader** is the second active window of your computer. Click on the **Indicate Element on Screen** option in the **Get Text** activity to enable UI identification mode. Once the identification mode is active, you will be able to highlight elements just by hovering the cursor on top of those elements of the PDF file.

10. Hover the cursor over the **Invoice Number** section of the document and let it highlight the region. Click on it to indicate the area to capture. This action configures the **Get Text** activity to capture data from that UI element of the document.

11. Select the **Get Text** activity, and examine the **Selector** property to make it dynamic to support multiple documents. Click on the button with three dots next to the **Selector** property to open the **Selector Editor** screen.

12. Click on the **Open in UI Explorer** option to open the selector in the **UI Explorer** window for better visibility. The UI Explorer window will look similar to *Figure 11.13*:

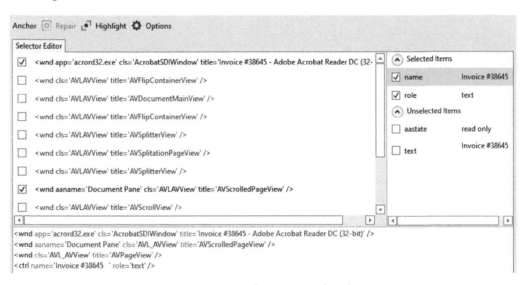

Figure 11.13 – Opening UI Explorer to view the selector properties

13. While examining the selector, you should see that the `title` tag explicitly focuses on the specific invoice document that you opened. In addition to this, the `name` tag looks for a specific invoice number. Locate the name tag within the selected items section and uncheck it. This action will remove the name tag from the selector so that the selector can handle any open document. Once the change has been applied, the selector will look similar to *Figure 11.14*:

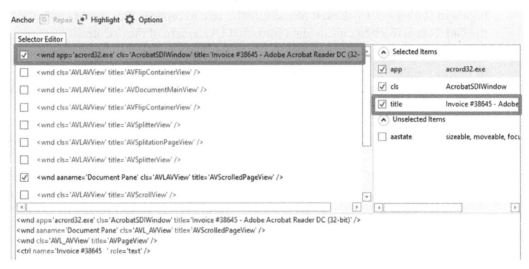

Figure 11.14 – Opening UI Explorer to view the selector properties

14. The next change is to make the name tag dynamic to capture any invoice number in documents that have the same layout and structure. We can introduce a wildcard character instead of the invoice number in the name tag. The name tag should be configured as follows: `name = 'invoice *'`.

Once the change has been applied, the full selector will look similar to *Figure 11.15*:

```
<wnd app='acrord32.exe' cls='AcrobatSDIWindow' />
<wnd aaname='Document Pane' cls='AVL_AVView' title='AVScrolledPageView' />
<wnd cls='AVL_AVView' title='AVPageView' />
<ctrl name='Invoice *' role='text' />
```

Figure 11.15 – The updated invoice number selector

15. Click on the **Validate** button and enable the **Highlight** option. The selector should highlight the invoice number field in the document and change the **Validate** button to green.

16. Click on the **Save** button to save and close the **UI Explorer** window.

17. Configure the **Output Value** of the **Get Text** activity by creating and providing a new string variable.

18. Add a **Write Line** activity below the **Get Text** activity and configure it to print the value in the string variable that you created.

19. Run the process to see whether the robot can extract the invoice number. You should be able to see the extracted number in the **Output** panel.

Use the same concept and extract other document values to become more familiar with document data extraction. Understanding the selectors and best practices for using selectors is very important. Using the knowledge gained in *Chapter 10, Exploring User Interfaces and User/Robot Interactions*, try finding the best selectors to capture the values. As you explore, you might realize that you cannot build a reliable selector to extract some values. In the next section, we will describe what approach you can take in scenarios where you cannot build a reliable selector to extract values from the document.

Extracting individual values using the Anchor Base activity

We were able to build a reliable selector for the document because the word "invoice" was always there in the document. However, if you look at the values, such as **Subtotal**, **Credit**, and **Grand total**, they only contain a number that could eventually change. The selector extracted for the **Subtotal** field is shown in *Figure 11.16*:

```
<wnd app='acrord32.exe' cls='AcrobatSDIWindow' title='Invoice #38645 - Adobe Acrobat Reader DC (32-bit)' />
<wnd aaname='Document Pane' cls='AVL_AVView' title='AVScrolledPageView' />
<wnd cls='AVL_AVView' title='AVPageView' />
<ctrl name='$40.00 USD  ' role='text' />
```

Figure 11.16 – The selector for the SubTotal field

As you can see in the sample selector, it does not contain a field that we can rely on to locate the correct field. We have an easy workaround to address such scenarios. We can use an **Anchor Base** activity to find an anchor (that is, an additional field that we can rely on) to extract the respective value. The **Anchor Base** activity consists of two sections; the **Anchor** section and the **Value** section:

- The **Anchor** section is dedicated to looking for a suitable UI element with a reliable selector next to the value that needs to be extracted. The **Anchor** section of the **Anchor Base** activity is configured with the **Find Element** activity to find the anchor element.

- The **Value** section of the **Anchor Base** activity is configured with the interaction that needs to be performed with the field that you need to read or write.

Now, we will try to update the same workflow by introducing an **Anchor Base** activity to extract the **Credit Total** value. Since we are trying to read a value, we can use the **Get Text** activity in the **Value** section of the **Anchor Base** activity. We will use the word `Credit Total` as a reliable anchor, as the text is static but the value is not.

To do this, perform the following steps:

1. Search for the **Anchor Base** activity from the **Activity** panel and place it below the **Write Line** activity.

2. Search for the **Find Element** activity and place it in the **Anchor** section of the **Anchor Base** activity.

3. Click on the **Indicate on Screen** option of the **Find Element** activity and indicate the word `Credit Total` in the document.

4. As you already know, the selector is pointing to a specific document once we indicate the element. Therefore, as we did in the previous section, we need to edit the title tag of the selector to make it dynamic. Navigate to **UI Explorer** and introduce the wildcard character, `"*"`, for the fluctuating parts of the title tag of the selector and save the changes. The modified selector looks similar to *Figure 11.17*:

```
<wnd app='acrord32.exe' cls='AcrobatSDIWindow' title='*|- Adobe Acrobat Reader DC (32-bit)' />
<wnd aaname='Document Pane' cls='AVL_AVView' title='AVScrolledPageView' />
<wnd cls='AVL_AVView' title='AVPageView' />
<ctrl name='Credit  ' role='text' />
```

Figure 11.17 – The dynamic selector for the Credit Total label

5. Now, use a **Get Text** activity and place it in the **Value** section (the right-hand side section) of the **Anchor Base** activity.

6. Configure the **Get Text** activity by indicating the **Value** portion of the **Credit Total** label in the document through the **Indicate on Screen** option.

7. Complete the configuration of the **Get Text** activity by providing a string variable for the **Output Value** property.

8. We have an additional property in the **Anchor Base** activity to define, where the anchored element is, with respect to the UI element that we need to get the value from. In our scenario, the `total Credit` label is positioned on the left-hand side of the total credit value. As a result, you need to change the **Anchor Position** property of the **Anchor Base** activity to **Left**.

9. Add another **Write Line** activity and print the **CreditTotal** value in the variable. The completed process workflow should look similar to *Figure 11.18*:

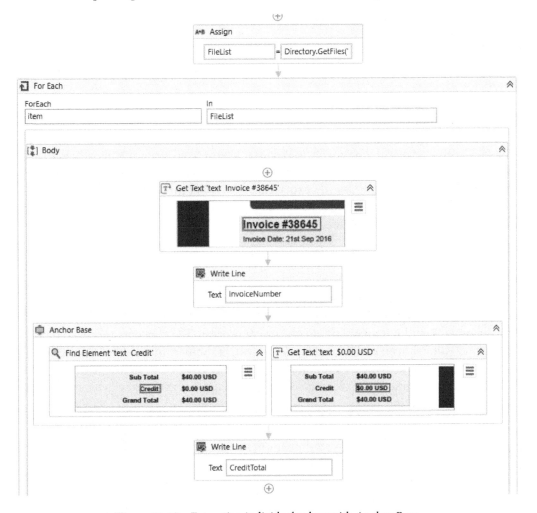

Figure 11.18 – Extracting individual values with Anchor Base

10. Run the process and examine the output. The sample output is shown in *Figure 11.19*:

Figure 11.19 – The sample output of individual value extraction

By now, you will be familiar with the basic actions that you can perform with PDF files to extract the data. There are more advanced functions that you can apply to documents to generate different types of documents that do not have a fixed structure. However, that is not within the scope of this chapter. Document processing is an exciting area in which you can use multiple technologies, as you experienced by going through the sections of this chapter. We highly recommend that you apply the knowledge you have gained so far and practice with different types of documents further.

Summary

This chapter introduced you to the topic of processing PDF files using UiPath. PDF files are a prevalent type of file that we interact with every day. Today, all organizations deal with documents, and it is a very time-consuming process. The concepts we covered in this chapter will help you easily extract graphs, text, and other information from PDF files using a simple set of activities. Additionally, the chapter covered the activities involved in PDF automation, extracting text/images from pages, and extracting key fields from a PDF file using UI automation.

The concepts you learned in this chapter will be very helpful in future projects. It is essential to practice how to best interact with PDF files and what activities to use based on different scenarios. Similar to PDF processing, emails also play a significant role in our daily activities. We read and send emails to communicate with other parties. UiPath also supports the automation of emails to improve the work-life of employees. In the next chapter, we will address how you can automate the actions you perform in emails. Email automation is a part of almost all the automation solutions that we build in the present day. Therefore, it is essential to learn how to interact with emails even though the process you automate does not have email processing activities.

12
Exploring UiPath Email Automation

Email is one of the most popular forms of digital communication and is widely used by individuals and organizations. When it comes to manual and repetitive tasks in our daily life, activities such as reading emails, performing business processes based on email inputs, and responding to emails consume most of our time. UiPath offers various email ways to read emails, filter emails, and respond to emails to help us automate repeated business processes.

As part of this chapter, you will become familiar with **email automation**, the different email automation types, and the different activities that support email automation. You will learn how to send and receive emails, respond to emails, attach and download document attachments, and use defined message templates for emails.

This chapter consists of the following sections:

- Exploring email activities
- Extracting email contents using Receive Messages
- Automating sending email messages
- Filtering and downloading attachments from an email

Technical requirements

This chapter requires you to have UiPath Studio and Robot installed, along with a good understanding of variables, data types, control flows, data manipulation, Excel and data tables, and selectors. You can refer to *Chapters 5 to 10* to gather all the required knowledge.

Exploring email activities

Email activities packages are used to automate email-related tasks that are performed using protocols such as IMAP, POP3, and SMTP, which we will explore in the upcoming sections. To identify the different email activities available, you need to install the UiPath Mail Activities package in UiPath Studio. In this section, we will explore how to install the UiPath.Mail.Activities package and then investigate different email activities using step-by-step instructions.

Let's get started:

1. **Create a new project**

    Create a new email project by clicking on **Process** in the **New Project** section of the UiPath home page view. This will open the **New Blank Process** window. Fill in the details for **Name (1)** and **Description (2)**, and click the **Create** button (**3**), as shown in *Figure 12.1*:

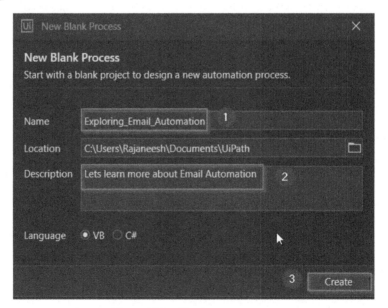

Figure 12.1 – Create new process

2. **Verify mail activities**

The **UiPath.Mail.Activities** option is available by default in the **Dependencies** branch of the project while creating the process, as shown in *Figure 12.2*:

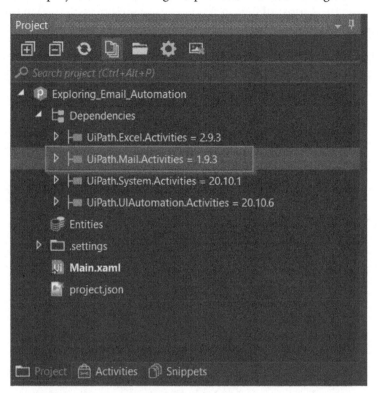

Figure 12.2 – Email activities dependencies

However, if it has been uninstalled or deleted by mistake, you may need to manually install the email dependencies from the packages.

3. **Install UiPath.Mail.Activities**

    Ensure that the **UiPath.Mail.Activities** option is not available in the **Dependencies**
    section, as shown in *Figure 12.3*. You can uninstall by clicking the dependency
    and clicking the **Uninstall** button if it is already present, as shown in the
    following screenshot:

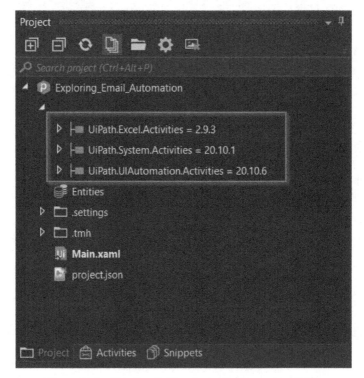

Figure 12.3 – Email activities dependencies not available

Now, click **Manage Packages** in the **Design** tab and perform the following steps, as
shown in *Figure 12.4*:

I.   Type UiPath.Mail.Activities in the **Search** textbox (**1**).

II.   Click on the **Official** (**2**) option on the left. This will populate the required
      package (**3**).

III. Click on the package (**3**), and click **Install** (**4**).

IV.   Click the **Save** button at the bottom of the screen to install the package:

Figure 12.4 – Installing email dependencies

4.   **Verify the installed package**

Expand the **Dependencies** section in **Project** to verify the UiPath.Mail.
Activities installed dependency, as shown in *Figure 12.5*:

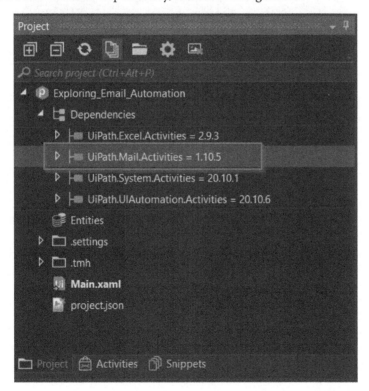

Figure 12.5 – Verifying installed dependencies

5. **Verify activities**

    Click the **Activities** (**1**) tab and type `mail` (**2**) in the **Search** field to verify the mail activities. You will see six different categories, **Exchange**, **IBM Notes**, **IMAP**, **Outlook**, **POP3**, and **SMTP**, along with **Create HTML Content**, **Save Attachments**, and **Save Mail Message**, as shown in (**3**) in *Figure 12.6*:

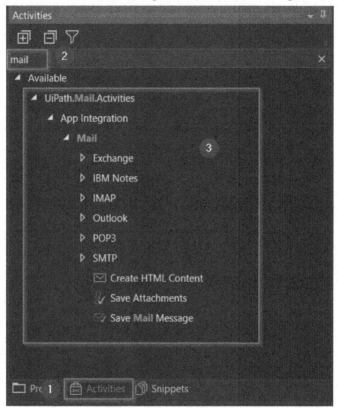

Figure 12.6 – Verifying installed activities

These activities are used for different automation purposes, which we will learn about in the upcoming sections. Please note that these activities will not be displayed without installing the `UiPath.Mail.Activities` package. Now let's look in to different Mail activities as follows:

I.   **Exchange**

Exchange refers to the Microsoft enterprise email solution and these activities can be used to perform various email operations such as sending emails, receiving emails, moving emails between folders, and deleting emails. The available activities are as shown in *Figure 12.7*:

Figure 12.7 – Exchange

II.   IBM Notes

The **IBM Notes** activities can be used to automate various email tasks in the IBM Notes client for sending emails, receiving emails, moving emails between folders, and deleting emails. The available activities are as shown in *Figure 12.8*:

Figure 12.8 – IBM Notes

III.   IMAP

The **Internet Message Access Protocol (IMAP)** is only used for receiving emails. There are also additional features to mark the email as **Read** and move emails within folders. The available activities are as shown in *Figure 12.9*:

Figure 12.9 – IMAP

IV.   **Outlook**

Outlook activities are used to automate email tasks on already configured Outlook accounts. They can perform various automation tasks, including sending emails, receiving emails, moving emails between folders, and deleting emails. As a prerequisite, the Microsoft Outlook application should be installed on your machine for the activities to function correctly. The available activities are as shown in *Figure 12.10*:

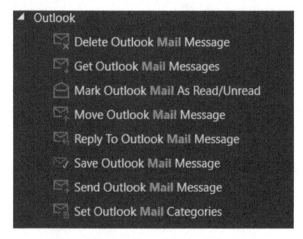

Figure 12.10 – Outlook

V.   **POP3**

The **Post Office Protocol (POP3)** is one of the oldest and less frequently used protocols and is only used for receiving emails. The available activity is as shown in *Figure 12.11*:

Figure 12.11 – POP3

VI.   **SMTP**

The **Simple Mail Transfer Protocol (SMTP)** is one of the most basic protocols and is only used for sending emails. The available activity is shown in *Figure 12.12*:

Figure 12.12 – SMTP

In this section, we have explored how to install the `UiPath.Mail.Activities` package and have verified the installed dependency. We have also seen a high-level introduction of each activity and we will explore all the important email activities in upcoming sections.

Extracting email contents using Receive Messages

In this section, we will learn how to automate receiving emails, where the robot will read the contents of an email in a Google (Gmail) account. We will be using IMAP to achieve this goal. Assume the email address and password are already passed as an argument within the workflow and we consider only the first five unread email messages:

1. **Create a process**

   Create a new process named `Email_Automation` in UiPath Studio. To proceed with this development, you need to send a sample email to the Gmail account.

2. **Send email**

   Send one test email to the Google email that needs to be automated, as shown in *Figure 12.13*:

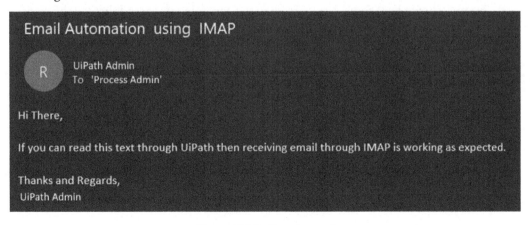

Figure 12.13 – Sample email

3. **Enable IMAP in Gmail settings**

You need to enable IMAP in your Gmail settings, as shown in *Figure 12.14*. To perform this, first, log in to your Gmail account and click the **Settings** icon, then, click the **See All Settings** button. Click on **Forwarding and POP/IMAP** on the **Settings** screen, as shown in *Figure 12.14*:

Figure 12.14 – Settings screen

Click on **Enable IMAP** in the **IMAP access** section, as shown in *Figure 12.15*:

Figure 12.15 – Enabling IMAP

4. **Create an app password in Google**

Next, you need to create an app password to use in UiPath Studio for accessing your Gmail to connect to IMAP. To perform this, create an app password by going to `https://myaccount.google.com/apppasswords`. Click the **GENERATE** button (shown in *Figure 12.16*) and copy the generated password that will be copied inside UiPath activities in the upcoming steps.

Figure 12.16 – Generating app password

5. **Create a workflow to receive email**

I.   Perform the below steps to create a Process workflow for automating receiving emails. Drag the **Get Password** activity inside the workflow as shown in *Figure 12.17*:

Figure 12.17 – Get Password activity

II.   Create the following variables to store the email ID, password, and actual
      emails. Enter the email address to be automated in the **Default** field, as shown
      in *Figure 12.18*:

Name	Variable type	Scope	Default
email	String	Sequence	"processadminhr@gmail.com"
password	String	Sequence	*Enter a VB expression*
Emails	List<MailMessage>	Sequence	*Enter a VB expression*

Figure 12.18 – Variables for the process

III. Click on the **Get Password** activity from *Step I*, enter the password copied
      in Step 4 of the previous section to the **Password (1)** field in **Properties**, and
      store the result in a variable named password (**2**), as shown in *Figure 12.18*:

Figure 12.19 – Get Password properties

IV.   Drag the **Get IMAP Mail Messages** activity to the workflow, as shown in
      Figure 12.19:

Figure 12.20 – Get IMAP Mail Messages activity

V.   Configure the **IMAP** settings properties for accessing emails from Gmail as shown in *Figure 12.21* and the following steps:

i.   In **Mail Folder** (**1**), enter `"Inbox"`.

ii.   In **Port** (**2**), enter `993`.

iii.   In **Server** (**3**), enter `"imap.gmail.com"`.

iv.   In **Email** (**4**), enter the `email` string variable, where you define the email address to be automated in the variables panel, as mentioned in *Step II of 5. Create a workflow to receive email.*

v.   In **Password** (**5**), enter the `password` variable obtained from *Step III of 5. Create a workflow to receive email.*

vi.   Check the **OnlyUnreadMessages** (**6**) checkbox.

vii.   In **Top** (**7**), enter `5`, to read only the top five unread emails.

viii. In **Messages** (**8**), enter the `Emails List<MailMessage>` variable to store all the emails.

Figure 12.21 – Configuring IMAP settings properties

VI. Given that you have read through the top five emails described in the previous steps, now, you can use the mail variable (1) to loop through each of the emails (2) to find the expected email using a **ForEach** activity, as shown in *Figure 12.22*:

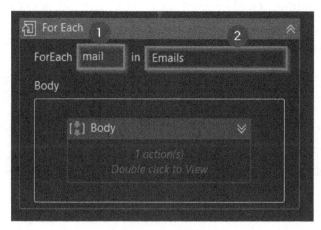

Figure 12.22 – For Each activity

VII. Configure the properties of the **For Each** activities to verify that **TypeArgument** is System.Net.Mail.MailMessage, as shown in *Figure 12.23*:

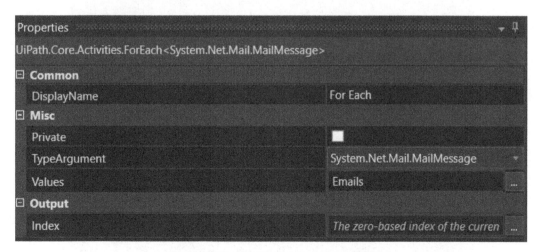

Figure 12.23 – For Each activity properties

VIII. Perform the following steps to filter the emails containing the IMAP subject, as shown in *Figure 12.25*:

i.   Add an `if` activity.

ii. In **Condition** (**1**), enter `mail.Subject.Contains("IMAP")`.

iii. Add an **Assign** activity in the **Then** section, and store the matched email to the **emailBody** (**2**) variable, as shown in *Figure 12.24*:

Figure 12.24 – Value of Assign activity

iv. Output the captured email using the **Write Line** activity (**3**).

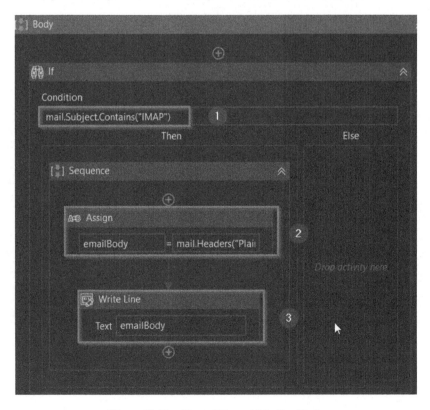

Figure 12.25 – If condition within For Each

V.   Run the project using the **Run** button, or *Ctrl + F5*, to verify the output in the
      Output panel is working as expected. Ensure the email you sent in *Step 2* is
      displayed as the output, as shown in *Figure 12.26*:

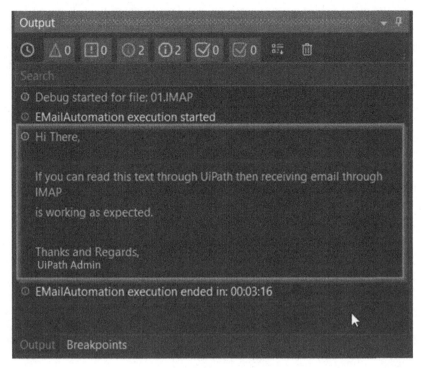

Figure 12.26 – Output panel

In this section, we learned about automating receiving emails from Gmail using IMAP
within UiPath Studio. In addition, we saw how a password can be securely created using
Gmail and passed to UiPath Studio. Finally, we explored many different activities, such
as Get Password and Get IMAP Mail Messages, and learned how to implement them in
automating emails. Now, let's see how to automate sending emails in the next section,
where we will automatically send an email along with attachments using UiPath Studio.

Automating sending email messages

In this section, we will learn about *automating sending emails*, where the robot will read the contents of an email in a Gmail account. We will be using SMTP to achieve this goal. Assume the email address and password are already passed as an argument within the workflow, and we are only focusing on the first five unread email messages, like our example in the previous *Extracting email contents using Receive Messages* section on reading emails. All you need is a Gmail account to send an email with an attachment, and another email configured in Outlook to receive the emails sent by UiPath Robot.

The following provides step-by-step instructions to send an email from UiPath Studio:

1. **Create a process**

   Create a new SMTPEmailMessages process in UiPath Studio.

2. **Configure the Gmail password using Get Password**

3. Add a new activity, **Get Password**, to the workflow, as shown in *Figure 12.27*:

Figure 12.27 – Get Password

Configure the app password created in *Step 4, Create an app password in Google* of the previous section, as shown in *Figure 12.28*:

Figure 12.28 – Get Password properties

4. **Set the input folder with the input files to be processed**

   Keep the input files to be processed in the Input folder. We have two files, Invoice1.pdf and Invoice2.pdf, which need to be attached to emails, as shown in *Figure 12.29*:

Name	Date modified	Type	Size
Invoice1.pdf	20/03/2021 7:54 PM	Adobe Acrobat D...	359 KB
Invoice2.pdf	20/03/2021 7:54 PM	Adobe Acrobat D...	43 KB

   Figure 12.29 – Input folder

5. **Define the input variable**

   Create an array of String variables for invoices to define the input files, as shown in *Figure 12.30*:

Name	Variable type	Scope	Default
invoices	String[]	_02_SMTPEmailMessages	{"Invoice1.pdf","Invoice2.pdf"}

   Figure 12.30 – Input files defined

6. **Process attachments**

   Add the **For Each** activity to the workflow, and use a variable invoice (1) to loop through each invoices (2) to send a separate email for each of the invoices, as shown in *Figure 12.31*:

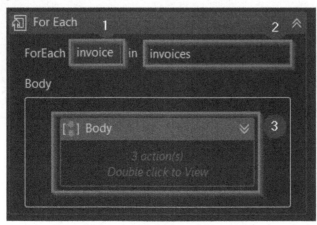

   Figure 12.31 – For Each invoice files

7. **Send the SMTP email activity**

Assign the `filename` (**1**) and full file path using the variable `filefullPath` (**2**) of the file using two **Assign** activities. Next, add the **Send SMPT Mail Message** (**3**) activity, as shown in *Figure 12.32*:

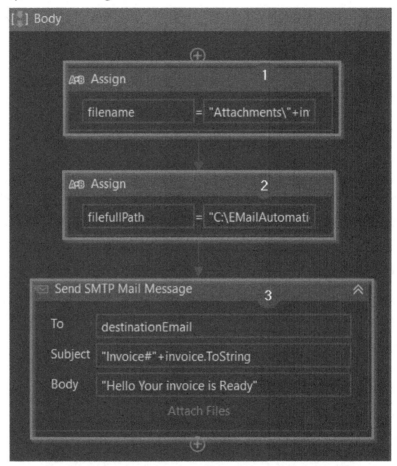

Figure 12.32 – Send SMTP Mail Message within For Each

Ensure the correct variable is assigned to `filename`, as shown in *Figure 12.33*:

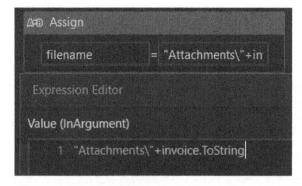

Figure 12.33 – Filename as a String

Ensure the correct variable is assigned to `filefullPath` so that the Robot can access the correct filenames, as shown in *Figure 12.34*:

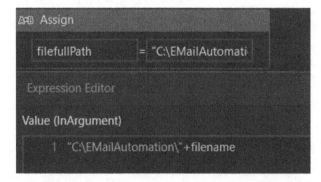

Figure 12.34 – Assign the full path of the input file

8. **Configure the properties of the Send SMTP Mail Message activity**

Configure the **Attachments** filename variable in the **(Collection)** field (**1**), update the **Email** section with the **Subject** and **Body** contents (**2**), update the **Host** details (such as **Port** and **Server**) to send the SMTP email (**3**), pass the email **Logon** details (such as **Email** and **Password**) (**4**), and finally, pass the **Receiver** details variable in the **To** field (**5**), which is the email ID of the receiver, as shown in *Figure 12.35*:

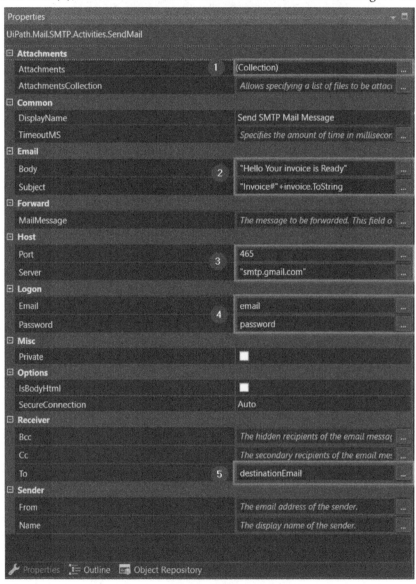

Figure 12.35 – Properties of Send SMTP Mail Message

Ensure the correct variable is assigned to **Attachments** so that the Robot can attach the correct document while sending emails, as shown in *Figure 12.36*:

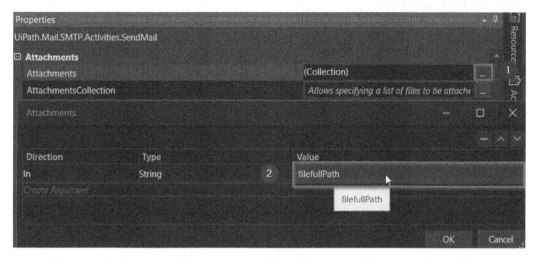

Figure 12.36 – Attachment of Send SMTP Mail Message

9. **Output verification**

Run the project using the **Run** button or *Ctrl + F5* to verify the output. Check the destination email to see if you received the two emails with attachments. Ensure the email you sent in *Step 7* is displayed as the output in your email, as shown in *Figure 12.37*:

Figure 12.37 – Output verification in the destination email

In this section, we have automated sending emails using UiPath Robot and SMTP. We used a Gmail account to send an email with attached documents using the **Attachments** properties, and an Outlook account to receive the email. Finally, we executed the Robot to verify the output. In the next section, we will look at how to automatically process the attachments from an email.

Automating filter and download attachments from an email

In email automation, processing attachments is one of the most essential tasks. In UiPath Studio, we will use the **Get Outlook Message** activities to read the attachments and store them in a destination folder. We are going to use the attachment documents from the output emails generated in the previous section (Step 9 of Automating sending email messages) to process the attachments. For all Outlook activities, the Outlook application needs to be installed on the machine in which the automation is executed. Finally, we will learn about various filtering options, such as email address and subject line.

Use the following step-by-step instructions to download the attachments:

1. **Create a new project**

    Create a new process from the UiPath Studio backstage view.

2. **Get the Outlook mail message**

    In the **Main** file, drag the **Get Outlook Mail Message** activity from the **Activities** panel, as shown in *Figure 12.38*:

Figure 12.38 – Get Outlook Mail Message activity

3. **Configure the Get Outlook Mail Message properties**

   Click the **Get Outlook Mail Message** activity to view the **Properties** panel. In the **Input** section, enter the Outlook account email address in the **Account** field (**1**) and the corresponding **MailFolder** (**2**) from where you will be accessing the email. Now, it is time to filter the expected emails from the **Options** section using the **Filter** field (**3**), where you need to enter the sender's email address. Alternatively, you can use **Subject**, or any other email parameters, to filter the emails. Enable the **OnlyUnreadEmails** option (**4**) and enter the **Top** field as 10 (**5**) to read the top 10 unread emails. Finally, save all the read emails to the emails variable in the **Output** field (**6**), as shown in *Figure 12.39*:

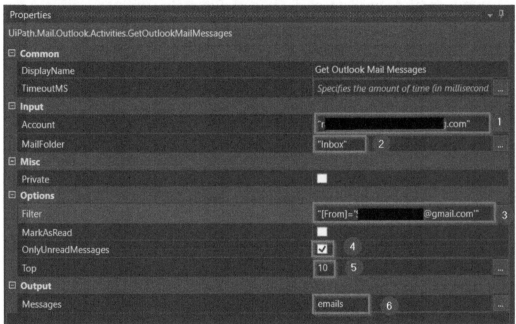

Figure 12.39 – Get Outlook Mail Message properties

4.   **Extract and save the attachments using the Save Attachments activity**

So far, we have read all the filtered emails and saved them into a variable called
`emails`. Now, we will process each of the emails using a **For Each** activity (**1**) and
check for the emails containing the subject line as `Invoice#` in the **Condition**
field (**2**). Extract the invoice number from the subject line using the **Split**
function (**3**) to create an `output` folder to save the attachments. Now, extract the
attachments using the **Save Attachments** activity (**4**), as shown in *Figure 12.40*:

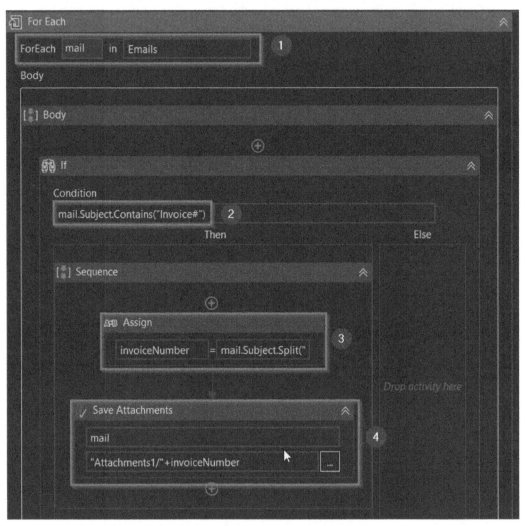

Figure 12.40 – Save Attachments properties

More information on creating an `output` folder to save the attachments is shown in *Figure 12.41*:

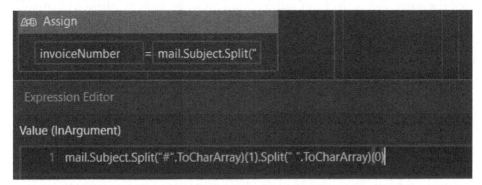

Figure 12.41 – Split function to create an output folder

5. **Output verification**

Run the project using the **Run** button or *Ctrl + F5* to verify the output. Check the destination folder to verify the attachments. Ensure the files you have sent from Gmail are displayed as the output in your project, as shown in *Figure 12.42*:

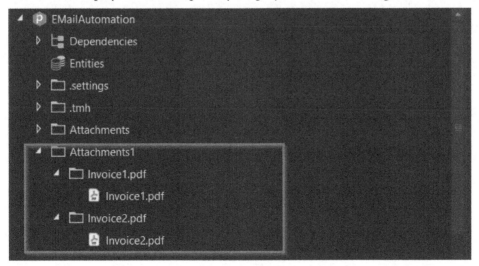

Figure 12.42 – Run project and output verification

In this section, we explored different features to process emails from the specified input email to read the subject, contents of the email, and download attachments. We also explored the properties of the **Get Outlook Mail Message** activity, where we learned the use of the fields, such as **Account** and **Mail Folder**. Finally, we used different options to filter the emails based on certain conditions, such as **Only UnreadMessages from** a list of emails, for example, the first 100 emails. These concepts can easily be applied to processing attachments in emails.

Summary

We explored everything about email automation in this chapter. We performed most of the email operations, such as sending emails, receiving emails, and downloading attachments automatically using UiPath Studio – operations that we frequently used to perform manually. In addition, we discussed various email protocols such as IMAP, SMTP, POP3, Exchange, and Outlook, and their usage. We also implemented practical examples to understand all the essential email automation concepts, from sending emails to receiving emails, filtering emails, and processing attachments.

In the next chapter, we will learn more about debugging. We will use UiPath Studio to easily troubleshoot, identify errors, and practice solving issues during any challenging situations while creating automation projects.

Part 3: Use Case and Exam Preparation

In this part, you will learn how to build an invoice processing automation with the help of the Dispatcher - Performer model. In the Dispatcher model, you will upload the details of the invoices to the Orchestrator queues, and in the Performer model, you will fetch the values from the queues and enter them into the CRM. After that, you will learn about the UiPath RPA (UiRPA) associate exam, where you will learn about the target audiences for the exam, exam topics and sections, how to register for the exam, and much more information on the exam. Finally, you will solve two practice tests for the UiRPA exam, assessing the skills you have learned so far.

In this part, we will cover the following chapters:

- *Chapter 13, Debugging*
- *Chapter 14, Invoice Processing – Dispatcher*
- *Chapter 15, Invoice Processing – Performer*
- *Chapter 16, How to Prepare and What to Expect*
- *Chapter 17, Mock Exam 1*
- *Chapter 18, Mock Exam 2*

13
Debugging

Software development projects will rarely be perfect, as various kinds of errors can hamper the project execution. **Debugging** is a multistep process that involves identifying and removing these errors/bugs from a given project to make it function correctly as intended and without errors.

Just like any other **Integrated Development Environment** (**IDE**), UiPath Studio offers several options to help you with the debugging process of locating bugs quickly, especially in large and complex workflows. It helps you view each activity's execution, verify what data it gets, and check whether there are errors in producing output. In addition, it provides a real-time engine that checks for errors while working with the workflow.

In this chapter, you will learn how to use the different debugging actions from the **DEBUG** ribbon bar, and how different debugging panels and breakpoints help rectify bugs during the debugging process. You will also learn how to test an individual activity and create a test bench with activities, and then how to work with the **Run from this Activity** option.

This chapter consists of the following topics:

- Understanding the debugging actions
- Working with the debugging panels
- Testing activities

Technical requirements

Before starting this chapter, please have UiPath Studio and Robot installed.

Later in the chapter, we will go through a process that causes runtime exceptions and fix it with the help of the **Debug** option in UiPath Studio.

You can download the process from the GitHub repository: `https://github.com/PacktPublishing/UiPath-Associate-Certification-Guide.git`.

Understanding the debugging actions

Debugging a single workflow or the entire project can be performed from the **DESIGN** and **DEBUG** ribbon bars. Clicking on the **Debug** options from the ribbon bar opens up the **Debug** panel. The following screenshot shows the **DEBUG** ribbon bar in UiPath Studio:

Figure 13.1 – The DEBUG ribbon bar

The **Debug** tabs allow the user to perform debugging of a single file or the whole project. The ribbon consists of several debugging actions. Let's understand each one of them in detail.

Debug File

Clicking on **Debug File** will start the debugging process for that particular workflow.

Stop

Clicking on the **Stop** button ends the debugging process irrespective of which activity is executing. The keyboard shortcut for the **Stop** button is *F12*.

Step Into

When you want to debug one activity at a time, select the **Step Into** option from the debug ribbon bar. When the **Step Into** action is triggered, the debugger opens and highlights activities in the workflow container, such as the `Flowchart` or `Sequence` activity. Clicking **Step Into** once will highlight the activity to be executed. Clicking on **Step Into** one more time will execute the highlighted activity and then highlight the next activity.

Using **Step Into** with the `Invoke Workflow File` activity opens the workflow in a new tab in *read-only* mode, and each activity inside it is executed one at a time.

The keyboard shortcut for **Step Into** is *F11*.

Note

Activities such as `Sequence`, `Flowchart`, and `Invoke Workflow File` are referred to as **containers**.

Step Over

Step Over is the opposite of **Step Into**. It does not open the current container and then debug one activity at a time. Instead, it executes the container in one go with all the activities present in it. It is useful when you want to skip containers with all the activities that are unlikely to trigger any issues during execution.

Also, when the debugger is inside the container and you hit the **Step Over** action, it will jump through all the activities in it one after the other, as with **Step Into**, but it will not highlight a particular activity.

The keyboard shortcut for **Step Over** is *F10*.

Step Out

The **Step Out** action completes the execution of all activities in a current container. After the execution of all activities, the control moves out of that container and then pauses the debugging. This action is beneficial when you are working with nested sequences.

The keyboard shortcut for **Step Out** is *Shift + F11*.

Retry

While debugging, when an activity has thrown an exception and you want to debug this activity again, choose the **Retry** action. **Retry** re-executes the previous activity and throws an exception if it is encountered once again during the debugging process. The activity that threw the exception is highlighted, and details about the error are shown in the **Locals** and **Call Stack** panels (you will learn about the **Locals** and **Call Stack** panels in the *Working with the debugging panels* section).

Ignore

While debugging, you can use the **Ignore** action to skip the current exception and resume execution from the next activity in the flow.

You can continue debugging the remaining set of activities by ignoring or jumping over the activities that threw the exception.

> **Note**
>
> The **Retry** and **Ignore** actions are available when an exception is thrown and the debugging process goes into a paused state.

Restart

In the middle of the debugging process, at times, if you want to debug the project from the start, choose the **Restart** action. This action restarts the debugging process from the first activity of the project.

Break

The **Break** action is available once the debugging process has started. You can pause the debugging process at any moment using the **Break** action. When the **Break** action is applied, the activity that is currently being executed will be stopped and highlighted in Studio.

You can choose the **Continue** action to resume the debugging process or the **Step Into**, **Step Out**, or **Stop** action, depending upon the situation.

Focus

Ideally, during the debugging process, execution goes into a paused state when an exception occurs or a breakpoint is encountered. The **Focus** action takes you back to the breakpoints you mentioned in your flow or the location of an error when debugging the flow in a paused state. The **Focus** action is an easy way to return to that particular activity and resume the debugging process.

Slow Step

The **Slow Step** action can be enabled both before or during the debugging process. When enabled, the **Slow Step** action highlights the activity that is executing. The **Slow Step** action comes with four different speeds – *1x, 2x, 3x,* and *4x.*

Debugging speed changes by one step from 1x to 4x with each click on the **Slow Step** button. Thus, debugging with **Slow Step** at 1x runs the slowest and at 4x the fastest. The speed determines how fast the debugger jumps from one activity to the next.

Execution Trail

Execution Trail shows the execution path while debugging. By default, the **Execution Trail** button is disabled. While each activity is getting executed, they are highlighted and marked with a color code, depending upon the execution status:

- Partially executed activities are marked with a golden yellow clock symbol:

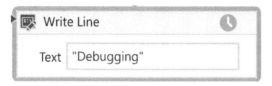

Figure 13.2 – A partially executed activity

- Successfully executed activities are marked with a green checkbox symbol:

Figure 13.3 – A successfully executed activity

- Activities that throw an exception are marked with a red color:

Figure 13.4 – An exception thrown by an activity

Highlight Elements

The UI element of a process is highlighted for each activity during the debugging process if the **Highlight Elements** action is enabled. Thus, you can use it both with a regular and a step-by-step debugging process – for example, if a Type Into activity is placed on a text field in a web form, during execution, the text field of the web form is first highlighted before the Robot types into that text field.

Log Activities helps you determine where issues might be occurring in your flow. All the debugged activities are displayed as *trace logs* in the **Output** panel if the **Log Activities** action is enabled. If the log feature is disabled, then trace logs are not displayed in the **Output** panel; instead, you only get to see the debug start and end time along with any exceptions thrown.

In addition, if connected to UiPath Orchestrator, logs are automatically sent to Orchestrator. If you disable the **Allow Development Logging** option from the **Robot Settings** tab in the **Add** or **Edit** user window, you can store the logs locally.

> **Note**
> The **Highlight Elements** and **Log Activities** actions can only be enabled before debugging and persist when you reopen the automation project next time.

Continue on Exception

When the **Continue on Exception** action is enabled during debugging and an exception is thrown, that exception is logged in the **Output** panel, and the execution continues with the further activities without stopping the debugging process.

Open Logs

Clicking on the **Open Logs** button opens up the locally stored logs folder. The folder path where logs are stored is %localappdata%\UiPath\Logs. The naming convention of logs is YYYY-DD-MM_Component.log – for example, 2021-07-08_Studio.log.

In this section, you have learned about the debug action menu of the ribbon bar. In the next section of the chapter, you will see the different debugging panels available in UiPath Studio.

Working with the debugging panels

Apart from the actions available in the **DEBUG** ribbon bar, UiPath Studio provides you with an array of panels that help you in the debugging process.

There are five panels available for debugging in UiPath:

1. The Locals panel

2. The Watch panel

3. The Immediate panel

4. The Call Stack panel

5. The Breakpoints panel

Each panel is marked in the following screenshot. Each number corresponds with the position of the panel in the preceding list:

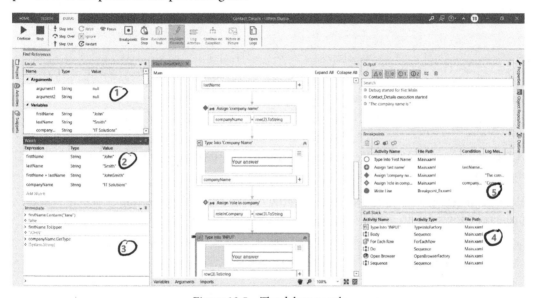

Figure 13.5 – The debug panels

Once debugging has started, all five panels become visible. But, first, let's look at each panel and understand what purpose they serve.

The Locals panel

The **Locals** panel window has three properties – **Name**, **Type**, and **Value**. The panel shows the following information with their corresponding properties:

- **Variables**: Displays all the variables within the scope of the executing container

- **Arguments**: Displays all the arguments of the executing workflow

- **Activity Properties**: Displays the properties of the previously executed activity and the current activity

- **Exceptions**: Displays the description and type of the exception

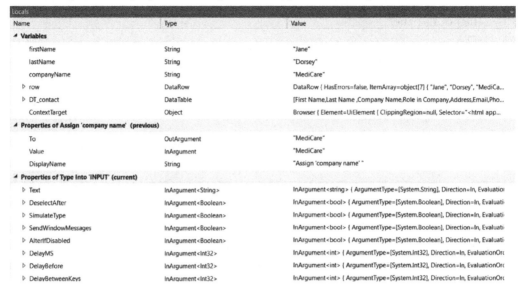

Figure 13.6 – The Locals panel

All the **Arguments**, **Properties**, and **Variables** categories can be compressed or expanded in the **Locals** panel.

When debugging is in a paused state, clicking on the pencil icon button under the **Value** property allows you to modify the variables' and arguments' values:

Figure 13.7 – The firstName variable value changed to Micheal from Jane by clicking on the pencil icon

Also, when debugging is in a paused state, you can inspect the values of items from the **Value** properties column by clicking on the magnifier button:

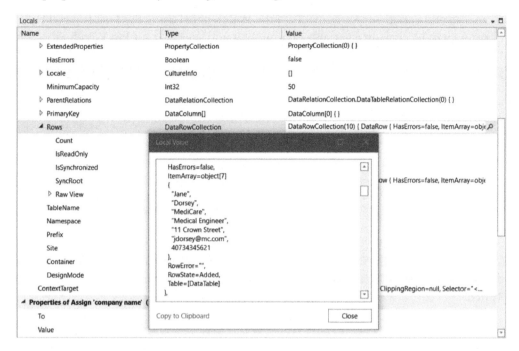

Figure 13.8 – Inspecting all rows inside a DataTable variable by clicking on the magnifier button

The Watch panel

The **Watch** panel window has three properties – **Expression**, **Type**, and **Value**.

You can display the values of variables, arguments, and user-defined expressions that are in the scope of the executing container. The values in the **Watch** panel are updated, depending on the execution of the related activity during the debugging process – for example, debugging a process inside a For Each activity. The values get updated in the **Watch** panel for every iteration:

Expression	Type	Value
firstName	String	"Jane"
lastName	String	"Dorsey"
firstName + lastName	String	"JaneDorsey"
companyName	String	"MediCare"
Add Watch		

Figure 13.9 – The Watch panel displaying the type and value of the variables and expressions

You can add variables, arguments, or expressions to the **Watch** panel by clicking on the **Add Watch** option in the **Expression** property.

You can also add variables or arguments to the **Watch** panel using the **Locals** panel by performing a right-click on a variable or argument and selecting **Add to Watch**:

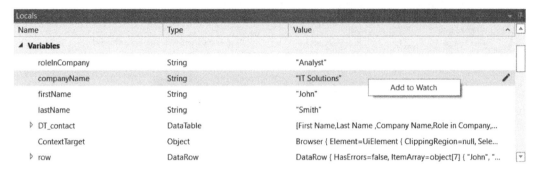

Name	Type	Value	
▲ Variables			
roleInCompany	String	"Analyst"	
companyName	String	"IT Solutions"	Add to Watch
firstName	String	"John"	
lastName	String	"Smith"	
▷ DT_contact	DataTable	[First Name,Last Name ,Company Name,Role in Company,...	
ContextTarget	Object	Browser { Element=UiElement { ClippingRegion=null, Sele...	
▷ row	DataRow	DataRow { HasErrors=false, ItemArray=object[7] { "John", "...	

Figure 13.10 – Adding a variable to the Watch panel from the Locals panel

Alternatively, you can add variables or arguments to the **Watch** panel using the **Variables** and **Arguments** panels. To do so, right-click a variable or argument and select **Add to Watch**:

Name ∨	Variable type	Scope	Default
roleInCompany	String	Body	*Enter a VB expression*
lastNam	String	Body	*Enter a VB expression*
firstNam	String	Body	*Enter a VB expression*
DT_cont	DataTable	Do	*Enter a VB expression*
compan	String	Body	*Enter a VB expression*

Context menu:
- 📋 Convert to Argument
- 📋 Copy
- 📋 Paste
- 🗑 Delete
- Add Annotation
- Edit Annotation
- Delete Annotation
- **Add Watch**
- 🔍 Find References

Variables   Arguments   Imports   ✋ 🔍 100% ∨ 🔲 🔳

Figure 13.11 – Adding a variable to the Watch panel from the Variables panel

The Immediate panel

The **Immediate** panel can be used for checking the data/output of a variable, arguments, or statements at a given point during the debugging process:

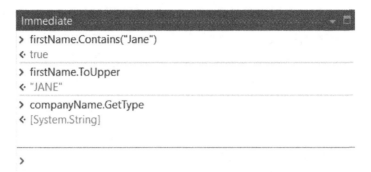

Figure 13.12 – The Immediate panel

To get the output, type the variable or argument name in the **Immediate** window and press *Enter*. The output doesn't get updated during the debugging process; rather, it keeps the history of previously evaluated statements.

Using the context menu, you can copy the previously evaluated expression or use the **Clear All** option to clear all lines in the panel. Using *Ctrl + spacebar* opens up IntelliPrompt, which helps to select the desired functions or properties associated with the variable or argument:

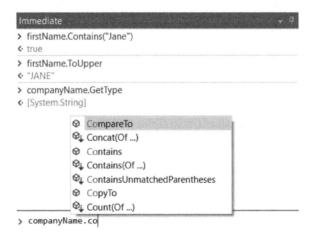

Figure 13.13 – IntelliPrompt using Ctrl + spacebar

The Call Stack panel

While debugging is in a paused state, the **Call Stack** panel displays the activity to be executed along with its parent containers:

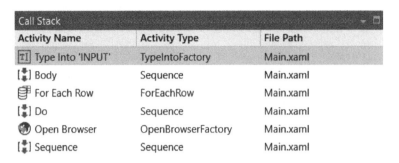

Figure 13.14 – The Call Stack panel

The **Call Stack** panel gets populated in the following two scenarios:

- When **Step Into**, **Break**, and **Slow Step** are used
- If the execution goes into a paused state because an error or a breakpoint was encountered

Double-clicking on an activity name in the **Call Stack** panel highlights the activity in the **Designer** panel. Also, when an activity throws an exception during debugging, it is marked in the **Call Stack** panel, and that particular activity is highlighted in red.

The Breakpoints panel

Before we start with the **Breakpoints** panel, let's understand what **breakpoints** are. As with any other IDE, UiPath Studio supports breakpoints. They are used to intentionally pause the debugging process on an activity that may trigger execution issues. A breakpoint can also be used to monitor the value of variables or arguments at that point and also take control of execution by using the **Step Into**, **Step Over**, and **Step Out** actions.

Let's now see how can you add, remove, or delete a breakpoint in UiPath Studio. We need to know how to add a breakpoint first, as the **Breakpoint Settings** tab is only available after that point.

How to place a breakpoint

You can add a breakpoint on an activity in the following three ways:

- Right-click on the particular activity for which you want the breakpoint and click on **Toggle Breakpoint** from the context menu:

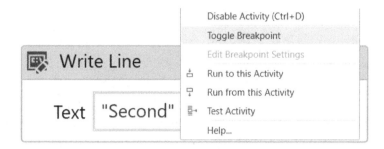

Figure 13.15 – Applying a breakpoint from the context menu

- Clicking on **Toggle Breakpoint** will apply the breakpoint to that particular activity, and it will be marked with a red disk at the top left of the activity. Breakpoints are always marked with a red disk:

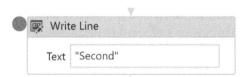

Figure 13.16 – A breakpoint applied to the Write Line activity

- Select an activity and click the **Breakpoints** action from the **DEBUG** ribbon bar:

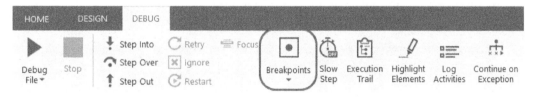

Figure 13.17 – Click on the Breakpoints button to apply a breakpoint

- Select the desired activity and press the *F9* key on your keyboard.

You can use any of these methods to apply breakpoints, depending on your preferences.

How to disable a breakpoint

Disabling a breakpoint will not pause the debugging process on a particular activity. The disabled breakpoint is marked with a red circle at the top left of the activity:

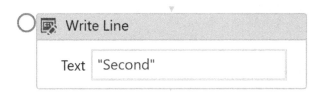

Figure 13.18 – A disabled breakpoint on the Write Line activity

You can disable a breakpoint using any one of the three ways used to create a breakpoint. So, you can either select the breakpoint activity and then click on **Toggle Breakpoint** from the context menu, click on the **Breakpoints** button from the **DEBUG** panel, or press the *F9* key from your keyboard to disable the breakpoint.

How to delete a breakpoint

You can delete a disabled breakpoint by repeating any one of the three steps used to create and disable a breakpoint. Either select the breakpoint activity and then click on **Toggle Breakpoint** from the context menu, click on the **Breakpoints** button from the **DEBUG** panel, or press the *F9* key from your keyboard to delete the breakpoint.

Now that we have learned how to add, disable, and delete breakpoints on an activity, let's see where we can see all the breakpoints of a particular process together.

The Breakpoints panel

The **Breakpoints** panel displays all the breakpoints in the current project, along with the workflow name in which they are contained:

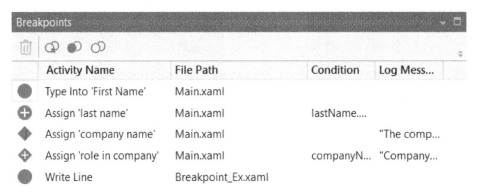

Figure 13.19 – The Breakpoints panel

The **Condition** column displays the condition (if any) set on a particular breakpoint, and the **Log Message** column displays the logged message set on that breakpoint.

You can delete, enable, or disable all the breakpoints in a project by selecting the appropriate action from the **Breakpoints** panel.

Clicking on the **Delete all breakpoints** button deletes all the breakpoints present in the workflow:

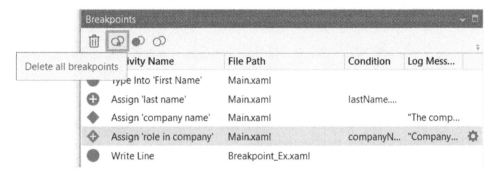

Figure 13.20 – Delete all breakpoints

Clicking on the **Enable all breakpoints** button enables all the disabled breakpoints present in the workflow:

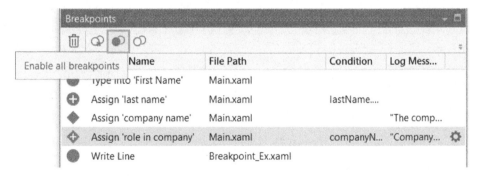

Figure 13.21 – Enable all breakpoints

Clicking on the **Disable all breakpoints** button disables all the breakpoints present in the workflow:

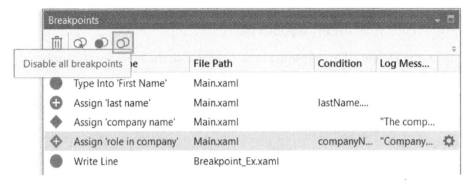

Figure 13.22 – Disable all breakpoints

Let's now see how you can parameterize individual breakpoints to meet a particular condition for the breakpoint to get executed.

Breakpoint Settings

Individual breakpoints can be further modified by clicking on the gear icon from the **Breakpoints** panel. This opens up the **Breakpoint Settings** tab for that particular breakpoint:

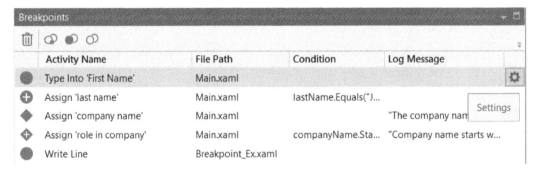

Figure 13.23 – The gear icon for Breakpoint Settings

The **Breakpoint Settings** tab has four parameters named **Condition**, **Hit Count**, **Log Message**, and **Continue execution when logging**:

Figure 13.24 – The Breakpoint Settings tab

Let's understand these four parameters in detail:

- **Condition**: Provide a conditional statement for the execution to break. If the condition on the breakpoint becomes TRUE, then the debugging is paused, and the corresponding activity is highlighted.

- **Hit Count**: This specifies the number of times the condition is met before debugging goes into a paused state – for example, a variable num default value is set as 1. If a breakpoint with the num Mod 2 = 0 condition is inside a While activity and **Hit Count** is set as 2, then debugging goes into a paused state when the condition is met for the second time:

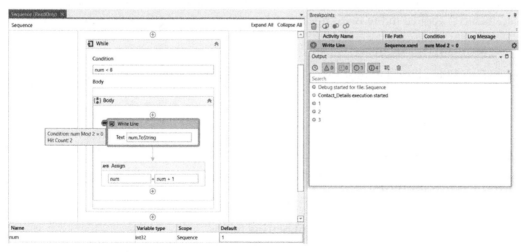

Figure 13.25 – Hit Count with Condition

> **Note**
> The maximum hit count value is 32,767.

- **Log Message**: You can add a `trace level` log message to the breakpoint when the condition is met. You can also add a log message when there is no condition provided.
- **Continue execution when logging**: This checkbox is only available if the **Log Message** parameter is set. If the checkbox is checked, the execution is not paused when the condition is met, and the specified message is logged in the **Output** panel:

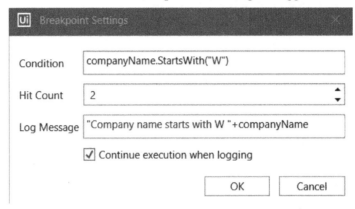

Figure 13.26 – Breakpoint Settings with all the parameters initialized

A breakpoint on an activity can be categorized in four ways, depending upon the parameter(s) applied in the **Breakpoint Settings** tab. The four categories are as follows:

- Standard breakpoints
- Conditional breakpoints
- Tracepoints
- Conditional tracepoints

Let's understand each one of them in detail.

Standard breakpoints

A standard breakpoint is one where no **Condition**, **Hit Count**, and **Log Message** parameters are added in the **Breakpoint Setting** tab.

Figure 13.27 – Breakpoints

Conditional breakpoints

Breakpoints where only the **Condition** and/or **Hit Count** parameters are added in the **Breakpoint Settings** tab are called conditional breakpoints:

Figure 13.28 – Conditional breakpoints

Tracepoints

Breakpoints where only the **Log Message** parameter is added in the **Breakpoint Settings** tab are called tracepoints:

Figure 13.29 – Tracepoints

Conditional tracepoints

Breakpoints where the **Condition** and/or **Hit Count** and **Log Message** parameters are added in the **Breakpoint Settings** tab are called conditional tracepoints:

Figure 13.30 – Conditional tracepoints

Different icons are made available for the different types of breakpoints in UiPath Studio. They are as follows:

Icons	Breakpoint
●	Enabled Breakpoint
○	Disabled Breakpoint
⊕	Enabled Conditional Breakpoint
⊕	Disabled Conditional Breakpoint
◆	Enabled Tracepoint
◇	Disabled Tracepoint
◈	Enabled Conditional Tracepoint
◈	Disabled Conditional Tracepoint

Figure 13.31 – A summary of breakpoint categorization

Let's now see the context menus available for individual breakpoints present in the **Breakpoints** panel.

The context menu for breakpoints

Right-clicking on a breakpoint from the **Breakpoints** panel opens up the context menu for that particular breakpoint:

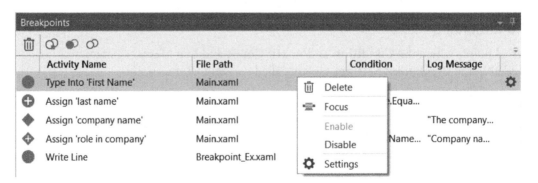

Figure 13.32 – The breakpoint context menu

The context menu displays five options:

- **Delete**: Deletes the selected breakpoints from the project.

- **Focus**: Navigates to the breakpoint in the **Designer** panel.

- **Enable**: This option is active on disabled breakpoints only. It enables the selected breakpoint.

- **Disable**: This option is active on enabled breakpoints only. It disables the selected breakpoint.

- **Settings**: Opens the **Breakpoint Settings** tab, where you can customize it by passing the parameters.

Now we have learned about the different debugging panels available in UiPath Studio and how to use them to detect and correct bugs in the workflow. Next, let's look at how we can perform tests on activities in UiPath Studio.

Testing activities

UiPath Studio allows testing activities while you are in the design phase of process automation. Depending upon the scenario within Studio, you can do the testing of activities in four different ways:

- Test Activity

- Create Test Bench

- Run to this Activity

- Run from this Activity

Let's understand each one of them in detail.

Test Activity

Selecting the **Test Activity** option from the context menu on a selected activity allows you to run a test on that particular activity. Choosing the **Test Activity** option will open it in debug mode, highlighting the selected activity.

You can use Test Activity in the following scenarios:

- For adding default values to properties and then testing it

- Using the **Locals** panel to add values for testing the activity

Let's understand more about Test Activity through a use case. Here, we will program a Robot that checks whether a number entered by the user is an even or odd number:

1. Create a new sequence named **Even_Odd** sequence, and inside it, create a variable named num of the datatype as Int32 (note that no default value has been assigned to the variable):

Name	∧	Variable type	Scope	Default
num		Int32	Even_Odd	*Enter a VB expression*

Figure 13.33 – An integer variable "num" declaration

2. Drag and drop the following three sets of activities inside the Even_Odd sequence:

- Input Dialog: Asks the user for a number
- If: Checks whether the number is even or odd and displays the appropriate message
- Write Line: Displays the even and odd messages:

Figure 13.34 – The Even Odd sequence

3. Before running the sequence, we will test the `If` activity to check whether the conditional logic is working correctly. To do so, select the `If` activity and right-click for the context menu. Then, select Test Activity from the context menu:

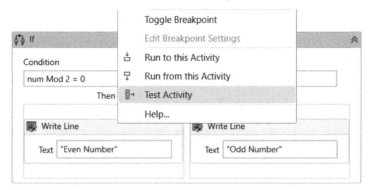

Figure 13.35 – Select Test Activity from the context menu

4. Clicking on Test Activity opens the `If` activity in debug mode and highlights the `If` activity. All the debugging actions and panels are made available:

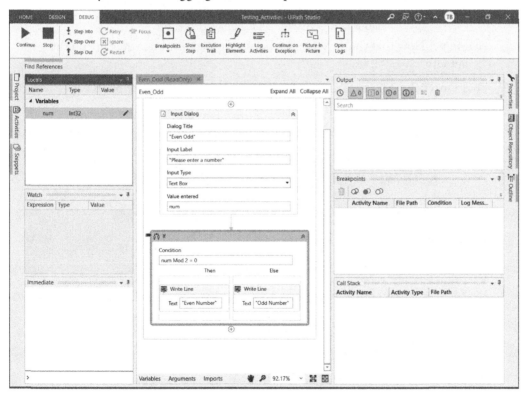

Figure 13.36 – The If activity opened in debug mode

5. Since the num variable was not assigned a default value, we can add a value to the variable using the Locals panel before testing the If activity. Clicking on the pencil icon allows us to edit the value of the variable. Here, we will pass 5 as the value to the num variable:

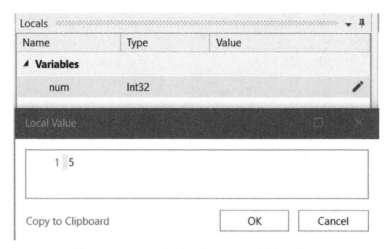

Figure 13.37 – Assigning the num variable with 5

Awesome! Now that the variable has been assigned a value, you can run the If activity.

6. To do so, click on Step Into or Continue from the DEBUG ribbon bar.

    In this case, the Write Line activity of the else block of the If activity got executed, and a message was written in the **Output** panel as Odd Number, which means that the condition written in the If activity was correct:

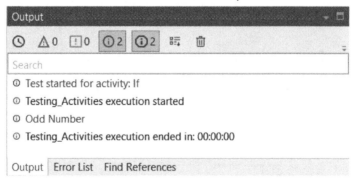

Figure 13.38 – Odd Number printed in the Output panel

Create Test Bench

Building automation in UiPath Studio is just like LEGO, where you keep on adding blocks to complete a character. For example, let's say you are building a LEGO robot. Ideally, you build the hands or legs of the robot individually to test whether they move correctly as expected and then attach them to the body. With the help of **Create Test Bench**, the same scenario can be created in UiPath Studio while building a bot. So, using **Create Test Bench** allows you to create automation building blocks that can then be individually tested and added to the final workflow.

From the **Activities** panel, you can choose any activity and create a test bench for it:

1. To do so, right-click on the selected activity and choose **Create Test Bench** from the context menu:

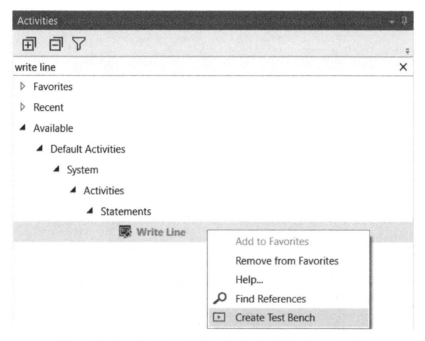

Figure 13.39 – Creating a test bench for the Write Line activity

Clicking on **Create Test Bench** will open it in a test bench workflow. The Test Bench workflow is a temporary sequence that's not part of the current project and is discarded when closed:

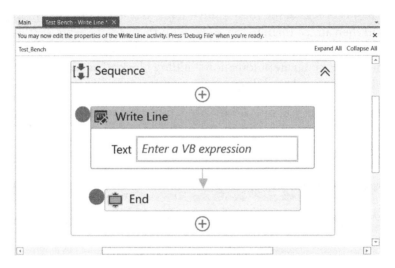

Figure 13.40 – A temporary test bench workflow created

The selected activity is automatically added to a new temporary sequence file not included in your project. You can edit the properties of this activity or add new activities and later debug the test bench workflow.

2. To save the file, use the **Save as** option in the **DESIGN** ribbon bar to add a filename, and save it to the same file path as your project. Later, you can use the **Invoke Workflow File** activity and call the sequence in the desired workflow.

> **Note**
>
> **Create Test Bench** does not work with the `Pick Branch` activity because it requires the `Pick` activity as a container to execute.

Run to this Activity

Let's say, for example, you have five activities inside a workflow, and you want to run till the second activity only. Then, choose the **Run to this Activity** option from the context menu by selecting the third activity.

Let's understand this concept with the help of an example. In the `Main.xaml` file, we have five `Write Line` activities inside a `Sequence` activity. The `Write Line` activities print messages starting from **"First"**, **"Second"**, and so on till **"Fifth"**:

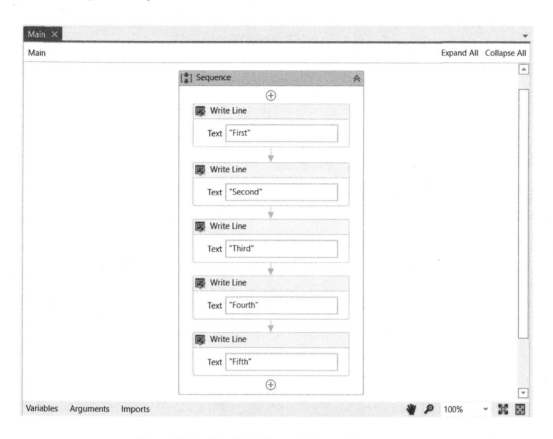

Figure 13.41 – The Write Line activities inside a sequence

In our scenario, we want the output till the second `Write Line` activity to be printed. To do so, right-click on the third `Write Line` activity in the **Designer** panel and click on **Run to this Activity** from the context menu:

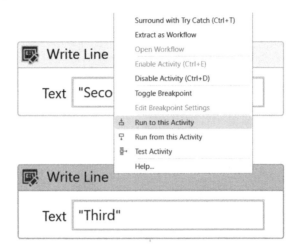

Figure 13.42 – Run to this Activity

This starts the debugging process, prints the value in the **Output** panel, and pauses before the third `Write Line` activity is executed while highlighting it in the **Designer** panel:

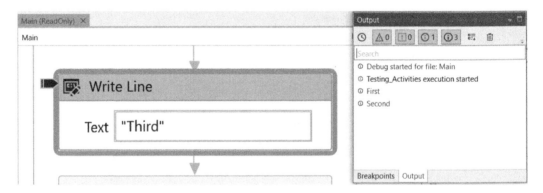

Figure 13.43 – The Write Line activity highlighted with the Output panel

> **Note**
> If a workflow is in a paused state while debugging and **Run to this Activity** is triggered, then the execution continues until this activity is reached.

Run from this Activity

The **Run from this Activity** option is the opposite of **Run to this Activity**. Here, you can start running the automation from any particular activity. Let's take the previous example and understand more about **Run from this Activity**.

In this scenario, we want the output from the fourth `Write Line` activity to be printed. To do so, right-click on the fourth `Write Line` activity in the **Designer** panel and click on **Run from this Activity** from the context menu:

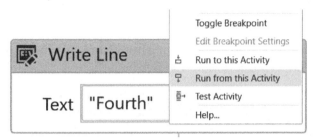

Figure 13.44 – Run from this Activity

It enters debugging in a paused state, allowing you to change the values of variables and arguments from the **Locals** panel. Then, you can choose the **Continue**, **Step Into**, **Step Over**, or **Step Out** actions from the **DEBUG** ribbon bar to start the debugging process. In our case, values from the last two `Write Line` activities are printed in the **Output** panel:

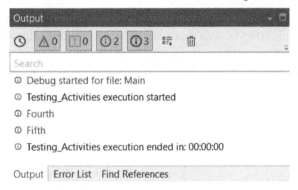

Figure 13.45 – The Write Line activities printed in the Output panel

> **Note**
>
> Using **Run from this Activity** on an activity added inside the `Try Catch`, `Switch`, `Parallel`, `Pick`, `Trigger Scope`, or `Retry Scope` container will result in an error.
>
> The debugging is restarted from the previously indicated activity if the **Restart** action from the **DEBUG** ribbon bar is used after the **Run from this Activity** action.

Testing activities plays a vital role in removing any errors while you are still in the building phase. **Test Activity** debugs an activity from the existing workflow where you can pass values of the variables or arguments using the **Locals** panel. **Create Test Bench** allows you to create a temporary sequence to play around with the activities before adding them to the workflow. Finally, **Run to this Activity** or **Run from this Activity** allows you to debug to or from a particular activity in the workflow. In the next section, you will gain hands-on experience in debugging a workflow.

Fixing the workflow

Now that you have learned all about debugging in UiPath Studio, let's apply the skills you have learned so far and debug a workflow to fix a bug.

Your co-worker was assigned to build a bot for the **Voter Registration** campaign. The Robot needs to fetch **First Name**, **Last Name**, **Email**, **Age**, and **State** information from an Excel file and insert them in the correct fields on the web voter's registration form.

The Robot is throwing an error at some point, and your co-worker needs your help to make it work. So, let's apply all the knowledge that we have learned so far on debugging and fix this workflow. You can download the code from the GitHub repository mentioned in the *Technical requirements* section of this chapter.

Let's examine the input data file and the workflow. The Voters Details.xlsx file contains four columns named **First Name**, **Last Name**, **Email**, **Age**, and **State**. In addition, it has multiple rows of data that have to be entered into the web form:

First Name	Last Name	Email	Age	State
Marie	Kenny	marie.kenny@ui.com	28	Maharashtra
Lloyd	Wong	lloyd.wong@ri.com	37	Karnataka

Figure 13.46 – A snippet of the Voters Details.xlsx file

The `Main.xaml` file consists of two main `Sequence` activities:

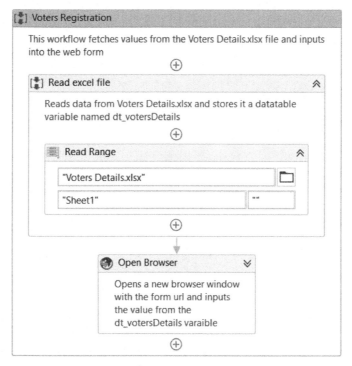

Figure 13.47 – The Voters Registration sequence

The two activities are as follows:

- The `Read excel file` activity: Reads data from `Voters Details.xlsx` and stores it in a `datatable` variable named `dt_votersDetails`.

- The Open Browser activity: Opens a new browser window with the form URL and inputs the value from the dt_votersDetails variable to the voter registration form. Five variables named firstName, lastName, email, age, and state are declared for the corresponding fields of the web form:

Figure 13.48 – The Open Browser sequence

In addition, the Open Browser activity has five Type Into activities inside a For Each Row activity to type in the details in the web form:

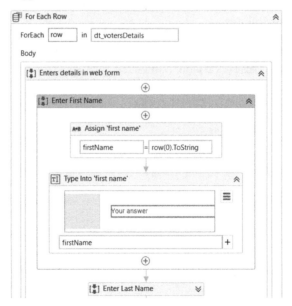

Figure 13.49 – The Type Into activity to enter values into the form

The voter registration web form has a total of five fields (here, we are just showing you two):

Voter Registration

* Required

First Name *

Your answer

Last Name *

Your answer

Figure 13.50 – A snippet of the Voter Registration form

Now that we have seen all the input files and the code, let's debug the automation and see what the error is. The bot does the registration of the first two individuals successfully. When entering the age of the third person, it throws an exception, and the debugging goes into a paused state. The Type Into activity for age is highlighted in the **Designer** panel, since it caused the exception. An error log is logged in the **Output** panel:

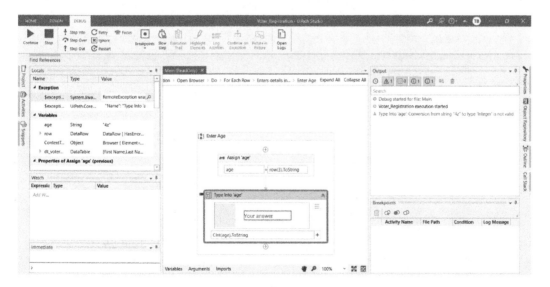

Figure 13.51 – An exception thrown at the Type Into activity

More about the exception can be found from the **Locals** panel by clicking on the magnify icon from the **Exceptions** section:

Figure 13.52 – The Exceptions window

From the exception, we can make out that it is `InvalidCastException`, which occurs when the conversion of an instance of one data type to another is not supported. In the `Type Into` activity for entering the age, the `Cint()` function is used for converting `String` to `Integer`. Since the typecasting couldn't happen, the exception was thrown:

1. Apply a conditional breakpoint at this **Type Into** activity with the condition as **Not age.IsNumeric** and restart the debugging process:

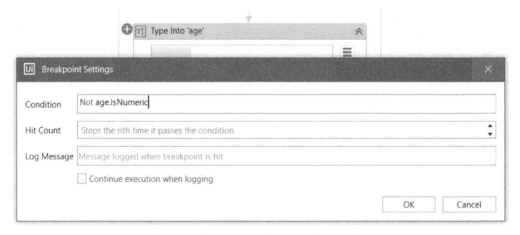

Figure 13.53 – A conditional breakpoint on the Type Into activity

The execution will then go into a paused state when the age cannot be converted to an integer. As expected, the debugging goes into a paused state while entering the age of the third person without throwing an exception.

2. Use the **Immediate** panel to check whether the data present in the **age** variable is numeric. Providing **age.IsNumeric** prints the answer as **false**:

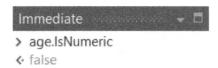

Figure 13.54 – The Immediate panel

3. Add the **age** variable to the **Watch** panel to check what value it is currently holding:

Expression	Type	Value
age	String	"4z"
Add Watch		

Figure 13.55 – The Watch panel

Now, we can see that the value of age is 4 z. Because of z, the typecasting couldn't happen, hence the exception was thrown.

4. Navigate to the **Locals** panel and change the value of **age** from **4z** to **48** by clicking on the pencil icon.

5. Click on **Continue** to resume the debugging:

Figure 13.56 – The Locals panel

The workflow continues to execute without any further errors. You have successfully debugged the automated voter registration process!

Summary

In this chapter, you have learned what debugging is and how it helps to troubleshoot and remove bugs from a process. First, you saw the various debugging action menus present in the **DEBUG** ribbon bar, which helps you navigate to perform debugging of a single file or an entire project. Next, you learned about the multiple debugging panels, which helps you fix the errors. You also learned about the testing activities within UiPath Studio while you are still in the building phase of the process development. Lastly, you debugged a workflow to fix a bug with all the skills you previously learned.

In the next chapter, you will learn how to build an automation project using the concept of a dispatcher and a performer.

14
Invoice Processing – Dispatcher

Henry's Food Mart is a chain of convenience stores in the US with headquarters in New York, and there are currently 400+ stores located in the US. The **invoice processing** process has been selected for RPA automation as part of the larger project initiative conducted within Henry's Food Mart's finance and accounting department.

The objective of this process automation is linked to the project business case and is primarily intended to do the following:

- Deliver faster processing of the invoices.
- Reduce redundant activities in the invoice processing.
- Improve overall performance and reliability by eliminating errors.

The invoice processing process reads through emails and downloads the invoices received in the form of an email attachment as a PDF. Then, it extracts customer information and invoice particulars from the invoices and enters them into the **order entry CRM**.

You will be building this process in two parts. You will follow the **dispatcher-performer** model and create two different processes. In this chapter, you will build the dispatcher model, and in the next chapter, you will build the performer model.

Here is what you will learn as part of this *Invoice Processing – Dispatcher* project:

- Creating and consuming orchestrator assets
- Using mail automation
- Manipulating data in UiPath Studio
- Automating PDF files to read data
- Modifying selectors
- Using regular expressions
- Working with the UiPath Studio data scraping wizard
- Creating and uploading data to Orchestrator queues
- Exception handling in UiPath Studio
- Logging in UiPath Studio

Technical requirements

Let's understand the requirements for this project:

- UiPath Studio Community/Enterprise/Academic Alliance Edition version 20.10 and above, connected to UiPath Orchestrator
- Access to the UiPath Orchestrator services
- A Gmail account
- Adobe Acrobat PDF Reader
- Access to the internet
- Read-write permission in the machine where UiPath Studio is installed

You can get the entire code for the invoice processing dispatcher at GitHub: `https://github.com/PacktPublishing/UiPath-Associate-Certification-Guide.git`.

The project overview

In this chapter, you will be designing the dispatcher model of invoice processing. Let's understand the process in detail. Here are the steps that you will need to perform:

1. Program a robot that will read the last unread emails from your Gmail account.

2. Program a robot that will download all the invoice attachments from the read mails. The conditions for downloading the attachment are as follows:

   - The subject line of the mail must be **Invoice-Henry-FM-Invoice Number-Customer Name**.

   - The naming convention of the attachment must be **Invoice-Henry FM-Invoice Number-Customer Name.pdf**.

3. Program a robot to save all invoice attachments in a folder named `Invoice`, created in the project directory.

4. Program a robot to extract the following relevant fields from the invoice:

   - **Customer Details**:

      - Customer Name

      - Customer Address

      - Customer Phone Number

      - Customer Email ID

   - **Invoice Particulars**:

      - Invoice Date

      - Invoice Number

   - **Order Information**:

      - Item Quantity

      - Item Description

      - Item Unit Price

      - Line Total Amount

      - Subtotal Amount

      - Shipping Amount

      - Total Amount

5. Program a robot to upload the following details to the Orchestrator queue:

    • Customer Details

    • Invoice Particulars

6. Repeat *steps 4–5* for the remaining invoices.

7. Program the robot to successfully end the process if all the attachments downloaded from the mail in *step 2* are processed.

Let's understand the entire process with the help of a diagram:

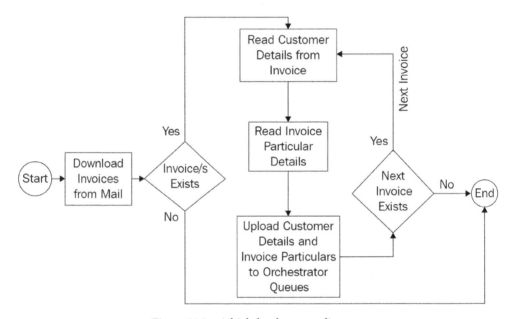

Figure 14.1 – A high-level process diagram

Before you begin designing the process automation, download all the provided invoices from the Input File - Invoice folder from this GitHub repository: https://github.com/PacktPublishing/UiPath-Associate-Certification-Guide/tree/main/Chapter14/Input%20File%20%E2%80%93%20Invoice.

Send a separate email for every individual invoice to your own Gmail account from where the bot will read the email. The subject line must be **Invoice-Henry-FM-Invoice Number-Customer Name** (the invoice number and customer name are present in the invoice file name) – for example, if the customer's name is Adam Smith and the invoice number is 8745, then the subject line of the mail should be **Invoice-Henry-FM-8745-Adam Smith**. Here are some examples:

☐ ☆ **me**   **Invoice-Henry-FM-5249-Wills Williams**

📄 Invoice-Henry F…

☐ ☆ **me**   **Invoice-Henry-FM-5250-Sam Will**

📄 Invoice-Henry F…

☐ ☆ **me**   **Invoice-Henry-FM-5321-Henry Dough**

📄 Invoice-Henry F…

Figure 14.2 – A snippet of the Gmail inbox with the subject line and attachment

Now that you have sent the invoices to your mail ID, let's start building the automation.

Setting up the project

Before we start building the process, let's first set up all the UiPath Studio configurations correctly:

1.   Open up UiPath Studio and create a new process with the name `Invoice_Processing_Dispatcher`:

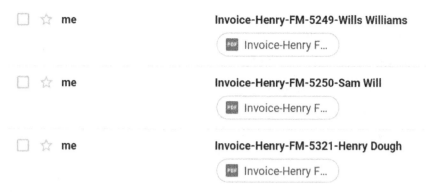

Figure 14.3 – Creating a new process

2. Click on **Manage Packages** from the **Designer** ribbon bar and update the project dependencies to the following versions:

    -   **UiPath.Excel.Activities – v2.10.4**

    -   **UiPath.Mail.Activities – v1.10.5**

    -   **UiPath.System.Activities – v21.4.1**

    -   **UiPath.UIAutomation.Activities – v21.4.4**

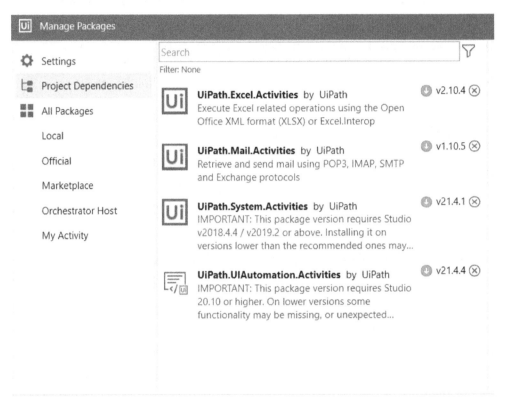

Figure 14.4 – Updating the dependencies

3. Now that you have updated the dependencies to the correct versions, let's also install one more dependency, **UiPath.PDF.Activities – v3.4.0**:

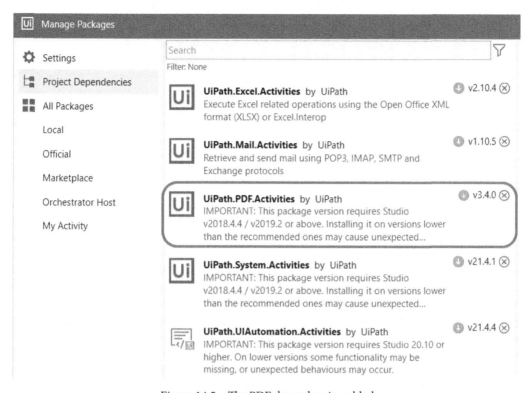

Figure 14.5 – The PDF dependencies added

4. In the Orchestrator web page under your tenant, navigate to the **Folders** section and create a new folder named `Packt`.

Now that you have configured everything that is needed, let's start building the process.

Downloading the invoice

In this section, you will design the bot to download all the invoices from the Gmail account. The following diagram explains the high-level process of downloading the invoices:

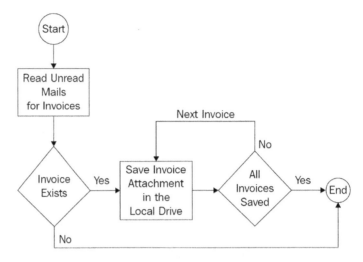

Figure 14.6 – Downloading the invoice

Downloading the invoices is the first step of the entire process. Let's build it:

1. Click on the **New** button from the **DESIGN** ribbon bar and select **Sequence**.

2. Name the sequence Download_Invoice and click on the **Create** button:

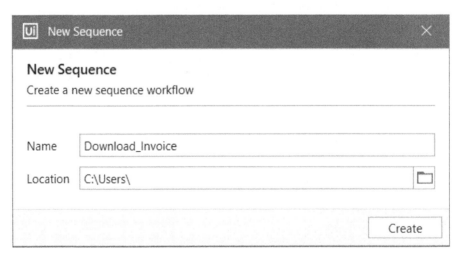

Figure 14.7 – Creating the Download_Invoice sequence

3. Log in to your `cloud.uipath.com` account and start the Orchestrator services. Under the **Assets** section, create an asset with the name `Mail Credential` and choose **Credential** for **Type**. Next, type in your Gmail ID **Username** and **Password** details and click on the **Create** button:

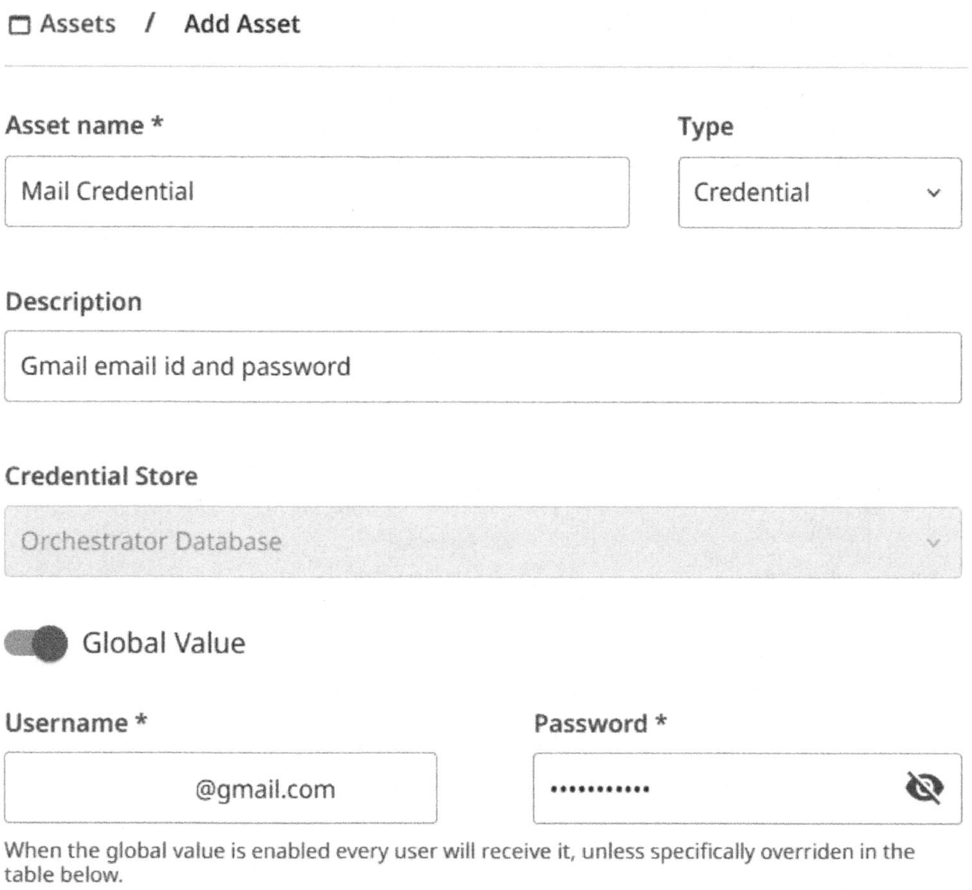

☐ Assets   /   **Add Asset**

Asset name *

| Mail Credential |

Type

| Credential   ⌄ |

Description

| Gmail email id and password |

Credential Store

| Orchestrator Database   ⌄ |

🔘 Global Value

Username *

| @gmail.com |

Password *

| ••••••••••   👁 |

When the global value is enabled every user will receive it, unless specifically overriden in the table below.

Figure 14.8 – Creating a credential asset to store the Gmail credentials

The **Mail Credential** asset in this scenario is created in the personal workspace folder. You can create the asset in the `Packt` folder if you wish to.

4. In Studio, inside the `Download_Invoice` sequence, drag and drop the `Try Catch` activity and then drop the `Get Credential` activity inside the `Try` block. Next, click on the **Properties** panel of the `Get Credential` activity. For the **Input** property, provide `"Mail Credential"` under **AssetName**. Then, under **Output**, create a new variable for the **Password** and **Username** properties using *Ctrl + K*. Type in `pwd` for **Password** and press *Enter*, and then type in `email` for **Username** and press *Enter* again:

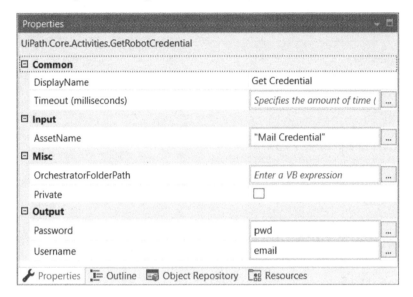

Figure 14.9 – The Properties panel of the Get Credential activity

5. Drag and drop the `Get IMAP Mail Messages` activity after the `Get Credential` activity. By clicking on the **Properties** panel of the `Get IMAP Mail Messages`, configure the properties as follows:

- **MailFolder** – `"Inbox"`.

- **Port** – `993`.

- **Server** – `"imap.gmail.com"`.

- **Email** – pass the `email` variable.

- **SecurePassword** – pass the `pwd` variable.

- **FilterExpression** - `"SUBJECT Invoice-Henry-FM"`.

- Check the **MarkAsRead** option.

- **Top** – `10`.

- Add a new variable called `mails` for the **Messages** property under **Output**:

Properties		
UiPath.Mail.IMAP.Activities.GetIMAPMailMessages		
⊟ **Common**		
DisplayName	Get IMAP Mail Messages	
TimeoutMS	*Specifies the amount of time in millisecc*	...
⊟ **Host**		
MailFolder	"Inbox"	...
Port	993	...
Server	"imap.gmail.com"	...
⊟ **Logon**		
Email	email	...
Password	*The password of the email account used*	...
SecurePassword	pwd	...
⊟ **Misc**		
Private	☐	
⊟ **Options**		
DeleteMessages	☐	
FilterExpression	"SUBJECT Invoice-Henry-FM"	...
FilterExpressionCharacterSet	"US-ASCII"	...
MarkAsRead	☑	
OnlyUnreadMessages	☑	
OrderByDate	NewestFirst	
SecureConnection	Auto	
Top	10	...
⊟ **Output**		
Messages	mails	...
🔧 Properties ᵇ≡ Outline ᴱ◙ Object Repository ᴸᴬᴬ Resources		

Figure 14.10 – The Properties panel of the Get IMAP Mail Messages activity

6. Next, use the `For Each` activity to iterate over all `mails`. Then, pass the `mails` variable in the `Value` section, change the argument name to `mail` from **item**, and change **TypeArgument** to `System.Net.Mail.MailMessage`.

7. Inside the body of the `For Each` activity, use an `If` activity where you will check whether the mail has the invoice as the attachment. Under the `If` activity condition, type `mail.Attachments.Count > 0 And mail.Attachments. Count < 2 And mail.Attachments.Item(0).Name.ToString. StartsWith("Invoice-Henry FM-") And mail.Attachments. Item(0).Name.ToString.EndsWith(".pdf"`.

8. The Boolean condition checks for a single attachment and the naming convention of the invoice. If the Boolean condition is TRUE, you will save the attachment; otherwise, log a message, with the log level as Info and a message saying "No invoice attachment in the mail".

9. Then, drag and drop the Save Attachments activity into the **Then** block of the If activity to download the invoice. Finally, pass the mail argument in the **Message** property. Now, type in "Invoice" (the folder name to save the invoice) in the **FolderPath** property of the Save Attachments activity.

10. In the **Arguments** panel, create an argument with the name out_isMail. Set the direction of it to Out and choose the argument type as boolean.

11. Then, use an Assign activity below Save Attachments, passing out_isMail in the **To** section and True in the **Value** section. You will be using the out_ isMail argument in Main.xaml later to read invoices:

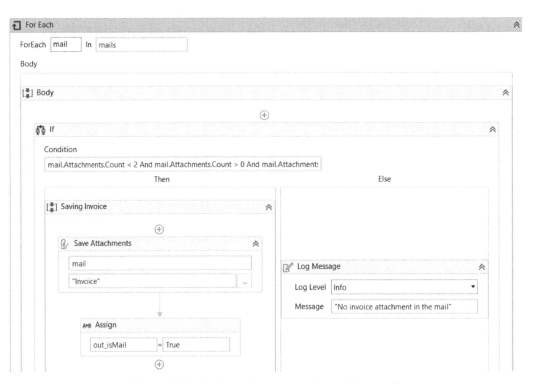

Figure 14.11 – Saving an invoice attachment from mail

12. Finally, inside the **Catches** block, catch `SystemException` and log a message. The **Log Level** value should be `Error` and **Message** should be `"Unable to fetch the mail, please check Logon or host properties setting"+vbLf+exception.Message+vbLf+exception.Source:`

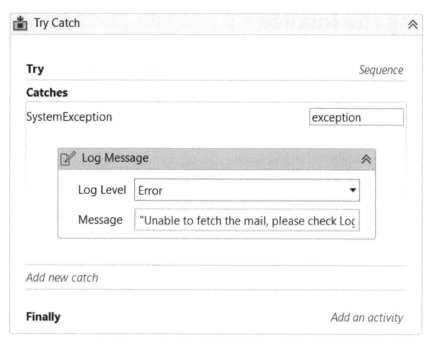

Figure 14.12 – The Catches block with the Log Message activity

Before finishing up with this `Download_Invoice` sequence, let's do a final check on it. The `Variables` panel of the `Download_Invoice` sequence should have three variables, as shown in the following screenshot:

Name	Variable type	Scope	Default
pwd	SecureString	Download_Invoice	Enter a VB expression
email	String	Download_Invoice	Enter a VB expression
mails	List<MailMessage>	Download_Invoice	Enter a VB expression

Figure 14.13 – The Variables panel

The **Arguments** panel of the `Download_Invoice` sequence should have one **Out** argument, as shown in the following screenshot:

Name	Direction	Argument type	Default value
out_isMail	Out	Boolean	Default value not supported

Figure 14.14 – The Arguments panel

Now that we have completed the downloading of the invoices from the mail, let's look at the next section on how to read the downloaded invoices to extract the required information from them.

Reading the invoice

In this section, you will read the invoices that have been downloaded from the mail. The following diagram explains the high-level process of reading the invoices:

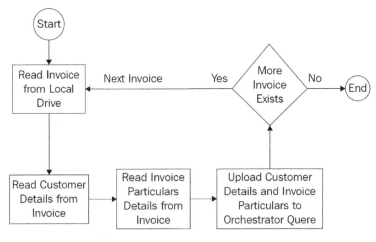

Figure 14.15 – Reading the invoice details

Here, you will be extracting the customer details and invoice particulars from the read invoices. Let's begin designing this process:

1. Let's start by creating a new sequence with the name Read_Invoice.

2. Then, in the **Variables** panel, create a variable with the name currentDirectoryPath, choose the type as String, and type Directory. GetCurrentDirectory() in the **Default** section.

3. Also, create two more variables, the first named invoices of the String[] type (an array of String) and the second named invoicePath of the String type.

4. In the Read_Invoice sequence, drag and drop the first Assign activity. Pass the invoices variable in the **To** section and Directory. GetFiles(currentDirectoryPath+"\Invoice") in the **Value** section. This will fetch all the names of the invoices from the Invoice folder and store them in the variable named invoices.

5. Next, drag and drop the `For Each` activity so that you can iterate over each invoice and extract information from them. Then, pass `invoices` in the **Values** section and change **item** to `invoice` in the `For Each` activity.

6. Add an `Assign` activity inside the body of the `For Each` activity and pass the `InvoicePath` variable in the **To** section and `invoice.ToString` in the **Value** section:

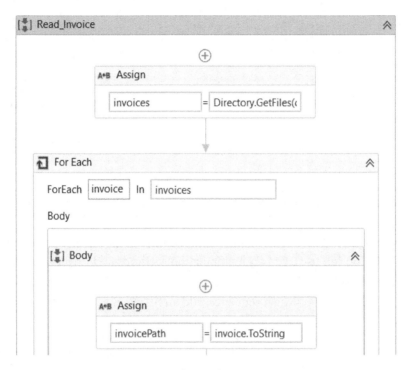

Figure 14.16 – The Read_Invoice sequence

Now that we can iterate over each invoice, let's first extract customer details from the invoice. After that, we'll extract invoice particulars too.

Extracting customer details

In this section, you will extract the customer details from the read invoice. The following diagram explains the high-level process of extracting customer details from the invoice:

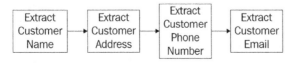

Figure 14.17 – Extracting customer details

In this sequence, you will extract the customer's name, address, phone number, and email from the invoice:

1. Let's start by creating a new sequence and naming it `Extract_Customer_Details`.

2. Create four `Out` arguments and one `In` argument, as shown in the following screenshot:

Name	∨	Direction	Argument type	Default value
out_customerPhoneNo		Out	String	*Default value not supported*
out_customerName		Out	String	*Default value not supported*
out_customerEmail		Out	String	*Default value not supported*
out_customerAddress		Out	String	*Default value not supported*
in_invoicePath		In	String	*Enter a VB expression*

Figure 14.18 – The Arguments panel

3. To extract the customer name, drag and drop a `Sequence` activity and rename it `Customer Name`.

4. If you look at the invoice name, it has the customer name already present in it. Therefore, you can use `String` manipulation methods and extract only the customer name from the complete string.

5. Inside the `Customer Name` sequence, add an `Assign` activity and pass out_customerName in the **To** section. Then, type in `in_invoicePath.Split({"-"},StringSplitOptions.None)(3).Split({"."},StringSplitOptions.None)(0)` in the **Value** section:

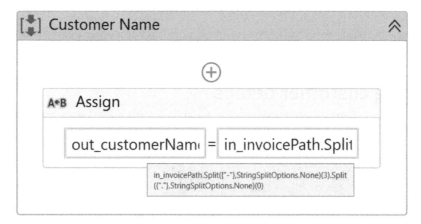

Figure 14.19 – Extracting the customer name

6. Let's now extract the customer address. We will use the Read PDF Text activity to read the invoice. Pass the in_invoicePath argument under the **FileName** property. Next, create a new variable for the **Text** property under **Output** using *Ctrl + K*; then, type in invoiceData and press *Enter*. All the invoice data read using the Read PDF Text activity will be saved in the invoiceData variable:

Figure 14.20 – The Read PDF Text activity

7. If you look at the invoice, the customer's address is between the customer's name and phone number. So, to find customer addresses, you will once again use the string manipulation methods.

8. Drag and drop a Sequence activity and rename it Customer Address.

9. Create a new variable with the name custNameIndex (to get the index position of the customer name from the invoice) of the Int32 type.

10. Inside the Customer Address sequence, add an Assign activity, pass custNameIndex in the **To** section, and type in invoiceData.IndexOf(out_customerName) in the **Value** section.

11. Drag and drop another `Assign` activity and pass the `out_customerAddress` argument in the **To** section and type in `invoiceData.Substring(custNameIndex + out_customerName.Length, invoiceData.IndexOf("Ph No:", custNameIndex + out_customerName.Length) - custNameIndex - out_customerName.Length)` in the **Value** section:

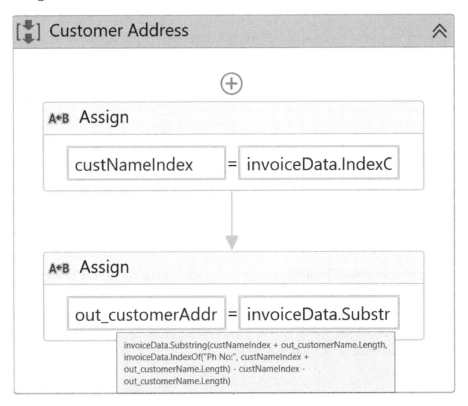

Figure 14.21 – Extracting the customer address

Let's now extract the customer's phone number. You will follow the same logic as the customer address. The customer phone number is between the **Ph No:** and **Email:** text. Again, you will use string manipulation methods here.

12. Drag and drop a `Sequence` activity and rename it `Customer Phone Number`.

13. Create a new variable with the name `custPhoneNoIndex` (to get the index position of **Ph No:** from the invoice) of the `Int32` type.

14. Inside the `Customer Phone Number` sequence, add an `Assign` activity, pass `custPhoneNoIndex` in the **To** section, and type in `invoiceData.IndexOf("Ph No: ")` in the **Value** section.

15. Drag and drop another `Assign` activity and pass the `out_customerPhoneNo` argument in the **To** section and type in `invoiceData.Substring(custPhoneNoIndex + 6, invoiceData.IndexOf("Email:", custPhoneNoIndex + 6) - custPhoneNoIndex - 6)` in the **Value** section:

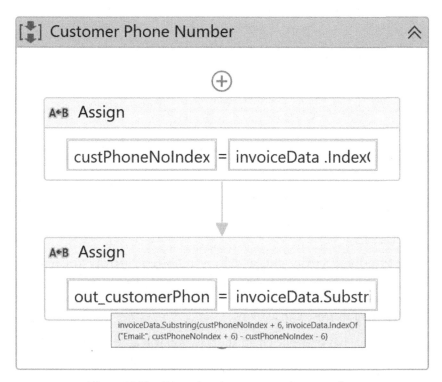

Figure 14.22 – Extracting the customer phone number

16. Let's now extract the customer's email address. To do so, you will use the **Regular Expression** (**RegEx**) technique, covered in *Chapter 7, Manipulating Data using UiPath*. Drag and drop a `Sequence` activity and rename it `Customer Email`.

17. Next, inside the `Customer Email` sequence, drag and drop the `Matches` activity.

18. Click on the **Configure Regular Expression** button to pass the email regex.

19. In the **RegEx Builder** window, from the **RegEx** drop-down menu, choose **Email** and click on the **Save** button:

Figure 14.23 – Selecting Email from RegEx Builder

20. In the properties section of the `Matches` activity, pass `invoiceData` under **Input**. Then, in the **Result** section, create a new variable (using *Ctrl + K*) named `emails`.

21. After the `Matches` activity, drag and drop an `Assign` activity to assign the email extracted from the `regex`. Pass `out_customerEmail` argument in the **To** section. Then, type in `emails.ElementAt(0).ToString` in the **Value** section of the `Assign` activity.

Since the invoice has only one email address, you will access it by the 0th index only:

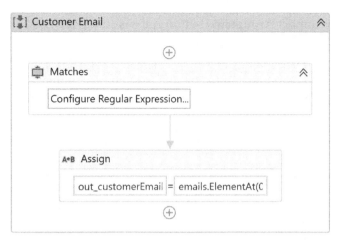

Figure 14.24 – Extracting the customer email

22. Return to the `Read_Invoice` sequence. From the **Project** panel, drag and drop the `Extract_Customer_Details.xaml` workflow below the `Assign` activity in the body of the `For Each` activity:

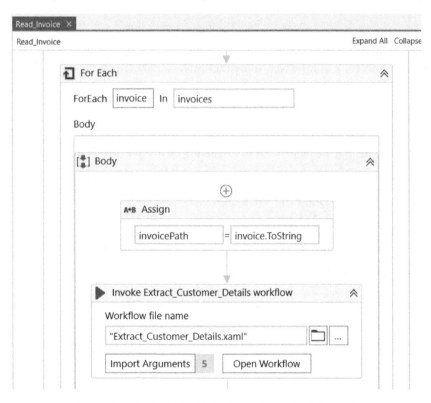

Figure 14.25 – Invoking Extract_Customer_Details.xaml

23. Click on the **Import Arguments** button and pass the `invoicePath` variable as the value to the `in_InvoicePath` argument.

24. Create four new variables using *Ctrl + K* named `customerName`, `customerAddress`, `customerEmail`, and `customerPhoneNo`. Then, pass them as **Value** to all the **Out** arguments, as shown in the following screenshot:

Name	Direction	Type	Value
in_invoicePath	In	String	invoicePath
out_customerName	Out	String	customerName
out_customerAddress	Out	String	customerAddress
out_customerEmail	Out	String	customerEmail
out_customerPhoneNo	Out	String	customerPhoneNo

Invoked workflow's arguments

Create Argument

OK   Cancel

Figure 14.26 – The import arguments

Now that we have successfully extracted the customer's name, phone number, address, and email, let's now look at how we can extract invoice particulars.

Extracting invoice particulars

In this section, you will extract the invoice particulars from the read invoice. The following diagram explains the high-level process of extracting customer details from the invoice:

Figure 14.27 – Extracting invoice particulars

In this sequence, we will extract the invoice date, invoice number, and order information:

1. Let's start by creating a new sequence and naming it `Extract_Invoice_Particular`.

2. Now, create three `Out` arguments and one `In` argument, as shown in the following screenshot:

Name	Direction	Argument type	Default value
out_invoiceNumber	Out	String	*Default value not supported*
out_invoiceDate	Out	String	*Default value not supported*
out_dt_invoiceParticulars	Out	DataTable	*Default value not supported*
in_invoicePath	In	String	*Enter a VB expression*

Figure 14.28 – The Arguments panel

3. Drag and drop the `Start Process` activity and pass the `in_invoicePath` argument in the **FileName** properties section. When the bot is running, the `Start Process` activity in this scenario will open up the invoice PDF file in Adobe Acrobat Reader:

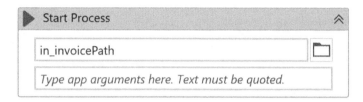

Figure 14.29 – The Start Process activity

4. Now, in the background, open any one of the invoices in Adobe Acrobat Reader (note that the Adobe Acrobat Reader used in this process is a 32-bit version). Then, in UiPath Studio, after the `Start Process` activity, drag and drop the `Attach Window` activity.

5. Next, click on **Indicate window on screen**, hover the mouse on **Adobe reader (Invoice)**, and then right-click on it. This will capture the invoice PDF.

6. Let's look at the selector of the `Attach Window` activity. The selector code looks as follows:

```
<wnd app='acrord32.exe' cls='AcrobatSDIWindow'
title='Invoice-Henry FM-Henry Dough.pdf - Adobe Acrobat
Reader DC (32-b*'/>
```

7. If you look at the `title` attribute, the value is `'Invoice-Henry FM-Henry Dough.pdf - Adobe Acrobat Reader DC (32-b*'`. Here, the customer name is also included, which means this will run only for the customer named `Henry Dough`, but we have multiple invoices and need to iterate over them, so this selector will not be valid for other invoices. Hence, we need to make the selector dynamic so that it will work for all the invoices.

8. To do so, add * wildcards to the selector (as discussed in *Chapter 8, Exploring UiPath Selectors*). Edit the selector and replace the customer name part with * and click on the **Validate** button. This turns green, which confirms that the new selector is correct.

9. After adding the * wildcard, your new selector code should look like this – `<wnd app='acrord32.exe' cls='AcrobatSDIWindow' title='Invoice-Henry FM-*.pdf - Adobe Acrobat Reader DC (32-b*' />`:

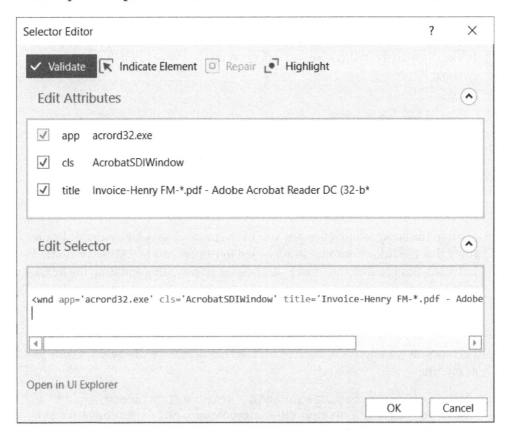

Figure 14.30 – The Selector Editor window of the Attach Window activity

10. Drag and drop the `Get Text` activity inside the `Attach Window` activity. You will use this `Get Text` activity to capture the invoice date from the PDF. Click on the **Indicate element inside window** action of the `Get Text` activity. Then, hover the mouse cursor on the **Date** field of the invoice and record it by doing a right-click, as shown in the following screenshot:

Henry's Food Mart
4628 Hillside Drive, Lafayette, Louisiana, 70506

INVOICE

Date: 16/07/2021|
Invoice No # 5321

Figure 14.31 – Capturing the date from the invoice

11. Let's look at the selector of this Get Text activity. In this case, the date mentioned in the invoice is captured by the selector. Here is the part of the selector:

```
<ctrl name=' Date: 16/07/2021 ' role='text' />
```

As we want it to be dynamic to work with any other date provided, we will use the dynamic selector concepts again. Replace the **16/07/2021** part with * and click on the **Validate** button. The **Validate** button turns green, which confirms that the new selector is correct. Your new selector code should look as follows:

```
<ctrl name=' Date: * ' role='text' />
```

* will make sure that it works for any date provided in the invoice:

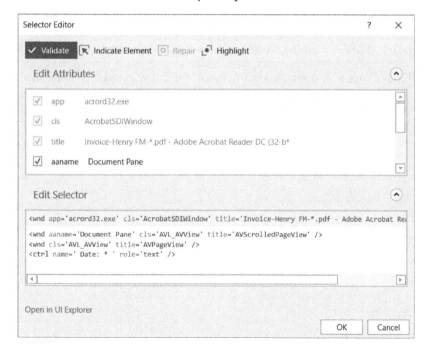

Figure 14.32 – The Selector Editor window of the Get Text activity for the invoice date

12. Now that we have captured the invoice date, let's save it into our already created argument. Under the **Properties** panel, pass out_invoiceDate in the **Value** section of the **Output** property.

   We have successfully extracted the invoice date. Now, let's extract the invoice number.

13. Drag and drop the Get Text activity below the Get Text activity of the invoice date. You will use this Get Text activity to capture the invoice number from the PDF.

14. Click on **Indicate element inside window**, hover the mouse cursor on the **Invoice number** field of the invoice, and then record it by doing a right-click.

15. Let's look at the selector of this Get Text activity. In this case, the invoice number mentioned in the invoice is captured by the selector. Here is the part of the selector:

```
<ctrl name=' Invoice No # 5321 ' role='text' />
```

   As we want the selector to be dynamic to work with any other invoice number provided, we will use the dynamic selector concepts again. Replace the **5321** part with * and click on the **Validate** button. The **Validate** button turns green, which confirms that the new selector is correct. Your new selector code should look as follows:

```
<ctrl name=' Invoice No # * ' role='text' />
```

   * will make sure that it works for any invoice number provided in the invoice:

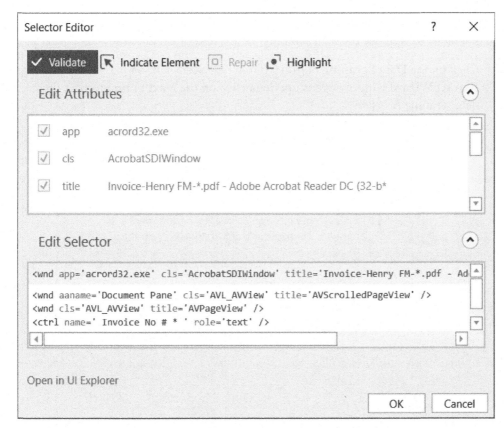

Figure 14.33 – The Selector Editor window of the Get Text activity for the invoice number

16. Now that we have captured the invoice number, let's save it into our already created argument. Under the **Properties** panel, pass `out_invoiceNumber` in the **Value** section of the **Output** property.

> **Note**
> The selector for the invoice date and invoice number is partially generated because both `Get Text` activities are used inside the `Attach Window` activity.

Let's extract the invoice particulars now. Since the data is structured data, presented in the form of a table, we will use the data scraping wizard tool of UiPath Studio to extract it:

1. Click on the **Data Scraping** button from the **DESIGN** ribbon bar. A new **Extract Wizard** window opens up; then, click on the **Next** button to start the data scraping process:

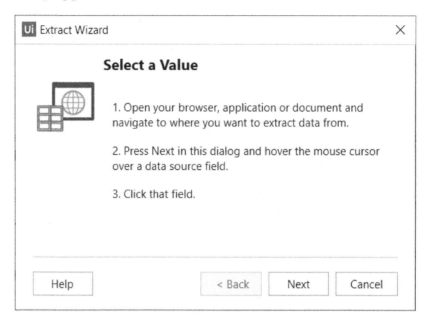

Figure 14.34 – The data scraping wizard

2. Hover the cursor over any of the table cells and right-click on it:

Qty	Description	Unit Price	Line Total
2	Avocado and chickpea pasta	10.00	20.00
5	Avocado and grapefruit bagel	8.00	40.00
1	Apricot and date crumble	10.00	10.00
1	Cheddar cheese and jujube salad	15.00	15.00
1	Mascarpone and mulberry salad	20.00	20.00
		Subtotal	105.00
		Shipping	2.00
		Total	$107.00

Figure 14.35 – Selecting a table cell

3. A new window appears, which shows all the extracted table cell values. Enter 0 (zero) in the **Maximum number of results** field and click on the **Finish** button:

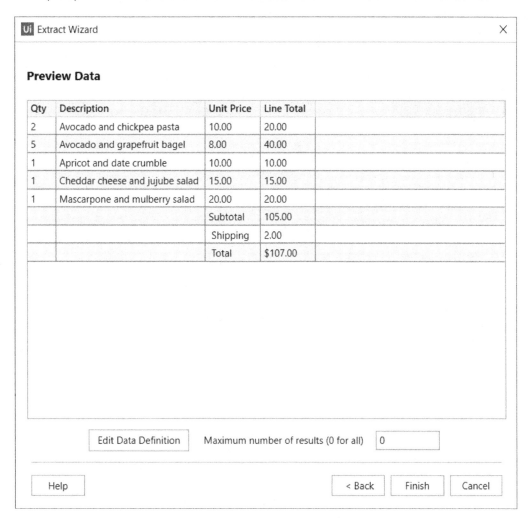

Figure 14.36 – The extracted table cells

4. Clicking on the **Finish** button places the `Extract Structured Data` activity in Studio inside an `Attach Window` activity:

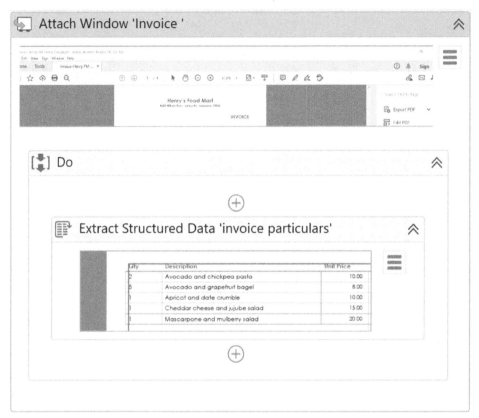

Figure 14.37 – The Extract Structured Data activity

5. Edit the selector for the `Attach Window` activity, since it contains the customer's name. The edited selector should look as follows:

```
<wnd app='acrord32.exe' cls='AcrobatSDIWindow'
title='Invoice-Henry FM-*.pdf - Adobe Acrobat Reader DC
(32-b*' />
```

6. The data scraping wizard will extract the data in a `DataTable` format. Save it into your already created `DataTable` argument. Under the **Properties** panel, pass out_ dt_invoiceParticulars in the **DataTable** section of the **Output** property.

7. Finally, drag and drop the `Close Application` activity, click on **Indicate element inside window**, hover the mouse on Adobe Acrobat Reader, and right-click on it. This will close the PDF reader after extracting all the required fields from it.

8. Return to the `Read_Invoice` sequence. From the **Project** panel, drag and drop the `Extract_Invoice_Particular.xaml` workflow below the `InvokeExtract_Customer_Details workflow` activity in the body of the `For Each` activity:

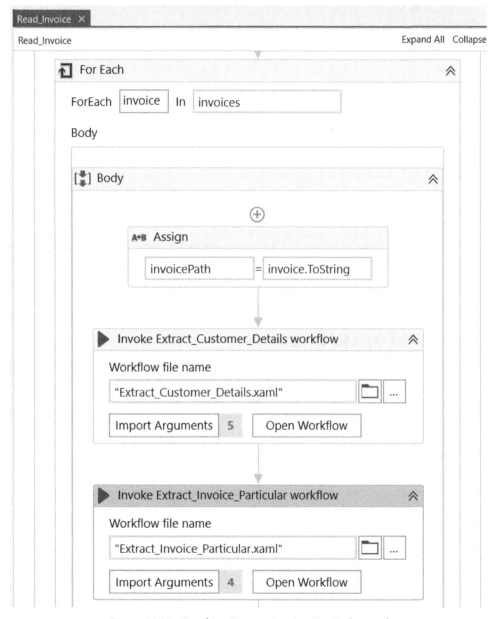

Figure 14.38 – Invoking Extract_Invoice_Particular.xaml

9. Click on the **Import Arguments** button and pass the `invoicePath` variable as the value to the `in_InvoicePath` argument.

10. Create three new variables using *Ctrl + K*, named `invoiceDate`, `invoiceNumber`, and `dt_invoiceParticulars`, and pass them as **Value** to all the **Out** arguments, as shown in the following screenshot:

Name	Direction	Type	Value
in_invoicePath	In	String	invoicePath
out_invoiceDate	Out	String	invoiceDate
out_invoiceNumber	Out	String	invoiceNumber
out_dt_invoiceParticulars	Out	DataTable	dt_invoiceParticulars
Create Argument			

Invoked workflow's arguments

OK   Cancel

Figure 14.39 – The import arguments

Congratulations! You have extracted all the necessary fields from the invoice. Let's upload all these values to the Orchestrator queues.

Uploading the invoice data to the Orchestrator queues

In this section, you will upload the customer details and invoice particulars to the Orchestrator queues. The following diagram explains the high-level process of uploading data to the queues:

Figure 14.40 – Uploading to the Orchestrator queue

Uploading the customer details and invoice particulars to the queue will help you build the performer model of this process where you can consume the data from the queue and then process it.

Let's get started:

1. First, let's create a queue in Orchestrator. Click on the queue section and create a new queue. Type in `HenryFoodMartInvoice` as the queue name and click on the **Add** button to create the queue:

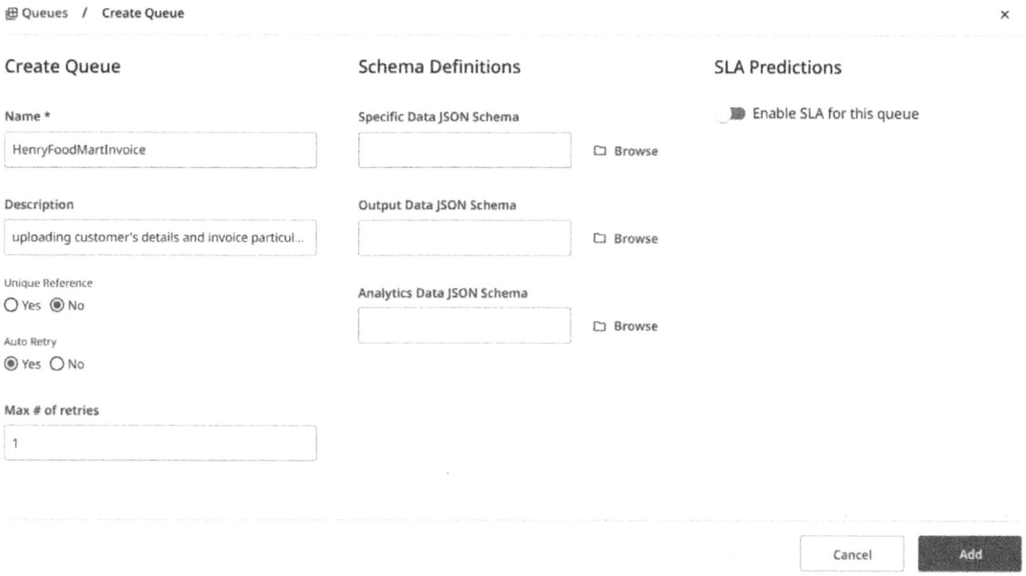

Queues / Create Queue   ✕

Create Queue   **Schema Definitions**   **SLA Predictions**

Name *   Specific Data JSON Schema   ⬤ Enable SLA for this queue

HenryFoodMartInvoice   ☐ Browse

Description   Output Data JSON Schema

uploading customer's details and invoice particul...   ☐ Browse

Unique Reference   Analytics Data JSON Schema
○ Yes ⦿ No   ☐ Browse
Auto Retry
⦿ Yes ○ No

Max # of retries

1

                                                          Cancel   Add

Figure 14.41 – Creating a queue

2. In Studio, create a new sequence and name it `Upload_To_Queue`.

3. Then, click on the **Imports** panel and search for the Newtonsoft.
    Json namespace and add it. You will use this for serializing the in_dt_
    invoiceParticulars arguments so that the entire DataTable can be added
    in a single transaction in the queue:

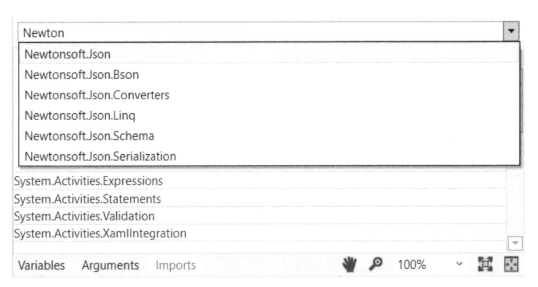

Figure 14.42 – Adding the Newtonsoft.Json namespace

4. Create seven In arguments, as shown in the following screenshot:

Name	Direction	Argument type	Default value
in_invoiceDate	In	String	Enter a VB expression
in_invoiceNumber	In	String	Enter a VB expression
in_customerName	In	String	Enter a VB expression
in_customerAddress	In	String	Enter a VB expression
in_customerPhoneNo	In	String	Enter a VB expression
in_customerEmail	In	String	Enter a VB expression
in_dt_invoiceParticulars	In	DataTable	Enter a VB expression
Create Argument			

| Variables | Arguments | Imports | | | 100% | ∨ |

Figure 14.43 – The Arguments panel

5. Drag and drop a `Try Catch` activity as the first activity.

6. Then, drag and drop the `Add Queue Item` activity inside the `Try` block. Then, under the **Properties** panel of the `Add Queue Item` activity, type in `"HenryFoodMartInvoice"` as the queue name in the **QueueName** section.

7. In this scenario, the queue was created under the folder named `Packt` in Orchestrator, so you must pass the folder name in the `Add Queue Item` activity properties. In the **Folder Path** section, type in `"Packt"`:

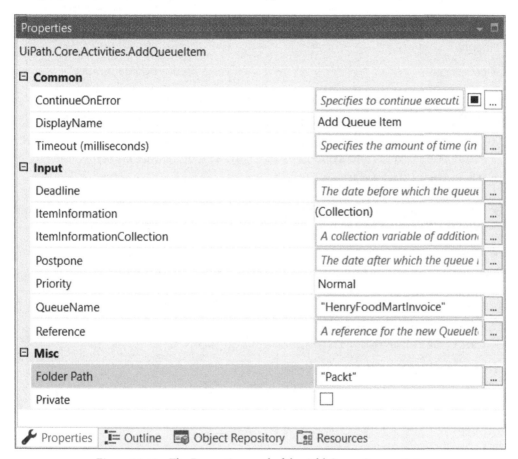

Figure 14.44 – The Properties panel of the Add Queue Item activity

8. Under the **Properties** panel, click on the ellipsis icon of the **ItemInformation** property:

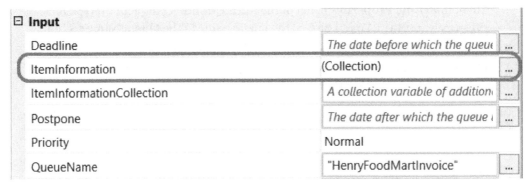

Figure 14.45 – The ItemInformation collection property

9. In the **ItemInformation** window, create seven arguments called `invoiceDate`, `invoiceNumber`, `customerName`, `customerAddress`, `customerPhoneNo`, `customerEmail`, and `invoiceParticulars` of the `String` type.

10. Let's assign values to all the arguments:

-   `invoiceDate = in_invoiceDate.Split({":"},StringSplitOptions.None)(1).ToString.Trim`

-   `invoiceNumber = in_invoiceNumber.Split({"#"},StringSplitOptions.None)(1).ToString.Trim`

-   `customerName = in_customerName`

-   `customerAddress = in_customerAddress`

-   `customerPhoneNo = in_customerPhoneNo`

-   `customerEmail = in_customerEmail`

-   `invoiceParticulars = JsonConvert.SerializeObject(in_dt_invoiceParticulars)`

After assigning all the values in the **Value** section, your **ItemInformation** window should look as follows:

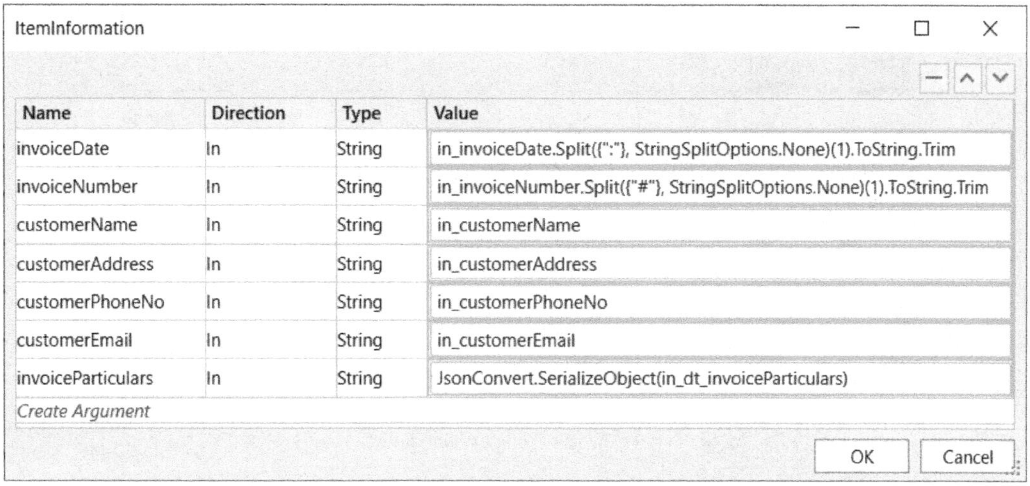

Name	Direction	Type	Value
invoiceDate	In	String	in_invoiceDate.Split({":"}, StringSplitOptions.None)(1).ToString.Trim
invoiceNumber	In	String	in_invoiceNumber.Split({"#"}, StringSplitOptions.None)(1).ToString.Trim
customerName	In	String	in_customerName
customerAddress	In	String	in_customerAddress
customerPhoneNo	In	String	in_customerPhoneNo
customerEmail	In	String	in_customerEmail
invoiceParticulars	In	String	JsonConvert.SerializeObject(in_dt_invoiceParticulars)
Create Argument			

Figure 14.46 – The ItemInformation window with all the values assigned

11. The invoice date and invoice number have extra characters in them. To get rid of them, use the Split() function with the appropriate delimiter. As mentioned earlier, the DataTable arguments have to be serialized before uploading to the queue. The SerializeObject() function of the JsonConvert class will help serialize it into a JSON object.

12. Finally, inside the **Catches** block, catch a SystemException.

13. Also, log a message, with **Log Level** as Error and **Message** as "Unable to Upload to Queue" + vbLf+exception.Message + vbLf + exception.Source.

14. Return to the Read_Invoice sequence, and from the **Project** panel, drag and drop the Upload_To_Queue.xaml workflow below the Invoke Extract_ Invoice_Particular workflow activity in the body of the For Each activity:

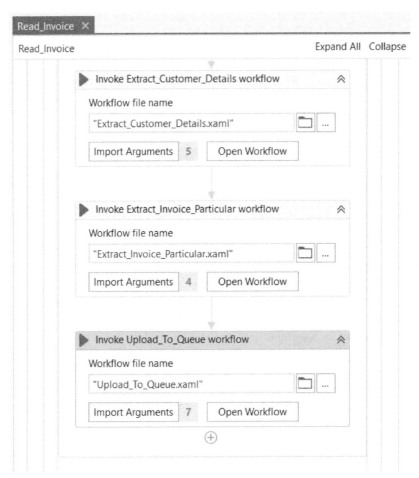

Figure 14.47 – Invoking Upload_to_Queue.xaml

15. Click on the **Import Arguments** button and pass the variables for all the seven In arguments, as shown in the following screenshot:

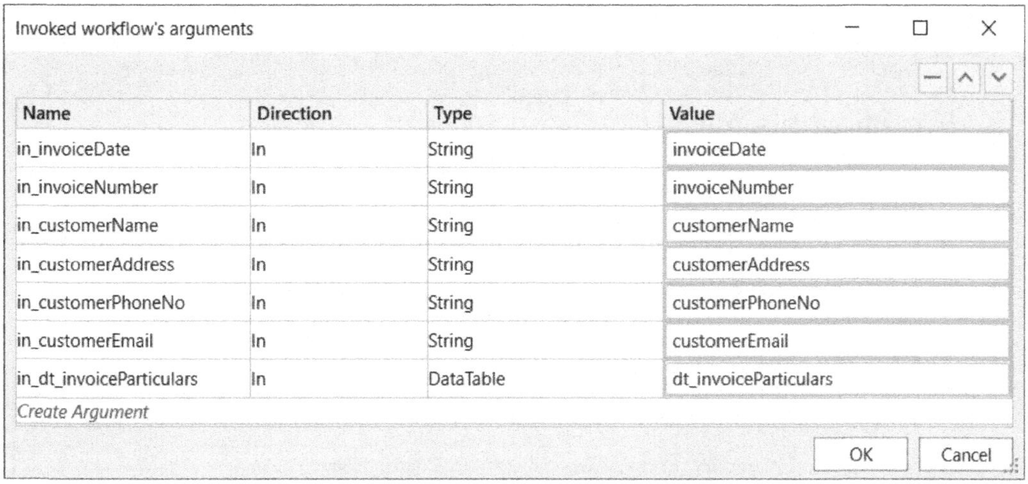

Name	Direction	Type	Value
in_invoiceDate	In	String	invoiceDate
in_invoiceNumber	In	String	invoiceNumber
in_customerName	In	String	customerName
in_customerAddress	In	String	customerAddress
in_customerPhoneNo	In	String	customerPhoneNo
in_customerEmail	In	String	customerEmail
in_dt_invoiceParticulars	In	DataTable	dt_invoiceParticulars
Create Argument			

Invoked workflow's arguments

Figure 14.48 – Importing the arguments

Now that you have completed the uploading to the queue section, it is time to assemble the Main.xaml file to run the process.

Assembling Main.xaml

It's time to run the process, but let's invoke the Download_Invoice.xaml and Read_Invoice.xaml workflows in the Main.xaml file before running the process:

1. In the Main.xaml workflow, create a variable named isMail of the boolean type. Then, drag and drop the Download_Invoice.xaml workflow in the Main.xaml workflow from the **Project** panel.

2. Click on the **Import Arguments** button and pass the isMail variable as the value to the out_isMail argument:

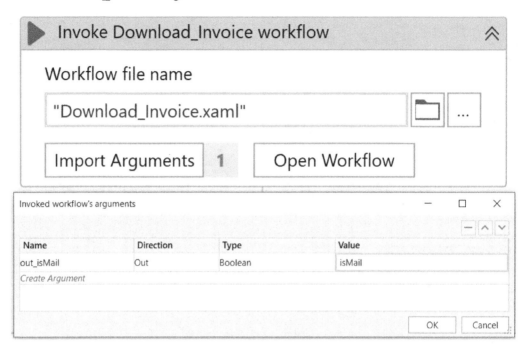

Figure 14.49 – The Invoke Download_Invoice workflow

3. Next, drag and drop the If activity and pass the isMail variable in **Condition**. If the isMail variable value is True, then you can start reading the invoices; otherwise, you will stop the process.

4. Drag and drop the Read_Invoice.xaml workflow inside the **Then** block of the If activity from the **Project** panel.

5. Below that, add a Log Message activity at the **Info** level and set the message to "All invoices details uploaded to queue".

6. In the **Else** block, add a `Log Message` activity at the **Info** level and set the message to "No invoice to process":

Figure 14.50 – The Main.xaml workflow

7. Now, let's run the entire process by clicking on the **Run** button from the **DESIGN** ribbon bar. The process completes without any errors, and all the invoice details are uploaded to the Orchestrator queue:

Figure 14.51 – The transaction item from the queue

Congratulations! You have successfully built the automation for the dispatcher model of invoice processing. Now, you can publish the code to Orchestrator to run the bot from the Orchestrator page or the UiPath Assistant.

Summary

In this chapter, you developed an automation process that scrapes relevant data from invoices for further processing. First, the robot read through emails and downloaded the invoices, received in the form of an email attachment as a PDF. Then, it extracted specific data from the invoices and uploaded them to the Orchestrator queue.

In the next chapter, you will learn how to build the performer model to consume values from the Orchestrator queues and punch them into the order entry CRM.

15
Invoice Processing – Performer

In **Henry's Food Mart**, the finance and accounting department has selected the **Invoice Processing** process for automation. The **Invoice Processing** process reads through emails and downloads the invoices that have been received in an email attachment as a PDF. Then, it extracts customer information and invoice particulars from the invoices and enters them onto the **Order Entry CRM** web page.

You started building this process by following the **Dispatcher-Performer** model. In *Chapter 14, Invoice Processing – Dispatcher,* you learned how to build an automation that downloads the unread invoices from emails, extracts the customer details and invoice particulars from each invoice, and then uploads them to the **Orchestrator** queue named **HenryFoodMartInvoice**.

In this chapter, you will build the **Performer** model to enter the invoice data onto the **Order Entry CRM** web page.

The following is a list of what you will learn as part of this *Invoice Processing – Performer* project:

- Browser automation
- Working with different types of workflows
- Consuming Orchestrator queues
- Modifying selectors
- Logging in UiPath Studio
- Handling exceptions
- Deserializing JSON
- Working with DataTables
- Updating the queue status

Technical requirements

Let's understand the requirements that you will need for this project:

- UiPath Studio Community/Enterprise/Academic Alliance Edition version 20.10 and greater, which must be connected to the UiPath Orchestrator service.
- Access to the UiPath Orchestrator service
- The Order Entry CRM web page
- A Google Chrome browser
- Access to the internet

You can get the entire code for the invoice processing dispatcher from GitHub at `https://github.com/PacktPublishing/UiPath-Associate-Certification-Guide/tree/main/Chapter15/Solution`.

Project overview

In this chapter, you will be designing the performer model of the invoice processing process. Let's understand this process in detail. Here are the following steps that you should perform:

1. Program a robot to start the Order Entry CRM web page.

2. Program the robot to read transaction items from the queue named **HenryFoodMartInvoice** in the Orchestrator workflow.

3. Program the robot to extract the following relevant fields from the transaction item that is read from the queue:

   - **Customer Details**:

     - Customer name

     - Customer address

     - Customer phone number

     - Customer email ID

   - **Invoice Particulars**:

     - Invoice date

     - Invoice number

   - **Order Information**:

     - Item quantity

     - Item description

     - Item unit price

     - Line total amount

     - Subtotal amount

     - Shipping amount

     - Total amount

4. Program a robot to enter the following details on the **Order Entry CRM** web page:

    - Customer details
    - Invoice particulars

5. Repeat *Steps 2*, *3*, and *4* for the remaining queue items.

6. Program the robot to successfully end the process if no new queue items are present in Orchestrator.

Let's understand the entire process with the help of a diagram:

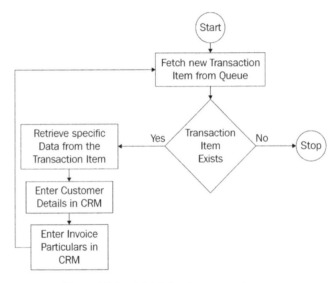

Figure 15.1 – A high-level process diagram

Now that you have understood the process overview, let's start building the automation.

Setting up the project

Before you start building the process, first, let's set up all of the UiPath studio configurations correctly:

1. Open up UiPath Studio and create a new process with the name of Invoice_ Processing_Performer:

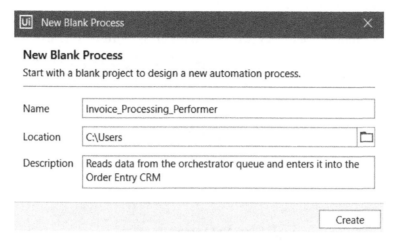

Figure 15.2 – Creating a new process

2. Click on **Manage Packages** from the **Designer** ribbon bar and update the current project dependencies to the following versions:

- **UiPath.Excel.Activities** - **v2.10.4**

- **UiPath.Mail.Activities** – **v1.10.5**

- **UiPath.System.Activities** – **v21.4.1**

- **UiPath.UIAutomation.Activities** – **v21.4.4**:

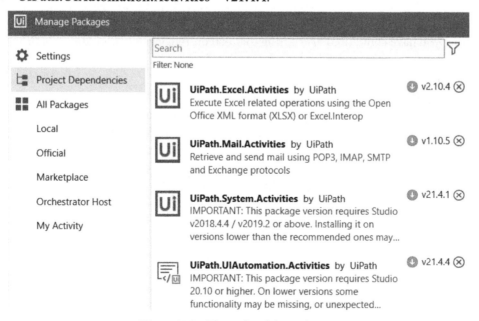

Figure 15.3 – The updated dependencies

3. Now that you have updated the dependencies to their correct versions, let's also install one more dependency, **UiPath.WebAPI.Activities – v1.7.0**:

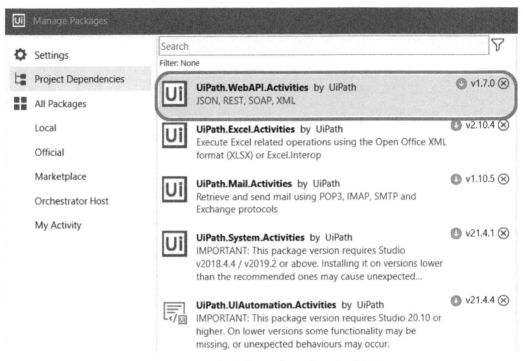

Figure 15.4 – The WebAPI dependencies added

Now that you have configured everything that is required, let's start building the process.

Starting the CRM

In this section, you will start the Order Entry CRM. Before you proceed with the building of the bot, download the Order Entry CRM from the **Input File – Order Entry CRM** folder from the GitHub repository at `https://github.com/PacktPublishing/ UiPath-Associate-Certification-Guide/tree/main/Chapter15/ Input%20File%20-%20Order%20Entry%20CRM`.

The Order Entry CRM has fields corresponding to the invoices, as shown in the following screenshot:

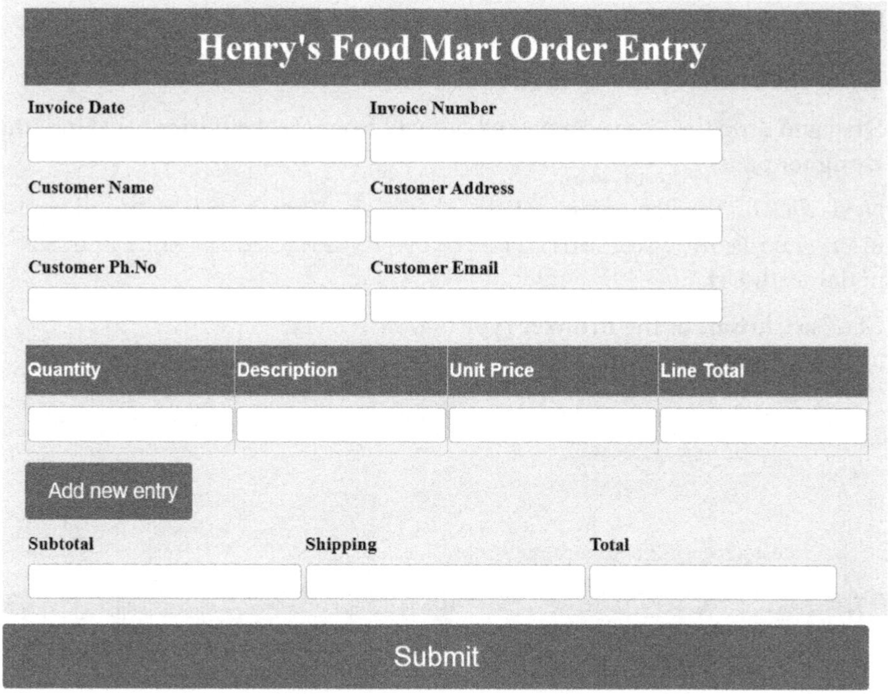
Henry's Food Mart Order Entry
Invoice Date
Invoice Number
Customer Name
Customer Address
Customer Ph.No
Customer Email
Quantity
Description
Unit Price
Line Total
Add new entry
Subtotal
Shipping
Total
Submit

Figure 15.5 – Order Entry CRM

Create a folder with the name of `CRM` in the project directory, and move the **Order Entry** CRM page into this folder:

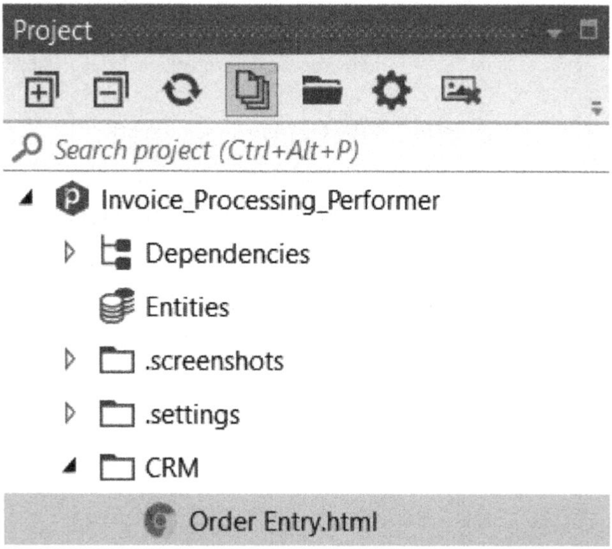
Project
Search project (Ctrl+Alt+P)
Invoice_Processing_Performer
Dependencies
Entities
.screenshots
.settings
CRM
Order Entry.html

Figure 15.6 – Order Entry CRM moved into the CRM folder

Now that you have downloaded the CRM, let's start building the automation:

1. In UiPath Studio, open the `Main.xaml` file.

2. Drag and drop the `Open Browser` activity from the **Activities** panel into the **Designer** panel.

3. Next, click on the **Properties** panel of the `Open Browser` activity and type in `Environment.CurrentDirectory+"\CRM\Order Entry.html"` underneath **Url**.

4. Choose **Chrome** as the **BrowserType** option:

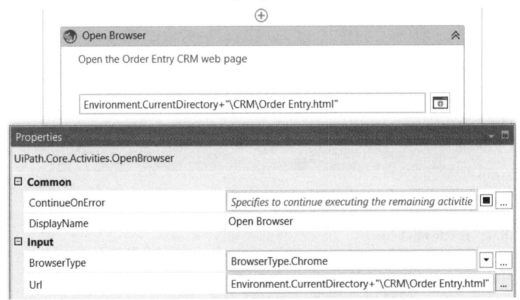

Figure 15.7 – The Open Browser activity

5. Drag and drop the `Maximize Window` activity inside the `Open Browser` activity. This will ensure that the Order Entry CRM web page always opens up in a maximized window.

Excellent! Now that you have opened up the Order Entry CRM web page, let's start reading the data from the queue. Then, we will enter the records into the CRM.

Processing the queue

In this section, you will read transaction items from the queue and enter them into the Order Entry CRM web page.

Let's start by building the workflow:

1. Create a new Flowchart workflow with the name of Read_From_Queue.

2. Next, drag and drop a Sequence activity, rename it to Fetch transaction item, and set it as the start node:

Figure 15.8 – The Fetch transaction item sequence set as the start node

3. Inside the Fetch transaction item sequence, drag and drop the Try Catch activity.

4. Inside the **Try** block of the Try Catch activity, drag and drop the Get Transaction Item activity:

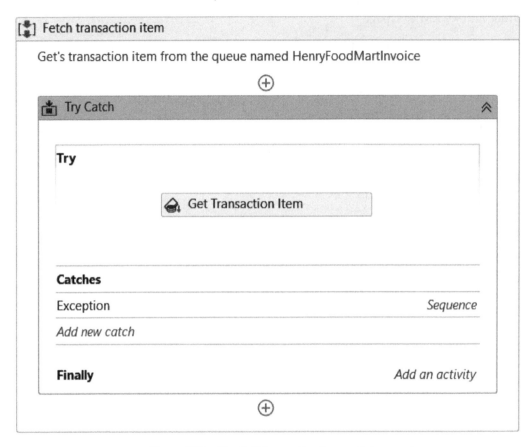

Figure 15.9 – The Get Transaction Item activity

5. Click on the **Properties** panel of the **Get Transaction Item** activity and pass in the following properties:

- **QueueName** = "HenryFoodMartInvoice"

- **Folder Path** = "Packt"

    In this case, the queue in Orchestrator is present in the folder named Packt. Therefore, to fetch the queue from the Packt folder, Packt has been passed in the **Folder Path** section.

- Add a new variable, called `transactionItem`, to the **TransactionItem** property under **Output**:

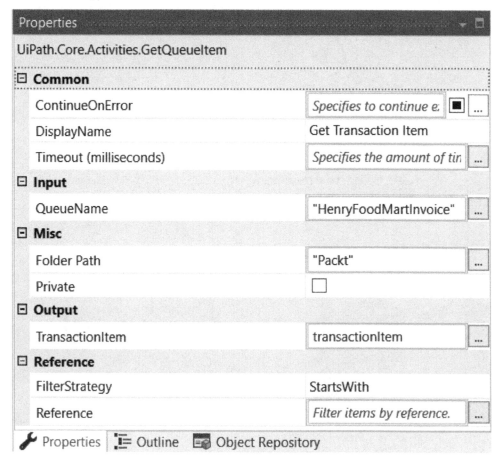

Figure 15.10 – The Properties panel

6. Inside the **Catches** block of the `Try Catch` activity, catch an `Exception` value and add a `Log Message` activity. The **Log Level** property should be `Error`, and the **Message** section should be `"No queue found at the mentioned folder path"+vbLf+exception.Message+vbLf+exception.Source`.

7. Navigate to the `Read_From Queue` flowchart workflow, and drag and drop the `Flow Decision` activity that connects to the `Fetch transaction item` sequence.

8. Type in `transactionItem IsNot Nothing` underneath the **Condition** property of the `Flow Decision` activity:

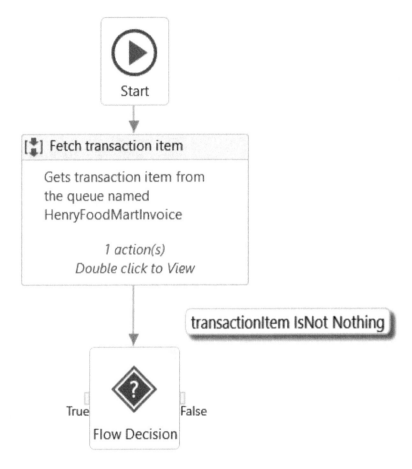

Figure 15.11 – The Flow Decision activity for checking a transaction item

This Boolean condition will give you two outcomes: either TRUE when transaction items are present in the queue or FALSE when there is no transaction item.

9. Drag and drop a `Log Message` activity connecting the `False` branch. Set the **Log Level** property to `Info`, and type `"No more transaction items present"` into the **Message** section:

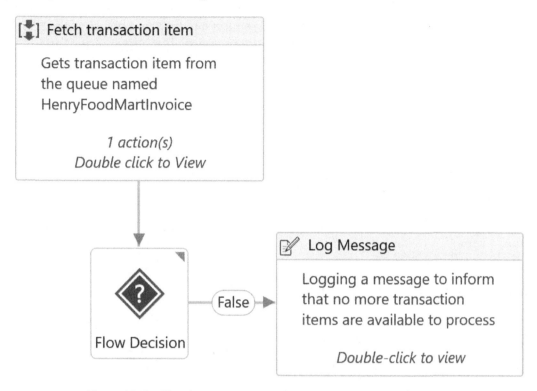

Figure 15.12 – Showing no new transaction items are present in the queue

If the `Flow Decision` activity condition is `TRUE`, you can go ahead and retrieve the **Customer Details** and **Invoice Particular** details from the transaction item. So, let's build the process in which to retrieve invoice details from the transaction item.

Retrieving data from the transaction item

In this section, you will extract the **Customer Details** and **Invoice Particular** details from the transaction item that has been read from the queue:

1. Drag and drop a `Sequence` activity and connect it to the `True` branch of the `Flow Decision` activity. Then, rename the `Sequence` activity to `Retrieve data from transaction`:

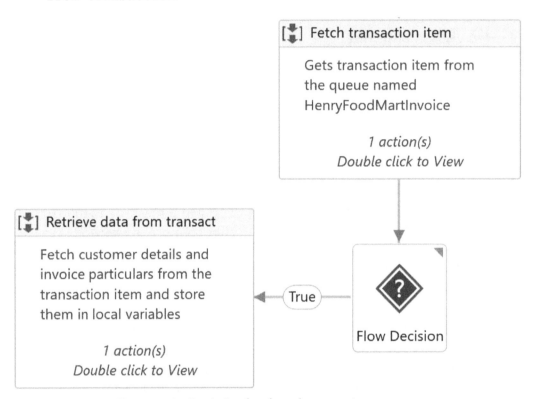

Figure 15.13 – Retrieving data from the transaction sequence

2. Inside the `Retrieve data from transaction` sequence, drag and drop the `Try Catch` activity.

3. Inside the **Try** block of the `Try Catch` activity, drag and drop a `Sequence` activity and rename it to `Fetching Invoice Date`.

4. Add an `Assign` activity inside the `Fetching Invoice Date` sequence. Under the **Property** panel, type `transactionItem. SpecificContent("invoiceDate").ToString` into the **Value** section. Next, in the **To** section, create a new variable, named `invoiceDate`, of the `String` type:

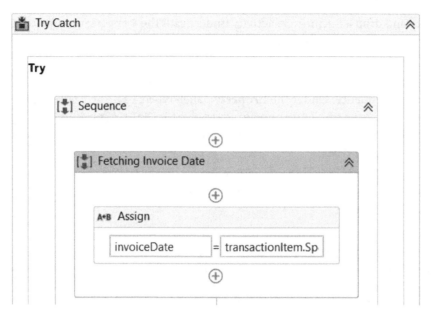

Figure 15.14 – Fetching Invoice Date

5. Drag and drop a `Sequence` activity underneath the `Fetching Invoice Date` sequence and rename it to `Fetching Invoice Number`.

6. Add an `Assign` activity inside the `Fetching Invoice Number` sequence. Under the **Property** panel, type `transactionItem.` `SpecificContent("invoiceNumber").ToString` into the **Value** section. Next, in the **To** section, create a new variable, named `invoiceNumber`, of the `String` type.

7. Drag and drop a `Sequence` activity underneath the `Fetching Invoice Number` sequence and rename it to `Fetching Customer Name`.

8. Add an `Assign` activity inside the `Fetching Customer Name` sequence. Under the **Property** panel, type `transactionItem.` `SpecificContent("customerName").ToString` into the **Value** section. Next, in the **To** section, create a new variable, named `customerName`, of the `String` type.

9. Drag and drop a `Sequence` activity underneath the `Fetching CustomerName` sequence and rename it to `Fetching CustomerAddress`.

10. Add an `Assign` activity inside the `Fetching CustomerAddress` sequence. Under the **Property** panel, type `transactionItem.` `SpecificContent("customerAddress").ToString` into the **Value** section. Next, in the **To** section, create a new variable, named `customerAddress`, of the `String` type.

11. Drag and drop a `Sequence` activity underneath the `Fetching CustomerAddress` sequence and rename it to `Fetching CustomerPhone Number`.

12. Add an `Assign` activity inside the `Fetching CustomerPhone Number` sequence. Under the **Property** panel, type `transactionItem. SpecificContent("customerPhoneNo").ToString` into the **Value** section. Next, in the **To** section, create a new variable, named `customerPhoneNo`, of the `String` type.

13. Drag and drop a `Sequence` activity underneath the `Fetching CustomerPhone Number` sequence and rename it to `Fetching CustomerEmail`.

14. Add an `Assign` activity inside the `Fetching CustomerEmail` sequence. Under the **Property** panel, type `transactionItem. SpecificContent("customerEmail").ToString` into the **Value** section. Next, in the **To** section, create a new variable, named `customerEmail`, of the `String` type.

15. Drag and drop a `Sequence` activity underneath the `Fetching CustomerEmail` sequence and rename it to `Fetching Invoice Particulars`.

16. Add an `Assign` activity inside the `Fetching Invoice Particulars` sequence. Under the **Property** panel, type `transactionItem. SpecificContent("invoiceParticulars").ToString` into the **Value** section. Next, in the **To** section, create a new variable, named `invoiceParticulars`, of the `String` type.

17. Finally, in the **Try** block, add an `Assign` activity underneath the `Fetching Invoice Particulars` sequence. Then, under the **Property** panel, create a Boolean variable named `flag` in the **To** section, and type `True` into the **Value** section.

    You will use this `flag` variable as a checker to verify whether an exception has occurred or not. If any exception is raised, then the `flag` variable will be initialized to `False`; otherwise, it will be initialized with `True` to continue forward.

18. Inside the **Catches** block of the `Try Catch` activity, catch an `Exception` value and add a `Log Message` activity. The **Log Level** property should be `Error`, and the **Message** section should be `"Transaction Item with the specified data not found "+vbLf+exception. Message+vbLf+exception.Source`.

19. Finally, in the **Catches** block, add an `Assign` activity underneath the `Log Message` activity. Then, under the **Property** panel, pass the `flag` Boolean variable into the **To** section and type `False` into the **Value** section.

20. Navigate back to the `Read_From_Queue` flowchart, and drag and drop the `Flow Decision` activity that connects to the `Retrieve data from transaction` sequence.

21. Pass in the `flag` variable underneath the **Condition** property of the `Flow Decision` activity. Doing this will ensure that if the outcome of the `flag` variable is `True`, you can proceed further with entering the details into the CRM. Else, if the outcome of the `flag` variable is `False`, that means there was an exception while retrieving data from the transaction item:

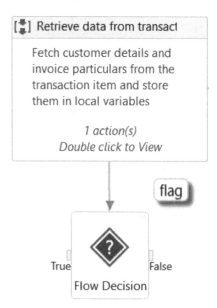

Figure 15.15 – The flow decision activity after fetching data from the transaction item

Now you have successfully retrieved the customer details and invoice particular details from the transaction item. Next, let's start entering the customer details and invoice particulars into the Order Entry CRM web page.

Entering the customer details

In this section, you will enter the customer name, address, phone number, and email in the Order Entry CRM web page:

1. Create a new `Sequence` workflow with the name of `Enter_Customer_Details`.

2. Create four `In` direction arguments and one `Out` direction arguments, as shown in the following screenshot:

Name	Direction	Argument type	Default value	
in_customerName	In	String	*Enter a VB expression*	▲
in_customerAddress	In	String	*Enter a VB expression*	
in_customerPhoneNo	In	String	*Enter a VB expression*	
in_customerEmail	In	String	*Enter a VB expression*	
out_flag	Out	Boolean	*Default value not supported*	▼
Variables Arguments Imports			✋ 🔍 100% ∨	

Figure 15.16 – The Arguments panel

3. Drag and drop the `Try Catch` activity inside the `Enter_Customer_Details` sequence.

4. Inside the **Try** block of the `Try Catch` activity, drag and drop the `Attach Browser` activity and attach the already opened **Order Entry CRM** web page.

5. Drag and drop the `Type Into` activity and indicate the **Customer Name** text field in the Order Entry CRM web page. Type in `in_customerName.Trim` underneath the **Text** property:

Figure 15.17 – Entering the customer name

6. Underneath the customer name `Type Into` activity, drag and drop a new `Type Into` activity and indicate the **Customer Address** text field on the Order Entry CRM web page. Type in `in_customerAddress.Trim` under the **Text** property.

7. Below the customer address `Type Into` activity, drag and drop a new `Type Into` activity and indicate the **Customer Ph.No** text field in the Order Entry CRM web page. Type in `in_customerPhoneNo.Trim` under the **Text** property.

8. Below the customer phone number `Type Into` activity, drag and drop a new `Type Into` activity and indicate the **Customer Email** text field in the Order Entry CRM web page. Type in `in_customerEmail.Trim` under the **Text** property.

9. Next, drag and drop an `Assign` activity. Pass the `out_flag` argument into the **To** section, and type `True` into the **Value** section.

10. Inside the **Catches** block of the `Try Catch` activity, catch an `Exception` value and add a `Log Message` activity. The **Log Level** property should be `Error`, and the **Message** section should be `"Error while entering Customer Details"+vbLf+exception.Message+vbLf+exception.Source`.

11. Below the `Log Message` activity, add an `Assign` activity. Pass the `out_flag` argument into the **To** section, and type `False` into the **Value** section.

12. Navigate back to the `Read_From_Queue` flowchart. From the **Project** panel, drag and drop the `Enter_Customer_Details.xaml` workflow into the **Designer** panel and connect it to the **True** branch of the **Flow Decision** activity:

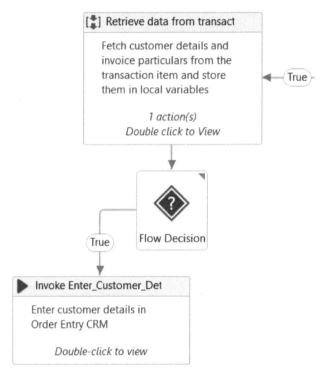

Figure 15.18 – Invoking the Enter_Customer_Details.xaml workflow

13. Click on the **Import Arguments** button of the `Invoke Enter_Customer_Details workflow` activity to open the **Invoked workflow's arguments** window:

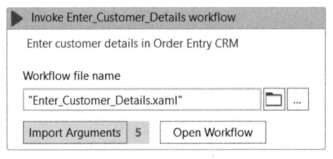

Figure 15.19 – Import Arguments

14. Pass the `flag`, `customerName`, `customerAddress`, `customerPhoneNo`, and `customerEmail` variables into the **Value** section, as shown in the following screenshot:

Invoked workflow's arguments   —   □   ✕

Name	Direction	Type	Value
in_customerName	In	String	customerName
in_customerAddress	In	String	customerAddress
in_customerPhoneNo	In	String	customerPhoneNo
in_customerEmail	In	String	customerEmail
out_flag	Out	Boolean	flag

OK   Cancel

Figure 15.20 – The Invoked workflow's arguments window

15. Finally, drag and drop the `Flow Decision` activity that connects to the `Invoke Enter_Customer_Details workflow` activity.

16. Pass the `flag` variable under the **Condition** property of the `Flow Decision` activity. Doing this will ensure that if the outcome of the `flag` variable is `True`, you can proceed further with entering the details of the invoice particulars in the CRM. Else, if the outcome of the `flag` variable is `False`, that means there was an exception while entering the customer details onto the Order Entry CRM web page:

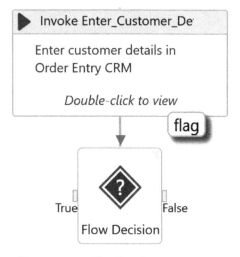

Figure 15.21 – The Flow Decision activity

Now that you have finished entering the customer details on the Order Entry CRM web page, let's move on enter the invoice particulars in the CRM.

Entering the invoice particulars

In this section, you will enter the details of the invoice particulars onto the Order Entry CRM web page. To do this, perform the following steps:

1. Create a new `Sequence` workflow with the name of `Enter_Invoice_Particulars`.

2. Create three `In` direction arguments and one `Out` direction argument, as shown in the following screenshot:

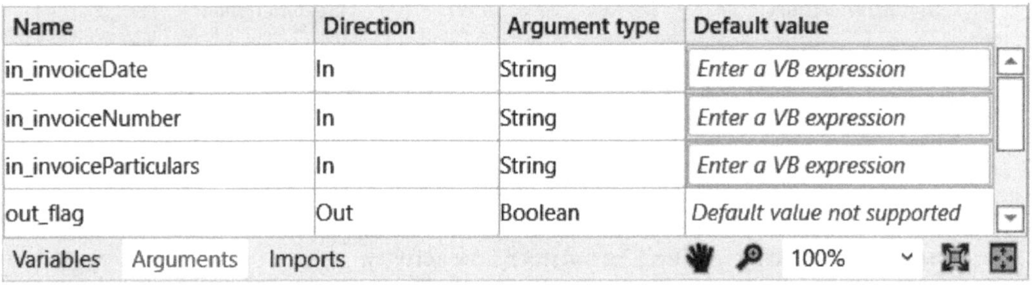

Name	Direction	Argument type	Default value	
in_invoiceDate	In	String	*Enter a VB expression*	▲
in_invoiceNumber	In	String	*Enter a VB expression*	
in_invoiceParticulars	In	String	*Enter a VB expression*	
out_flag	Out	Boolean	*Default value not supported*	▼
Variables Arguments Imports			🖐 🔎 100% ∨ 🔳 🔲	

Figure 15.22 – The Arguments panel

3. Drag and drop the `Try Catch` activity inside the `Enter_Invoice_Particulars` sequence.

4. Inside the **Try** block of the `Try Catch` activity, drag and drop the `Deserialize JSON` activity and configure the properties as follows:

    - Pass in `in_invoiceParticulars` under the **JsonString** field.

    - Select the **TypeArguments** property as `System.Data.DataTable`.

    - Create a new variable, named `dt_invoiceParticulars`, under the **JsonObject** field using *Ctrl + K*:

Figure 15.23 – Deserializing the JSON activity along with the Properties panel

Notice that the invoice particulars are in the form of the `DataTable` variable, and in *Chapter 14, Invoice Processing – Dispatcher*, you serialized the `DataTable` variable to `JSON`. In this case, the `Deserialize JSON` activity will deserialize the `JSON` output stored in the `in_invoiceParticulars` arguments into a new `DataTable` variable, named `dt_invoiceParticulars`.

5. Drag and drop the `Attach Browser` activity and attach it to the already opened **Order Entry CRM** web page.

6. Inside the `Attach Browser` activity scope, drag and drop the `Type Into` activity and indicate the **Invoice Date** text field in the Order Entry CRM web page. Type in `in_invoiceDate.Trim` underneath the **Text** property.

7. Below the invoice date `Type Into` activity, drag and drop a new `Type Into` activity, and indicate the **Invoice Number** text field in the Order Entry CRM web page. Type in `in_invoiceNumber.Trim` underneath the **Text** property.

8. Using the **Variables** panel, create three new variables named `dtCount`, `tableRow`, and `rowCount`, and choose the variable type as `Int32` for all three variables.

9. Below the invoice number `Type Into` activity, drag and drop the `Multiple Assign` activity and assign the following values to the `dtCount`, `tableRow`, and `rowCount` variables:

- `dtCount = dt_invoiceParticulars.Rows.Count`

- `tableRow = 2`

- `rowCount = 1`:

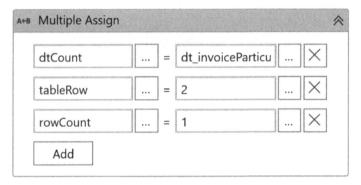

Figure 15.24 – The Multiple Assign activity

The `dtCount` variable determines the total number of rows present in the `dt_invoiceParticulars` DataTable variable.

The `rowCount` variable will determine the current row of the `dt_invoiceParticulars` DataTable variable in the loop. The `rowCount` variable is initialized with 1, and in every iteration, you will increase the values by 1.

The `tableRow` variable is used to enter the invoice particular onto the Order Entry CRM web page. The `tableRow` variable is initialized with 2, and in every iteration, you will increase the values by 1.

The following screenshot shows how the table row is marked on the Order Entry CRM web page:

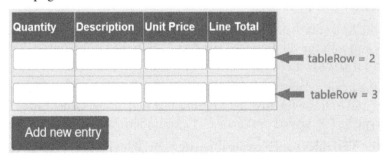

Figure 15.25 – The table row on the Order Entry CRM web page

10. Below the `Multiple Assign` activity, use the `For Each Row` activity and pass `dt_invoiceParticulars` into the **DataTable** property field.

11. Inside the body of the `For Each Row` activity, drag and drop the `Type Into` activity and indicate the **Quantity** text field on the Order Entry CRM web page. Type in `row(0).ToString.Trim` under the **Text** property.

Let's look at the selector for this `Type Into` activity:

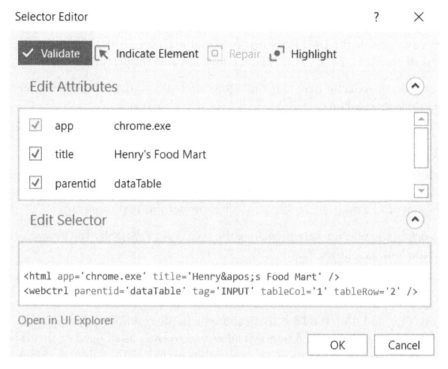

Figure 15.26 – The selector for the Type Into activity of the Quantity text field

If you look at the selector, it has a `tableRow='2'` attribute, which means it will type in the second row of the table for every iteration. However, you need to type in the new row for every new line item; hence, replace 2 with the `tableRow` variable.

The new selector should look as follows:

```
<webctrlparentid='dataTable' tag='INPUT'colName='Quanti-
ty'tableCol='1'tableRow='{{tableRow}}' />
```

> **Note**
>
> If the `tableCol` and `tableRow` attributes are not present in the selector, use the **UI Explorer** window and add them to the selector.

12. Below the item quantity Type Into activity, drag and drop a new Type Into activity and indicate the **Description** text field on the Order Entry CRM web page. Then, type in row(1).ToString.Trim under the **Text** property.

   Also, edit the selector here to include the tableRow variable. The new selector should look as follows:

   ```
   <webctrlparentid='dataTable' tag='INPUT'colName='Descrip-
   tion'tableCol='2'tableRow='{{tableRow}}' />
   ```

13. Below the item description Type Into activity, drag and drop a new Type Into activity. Indicate the **Unit Price** text field on the Order Entry CRM web page. Then, type in row(2).ToString.Trim under the **Text** property.

   Also, edit the selector here to include the tableRowvariable. The new selector should look as follows:

   ```
   <webctrlparentid='dataTable' tag='INPUT'colName='Unit
   Price'tableCol='3'tableRow='{{tableRow}}' />
   ```

14. Below the item unit price Type Into activity, drag and drop a new Type Into activity and indicate the **Line Total** text field on the Order Entry CRM web page. Then, type in row(3).ToString.Trim under the **Text** property.

   Also, edit the selector here to include the tableRow variable. The new selector should look as follows:

   ```
   <webctrlparentid='dataTable' tag='INPUT'colName='Line
   Total'tableCol='4'tableRow='{{tableRow}}' />
   ```

15. Next, drag and drop the If activity and type in the condition as rowCount = (dtCount-3). This condition will allow you to enter all of the data that is present in the dt_invoiceParticulars variable, excluding the subtotal, shipping, and total values. The subtotal, shipping, and total values are present in the last three rows of the dt_invoiceParticulars variable.

16. In the **Then** block of the If activity, add a Break activity. Once the bot reaches the subtotal field in the dt_invoiceParticulars variable, it will exit the For Each Row activity when it encounters the Break activity.

17. In the **Else** block of the If activity, add the following two activities:

   - The Click activity: Indicate the **Add new entry** button on the Order Entry CRM web page.

   - The Multiple Assign activity: Increment the value of tableRow and rowCount variables by 1:

Figure 15.27 – The If activity

18. Below the `For Each Row` activity, drag and drop the `Type Into` activity and indicate the **SubTotal** text field on the Order Entry CRM web page. Then, type in `dt_invoiceParticulars.Rows(dtCount- 3)(3).ToString.Trim` underneath the **Text** property.

19. Below the subtotal `Type Into` activity, drag and drop a new `Type Into` activity and indicate the **Shipping** text field in the Order Entry CRM web page. Then, type in `dt_invoiceParticulars.Rows(dtCount- 2)(3).ToString.Trim` underneath the **Text** property.

20. Below the shipping `Type Into` activity, drag and drop a new `Type Into` activity and indicate the **Total** text field on the Order Entry CRM web page. Then, type in `dt_invoiceParticulars.Rows(dtCount- 1)(3).ToString. Trim.Split({"$"},StringSplitOptions.None)(1)` underneath the **Text** property.

21. Use a `Click` activity and indicate the **Submit** button. The bot will click on the **Submit** button, and all the values entered in the CRM will be saved.

22. Below the `Attach Browser` activity, drag and drop the `Assign` activity. Pass `out_flag` into the **To** section, and type `True` into the **Value** section.

23. Inside the **Catches** block of the `Try Catch` activity, catch an `Exception` variable and add a **Log Message** activity. The **Log Level** property should be `Error`, and the **Message** section should be `"Error while entering Invoice Particular"+vBLf+exception.Message+vBLf+exception.Source`.

24. Below the `Log Message` activity, add an `Assign` activity. Pass the `out_flag` argument into the **To** section, and type `False` into the **Value** section.

25. Navigate back to the `Read_From_Queue` flowchart. From the **Project** panel, drag and drop the `Enter_Invoice_Particulars.xaml` workflow into the **Designer** panel and connect it to the **True** branch of the **Flow Decision** activity:

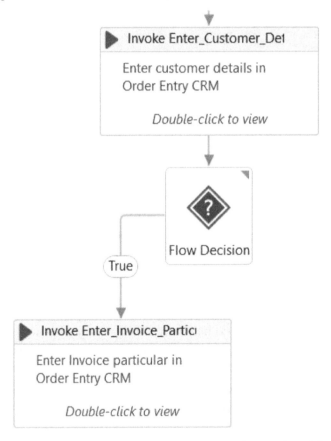

Figure 15.28 – Invoking the Enter_Invoice_Particulars.xaml workflow

26. Click on the **Import Arguments** button of the `Invoke Enter_Invoice_Particulars workflow` activity to open the **Invoked workflow's arguments** window:

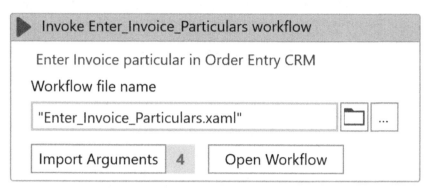

Figure 15.29 – Import Arguments

27. Pass the `flag`, `invoiceDate`, `invoiceNumber`, and `invoiceParticulars` variables into the **Value** section, as shown in the following screenshot:

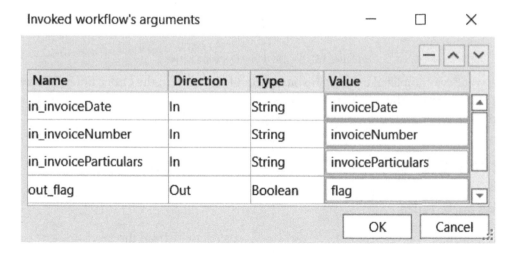

Figure 15.30 – The Invoked workflow's arguments window

28. Finally, drag and drop the `Flow Decision` activity that connects to the `Invoke Enter_Invoice_Particulars workflow` activity.

29. Pass the `flag` variable under the **Condition** property of the `Flow Decision` activity. Doing this will ensure that if the outcome of the `flag` variable is `True`, you can proceed further with the new transaction item. Else, if the outcome of the `flag` variable is `False`, that means there was an exception while entering the details of the invoice particulars onto the Order Entry CRM web page:

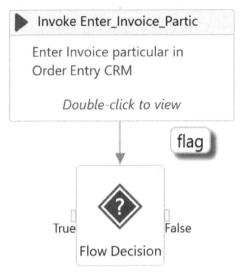

Figure 15.31 – The Flow Decision activity

Now you have completed entering invoice particulars details in the Order Entry CRM web page. In the next section, let's set the status of the transaction item depending upon the outcome of the `flag` variable in the `Flow Decision` activity.

Setting the transaction item status

In this section, for every transaction item read and processed, you will set the status to **Successful** or **Failed**:

- For the `True` branch of the `Flow Decision` activity from the `Invoke Enter_ Invoice_Particulars workflow` activity, you will set the transaction item's **Status** to **Successful**.

- For the `False` branch of the remaining `Flow Decision` activity, you will set the transaction item's **Status** to **Failed**.

So, let's set the status of the transaction item:

1. Drag and drop the `Set Transaction Status` activity that connects the `True` branch:

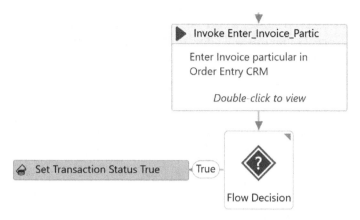

Figure 15.32 – A successful transaction

2. Edit the properties of the `Set Transaction Status`, as follows:

    • Set **Status** to **Successful**.

    • Pass the `transactionItem` variable into the **TransactionItem** text field.

    • For this process, queues were created in the folder named `Packt` inside the Orchestrator workflow. Hence, you will type `"Packt"` into the **Folder Path** section:

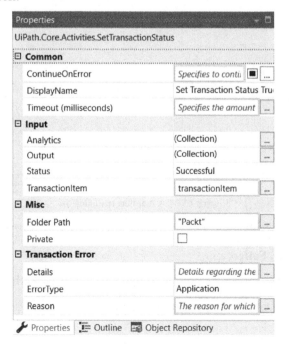

Figure 15.33 – The Properties panel of the successful Set Transaction Status activity

3. Connect the `Set Transaction Status` activity to the `Fetch transaction item` sequence. Doing this will allow the bot to go and fetch the next transaction item from the queue and process it.

4. Drag and drop a new `Set Transaction Status` activity connecting the `False` branch, as shown in the following screenshot:

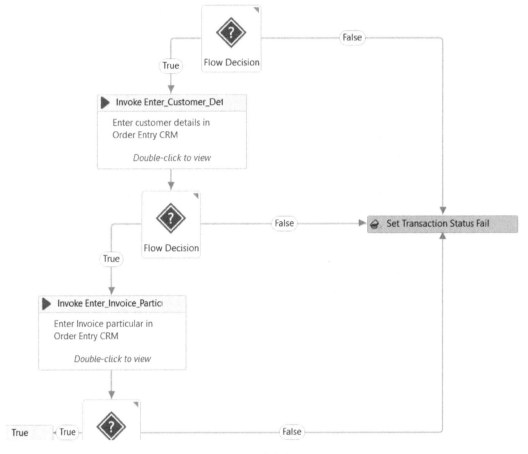

Figure 15.34 – A failed transaction

5. Edit the properties of `Set Transaction Status`, as follows:

    • Set **Status** to **Failed**.

    • Pass the `transactionItem` variable into the **TransactionItem** text field.

    • Type `"Packt"` into the **Folder Path** section.

- Set **ErrorType** to **Application**.

- Type "Failed while retrieving the transaction item or entering invoice data" into the **Reason** section:

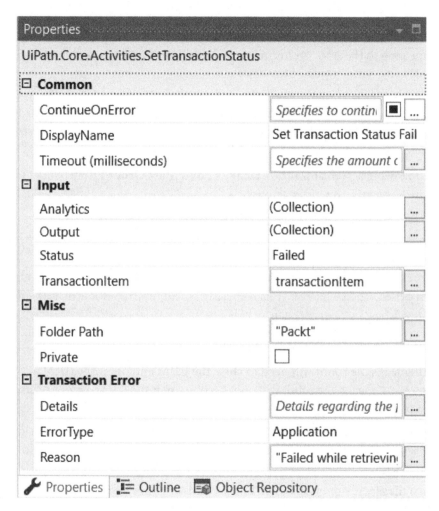

Figure 15.35 – The Properties panel of the failed Set Transaction Status activity

Setting the transactionItem status to **Failed** will update the status in Orchestrator from **In Progress** to **Retried**. A new transaction item with a **New** status will be added to the queue for every **Retried** status.

Now that the status of transactionItem has been set to **Failed**, let's look at how you can fetch the next transaction item from the queue.

Closing and opening the CRM

Since the status of the transaction item has been set to fail, before fetching the next transaction from the queue, you will need to close the Order Entry CRM web page and open the CRM again:

1. In the `Read_From_Queue` workflow, drag and drop a `Sequence` activity connecting to the `Set Transaction Status(Failed)` activity. Then, rename it to `Close and Open the CRM`.

2. Inside the `Close and Open the CRM` sequence, drag and drop the `Element Exists` activity and indicate **Henry's Food Mart Order Entry** on the Order Entry CRM web page. In the **Properties** panel, create a new variable under **Exists**, named `isCrmExists`, using *Ctrl + K*.

    The following screenshot shows **Henry's Food Mart Order Entry** being indicated by the `Element Exists` activity:

    Henry's Food Mart Order Entry

    Figure 15.36 – The Element Exists activity on the CRM page

    Before closing the CRM, you can check whether the CRM is open or has already been closed. The `Element Exists` activity will return a Boolean as the output:

    *   TRUE means the CRM is still open.

    *   FALSE means the CRM is not available.

    TRUE means the robot will need to **close the CRM** and **open the CRM** again, and FALSE means the robot will only need to **open the CRM** again because it is already closed.

3. To achieve the previously mentioned logic, you will use the `If` activity below the `Element Exists` activity. Pass `isCrmExists` into the **Condition** field.

4. In the **Then** block of the `If` activity, drag and drop the `Attach Browser` activity, attach the already opened **Order Entry CRM** web page, and place the `Close Tab` activity inside the scope of the `Attach Browser` activity.

5. Below the `Attach Browser` activity, drag and drop the `Open Browser` activity and type `Environment.CurrentDirectory+"\CRM\Order Entry.html"` into the **Url** field. Then, place the `Maximize Window` activity inside the scope of the `Open Browser` activity.

6. In the **Else** block of the `If` activity, drag and drop the `Open Browser` activity and type `Environment.CurrentDirectory+"\CRM\Order Entry.html"` into the **Url** field. Then, place the `Maximize Window` activity inside the scope of the `Open Browser` activity:

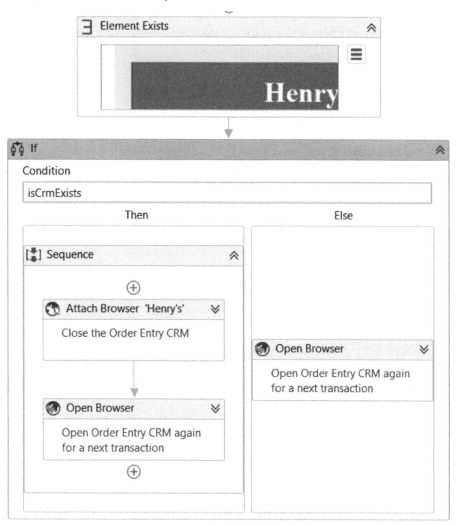

Figure 15.37 – The Close and Open the CRM sequence

7. Navigate back to the `Read_From_Queue` workflow and connect the `Close and Open the CRM` sequence to the `Fetch transaction item` sequence.

If the transaction item fails, you have successfully built a piece of logic to close and open the CRM again. Next, it's time to assemble the `Main.xaml` file to run the process.

Assembling the Main.xaml file

It's time to run the process, but let's invoke the Read_From_Queue workflow inside the Main.xaml file before running the process:

1. In the Main.xaml workflow, from the **Project** panel, drag and drop the Read_From_Queue workflow underneath the Maximize Window activity.

2. Add a Close Tab activity below it:

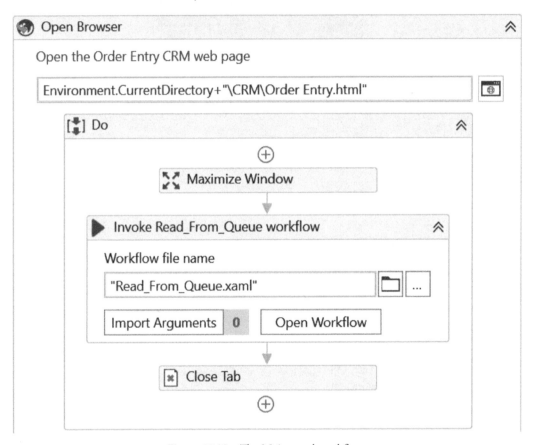

Figure 15.38 – The Main.xaml workflow

Now, let's run the entire process by clicking on the **Run** button from the **Design** ribbon bar. The process completes without any errors, and all the new transaction items from the queue have been processed and marked as successful:

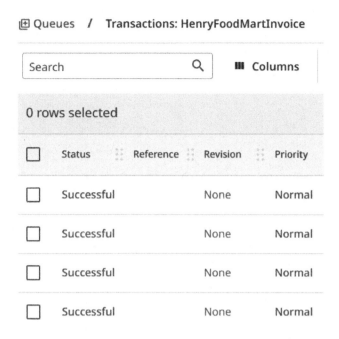

Figure 15.39 – A successful transaction item in the queue

Congratulations! You have successfully built the automation for the performer model of the invoice processing process. Now you can publish the code to Orchestrator to run the bot from the Orchestrator page or using the UiPath assistant.

Summary

In this chapter, you developed an automation process that fetches transaction items from a queue named **HenryFoodMartInvoice**. Later, you retrieved all of the specific data from the transaction item and stored it in a local variable. Once all the data was retrieved from the transaction item, you entered the customer details and invoice particulars on the Order Entry CRM web page.

Finally, you completed the dispatcher-performer model of the invoice processing process for Henry's Food Mart. In *Chapter 14, Invoice Processing – Dispatcher*, you downloaded the invoices from the mail and extracted the customer details and invoice particular details from the invoices, and uploaded them to the queue. In this chapter, you retrieved the customer details and invoice particular details from the queue and punched them into the Order Entry CRM.

In the next chapter, you will learn more about the **UiPath RPA Associate Exam (UiRPA)**.

16
How to Prepare and What to Expect

Are you planning to take the **UiPath RPA Associate Exam** to achieve the certification credential (**UiRPA**) and grow your RPA expertise? If so, this chapter, along with the information available on the UiPath Certified Professional website (`https://www. uipath.com/learning/certification`), will help you understand more about the exam and the certification credential. Preparing for a certification exam can be very stressful as it puts a lot of pressure on you to perform well, but these resources are designed to provide guidance and assistance as you prepare for the exam.

In this chapter, we will cover the following topics:

- Introducing the UiRPA and its target audience
- Exam sections and topics
- Question types and available practice tests
- Exam details and exam registration
- Managing your certification

Introducing the UiRPA and its target audience

The UiRPA certification exam is for anyone who works with the UiPath platform or wants to build their expertise in designing and developing RPA solutions.

This exam requires strong foundational RPA knowledge and/or hands-on experience. The exam assesses your problem-solving and process identification skills, as well as your ability to build simple automation solutions using UiPath Studio, Robot, and Orchestrator. In addition, the UiRPA certification credential is the first step to becoming an advanced RPA developer, solution architect, or RPA architect.

As of March 2022, the UiPath Certified Professional examination is categorized into two tracks:

- The *General Track*, which is for anyone who works with the UiPath platform and requires strong foundational technical knowledge and skills
- The *RPA Developer Track*, which is for anyone in a technical role who is looking to gain and/or possesses a deeper level of expertise in designing and developing complex RPA solutions in the Robotic Enterprise Framework

The UiRPA certification is included in both tracks.

The target audience for the UiPath RPA Associate exam includes anyone who is in a technical or semi-technical role. This includes anyone working as a junior RPA developer, RPA developer, solution architect, business analyst, or system administrator.

At a minimum, the qualified exam candidate should fit into one of the following categories:

- A graduate or college/university student who wants to pursue a career in the RPA industry
- A UiPath or UiPath Partner employee in a role such as pre-sales, services, support, and so on
- Someone who has 3-6 months' RPA hands-on experience

Now that you have a brief idea about the UiRPA exam, we will take a closer look at the exam's sections and topics.

Exam sections and topics

As an organization, UiPath has an array of products in its portfolio. However, the UiRPA certification exam tests you on the following three products:

- UiPath Studio
- UiPath Robot
- UiPath Orchestrator

It is important to understand each exam section and its associated exam topics. Having a clear understanding of this, as well as hands-on practice with the relevant products, will help you prepare for the exam. Let's do that now.

Exam sections

The UiPath RPA Associate exam contains the following exam sections:

- RPA Fundamentals
- UiPath Studio Overview
- UiPath Studio – Variables and Arguments
- UiPath Studio – Selectors
- UiPath Studio – Control Flow
- UiPath Studio – Data Manipulation
- UiPath Automation Concepts and Techniques
- UiPath Orchestrator Overview

Exam topics

Now, let's look at the topics within each section.

RPA Fundamentals

- Describe the processes that are suitable for automation and the processes that are executed with the different robot types; for example, attended versus unattended.
- Explain the functionality and interactions with UiPath Studio, Orchestrator, and Robot/Assistant.

UiPath Studio Overview

- Understand the debug functions and how they are used; for example, using breakpoints.

- Identify how to use Manage Dependencies and understand the significance of connecting an automation project to a version solution.

UiPath Studio – Variables and Arguments

- Describe the different variable types, how they are used, and the best practice for using the variable scope.

- Describe the functions and differences between variables and arguments, including how arguments are used, managed, and their best practices.

UiPath Studio – Selectors

- How dynamic versus static selectors are used.

- How partial versus full selectors are used.

- How and when to use Indicate Anchor in UI Explorer and the Anchor Base activity.

- Demonstrate and describe the use of a reliable selector and how to use UI Explorer to modify selectors.

UiPath Studio – Control Flow

- How to use Control Flow activities and workflow types such as sequences and flowcharts.

- Identify and describe the various Control Flow activities, such as If, Switch, While, DoWhile, For Each, and more.

- Explain the importance of error handling and how it can be implemented.

UiPath Studio – Data Manipulation

- Describe the importance and reasons why data manipulation is used; for example, converting from one data type into another.

- Explain how strings can be manipulated; for example, by using VB string methods and RegEx.

- Explain how to iterate and manipulate data on various collection types and data tables.

UiPath Automation Concepts and Techniques

- Identify and explain how email automation is used.

- Identify and describe Microsoft Excel and data table functions, as well as how Excel activities are used for data manipulation purposes.

- Describe the functions that are used to extract data from a PDF file; for example, reading native text or using OCR to scan PDFs.

UiPath Orchestrator Overview

- Identify and describe how UiPath Orchestrator queues and assets are used.

- Identify and explain how to publish projects to UiPath Orchestrator.

Now that you have become familiar with the exam topics, let's look at the types of questions you may be asked in the UiRPA exam.

Question types and available practice tests

The UiPath RPA Associate exam is not lab-based and does not include or require any project submissions. Rather, the exam includes the following question types:

- **Multiple choice**:

  - Straightforward questions with and without graphics

  - Scenario-based questions

  - Graphics as answer choices

  - Code as answer choices

- **Drag and drop**:

  - Designed to test a candidate's understanding of a particular "process"

  - Involves logical thinking and reasoning by the candidate

- **Simulation-based**:

  - Active screens allow interaction and automatic scoring with different display elements.

  - Emulates a user's interaction with UiPath Studio and/or Orchestrator displays.

  - Fully integrated with other question types.

  - No need to exit the testing event.

This book includes two practice tests – *Chapter 17, Mock Exam 1*, and *Chapter 18, Mock Exam 2*. These tests will allow you to practice before taking the proctored UiPath RPA Associate exam. In addition, the UiPath Certified Professional program offers a practice test at `https://uipath.onlinetests.app/assess.aspx?aid=UIPATH-RPAV1-PT&apass=uippassword`.

These practice tests are designed to help you prepare for the UiPath RPA Associate exam. They allow you to become familiar with the exam topics and the type of questions that you may come across in the proctored exam.

Exam details and exam registration

In this section, you will learn more about the exam and how to register for it.

Exam details

The following are some additional details about the UiPath RPA Associate exam:

- **Exam number**: UiPath-RPAv1
- **Exam title**: UiPath RPA Associate v1.0 Exam
- **Exam duration**: 90 minutes
- **Passing score**: 70%
- **Exam fee**: $150.00 (US dollars)

You won't be *marked negatively* if you choose the wrong answer. So, please attempt all the questions in the UiRPA exam.

Based on your location, the $150 exam fee may be subject to local taxes. In addition, students of UiPath Academic Alliance partner institutions are eligible for a 50% discount. If you are an educator, please contact the UiPath Academic Alliance team for student discount exam vouchers at `academic.alliance@uipath.com`.

Now, let's learn how to register for the exam.

Exam registration

UiPath Certified Professional exams are offered in secured proctored environments at **Pearson VUE test centers** worldwide, as well as through remotely proctored exam delivery at your private location through **OnVUE**.

To schedule the exam, visit `https://home.pearsonvue.com/uipath` to register, pay the exam fee, and schedule the day and time of your exam. If you have an exam voucher, you can enter the voucher number before the checkout process.

You should now have a brief understanding of how you can register for the exam. The next step is to understand how you can manage your certification credential once you have successfully passed the exam.

Managing your certification

All your exam and certification credential details will be saved on the UiPath Certification Manager (CertMetrics) website, where you can view and download your eCertificate and digital badge. CertMetrics is located at `https://www.certmetrics.com/uipath`. For tracking purposes, each eCertificate will include a unique verification code. If required, your employer can verify and validate your credential by entering the verification code on the UiPath Certification Manager verification page (`https://www.certmetrics.com/uipath/public/verification.aspx`).

Summary

In this chapter, you learned how to prepare for, register, and take the UiPath RPA Associate exam. This included details about the exam, the target audience for the exam, the exam's sections and topics, and the type of questions that you will come across. Finally, you were provided with additional exam details and learned how to manage your credential after successfully passing the exam.

If you require further information about the **UiPath Certified Professional Program**, its program policies, candidate agreement, and **frequently asked questions** (**FAQs**), please visit `https://www.uipath.com/learning/certification`.

We wish you all the best in successfully passing the UiPath RPA Associate exam and achieving the UiRPA credential!

In the next chapter, you will have the opportunity to practice for the exam by completing the first of this book's mock tests.

17
Mock Exam 1

This is mock exam 1. It is used to test your knowledge and give you a feeling of what the actual exam is like. This mock exam does not contain the actual exam questions. If you feel you are ready, take this exam without looking at the solutions. If you get a score of 70% or above on this one, you can be sure that you are ready to take the actual exam, and you will have a really good chance of passing.

So, what are you waiting for? Go for it:

1. Which type of robot can you provision from the UiPath Assistant using the Sign In functionality?

    A. Unattended Robot

    B. High-Density Robot

    C. Attended Robot

    D. Both Unattended and Attended robots

498   Mock Exam 1

2. What property can you use to ensure that the execution of an activity continues even after it fails?

   A. The `DelayAfter` property

   B. The `WaitForReady` property

   C. The `TimeoutMS` property

   D. The `ContinueOnError` property

3. Which key combination allows you to automatically create a variable from an activity's property field?

   A. *Ctrl + A*

   B. *Ctrl + K*

   C. *Ctrl + N*

   D. *Ctrl + P*

4. Which of the following best defines a partial selector?

   A. It contains all the required elements to identify a UI element, including the `root` node.

   B. It's generated by the Desktop recorder and does not contain a root node.

   C. It contains all the required elements to identify a UI element, excluding the root node.

   D. It's generated by the Basic recorder and does not contain a root node.

5. An array of string-named countries has been initialized with the following: `{"India","Dubai","Singapore","Nepal","Sweden","Maldives"}`.

   The `variable` panel is as follows:

Name	Variable type	Scope	Default
countries	String[]	Sequence	{"India","Dubai","Singapore","Nepal","Sweden","Maldives"}

   The `Main.xaml` workflow is as follows:

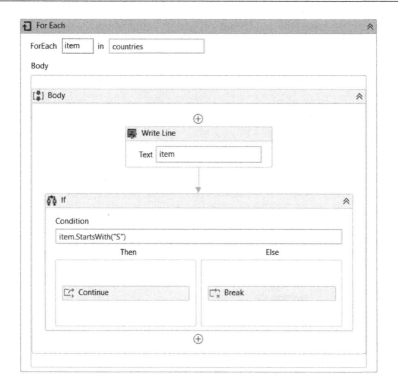

Based on the screenshots, which country names are printed by the **Write Line** activity in the **Output** panel?

A. India

   Dubai

   Singapore

   Nepal

B. India

C. India

   Dubai

   Singapore

D. India

   Dubai

   Nepal

   Maldives

6.   A developer has created an automation process that includes the following:

Here are the details of the **Build Data Table** activity – the data table is stored in a variable named dt_emp:

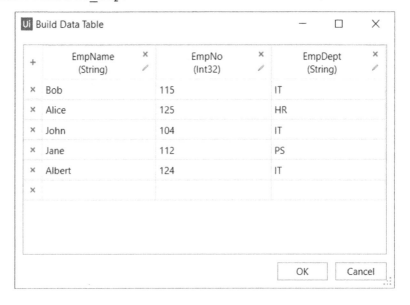

EmpName (String)	EmpNo (Int32)	EmpDept (String)
Bob	115	IT
Alice	125	HR
John	104	IT
Jane	112	PS
Albert	124	IT

Here are the details of the Filter Data Table activity:

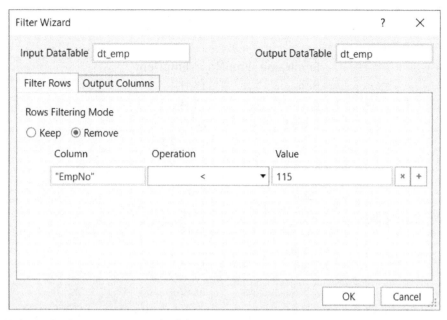

Here is the **Properties** panel of the **Write Range** activity:

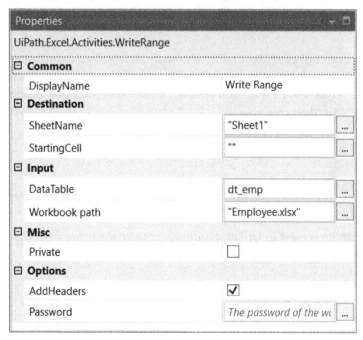

Based on the information shown in the screenshots, what is the output of the **Write Range** activity?

A.

EmpName	EmpNo	EmpDept
Bob	115	IT
Alice	125	HR
Albert	124	IT

B.

EmpName	EmpNo	EmpDept
Bob	115	IT
Alice	125	HR
Albert	124	IT
Jane	112	PS
Albert	124	IT

C.

EmpName	EmpNo	EmpDept
Alice	125	HR
Albert	124	IT

7. You have been tasked with building automation. It will read unread emails from a Microsoft Outlook account where the subject line should always read as How you doin'?. Which filter expression should be passed in the **Filter** property of the **Get Outlook Mail Messages** activity?

A. `[Subject] = 'How you doin''?'`

B. `"[Subject] = 'How you doin''?'"`

C. `Subject = How you doin'?`

D. `"[Subject] = 'How you doin'?'"`

8. Which activity is used in UiPath Studio to retrieve the value from the `Integer` asset type in UiPath Orchestrator?

A. `Set Asset`

B. `Set Credential`

C. `Get Asset`

D. `Get Credential`

9. What does publishing a package mean?

    A. Converting all workflows to a ZIP file

    B. Converting all workflows to `txt` format

    C. Converting all workflows to a NUPKG file

    D. Converting all workflows to a Git file

10. Which container activity retrieves the currently active window and enables the user to perform multiple actions within it?

    A. `Attach Window`

    B. `Attach Browser`

    C. `Get Active Window`

    D. `Open Browser`

11. Which key combination allows you to automatically create an `In` direction argument from an activity's `property` field?

    A. *Ctrl + A*

    B. *Ctrl + M*

    C. *Ctrl + N*

    D. *Ctrl + P*

12. What type of selector is generated when you use a **Click** activity in a container such as Open Application?

    A. Dynamic selector

    B. Partial selector

    C. Full selector

    D. Both partial and full selectors

13. How can execution be paused before a particular activity while debugging?

    A. By using a **Break** activity

    B. By using a `MessageBox` activity

    C. By using a `Delay` activity

    D. By using a breakpoint in `Debug` mode

14. What value will the following expression return?

    ```
    String.Format("Dear {0}, Welcome to the {1} club. You have
    been selected for the {3} club membership. Your user name
    is {0}123", "John", "RPA","elite","UiPath")
    ```

    A. Dear John, Welcome to the RPA club. You have been selected for the elite club membership. Your user name is John123

    B. Dear John, Welcome to the RPA club. You have been selected for the elite club membership. Your user name is UiPath123

    C. Dear John, Welcome to the RPA club. You have been selected for the UiPath club membership. Your user name is John123

    D. Dear John, Welcome to the UiPath club. You have been selected for the UiPath club membership. Your user name is John123

15. A developer is creating automation to read a series of page numbers from a PDF file. The page numbers are 2, 5, 8, 9, 10, 14, and 20. How should the `Range` property of the `Read PDF Text` activity be configured so that only these page numbers are read?

    A. Set the `Range` property to "2, 5, 8, 9, 10, 14, 20"

    B. Set the `Range` property to "2, 5, 8-10, 14 and 20"

    C. Set the `Range` property to "2, 5, 8-10, 14, 20"

    D. Set the `Range` property to "2, 5, 8-10, 14, 20-End"

16. Which of the following information cannot be stored in the Orchestrator asset?

    A. A periodic table of elements

    B. Email credentials

    C. A phone number

    D. The output of the **If** activity from Studio

17. Which UiPath component executes processes?

    A. Robot

    B. Studio

    C. Orchestrator

    D. A state machine

18. Which of these panels displays the information about an activity yet to be executed, along with its parent containers when a project is paused during debugging?

   A. **Locals panel**
   B. **Call Stack panel**
   C. **Watch panel**
   D. **Immediate panel**

19. What happens if you rename a variable from the **Variables** panel?

   A. You will have to change the name at all places where the variable is used.
   B. The name will be automatically updated in all the activities that use it.
   C. Errors and exceptions will be thrown during execution.
   D. The variable name cannot be edited from the **Variables** panel.

20. How can you improve the following calendar page selector to work only for the month of May in 2022?

   The selector code is as follows:

   ```
   "<html app='chrome.exe' title='UiPath - Calendar - Week of
   May 1, 2022' />"
   ```

   A. ```
   "<html app='chrome.exe' title='UiPath - Calendar - *
   2022' />"
   ```

   B. ```
   "<html app='chrome.exe' title='UiPath - Calendar - *
   />"
   ```

   C. ```
   "<html app='chrome.exe' title='UiPath - Calendar - Week
   of ?????, 2022' />"
   ```

   D. ```
   "<html app='chrome.exe' title='UiPath - Calendar - Week
   of May *, 2022' />"
   ```

21. Which activity should Brock use to write a data table into a string variable?

   A. For Each Row
   B. Merge Data Table
   C. Generate Data Table
   D. Output Data Table

22. What is the variable type in the Output property field of all **Get IMAP Mail Messages** activities?

   A. MailMessage

   B. Array<MailMessage>

   C. List(MailMessage)

   D. MailMessages

18
Mock Exam 2

This is mock exam 2. It is used to test your knowledge and give you a feel for what the actual exam is like. This mock exam does not contain the actual exam questions. If you feel you are ready, take this exam without looking at the solutions. If you get a score of 70% or above on this one, you can be sure you are ready to take the actual exam, and you will have a really good chance of passing.

So, what are you waiting for? Go for it! Answer the following questions:

1. Which of the following processes should not be chosen for RPA?

   A. Rule-based

   B. Voluminous

   C. Repetitive in nature

   D. A process with a high exception rate

2. How can execution be paused before a particular activity while debugging?

    A. By using a `Break` activity

    B. By using a `MessageBox` activity

    C. By using a breakpoint in `Debug` mode

    D. By using a `Wait Attribute` activity

3. Which key combination allows you to automatically create an `Out` direction argument from an activity's property field?

    A. *Ctrl + Shift + E*

    B. *Ctrl + Shift + M*

    C. *Ctrl + K*

    D. *Ctrl + P*

4. Can you store a `selector` in a variable?

    A. No.

    B. Yes, but the data type should be `Boolean`.

    C. Yes, but the datatype should be `String`.

    D. Yes, but the datatype should be `Int32`.

5. An array of `String` named `countries` has been initialized with the following: {**"India","Dubai","Singapore","Nepal","Sweden","Maldives"**}.

    The **Variable** panel is as follows:

Name	Variable type	Scope	Default
countries	String[]	Sequence	{"India","Dubai","Singapore","Nepal","Sweden","Maldives"}

The `Main.xaml` workflow is as follows:

Based on the graphics, which country names are printed by the **Write Line** activity in the **Output** panel?

A. India

   Dubai

   Singapore

   Nepal

B. India

C. India

   Dubai

   Singapore

D. India

   Dubai

   Nepal

6. Which of the following `String` methods will return the zero-based index of the first occurrence of a character in a string?

   A. `Concat`

   B. `Format`

   C. `IndexOf`

   D. `SubString`

7. A file called `Inspection.xlsx` has many duplicate entries. If the developer wants to remove the duplicates directly from the `Inspection.xlsx` file, which activity should be used?

   A. Remove Data Row

   B. Remove Duplicate Rows

   C. Remove Data Column

   D. Remove Duplicates Range

8. Queue items have many statuses that they go through. What does the **In Progress** status refer to?

   A. The item has just been added to the queue with the **Add Queue Item** activity.

   B. The item was added due to the failure of a previous queue item with auto-retry enabled.

   C. The item was processed and sent to a **Set Transaction Status** activity.

   D. The item was processed with the **Add Transaction Item** activity.

9. Which UiPath components ensure automatic workload distribution across Robots?

   A. Robot

   B. Studio

   C. Orchestrator

   D. State Machine

10. What is the **Manage Packages** option of the Design Ribbon bar used for?

    A. It enables you to download activity packages, libraries, and frameworks and update them, as well as add and remove them.

    B. It enables you to download activity packages, libraries, and frameworks, view the ones already installed on your computer, and update them.

C. It enables you to download activity packages, libraries, and frameworks, view the ones already installed on your computer and update them, as well as add and remove them.

D. It enables you to download activity packages and frameworks, view the ones already installed on your computer and update them, as well as add and remove them.

11. A developer has created an automation process that includes `Main.xaml`, as shown in the following figure:

The `Main.xaml` file invokes the `Number_Assign.xaml` workflow using the following arguments:

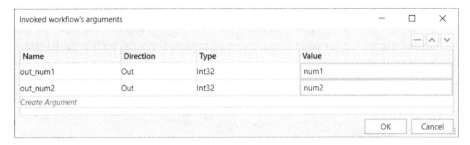

The `Main.xaml` file invokes the `Addition.xaml` workflow using the following arguments:

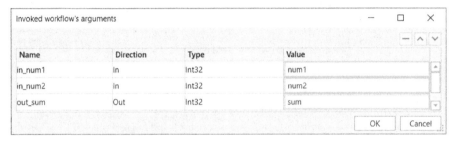

The `Number_Assign.xaml` workflow is as follows:

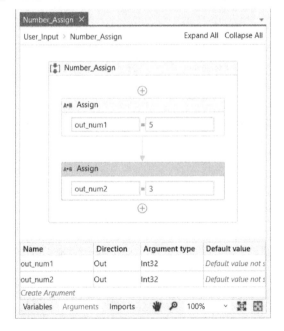

The `Addition.xaml` workflow is as follows:

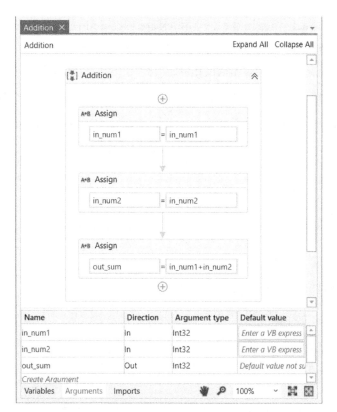

Based on the information shown in these figures, what is the output of the MessageBox activity in the `Main.xaml` file?

A. 80

B. 5

C. 8

D. 50

12. What role does the **Highlight** button in the **UI Explorer** window have?

A. It indicates a new UI element to replace the previous one.

B. It brings the target element to the foreground.

C. It enables you to choose an anchor relative to the target UI element.

D. It shows the status of the selector by checking the validity of the selector definition and the visibility of the target element on the screen.

13. When is the `Finally` block of a `Try/Catch` activity executed?

    A. When the activities in the `Try` block are executed with no error

    B. When the activities in the `Try` block are executed and have errors

    C. Every time, regardless of whether an exception occurred or not

    D. When the activities in the `Catch` block are executed and have errors

14. A developer has created an automation process, as shown in the following figure:

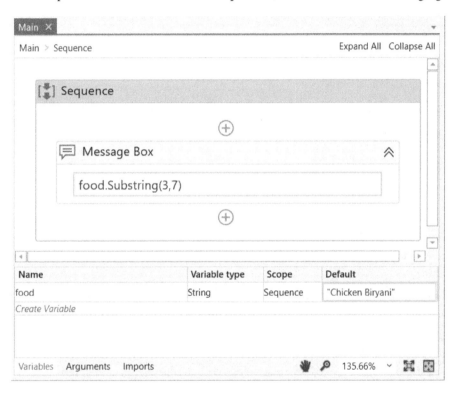

Based on the information shown in the figure, what is the output of the `Message Box` activity?

    A. `icken`

    B. `cken Bi`

    C. `icken B`

    D. `cken B`

15. What are the only types of delimiters supported in the Read CSV activity?

    A. Tab, comma (,), semicolon (;), caret (^), and pipe (|)

    B. Tab, comma (,), semicolon (;), slash (/), and braces ({ })

    C. Tab, comma (,), semicolon (;), slash (/), and pipe (|)

    D. Tab, comma (,), semicolon (;), caret (^), and braces ({ })

16. Out of the following options, when does a queue item go into the revision types of statuses?

    A. When the item was processed and sent to a **Set Transaction Status** activity

    B. When the item remained in the **In Progress** status for an extended period (approximately 24 hours) without being processed

    C. When the item has been manually selected from the **Transactions** page and marked as deleted

    D. When the transaction item is postponed

17. Which UiPath components are used for designing complex attended, unattended, and testing automation?

    A. Robot

    B. Studio

    C. Orchestrator

    D. State Machine

18. Test Bench for an activity can be created from where?

    A. Designer panel

    B. Activities panel

    C. Locals panel

    D. Watch panel

19. How can you pass data from one workflow to another?

    A. By using variables

    B. By using activities

    C. By using arguments

    D. By using packages

20. What does a gray **Validate** button in the UI Explorer window represent?

   A. Selector is being validated.

   B. Invalid selector.

   C. Selector modified, needs revalidation.

   D. Valid selector.

21. Which activity would you choose to loop through all the data table rows?

   A. `Do While`

   B. `For Each Row`

   C. `For Row`

   D. `While`

22. You are using a **Write Range** activity to write data in a `.xlsx` file that does not exist. What will happen when you execute this activity?

   A. Execution will happen without writing the data.

   B. It will create that file and then write the data in it.

   C. A runtime exception will be thrown.

   D. The process will not run due to validation errors.

Appendix

Mock Paper 1 Answers

1 – C

2 – D

3 – B

4 – B, C

5 – B

6 – D

7 – B

8 – C

9 – C

10 – C

11 – B

12 – B

13 – D

14 – C

15 – C

16 – A

17 – A

18 – B

19 – B

20 – D

21 – D

22 – C

Mock Paper 2 Answers

1 – D

2 – C

3 – B

4 – C

5 – C

6 – C

7 – D

8 – D

9 – C

10 – C

11 – C

12 – B

13 – C

14 – B

15 – A

16 – B

17 – B

18 – B

19 – C

20 – A

21 – B

22 – B

Index

E

530

Packt.com

Subscribe to our online digital library for full access to over 7,000 books and videos, as well as industry leading tools to help you plan your personal development and advance your career. For more information, please visit our website.

Why subscribe?

- Spend less time learning and more time c   with practical eBooks and Videos from over 4,000 industry professionals

- Improve your learning with Skill Plans built esp   you

- Get a free eBook or video every month

- Fully searchable for easy access to vital information

- Copy and paste, print, and bookmark content

Did you know that Packt offers eBook versions of every book published, with PDF and ePub files available? You can upgrade to the eBook version at packt.com and as a print book customer, you are entitled to a discount on the eBook copy. Get in touch with us at customercare@packtpub.com for more details.

At www.packt.com, you can also read a collection of free technical articles, sign up for a range of free newsletters, and receive exclusive discounts and offers on Packt books and eBooks.

Other Books You May Enjoy

If you enjoyed this book, you may be interested in these other books by Packt:

Democratizing Artificial Intelligence with UiPath

Fanny Ip, Jeremiah Crowley

ISBN: 978-1-80181-765-3

- Discover how to bridge the gap between RPA and cognitive automation
- Understand how to configure, deploy, and maintain ML models in UiPath
- Explore OOTB models to manage documents, chats, emails, and more
- Prepare test data and test cases for user acceptance testing (UAT)
- Build a UiPath automation to act upon Druid responses
- Find out how to connect custom models to RPA

N.ahmed

Lahiru Fernando